Business Administration

Fourth Edition

ARLENE DOUGLAS

GILL & MACMILLAN

Gill & Macmillan
Hume Avenue
Park West
Dublin 12
with associated companies throughout the world
www.gillmacmillan.ie

978 07171 4194 4

Print origination in Ireland by Carole Lynch

The paper used in this book is made from the wood pulp of managed forests.
For every tree felled, at least one tree is planted, thereby
renewing natural resources.

A CIP catalogue record is available for this book
from the British Library

Sadly my brother Brian passed away on 14 Nov 2011 and this book is dedicated to him.

How do you match the windswept clouds
that ride at speed crying of
Winter snows to the autumn lights
Safe be your flight

Contents

Preface

What is Business Administration?

Business administration involves managing the performance of an organisation and adapting to change. Organisations nowadays emphasise the importance of 'Lateral Co-ordination'. This means that managers need to know how their organisation works and many elements across the whole organisation are integrated, for example in marketing, finance and people (i.e. staff). This understanding, as well as a willingness to compromise, will help managers manage teams, projects and departments.

Business Administration includes the effective and efficient handling of challenges: managers and administrators are now required to respond quickly and flexibly to rapidly changing markets and environments.

What is Retail Administration?

Retail Administration equally emphasises 'Lateral Co-ordination', but specifically in the context of the retail environment.

Retailing is defined as the means by which goods and services are provided to consumers in exchange for payment. Retailing thus excludes wholesaling and business-to-business selling. Retailing can be segmented into three distinct categories:
- predominantly food stores
- predominantly non-food stores
- non-store retailing.

Chapter 7 of this book will focus on current trends in retailing and the retail sector in Ireland.

- This book is designed to help students studying FETAC Business and Retail Administration.

- Chapter 1 focuses on the organisation, different organisational structures, organisational change and the changing economic landscape, skills shortages, the need for organisational diversification, the prevalence of insolvencies, Organisational Management Systems (OMS), administrative supports and quality assurance systems. Company organisational profiles and charts are included in order to back up the detail in the chapter as well as sample questionnaires and examples of SWOT and PEST analyses that will help students research information on organisations of their choice.

- Chapter 2 incorporates details on business controls, Ireland's debt crisis, the Croke Park Agreement, NAMA, calculation of costs and selling prices, breakeven charts and cash flow forecasts.

- Chapter 3 focuses on banking, the euro and ECB, the Central Bank and commercial banks, the Government bailout, social networking, internet shopping, foreign exchange and an update on the insurance industry.

- Chapter 4 contains details on Human Resource management, workforce planning, employment legislation, induction procedures, risk assessments/safe work methods, and HR in a recession.

- Chapter 5 explains how meetings are planned, the protocol connected with them, reasons for them and the usual terminology connected with meetings.

- Chapter 6 details procedures regarding business documentation, checking and matching dockets and documents, spotting overcharges or undercharges, pricing, dealing with queries, preparing documents for dispatch and payments procedures.

- Chapter 7 introduces the reader to the retail sector, features of different types and sizes of retail outlet, retailing trends in Ireland with information on Retail Ireland, RGDATA, the Sale of Goods and Supply of Services Act, the Consumer Protection Act, the National Consumer Agency, Consumers' Association of Ireland, the European Consumer Centre, health and safety in retailing and customer complaint handling in retailing.

NOTE:

- Sample assignments are located at the end of each chapter.
- Practice questions appear at the end of every sub-section within the chapters.
- Student assignments, as appropriate, are given at the end of some chapters.
- Two sample FETAC examination papers for Business Administration and two for Retail Administration appear near the end of the book.

Please note future FETAC examination papers may be subject to change based on new programme modules.

1. The Organisation

Organisational Change in Recessionary Times

Organisational Change and Strategic Decision-making in the Face of Recession

Forfás, the Irish national policy and advisory board for enterprise, trade, science, technology and innovation, in its 2011 report entitled 'Statement on Competitiveness Priorities' says 'restoring the Irish economy to sustainable economic growth is essential both for reducing unemployment, restoring fiscal balance and for reducing the debt overhang to manageable proportions'. The report continues 'enhancing our international competitiveness is a necessary part of our recovery strategy. By competitiveness we mean the ability of businesses in Ireland to achieve success and increased share in international markets – leading to improved standards of living for all our citizens'.

In its report 'Making it Happen: Growing Enterprise for Ireland', Forfás emphasises the essential role of competitiveness and exports to the restoration of economic growth. It also says that stabilising the banking system and public finances, thereby reducing the debt/GNP ratio, will be a clear and immediate requirement to restore a stable economy fostering future economic growth.

The Changing Economic Landscape and Organisational Change

In the last four years, total employment in Ireland has fallen by over 300,000, or almost 15 per cent. Even though the working-age population has risen, the labour supply has fallen because some people have withdrawn from the labour market altogether. The unemployment rate has soared from 4.8 per cent to 14.2 per cent in this short period. In the construction sector alone, 166,000 jobs have disappeared, and this was the sector that was mainly responsible for fuelling the Celtic Tiger from 1997 to 2007. The accommodation and hospitality sector as well as the services sector and agriculture have also shed jobs. All economic sectors have experience a massive decline in employment, with the exception of public administration, health and education, over 70 per cent of which are state employees. In 2011, stronger export figures were recorded, however, further substantial improvement is needed in Irish competitiveness in the internationally traded sectors, particularly in manufacturing, export services and tourism, and this needs to result in an improved demand for labour, thus stimulating job creation.

The Response to Recession

ORGANISATIONS FOR THE FUTURE AND NEW AGE PRODUCTIVITY

A report, entitled 'The Games Sector in Ireland – An Action Plan for Growth (Oct 2011)', and carried out by Forfás, said that action needed to be taken to position Ireland as one of the most progressive and digitally advanced business environments.

Organisations need to change their strategies and develop business where demand is proven to exist. Parents are well aware that their children all know about gadgets and interactive games, and clearly a global demand appears to exist in this sector.

The Forfás report identifies six key opportunities for Ireland which include:

1. Developing an 'international cluster'.
2. Enhancing skills and experience by addressing short-term needs.
3. Attracting and developing a talent pool.
4. Building international visibility for the country.
5. Incentivising research and development efforts with Ireland-based firms.
6. Delivering next-generation broadband.

According to Martin Shanahan, Chief executive of Forfás, 'Games can also be a catalyst for growth in a host of other related activities in the digital economy including social networks, search engines, animation, film and video and e-learning.'

New organisations might therefore base their future business plans on sectors like games, film and animation and direct job creation as well as spin-off jobs could result from such developments.

Another sector that has been reported on is the environment and green technologies sector. According to the Forfás support guide for businesses, 'Developing a Green Enterprise', companies are becoming increasingly aware of the financial savings and competitive advantage that arise from adopting an environmentally sustainable and resource-efficient approach to their business. The increasing demand from consumers and clients for 'green' and sustainable products and services also provides new opportunities for enterprises to meet customer needs.

Refer to **www.forfas.ie.**

SKILLS SHORTAGES

Skills shortages were identified in a survey conducted by FÁS (SLMRU). The Recruitment Agency Survey (National Skills Bulletin 2011) indicated that positions were difficult to fill in the digital content and technology sector, in sectors such as engineering and utilities (e.g. metal working, production and maintenance fitters, electrical engineers, motor mechanics); ICT (e.g. computer installation and maintenance); high technology activities like pharmaceutical activities, medical devices, managerial, senior posts and sales positions. It also listed high-level niche area jobs such as accountants, tax experts, actuaries, business analysts, statisticians, planners, medical practitioners and chemists as difficult to fill.

Refer to **www.forfas.ie.**

Organisations in Ireland – Citizens' Information

Business Start-up Grants available in the Republic of Ireland

Financial support is a key requirement when starting up a new business and there are a number of schemes available to assist new and developing enterprises in the Republic of Ireland. The following list gives details of some bodies that may provide grants or other financial assistance:

CITY AND COUNTY ENTERPRISE BOARDS

Enterprise Boards provide financial assistance to develop economic and entrepreneurial activity at city and county level. City and County Enterprise Boards offer a variety of financial support packages to assist the start-up, development and expansion of small businesses in the manufacturing and services sectors employing ten or fewer people. Capital grants up to a maximum level of €75,000 are available for machinery and equipment purchases as well as for purchasing or altering business premises. Employment grants towards the cost of labour are available to incentivise job creation in new or expanding projects. A grant of up to €7,500 for each job, up to a maximum of ten jobs, may be provided.

Feasibility grants may be provided to assist with the cost of any necessary pre-start-up studies carried out for the purposes of assessing market interest in and demand for a proposed new product or service. These studies would also cover the appropriateness of any associated funding plans and the general viability and sustainability of the venture. The maximum feasibility grant available is €7,500 (Border, Midlands and West) and €5,100 (Southern and Eastern) per individual study.

Further information is available at **www.enterpriseboards.ie.**

ENTERPRISE IRELAND

Enterprise Ireland is the government agency responsible for the development and promotion of the business sector. Enterprise Ireland can provide financial support towards the cost of establishing, growing and expanding your business. The funding is typically a mix of equity and grants and is specifically intended to meet expenses in the areas of research and design, training, job creation and acquisition of capital assets. Enterprise Ireland has two distinct funding categories for start-up companies:

1. **Funding for exploring new opportunities:** This is preliminary funding towards costs associated with exploring new ideas or markets.

2. **Funding for high potential start-up companies:** Funding towards costs associated with establishing a new high potential start-up company.

Manufacturing or internationally traded services small or medium-sized (SME) companies employing 10-249 people or a high potential start-up companies can apply for these funding streams.

For further information see **www.enterprise-ireland.com**.

Education – a Route to Recovery and a Sustainable Society

It is a fact that recessions tend to hurt the less educated the most.

'The latest statistics reflect a nationwide increase in interest in upskilling in the face of economic downturn, with many people determined to enhance their skills base and level of education in order to make themselves more valuable to employers,' said Kevin Branigan, managing director of Learning Ireland – the group that managed the Irish National Education Database. Economic realities, economic uncertainty and the pursuit of learning for life have led to a rise in the demand for courses.

According to the OECD (Organisation for Economic Co-operation and Development) it is important to invest in education as there are growing advantages for those better educated and for those that engage in upskilling.

INNOVATION EMPHASISED AND HOPE FOR THE FUTURE

IDA Ireland emphasises the need for innovation in their newsletter *Innovation Ireland*. Continuous innovation plays a central role in Ireland's future as a knowledge-based economy. Recognising this, the Irish government put in place a national Strategy for Science, Technology and Innovation (SSTI) in the 1990s. Following from this, significant funding and support are available to fuel innovation across industry, research and education.

This strategy is now paying dividends, fostering a new generation of innovators, supporting exciting collaborative projects and delivering future solutions to the marketplace.

Refer to **www.idaireland.ie**.

Types of Business Organisation

The main types of business organisation that exist today are:

1. *SOLE PROPRIETOR:* This is an unincorporated (does not have company status) business organisation owned by one person who receives the profits and incurs the liabilities personally.

2. *PARTNERSHIP:* In Ireland, the partnership form tends to be used for professional practice, such as solicitors or accountants. Partnerships are normally formed by a partnership deed setting out the agreement and conditions of the partnership. A less common form is the limited partnership, which allows one or more general partners who manage the daily affairs of the business and one or more limited partners who provide a fixed capital investment with financial liability limited to the capital investment.

3. COMPANIES: These fall into two categories:

- *Public Limited Company:* This is the main form of incorporation for firms issuing stocks or bonds, having stockholders, and directors that manage the company. The company is incorporated under a Memorandum of Association and Articles of Incorporation, providing the name, share capital, and commercial objectives. There must be seven or more stockholders. There must be a minimum of two directors who manage the daily affairs of the firm and who are usually selected by the shareholders. Annual meetings are required with 21 days advance notice provided. It is also necessary to disclose financial statements and meet statutory requirements for reporting.

- *Private Limited Companies:* The requirements for formation and reporting of private limited companies are generally the same as for the public limited companies. This form is the most popular type of commercial organisation in Ireland – a head office might be located abroad. There must be between two and fifty shareholders, no debentures or shares should be issued to the general public, and there is no minimum level of share capital.

4. FRIENDLY SOCIETIES: These organisations are registered with the Registrar of Friendly Societies and are mainly made up of co-operative societies and group and community water schemes and enterprises.

Credit Unions, however, are now registered with the Registry of Credit Unions (RCU) (under the Credit Union Act 1997) as part of the Central Bank of Ireland's umbrella regulation. It is responsible for the registration, regulation and supervision of credit unions. In recognition of the unique nature of credit unions, a statutory position of Registrar of Credit Unions was explicitly created *within the Central Bank of Ireland* to assume responsibility for the regulation of credit unions.
Refer to **www.centralbank.ie.**

5. STATE BODIES – trading and non-trading

6. SEMI-STATE BODIES – trading and non-trading

7. CHARITIES

8. CARING GROUPS

Virtual organisations, and SMEs fit into one of the types of business organisation listed above – usually private companies or partnerships.

- Virtual organisations, such as virtual business schools, online tour operators, and Internet marketing companies, are some of the organisations that predominantly rely on Internet business and are called 'e-businesses'.

- SMEs are small and medium-sized enterprises that entrepreneurs develop when they find a niche in the market (where sufficient market demand exists) and with some state or semi-state help (e.g. IDA grants, funding from City and County Enterprise Boards, or through Business Expansion Schemes, which are offered by financial institutions to help small businesses get up and running or expand). SMEs' interests are represented by the SFA (Small Firms Association), by ISME (Irish Small and Medium Enterprises Association), and by IBEC (Irish Business Employers Confederation) in some cases.
  Note: The organisations mentioned here will be discussed in greater detail later.

What is an Organisation?

Chester Irving Barnard (1886–1961), author of *Functions of the Executive*, in his influential book on management presented a theory of organisation and the functions of executives in organisations. Baranard described an organisation as a 'system of co-operative human activities'. Organising involves the dividing up of tasks, the suitable allocation of these tasks to specialised personnel and the co-ordination and monitoring of the work in hand, to achieve agreed aims and objectives. According to Barnard:

- Everyone should know of the channels of communication.
- Everyone should have access to the formal channels of communication.
- Lines of communication should be as short and direct as possible.

Sole Trader

- This business person is the only owner of the business. Pubs, newsagents, hairdressers, restaurants, painters and decorators, bookshop owners, etc. can all trade as sole traders.
- If he/she wishes to trade under a trade name other than his/her personal name, he/she must register in Dublin Castle under the Registration of Business Names Act 1963 (See **www.irishstatutebook.ie**). It must be remembered however that if the business name is registered under the Registration of Business Names Act, it is not protected from being copied. If a sole trader or any business wants to protect its brand name, logo or sign, it should register a trademark. So business name registration does not guarantee any exclusivity to stop others from copying a business name, or from infringing a business name, or to stop you being sued from the holder of an existing registered trademark.
- The Safety, Health and Welfare at Work Act 2005 places responsibilities on all traders including the sole trader to ensure the health and safety of people at work

and of the public affected by work activities. He/she must put into place appropriate safety measures, having carried out a safety evaluation of the risks involved and potential hazards to health and safety. A safety programme must be written down in the form of a Safety Statement.

- He/she must keep the books of the business in order and submit monthly and end of year tax returns and must only register for VAT if certain annual limits are exceeded.
- **Advantages of being a sole trader:**
  (a) Speedy decision-making: no consultation required.
  (b) No profit-sharing.
  (c) Flexible hours.
  (d) No industrial relations problems.
  (e) Customer-friendly personal service ensures consumer loyalty.
  (f) Suits family-run business.
- **Disadvantages of being a sole trader:**
  (a) Unlimited liability: he/she is liable personally for all debts of the business. The business is not a separate legal entity.
  (b) Higher trade prices: since a small business does not buy in bulk as much as a larger one, not as many trade discounts can be gained. This causes a sole trader's costs to be higher and he/she passes on the cost to the consumer in the form of higher selling prices. Higher prices can cause decreased competitiveness and a loss of sales.
  (c) A larger capital requirement is necessary, funded only by the sole trader.
  (d) The business dies with the sole trader.
  (e) Complete competence in all areas of expertise is required, i.e. versatility, otherwise the business will not survive.
  (f) Administration overload can cause tax liabilities (owing money because books of the business are not in order).
- Sources of finance for the sole trader towards start-up:
  (a) Loans from banks and financial institutions.
  (b) Personal savings.
  (c) Hire purchase – getting assets like office equipment on loan.
  (d) Good credit terms – being allowed time by suppliers before purchases must be paid for. (Sources of finance are discussed in detail in Chapter 2.)

Many sole traders evolve into Partnerships or Limited Companies. However, many sole traders prefer to remain with this structure because of full profit-taking and control. It is advisable to have a good accountant to look after finances, tax returns and to implement changes in tax, VAT and employment legislation.

1. Briefly explain how in your opinion the onset of the recession has affected the Irish economy in relation to the organisational landscape and the need for future organisational diversification and growth.
2. Summarise the Safety, Health and Welfare at Work Act 2005.
3. Outline *three* advantages of the Sole Trader/Proprietor.
4. Outline *three* disadvantages of the Sole Trader/Proprietor.
5. How does the Registration of Business Names Act 1963 apply to the Sole Trader?
6. Why are Sole Traders' selling prices often higher than those of a larger trader?

Partnership

- This business operates on the basis of a minimum of two persons and a maximum of between twenty and fifty persons, depending on the business concerned.
- The partnership must register under the Registration of Business Names Act 1963 if the partners do not wish to trade under their own personal names.
- The Safety, Health and Welfare at Work Act 2005 applies also to the partnership (as it does to the sole trader).
- The books of the business must be kept in order. (VAT and other taxes must be paid regularly.)
- The partners usually draw up a Deed of Partnership to underpin the conditions of the agreement. Legally, if no written agreement like this is drawn up, the partners are covered under the Partnership Act 1890. Where the agreement is written up by the deed, the contents of the deed will overrule the conditions laid down by the Act.
- The Partnership Act 1890 states in general that profits and losses are to be shared equally. No new admissions are allowed without all the partners' consent. Disputes are settled by majority. Each partner can inspect the books and profits must be calculated before interest is paid to quasi-partners (partners who leave money in the business as a loan – explained below).
- There are four types of partner:
  (a) Active partner: one who participates fully in the running of the business.
  (b) Sleeping partner: one who contributes capital but does not take an active part in the running of the business.
  (c) Quasi-partner: one who retires and leaves his/her money in the business as a loan and is paid interest on the loan once profits have been calculated.
  (d) Limited partner: one whose liability or duty to pay debts is limited to the amount of capital which the partner invested – underpinned by the Limited Partnership Act 1907. With this type of partnership, one general partner with

unlimited liability must exist. The Investment Limited Partnership Act 1994 was designed to encourage collective investment in businesses, and was aimed at attracting American investors to the Financial Services Centre in Dublin by providing them with a certain degree of financial protection.

- Unlimited liability means the partner/s, i.e. general partners, would have to cover their business debts by dipping into their own private funds if company monies could not meet the debt. One general partner might have to cover another general partner's debt because the partners are jointly and severally liable. The business is not a separate legal entity from the persons who own it and the partners are not protected by limited liability in a general partnership. Unlimited partnerships are risky and require a high level of trust to operate efficiently and survive.

- On the dissolution of a partnership due to the death, bankruptcy or retirement of a partner, or due to the partnership's completion (job finished), expiry time (which would be outlined in the deed), or court order to dissolve due to illegal activities, the procedure to dissolve is as follows:
  (a) All assets are re-valued and sold (i.e. the realisation of the assets – liquidated – converted to cash).
  (b) Creditors are paid off.
  (c) Quasi-partners' loans are paid off.
  (d) Capital is repaid to the partners.
  (e) If there is any profit left over on the sale of the assets, it is divided according to profit-sharing ratios of partners. The dead partner's beneficiaries receive his portion.
  (f) Beneficiaries have the option of becoming sleeping partners (leaving the money in the business, allowing it to continue to operate) or quasi-partners (leaving the money in the business as a loan where interest will be paid to them).

- **Advantages of a partnership:**
  (a) Greater capital: greater possibility of expansion.
  (b) Greater specialisation – range of talents and expertise leads to improved productivity, speed and efficiency.
  (c) Division of liability (sharing the debts).
  (d) Consultation regarding decision-making.
  (e) Accounts not published, so privacy maintained regarding transactions.
  (f) Smaller-scale partnership arrangements benefit from the ability to give personal service and gain consumer loyalty as a result, e.g. hairdressers, window companies.

- **Disadvantages of a partnership:**
  (a) Unlimited liability (except in the case of limited partners): debts of company may have to be covered by dipping into personal funds.
  (b) The business is not a separate legal entity from the owners: owners can be sued personally for non-payment of debts.

(c) Differences of opinion can cause inefficiencies.

(d) Sharing of profits.

(e) The death of a partner means the automatic dissolution of the partnership.

(f) New partners cannot join without full agreement of all partners. This could deprive the business of new capital input.

- Examples of partnerships:
Doctors, solicitors, accountants, dentists, architects and many other regular businesses that trade either under their personal names or a trade name (in which case they must register under the Registration of Business Names Act 1963 in Dublin Castle).

- An example of limited partnerships that have grown is the amalgamation of the two largest accountancy bodies in the world, Coopers and Lybrand and Price Waterhouse, thus making a group of very powerful accountants.

PRACTICE QUESTIONS

1. Explain the differences between Active, Sleeping, and Quasi-partners.
2. What is the purpose of the Partnership Act 1890?
3. What is Unlimited Liability?
4. What is meant by 'The business is not a separate legal entity'?
5. Why would a Partnership dissolve?
6. What is the meaning of specialisation and how does it benefit a Partnership?
7. When a partner dies, explain the procedure that follows.
8. Outline *three* advantages of a Partnership.
9. Outline *three* disadvantages of a Partnership.

Companies

There are six main types of company:

1. **State bodies:** those totally funded by the government/state, e.g. the Army.
2. **Semi-state bodies:** those that are part funded by the government (public sector) and part funded by the private sector (firms and companies), e.g. the Electricity Supply Board (ESB).

State and semi-state bodies can be sub-categorised into trading and non-trading organisations as follows:

TRADING BODIES

Those which offer a service that you pay for.

Semi-state body examples are the Irish transport body CIE (Córas Iompar Éireann) (divided in three – Irish Rail (Iarnród Éireann), Bus Éireann (suburban) and Dublin Bus (city) transportation), ESB, Aer Lingus, Aer Rianta, and Bord na Móna (turf). An example of a state body is the Health Services Executive (HSE). Public hospitals are under the control of the HSE and public patients and out-patients have to pay for services.

Some essential services would be loss-making services and are semi-state for this reason. The government subsidises CIE for unprofitable routes in order to provide a full service to the public.

NON-TRADING BODIES

A semi-state body like the IDA (Industrial Development Authority), which looks after new and existing investment in Ireland, is a non-trading body providing important grants and incentives for any new iniatives. State bodies like the Army, Garda Síochána and the Blood Bank are non-trading bodies because they do not trade in goods or services for any fees, but they provide a free service to the public.

3. **Unlimited companies:** unlike partnerships, must register under the Companies Act but, similar to partnerships, do not enjoy the benefits of limited liability. Capital is provided by shareholders. Each individual amount is called a share.
4. **Companies limited by guarantee:** usually non-profit making like clubs registered under the Companies Act and liability is limited to the amount each individual member invests if the company gets into financial difficulty.
5. **Private Limited Company:** any business that applies to the CRO (Central Registrations Office) in order to gain limited liability and can place Ltd after the company name. Greater financial security is gained as the business is now a separate legal entity from the people that own it. Debts of the business are cleared by the business and money is not taken out of the owners' personal funds. The business, however, might be subject to Corporation Tax.
6. **Public Limited Company:** any well-established private limited company that has a good business track record and decides to float the shares of the business on the Stock Exchange, offering them to the public, and gaining a trading certificate allowing the business to place plc after their company name. The business is now a public company. More money or capital can be generated by going public through share capital. The company accounts have to be published and profit-sharing increases.

What is the CRO?

The Companies Registration Office is the statutory authority for registering new companies in the Republic of Ireland. It also deals with the registration of post-incorporation documents and ensures the enforcement of the Companies Acts (1963–2009) and companies' filing obligations.

The CRO (www.cro.ie) is where business people or the public in general can locate public statutory (or legal) information on Irish companies. Business people are also legally required to register with the CRO before commencing trading. The CRO operates under the rules of the Department of Enterprise, Trade and Employment.

Its website (search facility available) includes details of:

- The Register of Companies.
- Business names.
- Registered/disqualified persons.

The main functions of the CRO are:

- The incorporation of companies and the registration of business names.
- The receipt and registration of post-incorporation documents (after a business has been given company status).
- The enforcement of the Companies Acts in relation to the companies' filing obligations.
- Making information available to the public.

The CRO's website has been referred to as the main Irish companies' online registration environment.

There are three ways to register a business name, or a change made to a business name, with the CRO. You can register as:

- an individual (Form RBN1)
- a partnership (Form RBN1A)
- a body corporate (Form RBN1B).

(Forms can be downloaded from the CRO website, **www.cro.ie**.)

Formation of a Private Limited Company

(Converting from a Sole Trader, Partnership or Unlimited Company to a Private Limited Company)

You must decide on a company name. Look up the 'Frequently used numbers' section of the phone directory and find the Companies Registration Office – telephone (01) 804 5200. You must check with the office that the company name you have decided on is not already in use and you must get three forms:

1. An A1 form will be sent to you on request by the Companies Registration Office, more formally known as the Registrar of Joint Stock Companies.
2. A 'Memorandum of Association' form.
3. An 'Articles of Association' form.

    Both the memorandum and articles are in booklet form and must be purchased from a law stationery office. Look up 'Stationery Offices' in the phone book.

PROCEDURE

1. When the legal documents have been drawn up by yourself or by a solicitor (Solicitor's Act 1954) they must be lodged with the Registrar of Joint Stock Companies. They are:

(a) Memorandum of Association: containing information on the name and objectives of the company, a statement verifying that the company has limited liability, two signatures which are witnessed verifying the formation of the company, and the location of the registered legal office where all the legal documents are sent.

(b) Articles of Association: containing the list of internal rules and regulations connected with the company such as voting rights, powers and duties of directors, and procedures regarding meetings.

(c) A formal declaration of compliance with the Companies Act.

(d) A statement denoting the amount of Authorised or Nominal Share Capital of the company.

2. The documents are inspected by the Registrar and must comply with the Companies Act.

3. When the documents are verified, the Registrar issues a 'Certificate of Incorporation', the birth certificate of a limited company.

4. The company can now commence business with the protection of limited liability and can place Ltd after its company name.

   Note: Limited liability indicates that the company is a legal entity separate from the owners. Regarding debts of the company, the company is sued, not the owners. Refer to **www.cro.ie** for further information.

Formation of a Public Limited Company

(Converting from a Private Limited Company to a Public Limited Company)

The Companies Registration Office must be contacted (telephone (01) 804 5200) to clarify the requirements regarding capital turnover and size of business.

1. The company wishing to become public must satisfy the following conditions:

   (a) have a stated minimum authorised capital of which at least a quarter must be offered to the public.

   (b) have a minimum market value.

   (c) have a minimum number of shareholders.

   (d) have a healthy track record – positive working capital.

   (e) have a minimum profit level.

   (f) accept full disclosure on its operations – salaries, profits and strategies. This is the reason why some businesses are reluctant to go public.

2. The legal documents that must be lodged with the Registrar of Joint Stock Companies are:

   (a) Memorandum of Association – with at least seven signatures verifying the authenticity of the memo, as well as the other contents of the memo mentioned previously.

   (b) Articles of Association – contents mentioned previously.

   (c) A formal declaration of compliance with the Companies Act.

(d) A statement denoting the amount of authorised or nominal share capital of the company.

(e) A list of agreed directors.

(f) Directors' written consent to become directors.

3. Company makes application to Stock Exchange Council through a stockbroker where shares are quoted.

4. The company employs a merchant banker, and the stockbroker and the merchant banker together inspect the books of the company:

(a) to verify that the books meet the Stock Exchange Council's requirements regarding the financial state of the company.

(b) to verify the healthy future prospects of the company.

5. When the Stock Exchange Council accepts the company's application to trade on the Stock Exchange, the Registrar of Companies issues the company with a trading certificate.

TRADING CERTIFICATE

A public limited company must not commence business or exercise any borrowing powers until the trading certificate entitling it to commence business has been issued by the Companies Registration Office (CRO). Before such a certificate can be issued, the company must file *Form 70* in accordance with section 6 of the Companies (Amendment) Act 1983.

6. Before shares are quoted on the Stock Exchange, the company must produce a prospectus after receiving the trading certificate (the birth certificate of the public limited company).

PROSPECTUS

The word 'Prospectus' is defined in the Act as 'any prospectus, notice, circular, advertisement or other invitation, offering to the public for subscription or purchase any shares or debentures of a company'.

An offer to existing holders of shares or debentures is also regarded as coming within the scope of this definition.

7. Once the Trading Certificate has been received and the Prospectus has been organised, the company can now commence trading on the Stock Exchange, quoting the shares of the company, and can place plc after its trade name. Refer to **www. cro.ie** for further information.

Company Law

Irish company law is mainly laid down by the Companies Acts 1963–09. In addition, there is the Company Law Enforcement Act 2003, which aims to strengthen supervision and business compliance with some parts of company law. It was framed in response to a number of incidences of company fraud and malpractice that had been identified in the early years of the twenty-first century.

Areas that needed particular attention included:

- The appointment of a Director of Corporate Enforcement, to head a new multi-disciplinary agency to enforce company law, and to conduct investigations and prosecutions.
- More rigorous enforcement of the rules on filing annual returns and provision for 'on-the-spot' fines for late returns.
- Court powers, on the application of the Director, to order individual companies to comply with company law.
- Extended powers for the court to impose restrictions and disqualifications on individuals acting as directors.
- Costs of most investigations, prosecutions and court proceedings imposed on delinquent companies.
- New obligations on auditors to report suspected breaches of the Companies Acts by client companies.

In 2005 the then Minister for Trade and Commerce Michael Ahern gave the go-ahead for the new Investment Funds, Companies and Miscellaneous Provisions Act 2006. This Act allows a company to authorise a person to be its Electronic Filing Agent to simplify filing and doing business with the CRO.

Changes have also been introduced by the European Communities (Companies) (Amendment) Regulations 2007 Act with regard to new disclosure requirements of company information on websites and electronic communications. It is now mandatory to include the following information on all websites, electronic order forms and emails:

- Name of the company and its legal form.
- Place of registration of the company, the company number and its registered office.
- In the case of a company exempt from the obligation to use the word 'limited' or 'teoranta', the fact that it is a limited company.
- In the case of a company being wound up, the fact that this is so.
- If there is a reference to share capital of the company, the reference should be to paid-up share capital.

If a company has a website, it must display this information in a prominent and easily accessible place on the site.

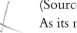

(Source: **www.lowtax.net**.)

As its name would suggest, the Company Law Consolidation and Reform Bill 2010 will consolidate the provisions of existing company law and related legislation into one single act.

For current information on Company Law Acts visit the Department of Jobs Enterprise and Innovation website: **www.djei.ie/commerce/companylawadmin.**

Changes to Private Limited Company Formation

In 2007 the Company Law Review Group suggested that Irish company law be consolidated into one Act, the Companies Consolidation Act 2008. This law is intended to change the profile of a private limited company from its current form.

The main changes are:

- The current memorandum and articles of association will be replaced by a single document.
- Companies will be allowed to have just one director and a company secretary instead of the previous requirement to have a minimum of two directors. The director and secretary must be different individuals.
- Clauses will be introduced so that companies' obligations to other parties are more copper-fastened and companies cannot any longer evade these obligations by using loopholes in company law.

Other Categories of Company

Other categories of company that are covered by the Companies Act include:

- Private Company Limited by Shares (private shares, 50 members only, no shares transfer).
- Non-resident Company. (The Finance Act 1999 rendered all incorporated companies resident in Ireland, with some offshore exceptions: now it is not as easy to benefit unfairly from favourable taxation conditions if you are a non-resident.)
- Public Company Limited by Shares (minimum seven members, maximum capital of €38,092).
- Company Limited by Guarantee (used for charitable and non-profit-making purposes such as a local community membership raising funds for buildings or facilities).
- Branch of Overseas Company (same CRO registration rules apply, with an authorised representative in Ireland).
- General Partnership (under Partnership Act 1890): partners are individually liable for debts of company.
- Limited Partnership (under Limited Partnership Act 1907): one or more general partners with unlimited liability and one or more limited partners where their liability or debt responsibility is limited to the amount they contributed to the business.
- Investment Limited Partnership (ILP) (under the Investment Limited Partnership Act 1994) allows collective investors to obtain double tax relief, which is unavailable to unit trust investors. The minimum share capital is €127,000 and at least two directors must be Irish. Partners must be approved by the Central Bank and monthly accounts must be submitted to the Central Bank.

What is Insolvency?

Insolvency means the inability to pay one's debts as they fall due. Usually used to refer to a business, insolvency refers to the inability of a company to pay off its debts. Business insolvency is defined in two different ways:

1. **Cash flow insolvency:** Unable to pay debts as they fall due.
2. **Balance sheet insolvency:** Having negative net assets, in other words, liabilities exceed assets.

A business may be 'cash-flow insolvent' but 'balance-sheet solvent' if it holds illiquid assets, particularly against short-term debt that it cannot immediately realise if called upon to do so. Conversely, a business can have negative net assets showing on its balance sheet but still be cash-flow solvent if ongoing revenue is able to meet debt obligations, and thus avoid default. This could be, for instance, if it holds long-term debt. Many large companies operate permanently in this state.

Insolvency does not automatically imply bankruptcy, which is a determination of insolvency made by a court of law, with resulting legal orders intended to resolve the insolvency.

Company Liquidity/Receivership Problems – What's Next for Companies in Ireland?

Irish insolvencies in the year to August rose to 1,090; Total company collapses in the 2008-2011 period to rise to 5,300 firms

Finfacts Team   1 September 2011

New statistics released today by InsolvencyJournal.ie reveal that corporate insolvency figures for August totalled 119, a 22 per cent drop from the July total of 152. The first eight months of 2011 saw a total of 1,090 corporate insolvencies, an increase of over seven per cent on the total recorded for the same period in 2010 (1,012).

Commenting on the figures, Ken Fennell of Kavanaghfennell, the firm which compiles the data commented: 'The decrease in August is not surprising as there is usually a seasonal reduction in the number of insolvencies. We had a comparable reduction in August last year.'

According to Fennell: 'Although the reduction in the number of receivership appointments is welcome we believe the banks and NAMA will continue to appoint receivers where they believe they have no alternative and they are of the view that such appointments will lead to greater recoveries. The recent outcome of the Start Mortgages case could also have some implications on future receivership appointments.'

With regard to industry totals, the total number of insolvencies in the construction industry so far this year totalled 278, a 10 per cent dip on the figures recorded for the same period during 2010.

'The overall trends in corporate insolvencies for the year to date would suggest that at least 1,600 companies will enter into some form of insolvency arrangement by the end of the year with construction and retail continuing to bear the brunt,' Fennell commented.

Source: www.finfacts.ie

What are the differences between Examinership, Receivership and Liquidation?

Examinership, Receivership and Liquidation – What's the Difference?

As the global economy continues to reel from the current downturn many businesses and individuals are facing what seem to be insurmountable financial problems. The event which demonstrates that an employer is in serious financial trouble can take various forms. Liquidation in the case of a corporate employer, bankruptcy in the case of an individual employer, are perhaps the most obvious examples. But there are other possible indications that an employer has serious financial problems such as receivership or the appointment of an examiner to a company.

The purpose of this article is to explain the distinct roles played by Liquidators, Receivers and Examiners as set under the Companies Acts.

Liquidation

Under Irish law, the liquidation or winding-up of a company, in other words, its legal death, can take one of two forms. It can be a winding-up by order of the court (also known as an official liquidation). Far more frequently, however, it will be a voluntary winding-up (which, in turn, may be either a members' voluntary winding-up, or a creditors' voluntary winding-up).

A Creditors' Voluntary Liquidation is the most commonly used procedure for dealing with an insolvent company. In summary, this process is usually initiated by the insolvent company, acting through its board. In a Creditors' Voluntary Liquidation, the liquidator is primarily concerned with the interests of the creditors.

A Members' Voluntary Liquidation is a mechanism whereby a solvent company, acting through its directors and members, decides to wind-up a company, primarily for the purpose of selling its assets and distributing the surplus to its shareholders.

Examinership

Examinership is an alternative to liquidation. The Companies (Amendment) Act 1990 introduced the examinership process to provide a mechanism for the rescue and return to health of an ailing, but potentially viable company.

An application is made to a court of law to appoint an Examiner; an application is usually made by the company itself, but it can be made by the directors, creditors, contingent or prospective creditors, including the employees.

The Examiner's primary function is to evaluate the company's viability, and if it is salvageable, the Examiner is responsible for developing a long-term survival plan. Once an Examiner has been appointed, the company goes under the protection of the court. This means that for a period in which the company is under examinership, no application can be made to wind up the company, nor can a receiver be appointed.

> ### Receivership
> Receivership is not usually initiated by the company itself, but rather by its creditors. It normally arises when the company has defaulted on a contract to repay loans or debts outstanding. The Receiver's primary role is to recover the money owing to the creditor and, in theory, the company can continue trading while in receivership.
>
> However, in order to recover the creditor's money the Receiver may have to sell off assets to the point that the company can no longer continue to operate. In those circumstances, the company is likely to end up in liquidation. Although historically and virtually exclusively a process used by banks as a means of recovery, it is a procedure of last resort in the lender-borrower relationship.
>
> Source: www.mlaw.ie.

What is a Public Private Partnership?

A Public Private Partnership (PPP) is a partnership between the public and private sector for the purpose of delivering a project or service traditionally to do with infrastructure, e.g. public road construction, school buildings, water treatment projects, etc. This type of partnership involves a public authority (such as a government department) delegating to a private organisation the responsibility for financing, executing and maintaining a project in return for the right to operate the facility for an extended period. This enables its investment to be amortised, that is, the private sector takes the financial risk.

Sample projects are listed on **www.ppp.gov.ie**.

Note: Irish Legal Acts referred to above and other Acts not referred to here are available as hard copy from the Department of Enterprise, Trade and Employment website (**www.entemp.ie**, under Company Law Financial Services Publications) or from the Government Publications Office, Molesworth Street, Dublin. Company Acts are also available to download from **www.cro.ie/en/downloads**.

What was the Financial Regulator?

In May 2003, the Irish Financial Services Regulatory Authority (IFSRA) was set up and was a distinct element of the Central Bank and Financial Services Authority of Ireland. The title of the organisation was then changed to the Central Bank Financial Services Authority of Ireland (CBFSAI).

Most recently following the tightening of regulations due to the global recession and the debt and banking crisis, the Central Bank of Ireland Reform Bill 2010 created a new single unitary organisation, the Central Bank of Ireland, with responsibility for both central banking and financial regulation. The Bank is headed by a Commission, chaired by the Governor. The Governor is supported by a Head of Central Banking and a Head of Financial Regulation.

The new structure replaces the Central Bank and Financial Services Authority of Ireland (CBFSAI) with its two component entities – the Central Bank and the Financial Regulator. Each has its own particular set of responsibilities and its own specific governance structure. With effect from 1 March 2010, the CBFSAI's statutory consumer information and education functions were transferred to the National Consumer Agency.

Friendly Societies

A friendly society was traditionally one that had an essentially community-based ethos and was a not-for-profit type of organisation. From the mid-1800s until 2003, the Registrar of Friendly Societies was the body that had statutory responsibility for the registration and general regulation of Friendly Societies, Trade Unions (social economy enterprises), Industrial and Provident Societies (mainly Co-operatives), Building Societies, and (from the 1960s) Credit Unions.

The most recent report on friendly societies entitled 'Registry of Friendly Societies Annual Report 2010' is available on the Department of Justice Enterprise and Innovation website at www.djei.ie.

These societies are categorised in the Report as follows:

The Registry of Friendly Societies deals with three different entity types, namely Industrial and Provident Societies, which in the main consist of co-operatives; Friendly Societies; and Trade Unions, which include employee unions, employer associations and trade associations.

The principal legislation governing these entities is:

* Industrial and Provident Societies Acts 1893-1978.
* Friendly Societies Acts 1896-1977.
* Trade Union Acts 1871-1990.

These societies are categorised in the Report of the Registrar of Friendly Societies 1994–1996 as follows:
1. Industrial and Provident Societies
2. Credit Unions
3. Friendly Societies registered under the Friendly Societies Acts.
4. Some trade unions.

INDUSTRIAL AND PROVIDENT SOCIETIES

These are divided in the following way:

Dairy societies, livestock breeding societies, meat-processing societies, livestock marketing societies, horticultural societies, egg and poultry societies, fishing societies, public utility societies. (Group water schemes and housing development are separate categories.)

Examples are Thurles Co-operative Creamery Ltd, Waterford Co-operative Society Ltd, Clover Meats Ltd, Donegal Potatoes Ltd, Goldenvale Co-operative Mart Ltd, Monaghan Poultry Growers Co-operative Society, Cappagh Group Water Scheme Society Ltd, Carlow Town Housing Co-operative Society Ltd, Clondalkin Community Enterprise Co-operative Society Ltd, and many others.

Most of the above-named industrial and provident societies are co-operative societies and have a co-operative organisational structure. The history of the co-op movement laid the foundation for the type of structures that exist today.

The co-operative movement had its origins in an English town in Lancashire called Rochdale. The father of the co-operative movement was a Welshman, Robert Owen (1771–1858). He gathered together a number of colleagues who called themselves the Rochdale Pioneers and they drew up a set of rules called the Rochdale Principles which still govern the thinking and conduct of co-operatives:

1. Open membership – anyone can join.
2. Democratic rule – one vote per person.
3. Limited return on capital.
4. Surplus profit to be distributed according to number of purchases.
5. No credit – cash sales only.
6. Some profit is set aside for educational purposes.
7. Neutral on political and religious issues.

CHARACTERISTICS OF THE CO-OPERATIVE

1. Must register under the Industrial and Provident Societies Act 1893–1978 with the Registrar of Friendly Societies and if they convert to companies they must conform to the Companies Act 1990.
2. Can be formed by eight or more people.
3. One person, one vote, irrespective of number of shares held.
4. A member may not own more than an agreed number of shares.
5. As more capital is acquired, no further authorised share capital can be issued.
6. Shares are non-transferable and a member must sell back shares to the co-op and they are withdrawn.
7. Surplus on profits is distributed to members in proportion to their holding. Some is used for educational purposes.

Retail co-operatives, producer co-operatives and worker co-operatives exist; however, the co-operative movement has undergone dramatic change in recent years and must now compete to survive. Many have become public companies, having successfully adjusted to the competitive position required in the business world today. Examples of plcs like this are Kerry Group plc and Avonmore Waterford plc (which merged in September 1997 to form Glanbia). Activities like milk processing, dairy produce trading, pig farming and meat processing are carried on by the Kerry Group. Talks of mergers or take-overs of any remaining suitable co-ops have been common in recent times due to the benefits attached to this type of venture:

1. Extra finance from share issues.
2. Top-class management improving efficiency and productivity.
3. Benefits attached to large-scale operations (economies of scale). Examples of economies or benefits are bulk buying with large discounts, lower advertising costs per unit output, and top-class specialised workers.

RETAIL CO-OPERATIVES

Some co-operatives, such as Thurles Co-operative Creamery Ltd, have a retail outlet (shop attached to the co-op). In this they sell fresh produce as well as a range of household items to the public. Retail co-operatives like this are listed in the Registry of Friendly Societies under 'Industrial and Provident Societies – Dairy Section'. Other co-operatives, such as knitwear co-ops, can also have shops attached to them. They are listed under the 'Other Productive Societies' section of the same publication.

What is a Credit Union?

A Credit Union is an organisation of people, for people. It exists only to serve its members, not to profit from their needs. History has shown that people can achieve far more through co-operation and working together than by individual effort. Credit Unions have ingrained this philosophy in their operations. They are are non-sectarian and non-political, and continue that Irish tradition of co-operative self-help.

Credit Union Operating Principles are founded based on the philosophy of co-operation, equality, equity (fairness), and mutual self-help. They are:

- Open and voluntary membership.
- Democratic control (one member one vote).
- Limited dividends on equity capital.
- Return of surplus to members.
- Non-discrimination in race, religion and politics.
- Services to members.
- Ongoing education (promoting the education of members, officers and employees).
- Co-operation among co-operatives (serving the best interests of members at local, national and international level).

- Social responsibility (extending services to those who need them; abiding by the interests of the broader community).

There are over three million members in Ireland and savings amount to approximately €12.6m. There are over 9,200 active volunteers involved in the movement and over 3,500 people are employed in Credit Unions in Ireland.

What is a 'Credit Union Chapter'?

Each Credit Union was traditionally a member of a particular Chapter (or geographical grouping), e.g. the Tipperary Chapter or the Limerick City Chapter. These chapters acted as a forum for the exchange of information, shared promotion and training programmes. There are 25 chapters, with Chapter Liaison Officers in charge of each individual chapter.

Credit Unions in the Republic of Ireland are now registered with the Registry of Credit Unions (RCU) (under the Credit Union Act 1997) as part of the Central Bank of Ireland's umbrella regulation. The Registry is responsible for the registration, regulation and supervision of credit unions. In recognition of the unique nature of credit unions, a statutory position of Registrar of Credit Unions was explicitly created *within the Central Bank of Ireland* to assume responsibility for the regulation of credit unions.

Refer to **www.centralbank.ie/regulation/industry-sectors/credit-unions/Pages/default.aspx** for further information.

Other committees such as a youth committee may be appointed from time to time

Figure 1.1 The Organisational Structure of the Credit Union

The members of a credit union elect a board of directors at its AGM (Annual General Meeting). The board is responsible for the control, direction and management of the affairs, funds and records of the credit union. Only credit union members are eligible for election to the credit union board and its committees. It is important, therefore, that members attend their AGM.

The Irish League of Credit Unions (ILCU) is the umbrella body for all credit unions in Ireland. It was set up in 1960 to represent and service affiliated credit unions on the island of Ireland. It now represents the interests of over 530 credit unions in Ireland.

Its main functions are to:

1. Promote the ideas and ethos (community-based) of credit unions.
2. Represent affiliated credit unions with government, the EU and other agencies.
3. Provide central services to credit unions.

The **Savings Protection Scheme Fund** protects the savings of individual members by making sure that the credit unions are financially and administratively sound and by providing remedial help to any credit union that shows signs of weakness in these areas. The savings of individual credit union members are protected up to a maximum of €12,700.

Credit Union services include:

*   Savings
*   Loans
*   Insurance
*   ATM/EFT facilities
*   Money transfer
*   Foreign exchange.

JOINING A CREDIT UNION

Joining your local credit union is easy: all you do is apply for membership. To be a member there may be an entrance fee of not more than €1/£1stg and you will need to hold minimum savings of between one and ten shares. After this members can continue saving regularly – even small amounts – which encourages the saving habit.

BENEFITS OF MEMBERSHIP

Members of credit unions enjoy many benefits associated with membership, including:

*   Control over members' own finances.
*   Encouragement and advice on a regular savings programme.
*   Loan availability at relatively low rates of interest that remain consistent even during times of economic turbulence.

- Security of savings through the credit unions fidelity bond and through the Irish League of Credit Unions Saving Protection Scheme.
- Loan Protection and Life Savings Insurance at no direct cost to the eligible member.
- The knowledge that their own savings are being used in their own community.
- All officials of credit unions, whether volunteers or staff, must be fidelity bonded.
- Under the rules of a member's credit union, confidentially is protected.
- The savings of eligible members are insured through Life Savings Insurance.
- Full financial statements are prepared and can be examined by members.
- Annual returns are independently audited and lodged with the relevant regulatory authority.

Savings are used to make loans to members. The interest received from loans and investments is used:

- To pay expenses
- To build up reserves.

The remaining income may be returned to members as a dividend. The rate of dividend can vary from credit union to credit union.

Credit unions to get €1bn boost

Friday, 7 October 2011

The Government will pump up to €1bn into credit unions around the country.

The move is being made to strengthen the balance sheets and boost the reserves of credit unions that have run into difficulties.

Although the majority of credit unions are healthy, Minister for Finance Michael Noonan said that others were 'on the brink of falling down a hole'.

'I seriously intend sorting out the credit unions and some of them we'll have to do immediately, but we won't do it in one big bang,' the minister has told the Seanad.

Around 20 of the 79 at-risk credit unions have experienced serious financial difficulties. These have sought financial aid from a fund set up by the Irish League of Credit Unions.

Almost €1bn worth of loans at the State's 400 credit unions are in arrears for 10 weeks or more. This represents gross arrears of 18 per cent of the €5.2bn loan book in the Republic.

Mr Noonan said that if the movement had been one large bank with individual branches, it would have no problems because the good ones would balance the bad ones.

'But individual credit unions have problems that are coming down the road quickly,' he said.

A commission set up earlier this year to examine the credit union sector is due to deliver an interim report next Tuesday. But Mr Noonan said that matters had been 'overtaken by events' and the Central Bank had requested that it urgently be given extra powers to deal with credit unions 'that are on the brink'.

Source: www.herald.ie/news/credit-unions-to-get-1bn-boost-2899719.html

Charities and Caring Groups

A charity is a not-for-profit organisation that must be constituted and operated exclusively for charitable purposes, e.g. St Vincent de Paul, Trócaire and Concern. It is a basic principle of charity law that an organisation's objects must be expressed in precise rather than broad or vague terms. This identifies it clearly as having a recognised charitable purpose.

There is no legal framework for the registration of charities in Ireland. However, the Office of the Revenue Commissioners, Charities Section maintains a database of organisations to which they have granted charitable tax exemption. A CHY reference number is then allocated to the charity.

Charitable organisations usually take one of three legal forms (as advised to them independently by a solicitor):

1. An unincorporated association with a Constitution or Rules.
2. A charitable trust established by Trust Deed.
3. A company governed by a Memorandum and Articles of Association.

Caring Groups are also not-for-profit organisations that fall under the 'charity' banner, but their services also consist of advice and counselling given by qualified trained volunteers e.g. CURA, the Samaritans and Alcoholics Anonymous. These organisations rely primarily on funding from donations and funds raised through charitable activities and events.

PRACTICE QUESTIONS

1. How do semi-state bodies and state-sponsored bodies differ?
2. Give *one* example *each* of:
    (i) a trading semi-state body
    (ii) a non-trading semi-state body
    (iii) a trading state body
    (iv) a non-trading state body.
3. Define the following:
    (i) Unlimited Company;
    (ii) Company Limited by Guarantee;
    (iii) a Private Limited Company; and
    (iv) a Public Limited Company.
4. What is the CRO?
5. Briefly explain Irish company law by referring to:
    (i) the Companies Act 1963–2009
    (ii) the Company Law Enforcement Act 2003
    (iii) the Investment Funds, Companies and Miscellaneous Provisions Act 2006

(iv) the European Communities (Companies) (Amendment) Regulations 2007 Act.

(v) The Companies Consolidation Reform Bill 2010.

6. What are the procedures for unlimited companies to become private limited companies?

7. What are the procedures for a private limited company to become public?

8. What is a public private partnership?

9. What is the Financial Regulator?

10. Name *three* types of friendly societies. What characteristics are common to each?

11. What are the main functions of the ILCU?

12. How have co-ops changed in status in recent years?

13. What are the Rochdale Principles?

14. What is a chapter with regard to credit unions?

15. Give a brief account of how credit unions operate.

16. In your opinion, will credit unions survive into the future? Why/Why not?

17. How are charities defined?

18. What is a Caring Group?

Features of Different Types of Organisational Structure

Factors Determining Organisational Design

1. **A Formal Organisation:** Functional divisions of labour that are based on the formal lines of authority affect the structure of an organisation.

   An organisation is structured to achieve specific goals with the formal functions of the organisation set out within a well-defined framework. Responsibilities are formally grouped to achieve specific tasks. Job specifications make the individual's position in the organisation clear. There are chains of delegated authority for different levels of decision-making and built-in channels of communication exist. Examples are banks, colleges, advertising agencies, software companies, etc.

2. **An Informal Organisation:** This operates alongside the formal framework, where individuals within the organisation form social groupings and relationships and often use informal methods to get things done. It is flexible and spontaneous and often speeds up the completion of tasks based on informal teamwork. Newcomers sometimes have to 'get accepted' into informal groupings.

The Organisational Hierarchy and Organisational Chart Shapes (flat, tall)

The lines of authority should be clearly defined in every organisation (i.e. every employee should be able to see clearly to whom he/she is responsible). Since the employee is answerable to somebody he/she is said to be, in the formal sense, a subordinate. The organisational structure is best displayed by constructing an Organisational Chart of the organisation in question. This chart represents a framework within which staff are designated to perform required activities.

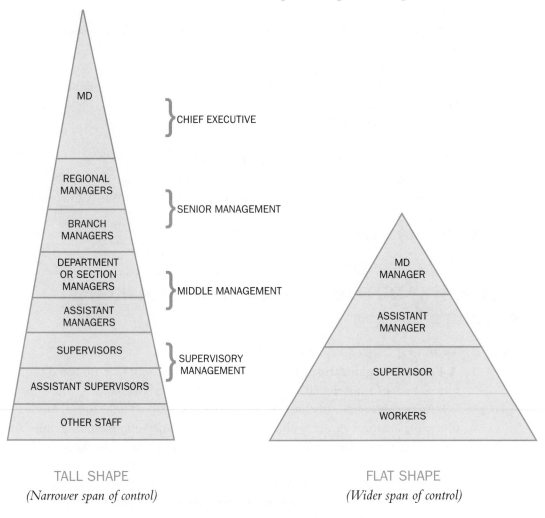

Figure 1.2 Organisational Pyramids

The main factors that dictate the shape of such a chart are referred to as the 'Principles of Organisation':

1. Unity of command and unity of purpose: is ensured when employees know who exactly they are answerable to (ideally one person) and no conflicts arise regarding authority.
2. Span of control: generally means one superior at the head of the organisation and a varying number of subordinates. The wider the span, the fewer the levels of

authority, the flatter the shape of the organisational chart. A narrow span of control will tend to create a tall structure (see Figure 1.2).

3. Amount of delegation: Delegation means the dividing up of responsibilities and spreading them out among subordinates. A high level of delegation results in a greater number of levels of authority.

4. Size of organisation: A greater division of work, specialisation and delegation is required in a larger organisation. The larger the organisation, the taller the shape of the chart; and the smaller the organisation, the flatter the shape of the chart.

5. Number and type of employees: The larger the organisation, the greater the labour force, and because of the need for greater departmentation and specialisation, there tends to be a greater number of levels of authority due to the workload and the need for delegation.

The horizontal and vertical dimensions of the pyramids are altered according to the factors listed above.

Question: Which in your opinion is more efficient?

TALL SHAPE

CHARACTERISTICS: larger business with more departmental divisions, specialisation and delegation; greater number and variation of type of employee; work involves more analysis, research and development.

ADVANTAGES:

1. Greater economies of scale (i.e. benefits) due to larger size, e.g. opportunities to specialise and divide up labour, increasing opportunities for improved productivity.
2. Greater efficiency in organisational methods.
3. Greater turnover – can afford to incorporate the most modern technology.

DISADVANTAGES:

1. Greater difficulty with maintaining unity of purpose due to communication problems – too many levels of authority.
2. Less consumer friendly – more informal due to size.
3. Decision-making may be slower due to time it takes to get from top to bottom and vital decisions might be made too late.

FLAT SHAPE

CHARACTERISTICS: smaller business with a small number of employees where work passes through fewer hands – few levels of authority.

ADVANTAGES:
1. Information and decisions pass from top to bottom quickly via fewer levels.
2. Top management are closer to the ground, ensuring efficiency – close and orderly planning and control of work.
3. Greater personal consumer attention and resulting consumer loyalty.

DISADVANTAGES:
1. Less specialisation or division of labour – usually lower wages for lower-level workers.
2. Smaller economies of scale.
3. Lower turnover – restricted ability to invest in expensive modern technology as it may not be cost effective.

PRACTICE QUESTIONS
1. How does a Formal Organisation differ from an Informal Organisation?
2. What is an Organisational Hierarchy and how is it illustrated?
3. What are the differences between a Tall and a Flat Organisational structure?
4. Which do you think is more efficient?
5. What is the meaning of the term 'Specialisation'?
6. How might it affect the shape of the Organisational Chart?
7. What is the meaning of the term 'delegation'?
8. What is the meaning of the term 'subordinate'?

Departments within an Organisation

(Role of Departments in achieving the Objectives of an Organisation)

Nearly every organisation has five main functional areas, to which departments can be linked, depending on the type of enterprise in question. These functional areas are:

1. **Technical:** including production, manufacture, and adaptation of materials (Production Department).
2. **Commercial:** including buying, selling and exchange (Purchases and Sales Departments).
3. **Financial:** activities designed to obtain capital and to make the best use of it (Financial Department).
4. **Accounting:** including payroll, tax returns, stock-taking and the preparation of balance sheets, cost statements and business statistics (Accounting Department).
5. **Managerial activities:** dealing with staff incentives and documentation, manpower planning and selection and general administration regarding staff (Personnel Department).

The divisions above would represent departmentation by function – a logical and traditional method which allows the division of work into specialist areas and is especially evident in large organisations. Within each department workers are specifically skilled and are allowed to concentrate on one task or a group of linked tasks. This process is referred to as specialisation or the division of labour. The aim is to increase efficiency and productivity in the organisation. Departmentation involves the clarification and grouping of tasks allotted to groups of people. It allows the organisation to complete targeted tasks that it has set itself.

The various means of departmentation are:

1. by function (functional)
2. by product (product – divisional)
3. by region (geographical or territorial)
4. by a mixture of the above (matrix).

DEPARTMENTATION BY FUNCTION

Further sub-departmental divisions are based on function.

DEPARTMENTATION BY PRODUCT

Managing Director (e.g. large supermarket)

sales		purchases		finance		production		personnel	
home	export	buying	stores	costing	records	assembly	service	recruitment	staff welfare

Figure 1.3 Functional Division of Organisation

Most companies have a mix of products at different stages of their life cycle. A single product might become outdated or unfashionable. Divisional managers might be given responsibility for a product or a brand line of products. This encourages expertise in sales and service areas.

Managing Director (e.g. a car, truck and aircraft components manufacturer such as Volvo)

Divisional Manager	Divisional Manager	Divisional Manager
Cars	Trucks	Aircraft Components

Figure 1.4 Product Division of Organisation

DEPARTMENTATION BY REGION OR TERRITORY (GEOGRAPHIC DIVISION)

Suitable for organisations where similar activities are carried out in widely different locations. On the spot decision-making is required based on local knowledge and the duplication of accounting tasks could be costly, e.g. insurance companies or travel agencies.

Managing Director (e.g. Dunnes Stores Branches Ireland)

Regional Manager North-east Branch	Regional Manager North-west Branch	Regional Manager Midlands Branch	Regional Manager South-west Branch	Regional Manager South-east Branch

Figure 1.5 Regional Division of Organisation

DEPARTMENTATION BY MIXTURE (MATRIX)

Within functional departments staff might be organised by region or by product. There may also be a subdivision of functions within product departments.

Functional departments organised by product:

Managing Director (e.g. Sales reps organised based on products) e.g. Roches Stores Ireland

Sales Reps

Hardware Products	Electrical Goods	Toys	Cosmetics	Groceries

Figure 1.6 Matrix Division of Organisation – Function by Product

PRODUCT DEPARTMENTS SUBDIVIDED BY FUNCTION

Managing Director (e.g. bank servies organised based on staff functions)
e.g. AIB, Bank of Ireland or Ulster Bank

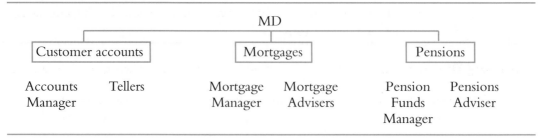

MD

Customer accounts	Mortgages	Pensions
Accounts Manager Tellers	Mortgage Manager Mortgage Advisers	Pension Funds Manager Pensions Adviser

Figure 1.7 Matrix Division of Organisation – Product by Function

Departmental divisions are dictated by the size, type of business, nature of work involved, numbers, shifts, type of customer, and equipment specialisation.

Departmentation is the division of work into different areas. Dividing people into groups within each department or sub-department and allocating a head of department will ensure a greater level of efficiency and specialisation, where the lines of authority and decision-making responsibilities are clearly defined.

Larger organisations find it cost effective to engage in this type of division of labour to increase sales and profits by utilising the expertise in each department, thereby linking the whole organisation in this way. Some of these organisations have a department specifically for research and development of product in order to out-manoeuvre their nearest competitors.

PRACTICE QUESTIONS

1. Define the term 'Departmentation'.
2. Name and explain the *five* main functional areas to which departments may be linked.
3. Pick an organisation and outline and discuss the duties attached to each functional area (i.e. Departments).
4. Pick any business and make illustrated divisions based on the process of:
    (a) departmentation by function (i.e. departments in a business such as sales, personnel)
    (b) departmentation by product (i.e. products in a business)
    (c) departmentation by region (i.e. branches in the country).

Environmental Features affecting an Organisation (A PEST plus C Analysis)

The factors that affect an organisation are:

1. POLITICAL AND LEGAL

Conservation and environmental groups backed by political pressure can affect an organisation's activities by highlighting health and safety risks usually linked to noise, water or atmospheric pollution caused by the organisation. Regulations like registration, tax and VAT returns, as well as health and safety regulations, laws regarding employment practices and legislation, trade union laws, etc. all restrict an organisation's activities.

Fiscal (tax and government spending changes and decisions) and monetary decisions, including changes in interest rates, sometimes have a profound effect on organisations.

2. ECONOMIC

The level of economic activity in an economy will dictate consumer income and purchasing power. The higher the level of disposable (spendable) income, the greater the demand for goods. Price and changing interest rates will also affect consumers' decisions to purchase. Government fiscal policies (budget decisions on taxes and government spending) and monetary policies (interest rates and the availability of credit in banks) influence the cost of living and exchange rates, and therefore this also directly influences demand for goods and services from the organisation. The value of the domestic currency will influence investment in industry based on business confidence and the ability to borrow to invest, as well as confidence in future healthy economic activity. The number of competitors and their current success will also impact on an organisation from an economic point of view.

3. SOCIAL AND CULTURAL

The ethical conduct of organisations is measured against legal and public standards. Organisations must carry out business in a responsible way that is both morally and legally acceptable. Certain attitudes, customs, beliefs and education, as well as behaviour and values, are generally adhered to by organisations. This will ensure that the business will remain a success or survive, whatever the case may be. Tribunals of inquiry are one example of social factors that will affect an organisation's reputation (e.g. the 1998 Blood Bank Tribunal) in a positive or negative way, depending on the outcome.

4. TECHNOLOGICAL

New high-tech equipment and computers have made work less time-consuming and more capital-intensive rather than labour-intensive. Work patterns have changed totally as a result. The need for retraining and constant modernisation of product due to processes and products becoming obsolete (out of date) has been highlighted in recent times. This can incur extra costs for organisations. The development of the Internet is good from an educational point of view as well as being a medium for payment (for example by credit card), intercommunications and advertising for a business all over the world.

5. COMPETITIVE FACTORS

If a similar business becomes established locally, it may affect the business – depending on the nature of the business. Retail organisations are more likely to be affected than services like hairdressers or beauty salons, which tend to retain custom based on customer loyalty because of the hands-on nature of these businesses.

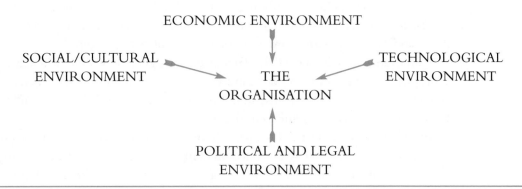

Figure 1.8 Environmental Factors impacting on an Organisation

Note: This analysis can be simply memorised by students, if they remember 'PEST plus C' (political, economic, social and technological factors that impact on an organisation, as well as competition factors).

Functions of Management

Henri Fayol (1841–1925) popularised the concept of the 'Universality of Management Principles', the idea that management should apply the same broad principles, no matter what sort of business is being managed. He is known as the 'father of modern operational management theory'. His work was published in 1949. He identified the following main functions of management:

1. ***PLANNING AND DIRECTING:*** to predetermine future action involving important areas like forecasting, objective-setting, decision-making and policy formation; also to direct events, as the organisation progresses towards achieving specific objectives. Planning is an essential element of good organisation and a manager must always be sure of goals.

2. ***ORGANISING/STAFFING:*** the activity of organising involves arranging and relating the work (a structure of tasks) to be performed, so that it can be accomplished most effectively by staff. It involves progressing plans from the decision stage to the activity stage by grouping tasks into specialised jobs for each individual, where each individual's responsibilities are clearly defined. Organising also involves delegating authority (dividing up tasks) and clearly defining the lines of authority so that each person knows who is superior and who is subordinate. It also involves the co-ordination and supervision of performance at all times. Staffing involves finding and training suitable successors, as well as the responsibilities for hiring and firing where appropriate.

3. *COMMUNICATION:* the key to good organisation where information flow is accurate and all inclusive with regard to staff. The manager will organise successfully by being open to change, by seeking new ideas and implementing them, and by incorporating new technology into the organisation.

Communication is one of the factors of management which, when used appropriately, is the key to good organisation and which influences the efficiency and effectiveness of an organisation. Efficiency means 'doing things right'. Effectiveness means 'doing the right things'.

Effectiveness comes first and is the key to managerial success – as dictated by the style of management and how the functions of management are undertaken. All the other functions rely on the existence of a good information system within the organisation. If planning is to be effective, i.e. if there is to be an effective planning environment, the goals, strategies and policies of the organisation have to be communicated appropriately to those who need to know them. The single greatest cause of unco-ordinated planning is a manager's lack of understanding of his goals, company strategies and policies when he is endeavouring to make decisions. Otherwise, a planning gap is caused by a lack of communication: senior management understand goals and plans; workers know what they have to do; but middle management do not understand how their departmental goals and policies tie in with those of the organisation as a whole. Effective planning is fostered when proper communication is established and all levels of management are given opportunities to contribute to plans which affect their areas of authority.

Efficiency can only be maintained when a high level of effectiveness is present and will be dictated by the individual skills, talents and styles of staff. Speed and efficiency with regard to work will gain the organisation a good reputation which will foster further future efficiency with results and productivity being based on good communication within the organisation.

4. *COMMANDING:* the activity of instructing subordinates, the demonstration of leadership skills. The roles regarding the 'Command' function can be subdivided into the following categories:

(a) Interpersonal: the manager is the figurehead, leader and facilitator for liaison purposes.

(b) Informational: the manager is a monitor, disseminator (sender of information in and out of the organisation), spokesperson (giving information to the organisation, having received it from either external or internal sources).

(c) Decisional: the manager makes decisions about internal disturbances, and is the initiator of change and innovation.

(d) Resource allocator: the manager takes charge of budgeting and the efficient management of time, money, materials, equipment and personnel.

(e) Negotiator: the manager must deal directly with staff, customers and suppliers.

5. **CO-ORDINATING AND MOTIVATING:** the activity of co-ordinating involves harmonising activities of the different groups within the organisation; making sure each section and subsection operates efficiently and relates its efforts to the others. Motivating involves encouraging greater work effort aimed at achieving better results, the activity aimed at satisfying needs and drives within the work situation.

6. **CONTROLLING:** activities and methods used by managers to ensure that previously agreed plans are in fact working (clarity of purpose, the awareness of objectives and targets). Henry Gantt, a specialist in scientific management, developed a type of bar chart which mapped actual and planned performances of the organisation based on agreed and established goals and standards. The chart provided a reviewing technique to compare target with actual performance over time. It allowed the effectiveness of the organisation to be judged in the light of specific targets. Based on mapping performance in this way, the organisation could take corrective action if a decline was detected.

Gantt chart

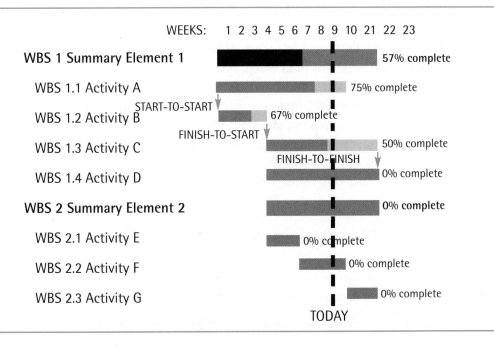

Figure 1.9 Work Breakdown Schedules in a Gantt Chart

WHAT IS A GANTT CHART?

A Gantt chart is a type of bar chart that illustrates a project schedule. It maps actual performance against planned or target performance. Gantt charts illustrate the start and finish dates of the elements of a project and includes the work breakdown structure of the project. Some Gantt charts also show the dependency relationships between activities. Gantt charts can be used to show current schedule status using percent-complete shadings and a vertical 'TODAY' line as shown in Figure 1.9.

Although now regarded as a common charting technique, Gantt charts were considered revolutionary when they were introduced. In recognition of Henry Gantt's contributions, the Henry Laurence Gantt Medal is awarded for distinguished achievement in management and in community service. This chart is used also in information technology (IT) to represent data that has been collected and continues to be an important tool in Project Management.

Gantt charts have become a common technique for representing the phases and activities of a project work breakdown structure (WBS), so they can be understood by a wide audience. WBS 1 and 2 can denote different phses of a project. The Gantt chart in Figure 1.9 shows three kinds of schedule dependencies (see orange arrows) and percentage complete indications.

PRACTICE QUESTIONS

1. List the environmental features that make an impact on an organisation and explain them briefly.
2. Carry out a PEST plus C analysis of an organisation of your choice.
3. What are the *six* functions of management?
4. Briefly explain each.
5. Why is the function 'communication' linked with organisation?
6. How does Effectiveness differ from Efficiency?
7. Explain the roles of the manager with regard to the command function.
8. Why is motivation so significant?
9. What is a Gantt chart and which function is it connected with?

Knowledge Management

Knowledge management is the method used by employers and managers to leverage knowledge to improve overall performance. (The analysis of performance in an organisation is known as performance appraisal.)

Knowledge Management Systems Involve:

1. Examining how an organisation's knowledge is maintained, accessed and exchanged. This knowledge comes from staff. Managers aim to encourage the sharing of knowledge and sometimes this requires a cultural change within the organisation.
2. Sharing information among different departments.

Modern management thinking aims to reinforce in employees' minds that if business performance improves due to intelligent sharing and use of knowledge, then everyone gains.

Advantages of Knowledge Management Systems Are:

1. The more people involved the easier it is to spread and collect information.
2. Employees are more involved in company decision-making and the development of the business, which in turn stimulates greater work effort and productivity and leads to much lower staff turnover.
3. They keep the organisation ahead of the curve and cut costs.

Knowledge management is an umbrella term for making more efficient use of the human knowledge that exists within an organisation. Sharing knowledge in any company is vital but in order for a knowledge management activity to succeed, it must be tied into a business strategy.

The major focus of knowledge management is to identify and gather content from documents, reports and other sources and to be able to search that content for meaningful relationships.

Knowledge management can also be defined as the twenty-first century equivalent of information management. It is essentially an industry trying to distinguish itself with specialised groupware and business intelligence (BI) products that offer a wide range of solutions.

What is Information Management or Knowledge Transfer?

Most customer service organisations today will admit that effective knowledge transfer is the most crucial element in resolving customer problems. When done correctly, knowledge transfer accelerates problem resolution processes, fuels customer satisfaction and leads to greater organisational efficiency.

Information management can be defined as the discipline that analyses information as an organisational resource. It covers the definitions, uses, value and distribution of all data and information within an organisation, whether processed by computer or not. It evaluates the kinds of data/information an organisation requires in order to function and progress effectively.

What is Data Administration/Management?

Information can now be stored on networked computer systems (via LAN; a local area network) and instead of the outdated practice of keeping information in hard-backed form in filing cabinets and the constant photocopying of sheets, businesses can use intranet and extranet systems to store information and allow staff and/or customers/clients limited or unlimited access. This also helps retain information for the business more efficiently.

Knowledge management: from lifelong employment to lifelong learning

Gerry McGovern

Knowledge management is often thought of as a process by which an organisation gets its staff to share their knowledge for the benefit of the organisation. Of equal importance to the success of knowledge management is how an organisation shares knowledge for the benefit of staff.

The traditional organisation made a promise to its staff: Work hard, show talent, and you will have a long and progressive career with us. Downsizing, outsourcing, and a general environment of rapid change, has meant that this promise is less common.

The response of many staff is to no longer expect lifelong employment. In fact, to stay a long time with a particular organisation is now seen in a negative light by many people. They want to stay fresh and move on before they are moved out.

The increase in interest in the discipline of knowledge management finds some of its roots in the decline of the lifelong employment promise. The organisation sees itself in danger of becoming a knowledge sieve, with knowledgeable staff continuously leaving, bringing their knowledge with them. A key question of knowledge management is: How do we tap this knowledge before it flows away?

Naturally, many staff have taken a cynical view. It looks to them that knowledge management initiatives are a way of draining knowledge from them. Some believe that once their best knowledge has been sucked out, they become even more dispensable.

The way to create a positive and realistic environment is to answer the question: What's in it for me? If you take away the promise of lifelong employment, what do you replace it with? Lifelong learning.

Lifelong learning is a direct response to the decline in lifelong employment. The age of lifelong employment was reflected by gradual change and a formal education for a fixed period that, by and large, lasted you through your career.

The age of lifelong learning is reflected by rapid change and the need to constantly update your skills. Rapid change has brought with it a tremendous rise in complexity. The emergence of the Internet combines access to vast quantities of information with powerful communication and collaboration tools.

Knowledge workers — those who get paid to think — live in a giant network that is constantly in flux. The opposite of a network is an individual. Hoarding of information is a natural defensive reaction, but it doesn't work if you want to succeed in a network.

In an Internet-driven economy, it simply pays to share. Getting connected and sharing is one of the surest ways to become a lifelong learner.

The organisation can offer a new set of promises to the knowledge worker:

- Our intranet will be full of useful things that will help you learn smarter and faster.
- We reward those who share and collaborate. The more quality knowledge you share the more your career will progress.
- Because everyone in this organisation shares, our collective knowledge is a powerful resource.
- We offer you opportunities to publish and promote your best ideas. This will enhance your reputation.
- In essence, we offer you a lifelong learning university. We provide you will the tools, content and environment that makes learning a form of sharing and sharing a form of learning.

Source: www.gerrymcgovern.com

In Summary:
- Knowledge Management is the collection of information from staff.
- Information Management is the analysis of information and business intelligence (often part of a business's R&D (research and development) function).
- Data Administration and Management refers to the modern, high-tech methods employed by businesses to store and transfer large volumes of information and enable access to this information by managers, staff and customers. (Examples are intranets and extranets.)

What is Facility Management?

A facility can be defined as a physical place where business activities are done – the building itself.

Facility Management has been defined by Tuveson as 'the co-ordination of the physical workplace with the people and work of an organisation' (*Facility Management in the 21st Century* (1998)).

The Facility Manager has a very responsible job, making facility plans in accordance with the needs and demands of business activities. It involves leadership skills and attempts to integrate the principles of business administration, architecture and the behavioural and engineering sciences.

In summary, it focuses on how to keep an organisation operating, specifically in relation to its buildings.

Examples of facilities include grocery stores, sports complexes, jails, office buildings, hospitals, hotels, retail outlets and government institutions.

The responsibilities involved in this type of management include a wide range of function and support services, including caretaking services and security, health and safety considerations, property and buildings management, space planning and accounting, telecommunications and mail and messenger services, management of records and other support duties.

It is the job of the facility manager to create an efficient environment that encourages productivity, safety (reducing the risk of liability, or of being sued), one that is pleasing to clients, customers and staff and meets legal and/or government requirements.

Different businesses generally have different facility needs in terms of buildings, space, an office or a suite of offices (urban/rural) and other physical aspects. A good facility manager will address these needs in the best and most cost-effective ways possible.

Typical responsibilities include:

- Monitoring operating efficiency within the organisation (identifying physical problems like machine breakdown, problems with products, deliveries, etc.) and finding solutions.

- Keeping a check on facility-related expenditure based on available monies.
- Real estate procurement (buying buildings for the business), leasing or sale of buildings, renovation or relocation of buildings.
- Monitoring of upkeep of buildings (high-capacity operation is essential).
- Ordering office supplies.
- Tracking and responding to environmental, health, safety and security issues. (Ergonomics – the design of tasks and work areas to maximise the efficiency and quality of employees' work.)
- Making sure business complies with codes and regulations.
- Planning future facility needs – e.g. new spaces, new wiring, lighting, technology/automation, wheelchair access, etc.
- Identifying needs for educating workforce in line with new plans and putting in place suitable training regarding standards and procedures (policy formulation).

Until recently, senior managers in Irish organisations have as a matter of course taken on the responsibilities of a facility manager. Now, however, in line with the knowledge economy, and due to senior managers' excessive workload and greater expectations of facilities by both staff and customers, many organisations employ facility managers for their expertise, in order to ensure that they have state-of-the-art, constantly updated and monitored facilities (buildings, etc.), in this increasingly competitive modern work environment.

Organisational Management Systems (OMS)

What are OMS Systems?

WHAT IS THE SMART HIRING WEB-BASED SOFTWARE (PART OF STRATEGIC MANAGEMENT)?

Decisions are the engines that drive our businesses. Top performance begins with smart hiring decisions. Managers can get the information they need about performance potential, job behaviours and job fit with computerised OMS systems, consisting of web-based software used to train organisations. They explain how to interpret the analysis and outputs quickly and simply. OMS systems can be integrated into in-house human resources systems and have the capability to get the information quickly, easily, and efficiently for all candidates for all jobs at all levels.

HOW DOES A MANAGER ENSURE THE RIGHT PERSON IS IN THE RIGHT JOB?

Despite better education and training, many business organisations have shown little improvement in making more accurate decisions about recruiting people. Why not? Too many people are still placed in the wrong jobs and kept there. They don't perform well, they are not motivated, and they are not happy. They build up defence structures that impede the performance of others. OMS systems employ two objective measurement and assessment tools:

- **The OMS questionnaire:** The questionnaire identifies personality traits, human motivating factors, and behavioural attributes, i.e. what makes the individual 'tick'.
- **JAX, the job analysis expert:** JAX measures job behavioural and motivational requirements and job-related talents and the behavioural needs of a given job role.

Matching the person to the job or vice versa is the secret of building a contented workforce. OMS systems are powerful, simple and visual, and include in them team-building programmes and can be integrated with other organisational training programmes. Organisations can even buy iPhone apps that use OMS systems. OMS systems allow managers to make faster, better-informed operating decisions, leading to higher individual and group performance, greater staff retention, and lower organisational costs.

Administrative Functions Supporting Effective Implementation of OMS systems

The office manager is the co-ordinator of the work system. They usually lead or manage a team of secretaries or administrative clerks. They take care of the assignment of tasks within the department, and the more complex tasks tend to come to their desk. An office manager is responsible for planning, organising and controlling the clerical aspect of the organisation, including the preparation, communication, co-ordination and storage of data to support production and other important operations of an industrial establishment. Often the office manager is also engaged in marketing.

Their tasks are also to monitor the work processes and to evaluate the outcome. The outcomes of work are intended for what can be called the final receiving system, as for instance, the client and other departments. The main office management function that OMS systems link with is Human Resources, and part of the office manager's role is to provide input to management on the development of policies and procedures that will integrate with the web-based OMS system used.

EXAMPLES OF ADMINISTRATIVE HARDWARE AND SOFTWARE SUPPORTS

Systems and network administrators have the main responsibility for management information systems (MIS) and locating suitable hardware and software for this purpose. They provide support through problem resolution and software installations as well as through educating the user in the use of supported applications. The users are usually the office manager and his or her team in conjunction with senior managers, line managers and department managers.

Hardware used: In most organisations regular high spec PCs (personal computers) are used in offices and in some graphics or print organisations, Mac computers are used.

Office managers and their teams receive training in different software packages, e.g. Microsoft Word, Access and Excel, and provide administrative support to senior, line and department managers as part of the organisation's day-to-day operational activities.

The Need for Quality within an Organisation

Quality control is part of an organisation's overall control mechanism used to maintain standards and to identify deviations that are unacceptable compared against an agreed standard of quality. It involves taking corrective action, if deviations are significant, to restore the agreed acceptable level of quality. The role of quality control is to ensure that appropriate standards of quality are set and that variances beyond the tolerances are rejected. It is, however, possible to mass produce items that are almost identical but are not defective and conform to quality standards.

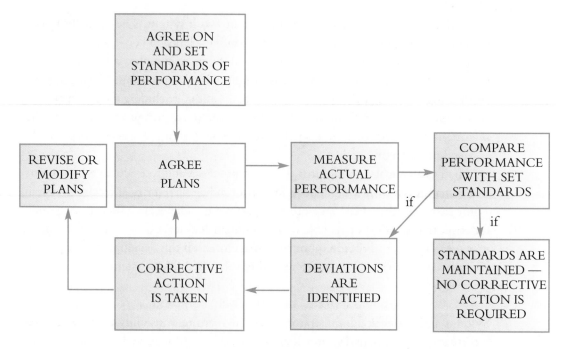

Figure 1.10   How Control is Maintained

Quality control is needed in an organisation because it is linked directly with such factors as:

1. **Price:** Businesses ascertain the quality of their products and charge selling prices which should correlate with these standards. Products such as highly priced porcelain will be subject to far higher quality controls than run of the mill household earthenware.

2. **Consistency:** Must be maintained to justify prices and for businesses to maintain competitiveness.

3. **Safety:** Products like pharmaceuticals and food require the highest standards of quality to ensure the good health and safety of the community. Vehicles in general, e.g. public transport vehicles, cars, etc., are also subject to intensive testing to ensure public safety.

4. **Legal requirements:** Pharmaceutical products are subject to health controls which are backed by legislation. The general public expect the highest quality with regard to products that they purchase. Legal action taken against businesses will affect their reputation and appropriate corrective action will be necessary to restore public confidence.

Quality Controls and Measures

THE MOST WIDELY USED TECHNIQUES

1. **100 per cent Inspection:** this is used when perfect quality is required, e.g. in the construction of a nuclear reactor plant or pharmaceutical product.

2. **Random Sampling:** where batch production takes place, 100 per cent inspection is not always necessary, nor is it always effective, where inspectors' ability to concentrate might be affected by noisy or busy surroundings. (Up to 15 per cent of defective items pass unnoticed, recent studies have shown.) Better results can sometimes be achieved by random sampling. Random sampling means that a batch is accepted or rejected on the basis of the number of rejects found after taking a random sample from the batch.

3. **Continuous Sampling:** this is used in mass-production systems, and entails an initial 100 per cent inspection until a predetermined number of correct items have passed in succession; then random sampling begins and continues until a further reject appears; then 100 per cent inspection is recommended, and the cycle is repeated if necessary.

4. **Quality Circles:** a quality circle is a group of people within an organisation who meet together on a regular basis to identify, analyse and solve problems in relation to quality, productivity or other aspects of day-to-day working arrangements using problem-solving techniques. The idea of quality circles is based on the Japanese ethos of quality.

ESSENTIAL FEATURES OF QUALITY CIRCLES

1. Membership is voluntary.
2. Group usually between five and ten members.
3. Group selects the problems to be tackled and methods of operation.
4. Leader is usually the immediate supervisor.

EFFECTIVENESS DEPENDS ON:

1. Commitment and support of top management.
2. Full consultation with staff.
3. A participative approach by management.
4. Delegation of decision-making.
5. Trust and goodwill on all sides.
6. An effective support structure of consultation and negotiation.
5. Group members will receive training in communication and problem-solving skills, quality control techniques and group processes.
6. The group recommends solutions to management and, where possible, has authority to implement agreed solutions.
7. Support of trade unions and/or staff representatives.
8. An effective training programme including development of quantitative skills.
9. Continuous monitoring and review of result.

BENEFITS OF QUALITY CONTROL

1. Reduction in costs of scrap or re-working.
2. Reduction in complaints from customers.
3. Enhanced reputation of company's products.
4. Feedback to designers and staff about performance of products and the machines required to produce them.

QUALITY CONTROL IN SERVICE-TYPE ORGANISATIONS

This concerns staff and their approach to clients as well as their skills and professional performance in these organisations (efficient human resource management). Quality with regard to service will be maintained by:

1. Attention to monitoring staff performance and refresher retraining to update staff.
2. Management should be open to new innovative ideas and be willing to implement them.
3. Lines of communication should be kept open to avoid staff-management relationship problems.
4. Corrective action should be taken to restore damaged reputation due to bad client-handling techniques.
5. Prompt and efficient response to client enquiries or problems should take priority.

6. Efficient manpower planning and back-up mechanisms for handling absenteeism. Manpower planning is the activity of matching the labour need with suitably skilled labour and making appropriate projections with regard to future expected shortfalls of labour in order to ensure efficiency and quality of service.
7. Maintain a professional image at all times.

Increasing Importance of Quality Systems in Different Types of Organisations

Quality IT systems (computer programs) are now available for organisations to purchase. The various techniques and processes in organisations are managed by these systems with specialised systems available to meet different organisational needs. A quality IT system can be designed to meet the needs of manufacturing-focused organisations that produce, for example, food or pharmaceuticals.

Other quality IT systems are available to meet the needs of service-focused organisations like recruitment or human resources agencies that deal in training and consultancy.

These IT systems main functions are to:

- Manage production or services.
- Assist in satisfying auditors that might inspect the finances of the business.
- Meet customer quality-reporting requirements: If customers have a query about quality systems there is a reporting facility available to the organisation.

The main aspects of quality IT systems often include the ability to:

- Capture data from different sources – Data Collection.
- Manage data.
- Analyse data.
- Report.

A Quality/Systems Assurance Manager usually has the overall responsibility of managing the IT system by generating reports for senior managers and by identifying defects and reporting the need for corrective action.

Quality Awards

The main quality awards presented to organisations are:

1. Quality Mark: information available from the Excellence Ireland Quality Association (EIQA).
2. QMark for Hygiene and Food Safety: information available from the Excellence Ireland Quality Association.
3. ISO 9000: information available from the National Standards Association of Ireland (NSAI).

Smaller organisations whose market share is mainly in the domestic market would tend to apply for the Quality Mark and/or the Hygiene Mark.

THE Q MARK

The Q Mark from EIQA has become one of the most sought-after trademarks in the Irish business world. To be awarded a Q Mark an organisation is independently audited on key operational criteria and business results.

Benefits of the Q Mark:
* widely known by consumers
* recognised as a reliable and trustworthy indicator of quality
* means significant operational efficiencies
* improves morale and teamwork
* will increase your bottom line.

The steps to achieving Q Mark certification are simple. If you have not sought Q Mark certification before, all you have to do is:
* fill in the application form
* submit it to EIQA
* wait for an audit to be scheduled
* have the audit completed and the result submitted to a board of independent assessors.

If your organisation passes the minimum threshold then it will be awarded the Q Mark for a period of twelve months.

Many organisations, particularly first-time applicants, may need some practical assistance such as training, a mock audit or some direct in-company help. EIQA will be happy to provide any or all such assistance.

THE HYGIENE MARK

The National Hygiene Mark Programme is open to any company in the food or non-food sector. Companies are assessed under the following headings (with some variations depending on the company):
* Structural Hygiene
* Operational Hygiene
* Food Storage and Protection
* Staff Facilities and Personal Hygiene
* Hygiene Management System.

A written report is issued and graded on a scale of A to F. A corrective action and surveillance system is in place.

ISO 9000

Companies with international links will tend to have a preference for ISO 9000. ISO 9000 registration is a logical move for a company demonstrably committed to quality, i.e. a company that already holds both or either of the other two awards. Some companies may consider ISO 9000 not relevant to their particular needs or too expensive, since generally speaking a small to medium-sized company can expect to pay significant costs plus expenses on consultation fees. Added to this is the staff time devoted to preparing the quality system and the cost of the audit of this system, as well as the production of a quality manual. The National Standards Association of Ireland (NSAI) is the certification body for ISO 9000.

THE MICHELIN GUIDE – STAR RATINGS

The Michelin Guide awards restaurants between one and three stars based on the quality of the cuisine served: *three stars* indicate that food, wine, décor and service are exceptional; *two stars* indicate perfection; and *one star* means that food is very good and there is a pleasant environment.

The Guide warns readers not to compare the very fancy 'de luxe' restaurant that has *one star* to a simpler restaurant 'where you can appreciate fine food at a reasonable price'. (Refer to **www.cuisinenet.com**)

FAILTE IRELAND QUALITY ASSURANCE

Tourism Accommodation Approval (B and B approval)
This organisation allocates Fáilte Ireland approval to bed and breakfast accommodation.

EXCELLENCE IN TOURISM (HOTEL, GUESTHOUSE, CARAVAN AND CAMPING PARK ACCOMMODATION APPROVAL)

This organisation awards different Fáilte Ireland grades of excellence to accommodation within the tourist industry as indicated above.

Q Mark for Hygiene and Food Safety

What is the Q Mark for Hygiene and Food Safety?

The Q Mark for Hygiene and Food Safety has been in existence since 1978 and is awarded to organisations that successfully complete a detailed audit of their food safety management systems. There are three levels of certification within the Q Mark for Hygiene and Food Safety as follows:

Level 1 Foundation

This is the basic level for entry into the Q Mark for Hygiene and Food Safety programme and is based around a specific Level 1 Foundation guidance document that is aimed at smaller organisations (less than 2000 square feet/185.8 square metres). The focus at this level is on basic compliance in all areas for the provision of safe food. Organisations that achieve Level 1 Foundation certification will have demonstrated an acceptable level of legal compliance during an unannounced audit. To achieve certification a score of 60 per cent or higher must be achieved during the audit.

Level 2 Sapphire

This higher level award is based upon a separate Technical Standard aimed at promoting continuous improvement and requires organisations to demonstrate standards of hygiene and food safety management above those required to achieve Level 1 Foundation certification. A minimum score of 60 per cent is required to achieve Level 2 Sapphire certification.

Level 3 Emerald

This is the highest level of certification in the Q Mark for Hygiene and Food Safety programme and is awarded to organisations that achieve a score of 75 per cent or higher in the unannounced audit. To achieve this, level organisations will have demonstrated that they are operating at the highest levels of food safety with a focus on continuous improvement.

All sectors of the food industry are eligible to join the programme and to receive the internationally recognised Q Mark for Hygiene and Food Safety certification. For details of the most suitable level for your organisation, contact for information info@eiqa.com or call 01 6604100.

Source: Excellence Ireland Quality Association (EIQA) www.eiqa.ie

How does the Q Mark for Hygiene and Food Safety Programme work?

The programme consists of two key documents:

1. The Hygiene and Food Safety Guidance Document for Level 1 Foundation
2. The Hygiene and Food Safety Technical Standard for Level 2 Sapphire and Level 3 Emerald

The key elements of the Hygiene and Food Safety Guidance document (Level 1 Foundation) are:

1. Management.
2. Food Safety Management Systems.
3. Auditing.
4. Structure and Services.

The key elements of the Hygiene and Food Safety Technical Standard (Level 2 Sapphire and Level 3 Emerald) are:

1. Planning and Commitment.
2. Approach.
3. Performance and Review.
4. Structure and Services.

The Audit Process

The unannounced audit is performed by an experienced auditor who will:
1. Review the organisation's food safety management system.
2. Inspect the premises and facilities.
3. Observe staff practices.
4. Interview staff and management.

Source: Excellence Ireland Quality Association (EIQA) www.eiqa.ie

BENEFITS OF THE Q MARK FOR HYGIENE AND FOOD SAFETY PROGRAMME:

- Enhances customer confidence: Third-party certification confirms that the organisation aspires to the highest standards of hygiene and food safety. This generates customer loyalty.
- Demonstrates an organisation's commitment using distinctive certification and marketing material based on the most widely used framework in Ireland.
- Provides the opportunity to benchmark against other organisations using the same framework, including Irish market leaders.
- Encourages and fosters excellent Hygiene and Food Safety Standards.
- Assists companies in adhering to the national and European Food Hygiene legislation and enables compliance with the latest industry codes of practice
- Ongoing EIQA marketing and advertising campaign promotes the Hygiene Mark brand. which creates brand awareness.
- Increases an organisation's competitive advantage.

EXAMPLES OF SUCCESSFUL ORGANISATIONS THAT HAVE COMPLETED THE Q MARK FOR HYGIENE AND FOOD SAFETY:

- Supervalu
- Centra
- Eurospar
- Londis
- Budgens
- Eurest
- Irish Prison Services
- McDonalds
- Musgrave Foodservices
- Johnston Mooney & O'Brien
- Wexford Creamery
- Fitzpatrick Hotel Group

Public Demand for Food Quality Assurance

In recent years the Food and Agriculture Organisation of the United Nations in conjunction with the World Health Organisation have produced publications relating to developing countries proving that there is growing consumer awareness of food safety and quality issues globally and increasing demand for safety and quality in the interests of public health and consumer protection.

According to Bord Bia (Irish Food Board), a Quality Assurance Scheme (QAS) for a food product is a programme whereby the food is produced to a set of standards (rules) and the producer or processor is inspected (audited) to ensure that production is in accordance with those standards. In the Bord Bia Quality Assurance Schemes all steps in the food chain from production to final packaging for sale to the end user are Quality Assured. These include the farm or growing unit, the meat factory or packing centre and any secondary processing food factory (smoking, curing, cooking etc).

There are three basic components in a quality assurance scheme:

- Standards.
- Audit.
- Certification.

What Products Carry the Q Mark?

Bord Bia operates Quality Assurance Schemes for the following: Bacon, beef, chicken, duck, eggs, fruit, lamb, pork, turkey and vegetables. A substantial number of farmers/producers and processors are members of these schemes and, therefore, a large range of food with the Bord Bia Q Mark is available from all the major supermarkets and other retail outlets.

WHAT FOODS CARRY THE BORD BIA Q MARKS?

Only food produced on approved Irish farms and processed in approved Irish factories can carry the Origin Ireland Q Mark. Currently all the members of the Bord Bia Quality Assurance schemes are on the island of Ireland.

IS THERE MORE THAN ONE VERSION OF THE BORD BIA Q MARK?

There are three main versions of the Bord Bia Q Mark. All members of the Bord Bia QAS are on the island of Ireland. Refer to **www.bordbia.ie.**

Figure 1.11 Bord Bia Q Marks

What is the Food Safety Authority?

The Food Safety Authority of Ireland's (FSAI) primary responsibility is to control the safety of food. It delegates some of its functions to other bodies such as the Health Services Executive and the Department of Agriculture, Fisheries and Food, but it retains the final responsibility.

A first for food-safety knowledge exchange
11 October 2011

*safe*food, the all-island agency responsible for promoting food safety and healthy eating, today launched eight new knowledge-exchange networks to promote the use of science-based knowledge to further enhance the integrity and reputation of the food supply on the island of Ireland.

By creating linkages between all the critical points of the food supply chain, the networks will enable greater knowledge-sharing and application, and ensure consumer expectations for a safe and healthy food supply can be met. The networks were officially launched at an event in Belfast today by Dr Andrew McCormick, Permanent Secretary at the Department of Health, Social Services and Public Safety. Since the beginning of 2011 more than 900 members have already joined.

The **safefood** knowledge networks were launched at an event which explored the application and value of knowledge exchange across all sectors of the food chain and how and where this exchange can be applied for the greatest benefit. Speakers included experts in the fields of international food business, knowledge exchange and international technology transfer and Research and Development.

Source: *safe*food
For more information on how to join the Knowledge Networks, visit www.safefood.ning.com.

What is the HACCP ?

HACCP (Hazard Analysis and Critical Control Point) is a food–safety management system which is a systematic approach to identifying and controlling hazards, whether microbiological, chemical or physical, which could pose a threat to the production of safe food. In simple terms, it involves identifying what could go wrong in a food system and planning how to prevent it. Since 1998 **HACCP has been a legal requirement for all food businesses.** Under current legislation, a food business is defined as '…any undertaking, whether for profit or not and whether public or private, carrying out any or all of the following: preparation, processing, manufacturing, packaging, storing, transportation, distribution, handling or offering for sale or supply of foodstuffs'. The FSAI has produced a new pack called 'Safe Catering – Your Guide to Making Food Safely' to aid businesses in implementing HACCP.

Refer to **www.fsai.ie.**

We must ensure our clean, green food island remains a recipe for success

Ivan Yates   Thursday, October 13, 2011

The good and great assembled in Dublin Castle, deliberating at the Global Irish Economic Forum, to conceive new ideas for our economic prosperity.

Their creativity included establishment of a new social networking website worldIrish.com, tourism initiative The Gathering to welcome emigrants in 2013, expanded graduate schemes, unpaid service on state boards and a diaspora awards scheme. It's a pity they seemed oblivious to Ireland's greatest strength — our natural resources — food and drinks. Ireland's world-class brands include Guinness, Bailey's, Jameson and Kerrygold. We are global leaders in food ingredients, infant formula and prepared consumer food products. There was no mention of our indigenous industries' global potential, nor any attempt to showcase our array of superb products to 70 million Irish worldwide. Preoccupation with global multinationals ignores the fundamentals of food security and net benefits to our economy. Take the IDA success story of Google, now employing 2,000 people in their European HQ in Dublin. Their 2010 accounts reveal on €10bn turnover, they contributed €2m in profits tax here. There are no repatriated profits from €24bn of output from agribusiness, seafood and timber sectors, delivering €9bn of exports.

HSBC's Global Research Unit, involving economists in 70 countries, produced The World in 2050 report. Their findings predict: world output will treble, while emerging states' output will increase fivefold; 19 of 30 top economies will comprise emerging states and China and India will be the largest and third-largest economies. Total world population will rise from 7 billion to 9 billion. They are going to be hungry.

Meeting demand for food is a crucial component of the global policy agenda. UN body, the Food and Agriculture Organisation, projects a 70 per cent increase in food production will be needed by 2050. Scope for extra areas for cultivation doesn't exist due to erosion of ecosystem quality and climate change constraints.

The challenge of meeting nutritional needs will be met by improvement in yields, adapting crops, extra investment and productivity. High-quality healthy foods will be especially in demand amongst richer consumers. Ireland — the Food Island — enters a period of sustained unprecedented opportunity. Recently, EU Agriculture Commissioner Dacian Ciolos published proposals to reform the Common Agricultural Policy, covering the period 2014-2020. The €387bn package involves annual expenditure of €55bn. Irish farmers will receive €1.3bn in direct payments. New measures seek to evolve a Common Environmental Policy, with 30 per cent of entitlements based on ecological sustainability; a ceiling of €300,000 will apply to any single farmer and production limitations will be abolished, such as national milk quotas in 2015. When all of these factors combine, the market outlook for 150,000 people employed in the sectors has never been better. Four decades of positive price prospects for agricultural commodities beckon.

There are considerable challenges in realising this potential. We need to develop competitive advantage through a cohort elite to 30,000 plus full-time professional farmers, who can produce clean, green, innovative, traceable produce. Allied to this must be a consolidated food processing industry that invests in additional capacity to achieve scale, matching retail giants. Sophisticated environmentally conscious consumer demands will pay a premium for added value. State agencies Teagasc, Bord Bia and Enterprise Ireland have to harness the best entrepreneurial talent, with reduced Exchequer support. This amounts to a national effort summarised in the vision of FoodHarvest 2020.

Source: *Irish Examiner*

Public Demand for Quality Health and Social Care

In the wake of public nursing home scandals and child abuse cases there is an increasing public awareness of the need for quality in health and social care in Ireland and there now exists a general public demand for quality and accountability. The following are some of the public bodies that have responsibilites in these areas.

Public Quality Authorities

WHAT IS HIQA?

HIQA is the national Health Information and Quality Authority.
The key objectives of HIQA are:

- **Healthcare:** To develop person-centred standards for healthcare services and to monitor compliance with these standards.
- **Social care:** The independent authority responsible for driving quality, safety and accountability in residential services for **children**, **older people** and **people with disabilities** in Ireland. HIQA produced standards to protect vulnerable people of all ages who are receiving residential care services and to ensure that these people are receiving an appropriate standard and quality of service.

Refer to **www.hiqa.ie.**

Additionally the following Irish childcare organisations were in 2011 allocated funding by the Department of Children and Youth Affairs **(www.dcya.gov.ie)** to promote quality in childcare:

- Barnardo's
- Childminding Ireland
- Forbairt Naíonraí Teoranta
- Irish Pre-school Playgroups Association (IPPA)
- Irish Steiner Waldorf Early Childhood Association
- National Children's Nurseries Association
- St. Nicholas Montessori Society of Ireland

Community Care Services

Public health services provided in the community in Ireland are sometimes referred to as 'Community Care Services'. They are generally provided by the Health Service Executive (HSE). Community care services may also be provided by voluntary organisations in conjunction with, or on behalf of the HSE. Community care services can include the public health nursing service, home help service, physiotherapy, occupational therapy, chiropody service, day care and respite care service.

THE SOCIAL WORKERS REGISTRATION BOARD

The National Social Work Qualifications Board (NSWQB) was in the past responsible for maintaining and promoting the quality of **social work** education and training in Ireland. It accredited training courses. In March 2011, the NSWQB was dissolved and its functions ceased. The NSWQB status as a competent authority in accordance with EU Directive 2005/36/EC transferred to the Social Workers Registration Board at CORU/Health and Social Care Professionals Council.

Quality Accreditation

There are many varied accreditation bodies, some national and some international, which award the ISO 9001 and ISO 140001 to manufacturing companies.

Some prestigious accreditations are awarded to companies that are part of particular industries. These accreditations are only awarded when a company demonstrates its commitment to providing high-quality, environmentally friendly services and safety management systems to both international and Irish operators. These accreditations have proven to be a major asset to companies that are trying to succeed in the highly competitive global market.

Organisations use these accreditations and display them on their products and use them as part of their product branding and their public relations with the view to generating more business.

1. What is Knowledge Management?
2. List two advantages of knowledge management systems in an organisation.
3. Distinguish between knowledge management, information management and data administration management.
4. What is facility management?
5. What are OMS systems?
6. Briefly explain the factors that dictate the need for quality in an organisation.
7. Explain the *four* main techniques used to maintain quality in organisations.
8. What are Quality Circles and have they a good chance of being effective, in your opinion?
9. What are the benefits of quality control in an organisation?
10. Why does quality control in service type organisations differ from quality control in manufacturing organisations?
11. Name the *three* main quality awards.
12. Why does ISO 9000 differ from the other two awards?
13. What are the Michelin Guide Awards?
14. How does Fáilte Ireland guarantee quality with regard to accommodation in Ireland?
15. What is the Q Mark for Hygiene and Food Safety and how does it work?
16. What is the Bord Bia Q Mark?
17. What is the Food Safety Authority?
18. What is HACCP?

How Students can Research Organisations

Methods to Collect Data

A survey is a framework used to collect primary data (raw data). Surveys are usually carried out using the following methods:

1. Observation or Direct Measurement.
2. Enumeration.
3. Personal Interview (face-to-face).
4. Telephone Interview.
5. Postal Interview.
6. Internet Interview.

OBSERVATION AND DIRECT MEASUREMENT

This describes the counting or measuring of items of data. The Roads Authority often employs this type of survey technique when it is carrying out a traffic survey. The survey can involve counting the number of cars that pass a particular location in a given time period.

ENUMERATION

This involves the distributing of questionnaires and the follow up collection of them. An example is the Census of Population. Due to the length and detail required on the Census Questionnaires, households need time to complete them. The collectors are called enumerators.

THE PERSONAL INTERVIEW

This is a face-to-face interview in which 'the interviewer' asks 'the respondent' (person being interviewed) a series of questions that are contained on the interviewer's questionnaire. The interviewer records the responses. Example: Detergent and washing powder manufacturers often use this survey technique. They carry out door-to-door household surveys, the results of which can be used as part of their advertising campaigns.

THE TELEPHONE INTERVIEW

This is an interview by telephone where the interviewer asks the respondent a series of questions that are contained in the interviewer's questionnaire. The interviewer records the responses.

THE POSTAL INTERVIEW

This questionnaire is posted to the respondent when a survey is being conducted.

THE INTERNET INTERVIEW

Many marketing research agencies have websites on the Internet and offer services including constructing questionnaires, fieldwork, collecting data, processing data and analysing the results of research. Companies and businesses find that this is a useful way of analysing business performance and making comparisons with competitors. Email (electronic mail) allows questionnaires to be sent to respondents via computer and increasingly the Internet is being used to collect data and show results and the analysis of these results.

Questionnaires and Questionnaire Design

A questionnaire is a group of questions compiled to do a survey. Types of questionnaires include:
1. The questionnaire for a Census
2. The questionnaire for the personal interview
3. The questionnaire for the telephone interview
4. The postal questionnaire
5. The Internet questionnaire.

QUESTIONNAIRE DESIGN

In order to put a useful questionnaire together – where information can be easily collated and coded – the investigator must be aware of different types of questions that can be asked.

OPEN-ENDED QUESTIONS: These are questions that lead to opinionated answers and are difficult to code but inject a useful level of variety and variability into a survey when they are constructed correctly. For example:

- Q What do you think of the performance of the current government?
- Q How in your opinion can we improve this product?

MULTIPLE-CHOICE QUESTIONS: These questions allow the respondent to choose from a range of options:

- Q What kind of telephone manner does Mary have?
  (a) Fair
  (b) Good
  (c) Very Good
  (d) Excellent

- Q What daily newspaper do you buy most often?
  Choose *one* only.
  Independent
  Times
  Evening Herald
  Examiner
  Belfast News
  Belfast Telegraph
  Irish Sun
  Irish Mirror

DICHOTOMOUS QUESTIONS: These questions allow the respondent to answer either yes or no.

- Q Will you support Labour in the coming General Election?
  Yes   No

- Q Did you shop on Grafton Street today?
  Yes   No

TYPES OF PROBLEM QUESTIONS: These are the type of questions that lead to unreliable answers and are best avoided.

- Leading Questions: Is it not true that Mary speaks well on the telephone? (The question is suggesting the answer is 'yes'.)
- Ambiguous Questions: Do you think that Mitsubishi Lancers are better than Volkswagon Jettas?
  (What does 'better' mean? – maybe cheaper or better quality? It is open to interpretation.)
- Irrelevant and Unnecessary Questions: Keep to the point and make sure that the survey only asks the questions that it needs to fulfil its purpose.

- Complicated Questions that involve other instructions: If the answer to this question is 'yes', enter a tick at the top of the form and move to question 53. If 'no' answer question 52.
- Unreasonable Calculations: How much do you clock up on your phone bill in a week?
- Multiple Questions: Do you travel to work by car or by bus or do you walk? Some people might use all three modes on different occasions.
- Questions containing difficult, not easily definable words: Do you think that President Clinton should be impeached?
- Offensive or Tactless Questions: Do you go to Mass every Sunday?
- Emotive Questions: Based on Catholic beliefs, do you think that contraception is acceptable?
- Questions based on Memory: How many times do you go to the supermarket in a year?

SWOT and PEST Analyses

The SWOT and PEST analyses should be carried out when the student has done all the fieldwork and all possible avenues of questioning have been exhausted. The student should then compile comprehensive analyses in these two areas based on both facts (data collected) and the student's own opinions of the organisation being examined.

SWOT ANALYSIS

SWOT stands for the Strengths and Weaknesses of the business as well as the Opportunities afforded to the organisation and the Threats that endanger its performance or continued existence.

Examples of questions useful for analysis:

Strengths:
1. Are management structures well organised? Are there good communication structures between management and staff?
2. Is technology future-focused and of help to staff?
3. Is the organisation well located?
4. Does infrastructure (road, rail transportation) benefit the organisation?
5. Are social conveniences for customers like car parking, crèche facilities etc. available to customers?
6. What type of pricing policy exists?

Weaknesses:
1. Is there bad management? How can it be improved?
2. Is there a problem with personal hygiene?
3. Is customer service poor?

Opportunities:
1. What future plans does the business have? — New ideas/possibilities/product or service diversification/more cost-efficient and higher quality operations?

Threats:
1. Has the conversion to the euro currency affected the business?
2. Have new European regulations affected the business?
3. Are new or existing competitors a problem?
4. Are the cost of new technology and the pace of business innovation causing products or services to be obsolete (out of date)?

PEST ANALYSIS

PEST means the Political, Economic, Social and Technological factors that affect the business in its own right, as well as in the context of the industry of which it is a part.

Examples of questions useful for analysis:

Political:

1. Have new political decisions had beneficial or non-beneficial effects on the business?
2. Has the business applied for and/or received any government grants?
3. Has the business had to register with particular bodies connected with the industry itself and/or connected with health, hygiene and safety? For example, leisure centres may look for grants from the Irish Sports Council.
4. Have the owners had to look for planning permission?
5. Has the government had to intervene to settle disputes and what effects has this had on the business?
6. Does the business play a part or benefit from the industry being placed high on the political agenda?

Economic:

1. Has the boom/recession in the economy affected the business/sales? Has new business developed? Has there been a positive or negative impact on the business?
2. Has expansion of product/service and/or premises taken place?
3. Have product and/or service diversification and/or change taken place?
4. Has new technology been employed due to the economic boom?
5. Have closures/job losses taken place due to the recession or are there more employed due to the boom? Is there a shortage of appropriately skilled labour?
   (A Business Employment Profile in the form of a chart would be useful and impressive — line graph, bar chart, pie chart — refer to 'Simple ways to illustrate the results of research.')

Social:

1. Has there been a change of ownership resulting in a new work ethos (competitive urge) which is more customer-orientated (more consumer-friendly atmosphere)?
2. Have new infrastructural developments (improved roads and rail accessibility) and better customer facilities like car parks and crèches made a direct impact on the business — by making it easier for people to avail of the service or to visit and purchase?
3. Have pollution and/or noise controls made it more difficult for the business to operate?
4. Have changes in fashion and popularity of certain products forced the business to change or lose money?

Technology:

1. Has the purchase of more modern equipment given the business the 'competitive edge' or have competitors won out in this way?
2. Has new technology meant redundancy or job losses (labour saving for management)?

Sample Assignment Brief

You are required to investigate and analyse topics appropriate to the structure and functions of any organisation of your choice. Please explore:

1. Internal organisational structures and functions.
2. External organisational structures.
3. The impact of these structures/functions on the performance of the organisation.

Choose either the company where you have completed your work experience or any other organisation of your choice.

Sample Questions for Student Research on 'The Organisation'

These questions or a sample thereof may prove useful to students when carrying out a personal interview (face to face) for any assignment on 'The Organisation'.

HISTORY & SIZE OF ORGANISATION

1. When was the business established?
2. Did it relocate and or change its name? (Is the business name registered in Dublin Castle?)
3. How many staff are employed? How many males/females?
4. What goods/services does the business offer?
5. How large (square footage/no. of floors etc.) is this branch of the organisation? Could I sketch a plan of the building? Or take a photo of it?
6. Are there branches nationally/internationally? Please specify.

ORGANISATIONAL STRUCTURE

7. Could you provide me with an organisational chart of the staff and departments displaying regional, functional and product and/or service divisions?
8. Are there many lines of authority (middle managers)? (Is there a flat or tall hierarchy?)
9. What are the functions of the staff mentioned on the organisational chart and/or other staff?

OWNERSHIP, INSURANCE AND BUSINESS CONTROLS

10. Who owns the business? Tick which category the business falls into:
    - Sole Trader
    - Partnership
    - Private Company

- Public Company
- Friendly Society
- State Body
- Semi-State Body
- Other – please specify.

11. Is there a Board of Directors?
12. How is shareholding split?
13. Has the business got a:
    - Certificate of Incorporation.
    - Trading Certificate.
    - Other?

    Can I include a copy in my project?
14. What general category of finance was used to set up the business? E.g. bank loan, overdraft, venture capital.
15. How is the business insured?
16. How are the following controls handled in the organisation?
    - Financial Control (Cash flow etc.)
    - Credit Control (Debt Collection and Payment/Credit terms).
    - Stock Control (EPOS, Stock-takes etc.)
    - Quality Control (quality testing, quality circles, etc.)
17. Does the business possess a quality mark? E.g. Q Mark, Hygiene Mark, ISO 9000, Star Ratings etc. If yes, is this beneficial?

INTERNAL ORGANISATIONAL STRUCTURES (COMMUNICATION AND STAFFING)

18. Is the business represented by any lobby group, e.g. ISME, SFA, IBEC?
19. How is the formal organisational structure arranged? E.g. timetable, roster, rota, shifts.
20. How do staff complete tasks informally? E.g. swooping shifts.
21. How are staff interest and motivation maintained? E.g. Staff days, bonuses, commission.
22. Tick which communication systems are used to make the business operate well and rate their effectiveness:

	Not Effective	Fairly effective	Very Effective
Intercom	❑	❑	❑
Meetings	❑	❑	❑
Notice boards	❑	❑	❑
Networked computer systems (e.g. staff email/ ICT access and usage)	❑	❑	❑
Internal phones	❑	❑	❑
Staff knowledge management	❑	❑	❑
Other	❑	❑	❑

EXTERNAL ORGANISATIONAL STRUCTURES

23. Have recent global events affected the organisation? In what ways?
24. Has the change to the currency and European Union affected the business? In what ways?
25. Have recent political decisions affected the business?
26. What types of advertising, marketing and PR methods are used by the business to gain exposure?

FUTURE FOCUS

27. Does the organisation have a five-year plan? What main plans are envisaged?

Student Analysis
(Impact of internal and external organisational structures/functions on the performance of the organisation)

Note: The student should carry out SWOT and PEST analyses (check previous information on this) and conclude by summarising what impact they think the functions and structures of the organisation have on its performance.

The student could take the following structure for this section:

My opinions on how effective and efficient the organisation is. (Being effective means making the right choices. Being efficient means having a tight and well-run organisation.)

The following are examples of how students could analyse the impact different structures or functions have on the performance of the organisation:

Efficiencies	How these efficiencies affect the organisation	Inefficiencies	How these inefficiencies affect the organisation
Good staff management interaction	Leads to good productivity and a happy working environment	Problem with customer service	Bad for company image
Up-to-date ICT and well-constructed website	Higher sales than nearest competitor	Frequent office equipment breakdown (photocopier)	Slows down completion of work and causes staff irritation

Simple Ways to Illustrate the Results of Research

Please refer to information on graphs and charts and the display of business information in Chapter 3. The following is a simple explanation and example of how to show the results of research in graphical form. The Chart Wizard in Microsoft Excel could be used to create these graphs.

Q1. How many staff are employed? Male/female?
Answer: 250 in total – 100 female and remainder male. There are 20 females in sales, 10 females in production and remaining females in administration. There are 50 males in sales and the remainder in production.

Summary Figures:

	Sales	Production	Administration	Total
Males	50	100	0	150
Females	20	10	70	100
				250

Staff Details

Staff Numbers

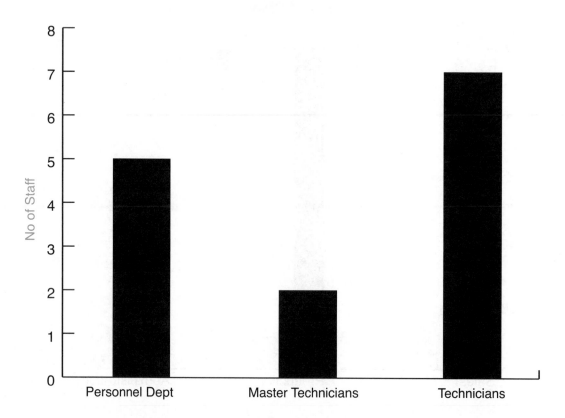

Sample Assignment Brief – 'The Organisation'

1. Candidates are required to investigate and analyse topics appropriate to the structure and functions of an organisation of the candidate's vocational area, e.g.
   a) internal organisational structures (staff structures, communications, quality, human resources, etc.)
   b) external organisation (PEST plus C factors affecting the business, suppliers, customers or clients, etc.)
2. Evidence will include reference to the impact of such structures and/or functions on the performance of the organisation, i.e. the candidate's opinion on efficiencies and inefficiencies of the organisation and how they affect its performance.

Sample Assignment

The Organisational Structure of St Munchin's — The Family Resource Centre, Limerick

Table of Contents
Introduction
Aim, Objectives and Methodology
History, Size, Type, Ownership and Services provided by St Munchin's
Internal Structures/Organisational Chart
External Structures (PEST plus C Analysis)
SWOT Analysis
Impact of the Structures on the Performance of the Organisation
Efficiencies and Inefficiencies
Conclusion
Bibliography
Appendix

Introduction

This project was compiled based on two weeks' work experience at St Munchin's Family Resource Centre, Ballynanty, Limerick.

Aim

My aim is to explore and analyse the internal workings of the centre and to look at external factors affecting it, and in so doing to make the reader more aware of how much the centre is needed by the community.

Objectives and Methodology

The primary data was collected by using a questionnaire and by observation. The questionnaire can be found in the Appendix. Secondary sources of information, including the centre's leaflets and the Community Link website, were also used.

Mission Statement

St Munchin's Family Resource Centre provides a safe, welcoming and supportive environment which encourages and enables our community to reach its full potential based on the principles of equality, empowerment and justice.

History, Size, Type, Ownership and Services Provided

St Munchin's is a non-profit-making organisation that exists to serve the community. Established by Sr Ursula in 1987, it was first set up in a normal three-bedroomed house. Significant expansion has taken place since then and the old centre was demolished in March 2007, having served the community for the previous twenty years. Funding has been secured for the new building. The centre is not owned by the people who run the centre but by Limerick Corporation.

Over the years the work and profile of the centre changed in many ways. In 1994, the International Year of the Family, St Munchin's Family Resource Centre was one of a small number of such centres (the other sister community centres include Our Lady of Lourdes Centre, Southill Community Services Centre, Moyross Community Enterprise Centre, and St Mary's) that were funded for the first time under the Department of Social Welfare.

The main rationale behind the funding was the perception of a possible gap in the statutory support for community development activities focused on support for family and tackling child poverty.

The centre's aims are listed on its website, indicating that it responds to the needs of the local community by providing:

- Structures that facilitate local people to support each other and search for ways to improve the quality of life in the area.
- Services in answer to the needs of families and family members.
- Support for those most disadvantaged and socially excluded.

It acts as a drop-in centre in the community and people are always welcome to come in for a cup of tea and a chat.

The following are the main services it provides:

SENIOR CITIZENS' OUTREACH AND SUPPORT

This provision includes meals on wheels, a counselling service, bereavement support, money advice and budgeting, chiropody, general information and a secretarial service.

Outreach visits the elderly, dinners are provided three times a week, minor repairs, cleaning and painting are looked after, alarms and lights installed for the elderly and a crafts group and clubs and social events are organised.

WOMEN'S GROUPS

The centre runs a local book project, a Young at Heart project, a mothers' group and a Follow Your Dreams mothers' group.

CHILDCARE AND CRECHE FACILITY

This facility (which includes an outdoor area) caters for up to 24 children per session ranging in age from three months to three years.

YOUTH SERVICES

These initiatives provide a combination of youth counselling, a Go 4 It programme (supported by Limerick Institute) and a first years' personal development club. There is also an after school club (for children aged eight to thirteen years), a homework club for six young people, computer clubs for twelve primary pupils and a summer project catering for sixty young people.

IT TRAINING AND COMPUTER CENTRE

ECDL classes are on offer, together with driver theory tests, beginners', intermediate and advanced computer training and anti-racism training.

FAIR TRADE PRODUCTS

Fair trade products are highlighted, promoted and used at the centre.

LITERACY PROJECT WITH A STEERING FROUP

Literacy research is carried out and funded by the Salesian Trust Fund and RAPID (a city rejuvenation group), the aim being to find out how many people in the community and parish area have literacy needs.

COMMUNITY EDUCATION

Lifelong learning and equality are promoted and literacy classes and art classes are also offered, either certified or non-certified, depending on the needs of the participants.

Organisation Chart of St Munchin's Family Resource Centre

BOARD OF DIRECTORS

CHAIRPERSON SECRETARY TREASURER

SUBGROUPS AND COMMITTEES

CENTRE CO-ORDINATOR

ADMINISTRATOR

Education Committee	Literacy Steering Group	PR Committee	Senior Citizens' Committee	Senior Citizens' Advisory Group	Bereavement Group Committee	After School Club Committee	Follow Your Dream Steering Group	Childcare Management Committee	Finance Sub-committee	Personnel Group
Administrator	Principal, St Lelia's	Community Person	Outreach Worker for the elderly	Outreach Worker	Manager	Centre Co-ordinator	Centre Co-ordinator	Centre Co-ordinator	Centre Co-ordinator	Centre Co-ordinator
Class Participant	HSCL Teacher	Development Workers (4)	Community Persons (3)	CDP	Outreach Worker for the elderly	Youth Services Co-ordinator	Youth Diversion Project, Moyross (2)	Barnardos Member	Admin Person	Management Committee Member
Development Worker	Learner	Management (1)	Senior Citizens' Club Leader	RAPID	Community Worker	Home/School Liaison Teacher	Youth Development Co-ordinator	PAUL Partnership Member	Management Committee Treasurer	MidWest Support Agency
ALSS VEC Tutor	Development Worker	Centre Co-ordinator	Development Worker	PAUL Partnership	Bereavement Facilitator	Staff ASC	Youth Project Worker	Childcare Manager		Crèche Management Committee Member
Chairperson	ALSS ALSS			Senior Citizens' Club Leader	Development Worker	Community Garda	Remedial Teacher	Parent Chairperson		HR Consultant
Centre Co-ordinator	Literacy Worker			Development Worker		Co-ordinator, School Completion Programme		Community Representative		
	Local Community (2)					Parent		Pre-school Parent Representative		
	Centre Co-ordinator					Resource Teacher		Crèche Parent Representative		
						Management Community Representative		Social Service Centre Member		
						ALSS: Adult Literacy Support Service				

Functions of Staff

- **Centre Co-ordinator**. Responsible to the Board of Management for all aspects of centre operations and sits on all the committees listed in the chart. It is her function to hire staff and to get approval for appointments from the Board of Directors.
- **Administrator**. Responsible for administrative duties connected with the centre, including wages and enrolment, and assisting the Centre Co-ordinator.
- **Development Workers**. Organise individual projects at the centre, e.g. women's groups, community education, PR, etc.
- **Child Services Co-ordinators** have a range of child-centred functions.
- **Youth Development Co-ordinator** is responsible for looking after all aspects of youth development and support.
- **Youth Project Workers** work with the Co-ordinator to help the youth project members.
- **Crèche Manager** manages the crèche.
- **Crèche Workers** look after the day-to-day running of the crèche.

The internal functions of the centre depend on the funding received. The centre is a company limited by guarantee and also a charity and they have a Chargeable Status Certificate, which means they are essentially non-profit-making and in existence for the good of the community. They are funded by the Department of Social Welfare.

Communications

Regular weekly meetings are held by each committee to discuss problems and/or future plans. Phone systems are efficient and there is also an email facility in the centre.

Advertising

The centre advertises using the Community Links website in co-operation with its sister centres. In the drop-in centre there are information leaflets available to any members of the community interested in visiting the centre or taking part in activities there.

Resources at St Munchin's

The communication systems in the centre are very high-tech in most areas. A computer room connects you to the Internet. The new Dell Dimension Computer is one of the newest additions to this room. There is a notice board in the main entrance to the building. Of the four telephones, three are for internal use only, in the reception, the crèche and kitchen. The telephone with the external line is located in the head office on the second floor of the building. Leaflets, the newspaper and sometimes the radio are also used to communicate with the public.

The centre is not recognised by any Quality Mark, but as there is a kitchen and crèche in the building there are occasional visits from health inspectors. They are always satisfied with the standards upheld by St Munchin's Family Resource Centre. The family resource centre has a Safety Statement that I was not allowed to include in this project.

External Structures

The external structures of St Munchin's Family Resource Centre are what happen outside the building. The tutors who take the education classes are all from outside the centre. Some are from primary schools or colleges and teach at the centre in the evening also.

As the centre cannot make a profit, they have to depend on grants and donations from people outside. Those who make such donations include the VEC, PAUL Partnership and also the Mid-Western Health Board. Without these donations the centre would not survive.

There are many visits from outside inspectors to ensure the centre maintains high standards for the public. All those unemployed who attend classes or visit the centre are from the community.

A PEST Analysis

Factors affecting the organisation:

Political Factors	Department of Social Welfare makes decisions regarding funding and allocation of numbers of staff
Economic Factors	The economic boom and the desire to have a good job helped people realise that going back to education is a good idea
Social Factors	Amenable surroundings and community spirit: good facilities to help the community participants
Technological Factors	New computers and generally efficient equipment
Competition Factors	Little competition evident: not a problem since this is a community initiative

A SWOT Analysis

Strengths	Good for community motivation and collective support for the area
Weaknesses	Could have better technology and buildings
Opportunities	Drive for more funding from the Department and new initiatives into the future
Threats	Cuts in funding

The Impact of the Structures on the Performance of the Organisation

This section is divided into the following headings:

* Efficiencies
* Inefficiencies.

The following information will show in my opinion the efficiencies and the inefficiencies of St Munchin's Family Resource Centre.

EFFICIENCIES

1. *Security*

The security system in the centre was very good. A camera in the main reception area is connected to a TV system showing everything that was happening in the reception area.

2. *The centre's good image*

When on my work experience I found that the centre had a good image which attracted people there.

3. *Interaction of staff*

All staff members interacted well with each other and with all members of the public.

INEFFICIENCIES

1. *Building facilities*

The centre is held in three houses. It would be better if more space was available.

2. *The use of only one external telephone*

The use of a telephone with an external line in the reception area would make the work in head office a lot easier.

3. *Depending on funds*

The dependence on funding means there is no job security in the centre. If funding stopped, staff would lose their jobs.

Conclusion

While completing my work experience and this project, my knowledge of St Munchin's Family Resource Centre has grown dramatically. I hope that some day the centre will not have to depend so much on grants as it does now.

Bibliography

Douglas, Arlene, *Business Administration*, Chapter 1. Dublin: Gill & Macmillan.
Website: www.communitylink.ie
Leaflets from St Munchin's Centre

Appendix

QUESTIONNAIRE

1. When was the business established?
2. Did it relocate or change its name at any time?
3. How many staff are employed?
4. What goods/services does the business offer?
5. Have you an organisational chart of staff and departments?
6. Is there a Board of Directors?
7. What are the functions of staff?
8. Has the business got a:
   – Certificate of Incorporation
   – Trading Certificate
   – Other?
9. Who owns the business?
10. Does any lobby group represent the business?
11. How is the formal organisational structure arranged?
12. How do staff complete tasks informally?
13. In your opinion how is the business
    – efficient
    – inefficient?
14. How are staff motivated?
15. What communication systems are used to make the business operate well?
16. Has the organisation got a five-year plan?
17. Is the business insured?
18. What general category of finance was used to set up the business?
19. What are the main factors that affect the business (negative/positive)?
20. How is finance controlled?
21. What types of advertising, marketing and PR techniques does the business have?
22. Has the business gained a Quality Mark?
23. Does the business have a Safety Statement?

2. Finance, Business Controls and Ratios

Why is Control so Important in Business?

It is a managerial task aimed at:

1. Setting standards.
2. Measuring performance against standards.
3. Feedback of results.
4. Correcting deviations that stray from set standards.

Refer to Gantt Chart, Figure 1.9 and How control is maintained, Figure 1.10 in Chapter 1.

Control is one of the functions of management. The different types of control necessary in business are:

1. PLANNING CONTROLS: This involves the determination of instructions to be used as directives for activities within the company and to determine standards that are to be used for comparison. There must be clear, unambiguous plans to enable managers to carry them out efficiently and effectively. (Refer to the Functions of Management in Chapter 1.)

2. FINANCIAL CONTROL: This involves budgeting – the formulation of plans for a given future period, expressed in quantitative terms; money management using cost and revenue controls.

The following are the different types of financial controls that are used, depending on the nature of the business in question:

1. **Non-budgetary Controls**
   Marginal Costing and Breakeven Charts:
   Marginal costing involves monitoring any extra costs incurred in a business and can help with price-fixing. Breakeven analysis is an extension of marginal costing. The breakeven chart maps total costs and total sales revenue and where the two lines intersect is the company's breakeven point. Below this line the company will see what output is making a loss, and above it what profit is being made on the other output. Total Costs are made up of Fixed Costs and Variable Costs.

   Fixed costs are for example rent, rates, permanent wages, insurance of premises – the type of costs that do not change as output or production increases.

Variable costs are for example part-time wages, raw material costs and overhead expenses like heat and light, telephone and general day-to-day bills that increase as output or production increases.

It is also important to note that there is a difference between direct and indirect costs.

Direct costs, like direct labour, are those costs that contribute directly to production. Production cannot take place without them.

Indirect costs, like indirect wages, selling expenses, administration and insurance, do not contribute directly to the physical production process. They are costs that are difficult to attribute to specific products or cost units. A good understanding of the terms mentioned will help students to answer the questions on breakeven charts, which will appear later in the section.

2. **Budgetary Controls**

This involves Standard Costing, which is costing out a job in terms of labour, materials and overheads. This is done together with monitoring total costs. Higher profits are gained by minimising costs.

Departmental Budgets are an integral part of the functional budget which forms part of the Master Budget of a business – the departmental expenditures being generally sales, production, stocks, administration, capital expenditure, R & D (research and development), cash and credit control (debtors and creditors), purchasing, and profit & loss and balance sheet forecasting.

A clearly defined financial policy allows management to authorise specific expenditures. The tight monitoring of costs using comparisons between actual and budgeted costs can allow the mismanagement of costs to be traced to a particular department. The correction of such deviations can then take place in order to minimise costs and maximise profit levels.

3. **Financial Ratios**

Liquidity, primary, current, sales, expense and operating ratios are used to measure efficiency and to summarise and assess overtrading, solvency and profitability in a business. Financial control can be maintained by observing the resulting ratios and making improvements where necessary.

4. **PPBS – Planning, Programming and Budgeting Systems**

This is a method used by government to control expenditure and to make decisions based on choices regarding money allocation for planned public expenditure. Calculations and benefit analyses are carried out by the programme.

3. CREDIT CONTROL: This involves the monitoring of debtors' and creditors' records – a system to ensure payment (into and out of the business): the means employed by a business to control the amount of credit it allows to its customers/debtors (the people that owe the business money) and to negotiate the amount of credit it is allowed to take from its creditors (the people to whom the business owes money).

The term 'credit terms' is the amount of time allowed to pay a bill. Suppliers can give 30 days (one month's credit), 60 days (two months' credit) or 90 days (three months' credit). Trade discount and settlement discount agreements are usually built into the terms of credit (discussed further in Chapter 6, 'Processing Business Documents').

4. QUALITY CONTROL: This involves the establishment of appropriate standards of quality. Variances beyond certain tolerances are rejected. The main methods used to control quality are 100 per cent inspection, random sampling inspection, continuous sampling, quality circles, and applying for quality awards (refer to the latter half of Chapter 1 for an explanation of these methods). Control charts are also often used and represent a graphical method to identify tolerance limits within which an item produced is acceptable and is not a reject. These charts have 95 per cent and 99 per cent tolerance limits.

5. STOCK CONTROL: Businesses must strive to maintain the optimum level of stock. This, however, depends on the following factors and the relationship between them:

1. The cost of holding stock – dictated by the type of goods in question – perishable/non-perishable, deterioration period, how long before the good becomes obsolete (out of date), and the cost of warehouse space.
2. Discounts available through bulk buying (warehouse space needed).
3. The variability of consumer demand.
4. On time, scheduled production supply to meet the demand: the shortage of materials or late delivery of materials can lead to major decreases in profits.

Keeping these factors in mind, a happy medium (optimum level) regarding stock levels must be reached, where a maximum and a minimum level of stock is set per item.

*   **Minimum Stock:** There exists the problem of holding the minimum amount of stock necessary to satisfy production (supply) and consumer demand, but at the same time not understocking. *Understocking* can lead to shortages of materials, with consumers switching to the nearest competitor (a loss of business and damaged reputation) – supply not keeping up with demand.
*   **Maximum Stock:** *Overstocking* can lead to excess supply (goods that do not sell) and the price must be reduced to dispose of the excess, like a sale (a loss-making venture). Purchasing managers often make use of the Economic Order Quantity formula (EOQ) to estimate acceptable levels of stock per annum:

$$EOQ = \sqrt{\frac{2DS}{IC}}$$

D = Annual demand
S = Ordering costs (storage & delivery)
IC = Annual cost of holding stock (like the cost of the administration of stock (documentation etc.) and the cost of the security of stock)

QUESTION

The annual demand (D) for a product is 3,000 units and the cost of placing an order is €8 (S).

The annual cost of carrying a unit of stock is 10% (IC).

Using the EOQ formula, work out:

    (a) How many units should be ordered each time.

    (b) How many times during the year the order should be placed.

ANSWER

$$EOQ = \sqrt{\frac{2DS}{IC}}$$

$$\sqrt{\frac{2 \times 3{,}000 \times 8}{10\%}}$$

$$\sqrt{\frac{2 \times 3{,}000 \times 8}{\frac{1}{10}}}$$

- Turn the divisor upside down and multiply – divisor is the fraction under the line in the case above.

$$48{,}000 \times \frac{10}{1}$$

Answer to Part (a)   692.82 = 693 units

                          Annual Demand = 3,000

                          Each Order = 693

Answer to Part (b)   4.3 = 4 times

- 693 units should be ordered each time – 4 times a year.

Average Cost is estimated as follows $\dfrac{\text{Total Cost}}{\text{Output (number of items produced)}}$

Weighted average cost is total cost weighted against proportion of income spent on goods.

6. REPLACEMENT COST OF STOCK: Any stock that does not sell or is damaged in transit or in the process of selling is calculated as wastage (e.g. perishable items or stock that goes off easily like vegetables, fruit and bread). In these cases consumers like these goods to be very fresh. The stock must be replaced. Sales agents who deliver bread, in particular, must bear the loss of bread that does not sell and the amount taken out is the replacement cost. Systems have been developed in recent times to minimise waste, helping to achieve low stock levels without causing shortages.

PRACTICE QUESTIONS

1. Why is control so important?
2. Revise how control is maintained (Fig. 1.10) and link it with the Gantt Chart (Fig. 1.9).
3. Name the *five* main controls that managers have to maintain in day-to-day business.
4. Distinguish between Fixed Costs and Variable Costs.
5. Distinguish between Direct Costs and Indirect Costs.
6. Explain how financial controls apply to business.
7. What is Credit Control?
8. Distinguish between a Debtor and a Creditor.
9. What is Quality Control? Link Fig. 1.9 with Quality Control.
10. With reference to Stock Control, what factors will affect a business that is looking to maintain an optimum level of Stock? Explain these implications in your own words.
11. Differentiate between Minimum Stock and Maximum Stock and the problems with both.
12. What is the purpose of the Economic Order Quantity formula?
13. When trying to estimate the cost of stock, distinguish between Average Cost, Weighted Average Cost and Replacement Cost.

Ordering Stock – Re-order Levels and Quantities

Re-order level: indicates when to purchase more stock.
Re-order quantity: indicates how much to purchase.

When shelf space is freed up, it indicates the speed at which stock is being bought up by consumers. This will dictate the need to re-order stock. Trained personnel in retail outlets carry out stock-takes on a regular basis, to make sure that the appropriate levels of stock are being maintained. In large retail outlets like supermarkets, it is usually the responsibility of individual sales distributors and agents to keep their shelf space well stocked and to contact their suppliers and make further deliveries based on the retail outlet's requirements. From time to time, based on changing consumer choice, seasonal factors and other factors, shortages occur and either the retail outlet manager, department manager or the stores supervisor will inform the sales distributor/agent of the extra requirements. Some unsold stocks, like bread and perishables, are taken back by the suppliers. However, this is not always the case.

LIFO/FIFO Stock Control

- LIFO, which stands for 'last in, first out' and FIFO, which stands for 'first in, first out', are terms commonly used in stock control. They simply mean how you handle your merchandise.
- FIFO, 'first in, first out', prompts the question, 'Do you restock the shelves by pushing the old items back to make room for new items of the same kind?' Then the last items stocked will be the first items sold.

LIFO, 'last in, first out', would be a typical stocking method for items that have no sell-by date associated with them, or at least one that is in the distant future (canned goods). Perishable items, like milk and eggs, are restocked from the back. This means that old items are pushed forward and, therefore, first selected by shoppers (FIFO restocking method). A lot of convenience stores have walk-in coolers behind their cold displays so they can stock from the rear. Some merchandise can be handled as LIFO and some as FIFO, depending on what it is and how fast you have to move it. (Source: www.wisegeek.com)

How the Retail Outlet Monitors Incoming and Outgoing Stock

In some supermarkets, deliveries are checked in through the stores area at the back of the supermarket. This is usually the responsibility of the stores supervisor.

1. COMPUTERISED STOCK CONTROL AND THE ROLE OF ELECTRONIC POINT OF SALE IN STOCK CONTROL (EPOS): In some supermarkets, a stock scanner is used to check in each individual delivery and to check out any returns (unsold/out of date stock) – last in, first out. A separate printout of the check-in and check-out is given to the agent/distributor. The number of goods sold is estimated by taking the number of goods delivered *minus* the returns.

Some supermarkets do not have stock scanners and in this case each agent has a separate stock card. The number of goods sold per day is noted on the stock card. The agent can estimate how many goods he/she should put on the shelves by looking at last week's sales column. An example of a stock card is shown on page 84.

Stock control computer programs incorporate stock ratios to indicate the efficiency of stock control in a business. Examples of these ratios are:

(a) Raw material/Total sales turnover
(b) Work in progress/Total turnover
   Both of these ratios show stock-holding in relation to amount sold – detects level of overstocking or understocking.
(c) Raw materials/Purchases, i.e. total purchases/average stock – shows how many times stock is turned over or replaced – indicating the frequency of restocking.

EPOS Systems: New Solutions for the Retailer and the Consumer

From the smallest huckster shop to video stores to supermarkets, electronic point-of-sale (EPOS) and scanning systems are in operation. What used to be seen as a high tech novelty are now part of the norm, but instead of functioning purely as a counting system (goods sold, stock received, stock remaining etc.), today's EPOS systems are focusing more and more on the consumer, for the mutual benefit of retailer and customer alike. Modern retailers are becoming ever more aware that information is everything, and the more they know about the erratic spending habits of modern society, the better they will be able to cater for its needs. Today's retailing wars are being fought with technology in the quest for understanding the customer, tracking their purchasing habits, adding systems that help them decide on a purchase, speeding up service and literally trying to take the hassle out of shopping.

What is becoming increasingly clear is that information technology systems are essential in helping solve the riddles of what people want to buy, why they buy it and what makes a happy shopping experience. Software is being created and updated for PC-based EPOS tills, which include a vast range of functions including bar code scanning, card readers, receipt printing, dockets, loyalty schemes and communications. The advantage this technology gives to the retailer is instant information on what products they're selling, which are the more popular and, most importantly, who they're selling it to. Proper use of this information has led

to the success of loyalty schemes introduced by retail chains over the last few years. Basic loyalty schemes offer the customer price reductions tantamount to the frequency of their visits to the outlet. Alongside, products can be given a boost in exposure to the consumer by the addition of extra points; for example, 'Buy a bottle of Yankee Cheez-in-a-Can today and receive 300 points!' This allows the popularity of the product to be gauged by the EPOS system; it will suggest whether Cheez-in-a-Can should be replenished and advise what time of year it sells best. Affinity schemes involve a wider network of companies based on the same premise (such as the 'SuperClub' card) and similarly give retailers a mutual boost, while attracting the same demographic of customers.

EPOS systems have also developed to account for theft or 'shrinkage', with compatible software being introduced to combat it. Most retailers have an idea as to when suspicious dealings are most likely to occur at the service till, such as the refund or exchange of goods, excessive voiding of transactions, and multiple manual entries of credit card details after the initial swipe. Although instinct is an advantage to any retailer, what EPOS systems offer is an effective means of detection. All of these events are identifiable while they take place, and the data can be processed quickly and efficiently. With EPOS systems in place with the relevant software, retailers have solutions that enable them to detect 'shrinkage' patterns and prevent theft before it occurs.

For the consumer, information technology in stores and shops adds a vibrant new element to the way they spend money. The introduction of easy to use touch-screen kiosks give customers access to services, from locating the deli counter to what wine might suit the lasagne they just bought. In Britain, some car showrooms allow the prospective buyer to create the car of their choice on-screen, while music stores give the customer a chance to browse through CDs, check the prices, listen to selected tracks and print a list of what they've chosen. With interactive kiosks in place, the next step is integrating them with the advantages of loyalty cards, allowing retailers access to a very comprehensive profile of what their customers want.

The attention being focused on the individual has led to concern from some consumers. There are those who think that personal information stored by retailers can be construed as intrusive. What people gain from the developments in EPOS technology is accurate pricing, a much higher level of service, and discount advantages through loyalty schemes. The customer's involvement in loyalty schemes is voluntary, and any information held by the retail company is available to the customer. On the subject of credit card confidentiality, the retailer cannot hold on to any credit information after the transaction has been completed. So with the initial fears of EPOS systems having been allayed, one can truly say that both retailer and consumer are helping each other into the next millennium.

New computerised stock control systems can monitor and track orders and balances and can indicate to the stock controller that stock renewal is required and 'best before' dates can also be estimated.

Other advanced stock control systems have good forecasting techniques incorporated into them in order to evaluate certain degrees of error, i.e. degrees of overstocking or understocking. The mistakes are noted and adjusted using statistical methods like 'exponential smoothing'. Using this method, stock levels are adjusted by a proportion of the most recent errors in stock numbers and a new forecast of stock requirements results. The Box-Jenkins statistical method is based on the adjustments of errors themselves, based on past errors. Both methods are accurate and satisfy the requirements of larger organisations and those that deal in stock that could be a risk to the health and safety of the community. Examples are pharmaceutical products and nuclear products.

EPOS means Electronic Point of Sale. The point of sale occurs at the check-out when the product has just been sold to the customer. Goods are checked through an electronic check-out scanner system where bar codes automatically program prices into the cash register. The till receipt is the proof of purchase and proof of the point of sale of goods to the customer. Using till details on how much stock is left, the outlet is a means of controlling stocks.

2. CONTINUOUS WRITTEN RECORD: This is based on the same idea as EPOS. However, the account of goods coming in and taken out is handwritten on stock cards. The supervisor takes account only of the difference between the goods that come in and returns taken out.

3. PERIODIC WRITTEN RECORD AND OBSERVATION: Trained personnel who work in the supermarkets/stores might do a check on the stock position at the end of every month. This would act as a double check on agents. Discrepancies possibly due to theft or numerical mistakes would be noted when sales volume is compared to till takings.

4. BIN CARDS: An account is also kept of changes in stock, in item order. For example, a bin card might exist detailing the change in the stock of jars of jam. The balance of the remaining stock of jam is recorded on the card (example of a bin card below).

| BIN CARD No. . . . . | | | |
| ITEM   Flour | | UNIT   1.5 KG | |
DATE	RECEIVED	ISSUED	BALANCE
1 Mar	12	3	9
5 Mar	–	4	5
8 Mar	12	4	13

It would probably not be cost effective for other smaller retail outlets like boutiques, jewellers and small shops to have a computerised stock control system. However, it is becoming the norm in most businesses now.

Note: Not all suppliers allow returns to be taken back. In most cases sales agents for bread and other perishable goods have to bear the cost of overstocking. To avoid this, they streamline stocks to a minimum level. Most shops such as clothes shops only return items when they are damaged or when more were delivered than were ordered.

Stock Card example (agents and sales distributors fill these cards in on a daily basis in some retail outlets).

* Stock Sales column – indicates the quantity sold the previous week.
* Floor Order column – the aim is to match or improve on the quantity sold the same day the previous week. This will, however, depend on the amount still on the shelves from the previous day.

For example on Friday, where 20/16 appears, this indicates that 20 items were sold that day last week. Only 16 items are replaced because 4 must have been left unsold on the shelf from the previous day. The previous week's sales (Stock Sales column) provide a guideline as to how many items should be put on the shelf to avoid shortages occurring.

Stock Turnover is measured using the following formula:

$$\frac{\text{Cost of Sales}}{\text{Average Stock}}$$

Average Stock is Opening Stock *plus* Closing Stock divided by 2.

Stock turnover describes the number of times stock is replaced. Jewellers generally have low levels of stock turnover because the goods for sale are expensive. Shops, supermarkets and pubs would have high levels of stock turnover, with perishable goods (milk, fresh cream) and fresh goods (bread, some vegetables such as carrots and broccoli) having a very short shelf life. The deterioration period, together with the fluctuation of consumer demand, will dictate the profitability of the retail outlet. The level of stock turnover will be indicated by the stock re-order levels.

STOCK AND ORDER CARD

Department 16 Bread & Cakes   Sales from :
Order from:

Store
Supplier
Phone
Product Description

MONDAY		TUESDAY		WEDNESDAY			THURSDAY			FRIDAY			SATURDAY			SUNDAY	
Stock Sales	Floor Order	Stock Sales	Floor Order	Stock Sales	Floor Order	Stock Order	Floor Sales	Stock Order	Floor Order	Stock Sales	Floor Order	Stock Order	Floor Sales	Order	Order	Sales	Order
3		2		3	3		1	3		3	4		4			0	
1		1		2	2		4	3		3	5		3			0	
2		1		2	3		5	3		6	4		6			0	
3		5		7	8		11	6		20	16		18			0	
3		4		7	16		7	-		15	9		10			0	
5		7		13	-		7	8		18	15		12			2	
0		0		0	-		0	-		0	-		0			0	
1		7		7	2		8	10		14	5		8			0	
4		7		5	9		7	-		13	9		9			0	
2		0		2	6		2	-		2	6		3			4	
3		1		2	5		6	7		3	5		8			0	
0		1		5	-		5	10		8	10		11			0	
0		2		3	-		9	10		2	5		4			0	

Total:

Signed for . . . .   by: . . . .

Supplier: . . . .

Factors that Influence the Levels of Profits and Stock Turnover of a Retail Outlet

The following factors have beneficial influences on the levels of stock turnover and profitability:

1. More competitive prices.
2. Supplier advertising via television, radio, newspapers, direct mail, leaflet drops, personal selling (e.g. cooking food in a supermarket), public relations exercises (creating an image that the public relates to the product) and special offers will usually increase consumer demand. Publicity in the form of the short sharp shock method is a marketing technique that can also increase sales.
3. Sunday and late opening hours will increase stock turnover.
4. Customer service: consumer friendly shop layout, self-service with helpful and friendly back-up customer service and free home delivery.
5. Material service: safety and hygiene, as well as the assurance that the outlet is always well stocked, with a wide and varied choice of stock which is always fresh. If the lines of authority are clearly defined when problems arise, prompt and efficient service should be provided in response to customer complaints, returns and replacement of damaged goods.

The following factors have undesirable effects on the levels of stock turnover and profitability:

1. High prices in relation to competitors can discourage demand.
2. The deterioration period together with the fluctuation of consumer demand, which can sometimes be unpredictable and perhaps seasonal, will dictate levels of wastage and unanticipated losses.
3. When supply falls short of demand due to badly managed re-ordering, failure to deliver or late delivery, the nearest competitor could win out (the substitution effect). This depends greatly on individual suppliers' relationships with their sales distributors and sales agents.
4. If stock returns are not taken back by suppliers, sales agents will streamline stock, which is likely to cause understocking and shortages from time to time.
5. The cost of holding stock and warehouse space will dictate stock re-order levels and quantities.

Breakeven Charts

PRACTICE QUESTION

Morton and Murphy Ltd project sales for the next twelve months at 100,000 units sold at €10 per unit.

The firm expects the following expenses:

Direct material cost	€3 per unit
Direct wages cost	€2 per unit
Administration expenses	€150,000
Rent of the premises for the year	€100,000
Advertising fixed budget (yearly)	€10,000

Based on the twelve-monthly financial information given:

A. Make the appropriate pre-calculations to prepare to draw a Breakeven chart.
B. Draw a Breakeven chart and include the following detail on it:
   (a) The Breakeven point.
   (b) The 100% Present Capacity position.
   (c) The Profit or Loss when 20,000 units are produced.
   (d) The Profit or Loss when 60,000 units are produced.
   (e) Comment on your findings.

SOLUTION

In order to draw the chart, Variable Costs must be grouped together and then Fixed Costs must also be totalled. Sales *less* Variable Costs = Contribution (an amount that is contributed to the business – a type of profit figure). When Fixed Costs are then deducted, depending on how high these fixed costs are, an overall loss could result. If Fixed Costs are lower than Contribution, then a profit will result.

QUESTION (A) PRE-CALCULATIONS

	€	€
Sales (100,000 x €10 per unit)		1,000,000
Less VARIABLE COSTS		
Direct Material costs	300,000	
Direct Wage costs	200,000	
Administration expenses	150,000	
TOTAL VARIABLE COSTS		650,000
CONTRIBUTION		350,000
Less FIXED COSTS		
Rent of premises for year	100,000	
Budgeted advertising	10,000	
TOTAL FIXED COSTS		110,000
Net profit		240,000

TOTAL COSTS (650,000 + 110,000) = 760,000

PROCEDURE TO DRAW THE CHART

1. Graph paper must *always* be used to ensure accuracy.
2. 'Output or number of units produced' is plotted on the X axis and 'Sales revenue' is plotted on the Y axis.

3. The 100 per cent Capacity line should be drawn in first – vertical line.
4. Then the Total Costs line should be drawn in – horizontal line.
5. The Sales line should extend from the Origin to the Present Capacity Sales revenue level.
6. The Variable Costs line should extend from the Total Costs line. It should intersect the sales line at the Breakeven point which can now be read from the graph, above which there is a profit and below which there is a loss made.
7. To read the profit figure or the loss figure from the graph, draw a straight dotted line from the given output level intersecting both the Sales line and the Variable Costs line.
8. If a loss is detected, the output level will be below the breakeven output level and the straight dotted line will hit the Sales line first. The loss is the DIFFERENCE between the two intersections and is read from the Y axis.
9. If a profit is shown, the output level will be above the breakeven output level and the straight dotted line will hit the Variable Costs line first. The profit is the DIFFERENCE between the two intersections and is read from the Y axis.

QUESTION (B) (a) TO (d) Breakeven Chart Morton & Murphy Ltd

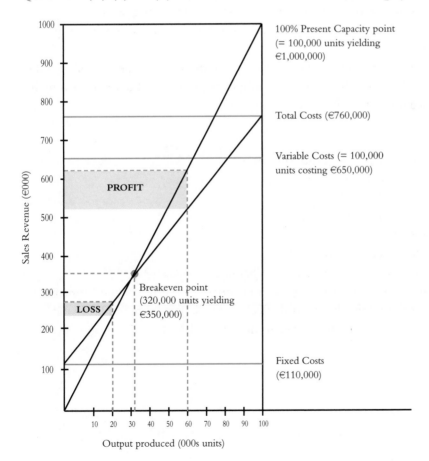

QUESTION 1B (e) COMMENT

The Breakeven point indicated on the chart is where 23,000 units of production yield €230,000 in Sales revenue. Any output/production level below this will show a loss, and above it will generate a profit.

The 100% present or current capacity line indicates the maximum point of production to which the business can go, given present resources available. This business is capable therefore of generating a maximum of €1,000,000 (€1m) in Sales revenue by producing 100,000 units. This would always be difficult to achieve due to problems that occur, like employee absenteeism, shortages or damaged materials, machinery breakdown and other unpredictable occurrences.

The first small shaded area represents the Loss that would be incurred if the business only produced 20,000 units. This amount (€270,000 *minus* €230,000 = €40,000 loss made) means 20,000 units is too low a level of production and indicates an under-utilisation and wastage of resources. This means that resources like labour and materials would not be used to the fullest capacity at this level of output.

The large shaded area represents the Profit that would be generated if the business produced 60,000 units. This profit (€600,000 *minus* €515,000 = €85,000 profit made) indicates good productivity (output per person) and the level of production is above breakeven point. Resources are being well employed to generate a good profit. The business is, however, a good distance away from optimum capacity.

The Fixed Costs line indicates costs that remain the same irrespective of any other activities in the business. In this case a set figure for rent and also for advertising has been agreed and will not change over the year.

PRACTICE QUESTIONS

1. What are Re-order Levels and Quantities?
2. How are stock levels monitored in retail outlets?
3. What are Stock Ratios?

4. What do LIFO and FIFO stand for?
5. What is EPOS?
6. How is a Stock Card written up?
7. How is Stock Turnover calculated? What does it indicate?
8. Explain *five* factors that have a good effect on Stock Turnover and Profitability.
9. Explain *five* factors that have a bad effect on Stock Turnover and Profitability.
10. The financial breakdown of the business owned by James and Sons Ltd is as follows:

	€	€
Sales (3,000 units at €120 each)		360,000
Direct labour	100,000	
Direct materials	50,000	
Factory overheads – variable	12,000	
– fixed	18,000	180,000
		180,000
Selling expenses – variable	30,000	
– fixed	16,000	
Other fixed overheads	12,000	58,000
Net profit		122,000

From the information provided:

(A) Make appropriate pre-calculations to draw a Breakeven chart.

(B) Draw a Breakeven chart and include the following details on it.

   (a) The Breakeven point.
   (b) The 100% present capacity position.
   (c) The profit or loss when 250 units are produced.
   (d) The profit or loss when 1,250 units are produced.

(C) Comment on your findings.

Sources of Finance for Business

The acquisition of money, often called capital, is the first step necessary to set up or develop businesses. Different interpretations of capital exist but it usually means money either in a liquid (cash) or non-liquid form (in the form of an asset). Together with the other three factors of production – Land (premises), Labour (workers), Enterprise (the entrepreneur co-ordinates activities) – Capital is the basis of successful business start-up or expansion. The four factors are known as the Factors of Production.

Business people usually avail of the following possible Sources of Finance to commence or develop businesses:

1. Bank or financial institution loans.
2. Personal savings.
3. Loans from family or friends.
4. Grants and incentives from public bodies (like the IDA, Forbairt).
5. Investment by promoters, partners or shareholders.

Capital can be defined as follows:

FIXED CAPITAL: the non-liquid form of capital – money in the form of land, buildings, machinery, equipment – usually not for resale and used as part of the running of the business.

WORKING CAPITAL: the difference between Current Assets and Current Liabilities of a business. Current liabilities generally consist of creditors (the people to whom the business owes money) and short-term loans. The lesser the current liabilities of a business the better because it allows for more working capital or current accessible money for immediate use in the business. Current assets are generally stock, debtors (the people who owe the business money) – there is money out there to be collected. The more debtors there are, the better. A healthy working capital figure ensures that the business has sufficient funds in the form of current assets to cover its current liabilities.

VENTURE CAPITAL: This is investment received from an investor who wishes to take a high risk, keeping in mind the possibility of making a higher than average positive return, as well as the possibility of making a negative return. An example of a venture capitalist is Richard Branson. Some promoters would also fall into this category.

SOCIAL CAPITAL: This refers to the infrastructure of the state i.e. roads, state schools, hospitals, public libraries. The basis for this public capital is through government spending of public monies

Short-Term, Medium-Term and Long-Term Finance

The sources of finance mentioned previously can be broken down into the following categories.

SHORT-TERM FINANCE (DURATION = UP TO ONE YEAR)

1. **Bank overdraft:** involves permission to overdraw an account in a bank to a specific amount, as sanctioned by the bank manager. It is a cheap source of finance, only available to customers who have a satisfactory record. Interest charged is allowable against profits or taxes. The facility can, however, be withdrawn at any time.
2. **Bill of Exchange:** could be described as similar to a post-dated cheque of sorts which is given in exchange for goods delivered. A bill may be discounted by the holder, should they require finance immediately, and the level of discount is normally agreed at the outset. The basic criterion applied to a bill transaction is that it should be self-financing by the date of maturity – this is usually thirty, sixty or ninety days, but can be arranged for longer periods. It is an unconditional order requiring the person to whom it is addressed to pay on demand a certain sum of money at an agreed fixed future date (an IOU).

Used in trade finance, a Bill of Exchange for a business is an unconditional order in writing, addressed by one person to another, signed by the person giving it, and requiring the person to whom it is addressed to pay on demand or at a fixed or determinable future time a sum certain in money to or to the order of a specified person, or to bearer It is one of the key financial instruments in international trade and is a key instrument used for business trade finance.

3. Amounts due to be paid by Debtors still outstanding, but yet to be collected: these amounts can be used by a business as finance. Debtors are current assets to a business in this way.

4. Credit terms agreed by Creditors (people to whom the business owes money): When a business purchases goods on credit, rather than demanding payment up front, creditors allow either thirty or sixty days before the payment is due. This time lapse allows the business to use the money it has to finance the business until creditors' payments fall due. Businesses like Dunnes Stores can sell goods for cash (cash up front) and purchase their materials on credit, sometimes availing of ninety days' credit. During this time they can bank their takings and earn interest, thus benefiting. This method of financing, involving rapid turnover generating small profits, is often called 'Leaning on the Trade' or Trade Credit Taken.

5. **Letters of Credit:** requests from the issuing bank to its foreign agent to honour all cheques presented by the holder only up to the limit specified in the letter of credit. It is an undertaking of a bank to honour demands for payment and is usually the means by which trade is carried out between companies in different countries.

Used in trade finance, exporting and international trade standard, a commercial Letter of Credit is a document issued mostly by a financial institution, which usually provides an irrevocable undertaking to pay. The letter of credit can also be payment for a transaction, meaning that redeeming the letter of credit pays an exporter.

Letters of credit are used primarily in international trade transactions of significant value, for deals between a supplier in one country and a customer in another.

In executing a transaction, letters of credit incorporate functions common to giros and traveller's cheques. Typically, the documents a beneficiary has to present in order to receive payment include a commercial invoice, bill of lading and documents proving the shipment was insured against loss or damage in transit.

6. **Factoring:** the sale of debts for less than their actual value to a finance company – this company being called 'the factor'. The debtors are no longer the debtors of the supplier but the debtors of the factor. It means immediate cash to finance the business. A loss is made, however, where the value of the debtors might have been €100,000 and sold to the factor for €94,000.

7. **Taxation and Expenses Due:** There is a period of time, i.e. six to twelve months, before interest is levied on unpaid business taxes. A business can allow

the money that is to be used for payment to accumulate interest. It is sometimes used for something else and in this way acts as a short-term loan to the business. Unpaid VAT and taxation on profits are often used as finance for businesses in this way. The same criterion can be applied to overheads and short-term expenses like ESB bills, rent and rates and advertising bills. If payment can be delayed, the money acts as short-term finance.

MEDIUM–TERM FINANCE (DURATION ONE TO FIVE YEARS)

1. **Term Loan:** These are usually designed to finance the purchase of fixed assets. Repayments are made by agreed stated amounts as negotiated. Repayments are usually paid monthly or quarterly and the borrower knows exactly what his commitment is. Term loans are usually more expensive than overdrafts.

2. **Hire Purchase:** Also called Instalment Credit, it is a method of paying for equipment in instalments, while gaining possession of the equipment immediately. An example is payment for televisions, fridges etc. as part of the household ESB bill. An initial contract is signed on receipt of the article purchased and the repayment might be six payments over a year, every two months, included on the ESB bill. The purchaser does not own the article, however, until the final instalment is paid. A computer might be purchased over five years in the same way.

3. **Leasing:** This gives a business the opportunity to use an asset, without ever owning it, for a specified number of years for set payments. The ownership of the article will never pass from the leasing company. This is availing of non–liquid capital to advance a business.

LONG–TERM FINANCE (DURATION FIVE YEARS AND OVER)

1. **Mortgages:** Loans for the purchase of houses, premises or buildings for a duration of over five years, usually for twenty or more years.

2. **Investment/Owner Capital:** Promoters, partners, shareholders, venture capitalists can all be owners of a business and are responsible for investing and contributing long-term capital to the business. The more the investment, the greater the ability for a business to grow and expand and to become more competitive by being able to purchase the most modern equipment and to employ highly skilled staff and pay them accordingly.

   Ordinary shareholders, preference shareholders and debenture holders contribute the capital to the business. These shares are said to be the Equity Share Capital of the business – this means the holders are entitled to the equity or balance of profits.

   Ordinary shareholders are the risk-takers because there is no guaranteed dividend (money paid out of profits, not out of the original capital). They are the last people to get money. (Generally they have voting rights.)

Preference shareholders carry a fixed dividend and must be paid before ordinary shareholders. (Generally they have less or no voting rights compared to ordinary shareholders.)

Debenture holders contribute the capital in the form of a long-term loan, carrying a fixed rate of interest and a specified repayment date (maturity date). Debenture holders are paid before the other shareholders, even if profits are inadequate to cover the repayment. There is a risk of court action if a business defaults on the interest payments, and this could force receivership. (Generally they have no vote.)

3. **Sale and Lease Back:** Large companies often run short of ready finance and may decide to sell their premises to an investment institution. These companies then lease the same buildings or offices (a long-term lease – usually twenty years) from the investment institution Business continues as before, but on a rental basis. The rent is reviewed every few years. Ready finance is received up front on the sale of the premises, allowing the business to become liquid again, despite having to pay rent in exchange.

4. **Government and semi-state grants:** New domestic small businesses as well as export-orientated businesses tend to gain finance in the form of grants because these producers help to improve the balance of trade through import substitution and capital inflow.

Other Sources of Finance

Where financing is not readily available from credit institutions, there may be other sources of finance.

What is Venture Capital?

A seed-funding option, venture capital (VC) is financial capital provided to early-stage, high-potential, high-risk, growth start-up companies. The venture capital fund makes money by owning equity in the companies that it invests in. The companies looking for investment usually have a novel technology or business model in high technology industries, such as biotechnology, IT or software, etc.

The typical venture capital investment occurs after the seed funding round as a growth funding round (also referred to as Series A round) in the interest of generating a return through an eventual realisation event, such as an IPO (initial public offering) or trade sale of the company.

Venture capital is a type of private equity. All venture capital is, therefore, private equity, but not all private equity is venture capital.

Business Angels

An angel investor, or angel (also known as a business angel or informal investor), is an affluent individual who provides capital for a business start-up, usually in exchange for convertible debt or ownership of some equity. A small but increasing number of angel investors organise themselves into angel groups or angel networks to share research and pool their investment capital.

Unlike venture capitalists, angels typically invest their own funds and manage the pooled money of others in a professionally managed fund.

The Halo Business Angel Partnership is the new national business angel network in the Republic of Ireland, bringing together the private equity activities of Enterprise Ireland, InterTradeIreland and the Irish Business and Innovation Centres. It is a nationwide service with the role of facilitators, not investment advisors. Before making any investment-related decisions, both sides take professional advice.

The aim is to develop and foster the growth of private equity and business-angel activity in Ireland by matching private investors with pre-screened investment opportunities in start-up, early-stage and developing businesses. In this way, the difficulty faced by early-stage and growing companies in raising funds on reasonable terms can be helped. The Halo Business Angel Partnership is managed by Dublin Business Innovation Centre Limited as part of its ongoing support to start-up and developing enterprises.

Dragons' Den

Dragons' Den is another way that could lead to securing investment finance. This series of reality television programmes features entrepreneurs pitching their business ideas in order to secure investment finance from a panel of venture capitalists. The format is owned by Sony Pictures Television International.

Enterprise Boards

The 35 County Enterprise Boards (CEB) were established in Ireland in 1993 to provide support at local level for small businesses ('micro-enterprises') with 10 employees.

The CEBs provide direct-grant support to new and existing enterprises and promote entrepreneurship, capacity building and women in business to micro-enterprises in the commercial sphere. The CEBs are uniquely positioned to understand local needs and know the background and track record of those applying for support and assistance.

The CEBs are co-funded by the Irish government and EU Structural Funds.

The CEBs support both new and established businesses with a range of supports including:

- Advice
- Mentoring
- Grants
- Supports for Training and Growth.

Refer to www.enterpriseboards.ie.

What is Sub-prime Lending?

Sub-prime lending refers to the practice of making loans (extending credit) to borrowers who do not qualify for market interest rates because of problems with their credit history: the type of borrowers who would otherwise not have access to the credit market. A sub-prime loan is offered at a higher rate than regular loans due to the increased risk. Sub-prime borrowers typically have histories of payment defaults and bankruptcy.

This type of lending has a number of credit instruments including sub-prime mortgages, sub-prime car loans, and sub-prime credit cards. Sometimes these types of high interest loans also have regular higher fees and up-front charges attached as part of the loan payment agreement. Many house repossessions have resulted from the inability of sub-prime borrowers to keep up with the payments.

Many opponents of the sub-prime lending industry have criticised loan companies, suggesting that they engage in predatory practices – targeting borrowers who do not have the financial resources to meet the terms of the loans they are offered over the longer term.

Ireland's Debt Crisis – The Journey from Boom to Recession to Recovery

During the Celtic Tiger years Ireland's economy expanded rapidly from 1997 to 2007 helped by low corporation tax and generous credit expansion by the banks and financial institutions. The vastly overrated pricing of properties and very high rates of lending from the banks led to a what was called a 'casino culture' in the Irish property market, which fuelled the inevitable bust that followed. European banks also gave large loans that many Irish recipients were not in a position to pay back.

The European Central Bank's low interest rates also helped the property bubble to expand until eventually in 2007 the cracks were evident. By late 2008 the bubble had burst due to the global financial crisis (2007 – 2010). Irish banks were overexposed to the Irish property market, the main one to enter the spotlight being Anglo Irish Bank. By December 2009 its share price dropped to an all-time low, prompted by the resignation of its director from the board of the Irish Stock Exchange. In 2008 the Irish economy entered recession and by 2009 Ireland entered into an economic depression.

GDP (Ireland national income) fell by 8.5 per cent from the previous year and unemployment rose to 11.4 per cent. By the latter end of 2009, GNP continued to decline, and property values and sales collapsed. Developers were in trouble with loan repayments, and nearly 40,000 people left Ireland. Emigration rose to a level not seen since the late 1980s. In Sept 2008 Ireland officially declared that it was in recession. The Government issued an unlimited bank guarantee favouring six banks, which cost the Irish people more than had been estimated. Minister Brian Lenihan guaranteed the debts of not just the Irish banks, but of the speculators and bond holders who take financial risks as a central part of their professional activity. This resulted in intervention by the EU (European Union) and IMF (International Monetary Fund) in late 2010 following the establishment of NAMA, the National Assets Management Agency (to be explained later).

Much industrial unrest was evident in the workplace following controversial measures introduced as part of the government 2008 budget. Many public demonstrations resulted following the introduction of an income levy for all workers over a certain income threshold, proposals for the withdrawal of the medical card and the reintroduction of university fees.

According to Irish Economist David McWilliams: 'Why should we trust the people who got us into this mess in the first place? They were wrong then and they are wrong now. The politicians, bankers and developers think they can hand us the bill and walk away from the carnage. They want us to follow a route that will make things worse for the ordinary man on the street while saving the bankers at the top of the tree, insisting that there is no other way.' (Refer to **www. davidmcwilliams.ie/follow-the-money.**)

In the last four years, total employment in Ireland has fallen by over 300,000, or almost 15 per cent. The unemployment rate has soared from 4.8 per cent to 14.2 per cent in this short period. In the construction sector, mainly responsible for fuelling the Celtic Tiger from 1997 to 2007, 166,000 jobs have disappeared.

What was MABS?

MABS, the Money Advice and Budgeting Service (Ireland), was a national, free, confidential and independent service for people in debt or in danger of getting into debt. A linked website between MABS and the Citizens Information Board – **www.keepingyourhome.ie** – provided advice on mortgage arrears and help for those having difficulties paying their rent or making mortgage repayments.

Mortgage Proposals would give Homeowners 'New Start'

Due to the recession many homeowners got into difficulties with mortgage arrears and were unable to pay off their mortgage or house loans.

In the Keane report commissioned by the Irish government, it was noted that mortgage arrears were influenced by three factors: affordability, negative equity and future prospects.

1. **Affordability:** Changes in people's ability to meet their monthly mortgage obligation due to changes in factors such as employment, salaries, tax, is the key driver of mortgage arrears.
2. **Negative equity (LTV – loan to value):** Negative equity has not of itself given rise to mortgage arrears. It does, however, influence the scale of loss that the mortgage holder and the bank face and, as a result, the potential solution.
3. **Future prospects:** While the scale of the problem can be estimated for each mortgagee now, the bigger difficulty is in determining how their income, interest costs and house value will fare in the future. Age, and how many future years of earning capacity an individual has, is also a very important consideration.

Irish Minister for Finance Michael Noonan said that the approaches set out in the Keane report would help people make a new start with regard to their mortgages.

SUMMARY OF RECOMMENDATIONS IN THE REPORT

MORTGAGE-TO-RENT SCHEMES

Mortgage holders sell their property to the mortgage company and lease it back from the company.

TRADE-DOWN MORTGAGES

Mortgage holders trade down to a lower value property and take the negative equity with them.

SPLIT MORTGAGES

The concept of splitting a distressed mortgage into an affordable mortgage and warehousing the balance, in other words paying off the affordable part and postponing the rest, perhaps until the house is sold in the future.

SALE BY AGREEMENT

This would involve selling the property and paying over the amount realised (it was sold for) agreeing on a time to pay off any shortfall.

What was 'Towards 2016'?

The seventh social partnership agreement, titled 'Towards 2016', was concluded in June 2006, with pay terms due to run to early 2008. These provided for wage increases set at 10.4 per cent over a 27-month period. It also included increased enforcement measures for employment protection and compliance with established labour standards. The trades unions, through the Irish Congress of Trades Unions (ICTU), voted in early September 2006 to accept the agreement, however the largest nursing (INO) and retail (Mandate) unions opting not to participate in the vote. On the same day IBEC, the main employers' union also announced its acceptance of 'Towards 2016'.

The second stage of 'Towards 2016' pay terms were agreed in September 2008 and accepted by the ICTU. In the face of rapidly rising unemployment and deteriorating public finances, unions which had previously opposed or abstained from the pay agreements were more supportive of the agreement. The second stage pay terms provided pay increases, payable in two stages, following a three-month pay freeze in the private sector and an 11-month pay freeze in the public service. The terms were accepted by IBEC, the main employers' union, on the same day but the Construction Industry Federation (CIF) withheld consent as it had sought a 12-month pay freeze for employees in construction. The terms also included an additional 0.5 per cent wage rise for those earning less than €11 an hour and maintained the inability-to-pay provisions for companies in financial or trading difficulties.

In March 2010, under the banner of 'social dialogue', the ICTU public service unions and the Government negotiated a three-year pay freeze, marking the abandonment of pay terms of the second stage of the 'Towards 2016' agreement.

The 'Government for National Recovery 2011-2016' Document

Following the virtual abandonment of the seventh social partnership agreement 'Towards 2016', the 'Government for National Recovery 2011-2016' document was produced in the face of partnership collapse. The second stage pay terms, described as a 'transition agreement', effectively collapsed at the end of 2009 when the Government imposed income cuts of between 5 and 8 per cent for about 315,000 public servants in its Budget. This new National Recovery document contained promises that the Government would restore Ireland's finances, radically reform an outdated system of administration and rebuild Ireland's reputation on the international stage and protect the vulnerable. It also promised burden-sharing on an equitable basis by forging a new Ireland built on fairness and equal citizenship. Refer to **www.socialjustice.ie.**

An Bord Snip Nua

In 2008 the Irish government set up the Special Group on Public Service Numbers and Expenditure Programmes (also known as An Bord Snip Nua) or the expenditure review committee. This advisory committee, headed by economist Colm McCarthy, was to recommend cuts in public spending. It issued its findings, commonly known as the **McCarthy report**, on 16 July 2009 in two volumes. The Report recommended approaches to a potential €5.3bn in savings, including recommendations for 17,300 public service job cuts and a 5 per cent drop in social welfare.

National Asset Management Agency (NAMA)

The National Asset Management Agency (NAMA) was established in December 2009 as one of a number of initiatives taken by the Irish government (listed in the 'Government for National Recovery 2011-2016' document). The Agency was set up to address the serious problems which arose in Ireland's banking sector as the result of excessive property lending. NAMA acquired loans (land and development and associated loans) with a nominal value of €72.3 billion from participating financial institutions. Its objective was to obtain the best achievable financial return for the State on this portfolio over an expected lifetime of up to ten years. For approximately €54 billion, NAMA purchased loans with a book value of around €77 billion. This is an estimated discount of 30 per cent.

Why was NAMA set up?

NAMA was set up to buy assets, i.e. loans, from banks, aiming to take the riskier loan classes away from the balance sheets of the banks and make the banks safer and more secure for depositors and investors. It was seen as the best approach to ensure stability in Ireland's financial system and intended to exist in order to free up the banks to lend to businesses and households. Refer to **www.fiannafail.ie.**

WHO HAS ENDORSED NAMA?

NAMA was endorsed by the European Central Bank, EU Commission, International Monetary Fund, Organisation for Economic Co-operation and Development. NAMA was seen as arguably the most effective solution to the issues confronting the banking sector and the economy at the time of the crisis in 2009.

Life in NAMA limbo

Ian Kehoe   11 September 2011

Big-name property developers who were once flying high now find their fates inextricably linked to the NAMA juggernaut. The figures are familiar at this stage: 850 borrowers who got 11,000 loans totalling more than €70 billion. Those loans have been transferred to the National Asset Management Agency (NAMA)

But behind the staggering numbers of NAMA are the developers who borrowed big and built big during the boom, and have now either been forced to adapt to NAMA or get left out in the cold in the bust. Since its establishment, NAMA has been dealing with these developers, with varying levels of success. Its immediate focus has been on the top 180 developers who, between them, borrowed more than €62 billion. The remaining 670 'smaller' borrowers are being handled by the banks, but they remain debtors of NAMA.

All the developers have been told to submit business plans to NAMA, outlining what assets they intend to sell and how they propose to pay back their debts. If a developer's plan is accepted, he could be paid a salary – most are being paid between €75,000 and €100,000 a year – and a cut of future profits.

If not, a receiver will be appointed over the assets behind the loans, giving NAMA the right to sell the properties and recoup some of what is it owed.

Source: *The Sunday Business Post* www.thepost.ie

What was the Troika of Lenders?

This referred to the troika, or trinity, of the European Commission, the European Central Bank and the International Monetary Fund, all of which monitored the financial activities within the European Union.

State is meeting bailout targets, says troika

Simon Carswell and Harry McGee

21 October 2011

'The Government is meeting the targets set under the €85 bailout plan, but there are domestic and international risks and more sacrifices to be made', the so-called troika of lenders has warned. The troika of the European Commission, the European Central Bank and the International Monetary Fund praised Ireland for sticking to the bailout programme. 'Ireland is not yet out of the woods and it will be a long journey but it is making real progress,' said Istvan Szekely, the commission country director for Ireland. In its latest quarterly review of the plan, the troika said a balance must be struck between correcting the public finances and growing domestic demand in the economy. IMF Deputy Director Ajai Chopra said outside investors did not just want fiscal adjustment in Ireland but also economic growth.

The troika warned that unemployment remained 'unacceptably high' and that further reforms of the 'sheltered' legal, medical and pharmacy professions – and the privatisation of State companies – would lower costs, including electricity costs, for consumers. 'We want to make the consumer king and we are close to the coronation here,' said Mr Szekely. Pointing to one example of high costs, he said that in Brussels, where he lives, it costs half of what it does in Ireland to visit a GP. The sale of public companies would lower costs and raise revenue for the Government, he said. The troika said it had assessed the cost of all possible spending cuts and tax increases for the December budget but that the scale and type of savings sought was for the Government to decide.

The Minister for Finance, Michael Noonan, hinted at an earlier press conference that he may not need to seek savings substantially beyond €3.6 billion in the budget to meet the troika's deficit target of 8.6 per cent of GDP next year. The Government has faced calls to seek savings of greater than €4 billion in this year's budget. Mr Noonan said the troika had not objected to finding budget alternatives to income tax rises and social welfare rate cuts. 'The troika made it clear that they had no difficulty in substituting one fiscal measure for another with an equal value,' he said. The Government would not break its promises on income tax or social welfare cuts, he said. The Minister said the Fiscal Advisory Council's suggestion of a more ambitious 1 per cent deficit target by 2015 – instead of 3 per cent – was 'a bridge too far'. 'To pull it back to 1 per cent would mean an additional correction of €4 billion … It's a very big ask,' said Mr Noonan. 'The final figure for this year's savings depends on tax receipts in October and November', he said. Minister for

Public Expenditure Brendan Howlin said there would be no fire sale of State assets and companies to generate €2 billion. The troika said it has not set any deadlines on the disposal of assets as it did not want to remove room to manoeuvre in the sale process.

Mr Chopra said that generally the troika had no concerns about the programme targets being met. 'There is a very significant meeting of minds on the objectives and the way to meet those objectives,' said the IMF mission chief. He said the EU debt crisis and a weaker global economic outlook posed risks to Ireland's recovery, which has been driven by exports. Ireland was trying to address mortgage arrears in a 'sensible' way through tailored, case-by-case solutions that retain an incentive to continue repaying, he said. The troika said that it would have to work with the Government to consider opportunities to tackle youth unemployment. 'No one wants to have a lost generation,' said Mr Szekely.

Source: *The Irish Times*

What were the NewERA Proposals?

The NewERA Proposals documented the plans for the restructuring of the semi-state sector. It consisted of the selling off of state assets to raise revenue for infrastructure. NewERA was a long-term financial investment by the State in commercial sectors of the economy – energy, telecoms and water, aimed at earning a financial return, paid for through user charges on households and businesses, and not through general taxation. NewERA was targeting a total commercial investment of just over €18.2 billion. NewERA investments were planned to stimulate the construction sector and the wider economy in the face of the recession, supporting just over 105,000 additional jobs in four years. The new jobs were to be spread evenly between regions and skill levels.

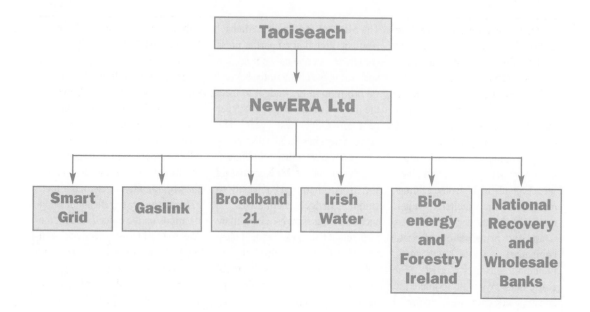

Fig. 2.1 A restructured semi-State sector

- **Smart Grid:** A merger of ESB Networks and Eirgrid.
- **Gaslink:** The existing state operator of the gas network to absorb Bord Gais networks to become the owner and operator of the gas network.
- **Broadband 21:** Will amalgamate the telecom assets of existing state companies, including Bord Gais, the NRA, the ESB and the MANs (Metropolitan Area Networks) which are managed for the State by Enet.
- **Irish Water:** Will take over the water investment and maintenance programmes of the 34 existing local authorities.
- **Bioenergy and Forestry Ireland (BFI):** Will merge Bord na Mona and Coillte.
- **National Recovery Wholesale Bank:** A wholesale bank that will provide financing directly to energy utilities to fund retrofits for houses with poor energy ratings.

Refer to **www.new-era.ie.**

Public Service Reform

Croke Park Agreement – Public Service Agreement (2010-2014)

The Croke Park Agreement (also known as the Public Service Agreement 2010-2014) was aimed at re-organising the public service i.e. public service reform. The core concern for the Government was to restore the public finances and to reduce the deficit to less than 3 per cent of GDP by 2014, in part by achieving sustainability in the cost of delivering public services relative to State revenues.

To help achieve that goal, the Government intended to restructure and re-organise the public service significantly. The Agreement details were compiled based on:

- The recommendations arising from the Reports of the Special Group on Public Service Numbers and Expenditure programmes.
- The Local Government Efficiency Review Group.
- The National Strategy for Higher Education.

In order to achieve an integrated public service that was leaner and more effective, and focussed more on the needs of the citizen, the parties to the Agreement recognised that, in the context of reduced resources and numbers, the public service would need to be re-organised, and public bodies and individual public servants would have to increase their flexibility and mobility to work together across sectoral, organisational and professional boundaries.

In the agreement it was acknowledged that public servants had:

- Made a very significant contribution towards the recovery of the economy over the last two years with over €3 billion saved from the potential public service pay and pensions bill.
- The general round pay increases under the terms of the Review and Transitional Agreement due in 2009 were not paid.
- A general moratorium on recruitment and promotion was applied to most of the public service, and incentivised early retirement and career break schemes were introduced.
- A pension-related deduction of an average of nearly 7 per cent was applied to all the earnings of all public servants.
- A reduction in rates of pay and allowances took effect on 1 January, 2010.

SUMMARY OF CHANGES INCLUDED IN THE AGREEMENT

- Reduction in public service numbers.
- Redeployment in the integrated public service
- Reconfiguring the design and delivery of public services – centralisation and mergers.
- Introduction of Performance and Skills Management systems.
- Implementation of sectoral agreements (sub-agreements that formed part of this Public Service Agreement relating to specific sectors of employment).
- **Public Service Pay Policy:** There will be no further reductions in the pay rates of serving public servants for the lifetime of this Agreement. This commitment is subject to compliance with the terms of thisAgreement.
- **Public Service pensions:** As announced in the 2010 Budget, the Government introduced a new single pension scheme for all new entrants to the public service.
- **Performance Verification:** The Agreement was to be monitored by the formal Implementation Body.
- **An agreed mechanism to resolve disagreements while implementing the agreement:** The Government anticipated problems in the face of pay cuts and reduced staff numbers, so part of the agreement directed unions to use the C and A Machinery where industrial relations matters could be referred to the LRC or Labour Court to ensure a **stable industrial relations climate to minimise the effects of disputes.**

The Agreement stated that a stable industrial relations climate had important benefits for the general public and the public service itself. These benefits included:

- The provision of uninterrupted services.
- Improved productivity and staff morale.
- Increased public confidence.
- The maintenance of Ireland as a desirable location for foreign direct investment.

PRACTICE QUESTIONS

1. List two short-term, two medium-term and two long-term sources of finance.
2. What other sources of finance exist. Name *four* sources and explain them.
3. What are the differences between Fixed Capital and Social Capital?
4. What are the differences between Working Capital and Venture Capital?
5. What are the differences between a Bank Overdraft and a Term Loan?
6. What is a Bill of Exchange?
7. How do Letters of Credit and Credit Terms differ?
8. Why are Debtors regarded as sources of short-term finance and how is Factoring connected with debtors?
9. Why is Taxation regarded as a source of short-term finance?
10. Are Leasing and Sale and Lease Back one and the same?

11. Define Hire Purchase, giving a current example.
12. How do Ordinary, Preference Shareholders and Debentures differ with regard to ownership of a business?
13. What is Equity Share Capital?
14. Explain the following: Dividend, Sale and Lease Back, and Government/semi-state grants.
15. Why are domestic entrepreneurs given grants?
16. What is sub-prime lending? What do sub-prime lenders do?
17. Explain the sub-prime lending crisis.
18. With regard to Ireland's debt crisis give a brief account of Ireland's journey from boom to recession to recovery.
19. What was NAMA and why was it set up?
20. In your opinion was the set up of NAMA a good idea?
21. What was MABS?
22. Explain briefly what were the recommendations of the Keane report.
23. What was the Troika of Lenders?
24. What were the NewERA Proposals?
25. What was the Croke Park Agreement (Public Service Agreement (2010–2014))?

Seed, Start-up and Expansion Capital

Under the EU **Community Guidelines on State Aid to promote Risk Capital Investments in Small and Medium-Sized Enterprises**, Member States are required to collect data on a beneficiary company's stage of development. Those guidelines contain definitions of 'seed capital', 'start-up capital' and 'expansion capital', as follows:

- **Seed capital:** means financing provided to study, assess and develop an initial concept, preceding the start-up phase.
- **Start-up capital:** means financing provided to companies, which have not sold their product or service commercially and are not yet generating a profit, for product development and initial marketing.
- **Expansion capital:** means financing provided for the growth and expansion of a company, which may or may not break even or trade profitably, for the purposes of increasing production capacity, or market.

SUMMARY OF THE SEED CAPITAL SCHEME (SCS)

Introduced in 1984, the Seed Capital Scheme (SCS), in conjunction with its associated scheme, the Business Expansion Scheme (BES) , are tax relief incentive schemes. The BES provides tax relief for investment in certain corporate trades, while the SCS provides for a refund of tax **already** paid by an individual, when that individual sets up, and takes employment in, a new qualifying business.

Both schemes have broadly taken the same format over a number of years and, because they are a form of State-aid (at the level of the enterprise), any changes to the scheme require the approval of the European Commission, to ensure that it remains compatible with EU law.

If you are an employee, an unemployed person or were made redundant recently and are interested in starting your own business you may be entitled to avail of the tax refund available under the Seed Capital Scheme.

An employee who leaves employment and invests by means of shares in a company, which carries on a new business may claim a refund of income tax paid in previous years. An unemployed person may also avail of this facility. Refer to **www.revenue.ie.**

The BES scheme ended officially in 2006. In 2010, the Business Expansion Scheme, which helps companies to gain access to capital investments, was revamped and renamed as the Employment and Investment Incentive introduced in the Finance Act 2011.

Employment and Investment Incentives Scheme (EII) (formerly the BES Scheme)

Padraig O'Feinneadha

Employment and Investment Incentives (EII) Scheme, introduced in the Finance Act 2011, is a replacement for the Business Expansion Scheme, which had been introduced in 1984. The Business Expansion Scheme (BES) was introduced initially to encourage employment in manufacturing companies. Over the years this expanded to include various types of tourism undertakings, internationally traded services, building of advanced factories and various green-related businesses. The number of projects receiving investment and the level of investment has been in decline.

The EII was introduced in an attempt to increase the amount of equity available to companies in these difficult economic times. A summary of the main features are outlined below.

Qualifying Trades
The type of trade that qualifies under the new incentive scheme is much broader than that which qualified under the BES. All trades qualify under the new incentive scheme except for the following:

1. Dealing in commodities or futures or in shares, securities or other financial assets.
2. Financing activities.
3. Provision of services, which would result in a close company that provides those services being treated as a service company. (A close company is a company controlled by five or fewer participators or is controlled by any number of participators who are directors. Most Irish resident companies are what are called 'close' companies.)
4. Dealing in or developing land.
5. Occupation of woodlands.
6. Operating or managing hotels, guest houses, self-catering accommodation.
7. Operating or managing nursing homes or residential care homes.
8. Operations carried on in the coal industry or in the steel and ship-building sectors.

Amount of Capital Available

The amount of capital that a company or its associated companies can raise under the scheme is a lifetime limit of €10 million. The limit applies to all funding under the scheme raised since 1984. In one year the maximum amount that can be raised is up to €2.5 million.

Source: Institute of Certified Public Accountants in Ireland: www.cpaireland.ie/UserFiles/ File/Accountancy%20Plus/A%20June%2011%20Article%20PDFs/Employment%20and%20 Investment%20O%20Feinneadha.pdf

Revamp for Business Expansion Scheme

Budget 2011 – Companies that create jobs to be rewarded

The Minister told the Dáil that there will be no change to the country's 12.5 per cent corporate tax rate and he said he welcomed recent comments by European finance ministers, who understand the 'importance of this issue to Ireland'. Minister Lenihan said that the Business Expansion Scheme, which helps companies to gain access to capital investments, is to be revamped and renamed as the Employment and Investment Incentive. The new scheme needs approval from the European Commission, and the existing scheme will continue until this has been received. Under the new scheme, Mr Lenihan said that the limit that can be raised by companies will be increased from €2m to €10m. The amount that can be raised in any 12-month period will be increased from €1.5m to €2.5m. Certification requirements will also be simplified. The Minister said the three-year corporation tax exemption for start-up companies starting a new trade in 2011 will be extended and amended so that the relief will be linked to the amount of employers' PRSI paid by the company. He said this change will focus the relief on employment creation, rewarding companies that create jobs.

Source: www.rte.ie/news/2010/ 1207/budgetbusiness-business.html

Development Finance

This is expansion capital and is regarded as being less risky than seed capital because the business has a guaranteed track record.

Ways of Raising Development Money

- Traditional financing sources, e.g. banks and venture capital firms.
- Equity Investment (in shares in the business) – issuing shares (share capital). Different company share details are on public record and available from **www.cro.ie**.
- Investment Fund Managers will fund small speculative infrastructure projects – the investor will expect returns in excess of their standard yield.
- Project Finance – some investment banks will advance funds for projects.
- Creating Debenture or Loan Notes (Loan Capital) – interest has to be paid to debenture holders.
- Factoring – selling some debts to a finance company at a discount.
- Sale and Lease Back of high-depreciation equipment that costs the business money – a bank may agree to raise finance based on the value of these assets.
- Lease and Lease Back – assets are leased to the bank, not sold to them, for an upfront lease payment

What was an IPO?

The term 'IPO' meant Initial Public Offering and was central to the dot-com era in the late 1990s during the technology bull market (rising shares). The term 'siliconaire' described the dot-com entrepreneurs in their early twenties and thirties who suddenly found themselves gaining from the proceeds of their Internet companies' IPOs due to positive share deals.

The IPOs were the first sale of stock by these private, small, young internet-based companies *seeking capital to expand* and this was also done by larger privately owned companies wishing to gain public company status. These were very risky investments and it was difficult to predict what stock values would result: however, the positive entrepreneurial economic environment of the era benefited many young business people.

Matching the Sources of Finance with Particular Needs of the Organisation or the Individual

Long-term finance is usually sought by businesses who run short of finance or wish to commence or expand businesses, where the amount of capital required is large. The decisions and commitments are long term and costly and require serious consideration before they are undertaken.

Medium-term finance need not necessarily apply to a business. Someone might want to buy a home computer for their children or change a car by availing of a term loan. They might wish to lease a photocopier or buy the computer in instalments by availing of hire purchase.

Short-term finance is usually required by businesses. A bank overdraft, however, can be sought by ordinary individuals who have a good track record with their bank. It will be reviewed after a year, whereas a term loan (medium-term finance) might have a repayment deadline of up to five years. Other sources like credit terms and taxation and expenses due represent short-term ways of maintaining the use of money, that would otherwise be used to pay creditors, to finance the business. (This concept is explained under 'Short-term Finance' in the previous section.) Also, quick money can be acquired by factoring, but a loss is made in the short term.

Cash Flow Forecasts

These are charts which analyse a business's inflows of money compared with outflows of money in order to predict whether a business will have enough money coming in to adequately cover outgoing expense payments due. Every business should compile a cash flow prediction chart or forecast each year or half yearly depending on the business. Typical inflows are sales, loans, investment capital raised, grants and refunds.

Typical outflows are interest on loans, purchases, wages, commission, advertising, rent and rates, light and heat, telephone, administration expenses, general expenses, personal drawings, and any capital expenditure like spending on fixed assets (office equipment/furniture, premises, plant, motor vehicles for the business).

THINGS TO BE KEPT IN MIND WHEN COMPILING A CASH FLOW CHART

1. Debtors' and Creditors' Credit Terms: For example, if we allow our debtors (people that owe us money) one month's credit, this means that if we bill them in January, the inflow will not occur until February (February entry into chart).

   If our creditors (people we owe money to) allow us two months' credit, this means that if they bill us in January, we will not have to pay until March – outflow will not occur until March (March entry into chart).

Important: It is only at the moment that the inflows and outflows occur that the figures are lodged into the cash flow chart and **not when the bills are dated**. This appears to be the most common mistake made by students.

2. Terms like 'month in arrears' and 'in the month incurred': Wages paid out by us a month in arrears (often referred to as a lag in the payment of wages by a month) means, for example, work done by employees in July will not be paid for by us until August (August entry into chart).

   Expenses paid out by us per month or in the month incurred means, for example, in June itself (June entry into the chart).

3. If a wage increase of 15 per cent is due from June onwards, the increased figure will appear in the months from June onwards (including June). *Note:* the wages · figure *never* reverts back to the original amount.

4. Terms like 'quarterly in arrears': Bills due for payment quarterly in arrears means at the end of every three months. Sometimes the first payment date due will be given, for example, a light and heat bill of €2,000 payable quarterly in arrears beginning on 1 February. Entries into the chart would be €500 in February, €500 in May, €500 in August and €500 in November. If no first payment date is given, and the chart is a twelve-monthly forecast starting in January, the entries into the chart would be €500 in March, €500 in June, €500 in September and €500 in December.

5. A cash purchase of goods: This is recorded in the chart as stock – an amount bought and paid for on the same day. March cash purchases of goods for stock, paid for immediately, is entered into the chart as an outflow in March only.

6. Calculation of Commission: (This exercise is probably the one that students find the most difficult.) If staff are to receive a 5 per cent commission of total sales, it means that the calculations should be worked on the question given and not the chart the student is compiling. Cash and Credit Sales will be listed in the question and these are added per month to get each month's Total Sales.

   For example, if the sales information in the question is:

SALES	Cash	Credit
January	2,000	3,000
February	5,000	2,500

and the commission is to be calculated at 5 per cent of Total Sales, payable to staff each month one month in arrears, then 5 per cent of €5,000 = €250 is entered into the chart in February. (This represents January wages not paid out until February.) Five per cent of €7,500 = €375 is entered into the chart in March. (This represents February wages not paid out until March.)

7. If new equipment or machinery is purchased, it is entered once in the month that it is purchased. The equipment is assumed to be purchased and paid for immediately, unless other information is provided where a lease exists. If this is the case, it becomes an ongoing bill that is either paid monthly or perhaps quarterly.

Note: Depreciation has *nothing to do with cash flow*, so it is ignored in this regard.

PRACTICE QUESTION

Frank Smith is expected to have the following inflows and outflows of money from 1 January to 30 June 2013. The cash balance at 1 January was €1,000.

1. Expected Sales

Month	Cash €	Credit €
January	2,300	1,000
February	2,000	1,500
March	3,000	1,800
April	2,800	1,400
May	3,300	1,500
June	3,500	1,900

2. Expected Expenses

	Jan	Feb	Mar	Apr	May	June
Purchases (credit)	700	1,500	1,300	1,000	1,000	1,000
Cash purchases	300	2,000	800	1,000	1,100	1,400
Wages	1,000	1,000	1,000	1,000	1,500	1,500
Purchase of office equipment		7,000				
Rent and rates	300	300	350	350	350	350
Administration	70	60	60	60	60	65

3. Purchases are on credit, where one month's credit is taken from suppliers.
4. Debtors are allowed two months' credit.
5. Commission is 2 per cent of total sales and is paid to employees one month in arrears.
6. A yearly light and heat bill of €2,000 is payable quarterly in arrears, with the first payment starting in February.
7. The lag in the payment of wages is one month.
8. Administration expenses are payable a month in arrears.
9. Any other expenses are paid out in the month incurred.

Based on the information given, you are required to:
(a) Compile a Cash Flow Forecast for Frank Smith for the period 1 January to 30 June 2013.

(b) Identify the sources of shortfall of cash.

(c) Recommend any provisions that should be put in place to avoid shortfalls of cash.

SOLUTION TO PRACTICE QUESTION

(a) Cash Flow Forecast for Frank Smith for the six months ending 30 June 2013.

CASH INFLOWS	Jan €	Feb €	Mar €	Apr €	May €	Jun €
Cash sales	2,300	2,000	3,000	2,800	3,300	3,500
Credit sales	–	–	1,000	1,500	1,800	1,400
TOTAL INFLOWS	2,300	2,000	4,000	4,300	5,100	4,900
CASH OUTFLOWS						
Cash purchases	300	2,000	800	1,000	1,100	1,400
Credit Purchases	–	700	1,500	1,300	1,000	1,000
Wages	–	1,000	1,000	1,000	1,000	1,500
Commission		66	70	96	84	96
Office equipment		7,000	–	–	–	–
Rent and rates	300	300	350	350	350	350
Admin. expenses	–	70	60	60	60	60
Light and heat	–	500	–	–	500	–
TOTAL OUTFLOWS	600	11,636	3,780	3,806	4,094	4,406
NET (inflows – outflows)	1,700	–9,636	220	494	1,006	494
BALANCE 1/1/13	1,000	2,700	–6,936	–6,716	–6,222	–5,216
BALANCE 30/6/13	2,700	–6,936	–6,716	–6,222	–5,216	–4,722

(b) Mr Smith will experience a shortfall of cash in February. This is due to the proposed purchase of office equipment. Cash inflows for credit sales are not due in until March and this is also a major cause of the shortfall.

(c) The following provisions should be put in place to avoid the cash shortfall:

1. Either postpone the purchase of the office equipment or acquire a loan to cover it in January.

2. The length of payment time allowed to debtors needs to be reviewed and reduced to one month's credit. Money from credit sales would come in in February if this could be agreed.

PRACTICE QUESTIONS

1. Distinguish between Commencement and Development Finance. What bodies provide these monies?

2. List two ways of raising development finance.
3. What were the purposes of the (a) the BES and (b) the SCS?
4. What were IPOs and how were they linked to development finance?
5. Why are Cash Flow Forecasts so vital to organisations?
6. Is Depreciation part of a cash flow chart?

Note: In order to understand fully the detail in the following section, the student should be able to prepare a cash flow forecast following the example given.

Credit Control and Cash Flow/Liquidity

The frequency of cash inflows and outflows will be regulated by the credit terms agreed between purchaser and seller. Control on credit allowed means, in simple terms, chasing up money that is due to you. It is in the interest of all retail outlets to have a tight credit control policy.

LIQUIDITY RATIO

Accountants measure liquidity using the Liquidity Ratio which ideally should be 1:1.

Formula: $$\frac{\text{Current Assets } less \text{ Closing Stock}}{\text{Current Liabilities}}$$

Answer will be CA *less* CS: CL

Current assets consist of valuable items in a business that can be easily converted into cash. Debtors (people who owe you money) are an example – money due to come in. Current liabilities consist of debts that we owe to creditors (people to whom we owe money). Closing stock is excluded because it is regarded as the current asset that is the most difficult to convert into cash. A business's current assets must be able to cover its current liabilities. In other words, the money it has must be able to cover the money it owes.

If a business shows a liquidity ratio of 2.5:1 this indicates a bad credit control policy and an under-utilisation of resources (meaning credit control personnel are not doing their job properly and debts are not being collected on time). There is a danger in this case that outstanding debts could turn into bad debts and would have to be written off – causing unnecessary losses that could be avoided.

If a business shows a liquidity ratio of 5:1 this indicates that its current assets are unable to cover its current liabilities, so even if the debtor payments due are collected on time, there would not be enough money generated to allow current liabilities to be paid off. The business in this case has a very serious liquidity problem and must substantially increase sales and profitability in order to break even.

Cash flow charts were discussed in the previous section. Since they are a means of measuring future requirements with regard to money needs, they therefore help a business to avoid shortfalls of cash and allow for appropriate future cash planning.

Ipso data shows cheque use in decline

Emma Kennedy   Sunday, August 21, 2011

The number of cheques written in Ireland dropped by 11 per cent to 91million last year, the fifth successive year of a decline in cheque usage, according to new figures from the Irish Payment Services Organisation Limited (Ipso).

According to Ipso's figures, the number of cheques written in Ireland has fallen from a peak of more than 131 million in 2005,with a 27 per cent decline in cheque usage over the last three years. Ipso chief executive Pat McLoughlin said that consumers and businesses were moving towards cards and electronic payments. Ipso estimated that a significant switch to electronic payments and card payments could boost the Irish economy by €1 billion per annum. However, McLoughlin said that Ireland still lagged behind other European countries in terms of cheque usage. Cheques still account for more than twice the value of electronic payments here, according to Ipso's figures. McLoughlin said that Ireland was one of three EU countries who continued to make significant use of cheques, alongside Britain and France. 'Cheques here are largely business usage now,' McLoughlin said. 'They are still very much a feature of business.' However, he

said research carried out by Ipso had shown that 62 per cent of businesses would prefer to receive all payments electronically. He added that 70 per cent of those surveyed had agreed that electronic payments and card payments improved credit control and reduced administrative costs. However, the research showed that only 19 per cent of businesses had encouraged customers to move away from cheques in favour of electronic payments and card payments.

The latest batch of payment statistics from Ipso, published last week, showed that Irish consumers continued to rely on cash more than the rest of Europe, but were beginning to change their payment habits. Irish consumers are the biggest users of ATMs in Europe, withdrawing more than double the amount of cash that an average European does each year. Ipso's figures showed that consumers in Ireland made about 40 ATM withdrawals each year, taking out about €5,000 per capita each last year.

ATM usage here peaked in 2008, with consumers withdrawing an average of €6,500 each that year. Nonetheless, ATM usage has been declining here since then. Meanwhile, the number of new

debit cards issued here last year was more than 330,000, meaning there are now 3.4 million debit cards in issue in Ireland. Irish consumers carried out about 200 million debit card transactions in 2010. According to Ipso, the total spend on cards in Ireland last year was €22.8 billion, marking the first time that the value of card transactions exceeded the value of ATM withdrawals, which was €22.3 billion last year.

Figures for the first half of 2011 show a continued rise in card usage and a continued decline in ATM withdrawals. Non-cash transactions accounted for just over a third, some 36 per cent, of Irish transactions last year. This compares with an EU average of 96 per cent, as consumers on the continent leave cash behind in favour of alternative payment options. The latest data from Ipso also showed a rise in the number of Irish people using internet banking services over the past four years.

There are now almost three million customers registered for online banking. IPSO recently reported that customers made 10.7 million online payments in the first quarter of this year, a 17.3 per cent increase on the same period last year.

Source: *Sunday Business Post*

Impact of Credit Control Policy on the Liquidity and Profitability of a Business

A tight and regulated credit control policy is essential to ensure *on time* cash inflow and outflow.

DEBT COLLECTION

Making sure that debts are collected and money is received when it is supposed to be received will:

1. Reduce the liquidity ratio and bring it nearer to the ideal 1:1 ratio.
2. Allow accurate cash flow forecasting, with planned spending being postponed if a shortfall occurs. If spending is essential, loan arrangements can be put in place.
3. Skilled credit control personnel will be able to estimate monies that are likely to be paid late, as well as possible bad debts. Money can then be put aside to cover these eventualities.
4. Future investments can be confidently planned, e.g. the purchase of new premises or equipment.
5. Costs can be minimised once sufficient monies are collected to pay off debts. This, combined with appropriate price competitiveness, advertising mechanisms, materials and customer service, will ensure a higher level of sales and will increase profit margins.

DEBT PAYMENT

Making sure that money owed by the business is paid out to creditors on time will:

1. Avoid unnecessary interest accruing on loans, overdraft facilities and credit cards.
2. Ensure a good reputation with regard to debt payment and will help to gain new customers/sales through goodwill (reputation).
3. Allow an accurate picture to be drawn with regard to how much money is available to either put aside or invest.
4. Uphold good reputation with regard to business management and profitability and attract new investors. Greater capital investment means business expansion and further profitability.

Once a business remains within the credit term agreed (payment within a month or two months) and once this degree of flexibility is respected, creditors will usually be thankful for the business and may put more business in the direction of the company.

When a business has:

1. a satisfactory level of stock turnover, as indicated by how many times stock is replaced (empty shelves that are efficiently restocked) – discussed previously under the heading 'Stock Control';
2. an effective and efficient Credit Control Policy, indicating a well managed cash flow record; and
3. a 1:1 Liquidity Ratio (or as near to this as possible), indicating that the business has enough money in current assets to cover its current liabilities;

this will imply that the retail outlet is operating at a high level of efficiency and profitability and it has a healthy turnover per annum.

PRACTICE QUESTIONS
1. What is Credit Control?
2. How might a business know that there is a problem with its credit control policy?
3. What does a Liquidity Ratio of 3:1 indicate?
4. What does a Liquidity Ratio of 8:1 indicate?
5. How are Cash Flow Forecasts linked to Credit Control policy?
6. Why would e-payments help a business's cash flow and credit control?
7. Explain *five* benefits of prompt debt collection.
8. Explain *four* benefits of prompt debt payment.
9. Why might efficient cash flow and credit control policies indicate profitability?

Unit Cost and Selling Price Calculations

The easiest way to understand Cost Analysis, and how selling prices are arrived at, is to take a question as follows:

PRACTICE QUESTION
You are the administrator of a restaurant and in the business of monitoring costs. The following information is made available to you:

Ingredients to produce ten portions of Irish stew.

1 kg lamb	@ €1.35 per kg
1 kg potatoes	@ 4c per kg
1 kg onion	@ 13c per kg
2 leeks	@ 5c each
1 head celery	@ 10c
1 kg button onions	@ 18c per kg
1 bunch parsley	@ 5c

You are required to:

(a) Calculate the Total Cost of the ingredients used.

(b) Find the Average Cost per portion.

(c) Work out the Selling Price so that the business can achieve a 40% profit on materials.

(d) Calculate the profit in money terms.

SOLUTION

(a) Cost of ingredients Total = €1.95

(b) Average Cost per portion = $\dfrac{€1.95}{10}$ = 20 cent

(c) Selling Price = Cost *plus* Profit (the Selling Price formula is a formula that must be learned)

Selling Price is always 100%

Therefore 100% = Cost *plus* Profit

Related to question:

$$100\% = Cost + 40\%$$

therefore   Cost = 60%

from (a)   Cost = €1.95

$$60\% = €1.95$$

What are we looking for? Answer 100% Selling Price

So $1\% = \dfrac{€1.95}{60}$

$100\% = \dfrac{€1.95 \times 100}{60}$

Answer = €3.25

The Selling Price that would be charged for the dish is €3.25

(i.e. $\dfrac{€3.25}{10}$ = 33 pence per portion based on 10 portions, which was not asked).

(d) The Profit in money terms is found in the following way:

Apply the Selling Price formula again but this time in money terms rather than in percentage terms.

Selling Price = Cost + Profit

€3.25   = €1.95 + Profit

Answer: therefore Profit = €1.30

It is important to note that different businesses have different profit margins and therefore the percentage profit levels will vary. Larger businesses can afford to charge lower selling prices because they can avail of large trade discounts through bulk buying or buying raw materials cheaper abroad. They create unmatchable price levels (too price competitive) that have contributed to smaller traders having to close their businesses.

Specialised businesses often have to charge higher prices because it is more expensive for them in terms of their costs and they combat their cost problems by passing on the cost to the consumer in the form of higher prices.

Warning! The last practice question only deals with material costs in the catering industry.

There are three main costs in every business.
1. Materials (e.g. shampoos and conditioners for hairdressers and food and drink for chefs).
2. Labour (payment for labour is wages – a rising cost in business).
3. Overheads (like electricity bills, telephone bills, insurance, advertising, stationery).

All three costs have to be taken into account when a business is setting selling prices.

Competitors' prices also have to be considered. It must be remembered that unless a business can secure a solid market share, it cannot charge extraordinarily high prices, because consumers generally look for a mixture of 'value for money' and 'quality'. Some consumers will continue to buy a good or avail of a service based on consumer loyalty.

Securing a good reputation (through advertising and a good marketing strategy) and resulting consumer loyalty will allow greater flexibility regarding selling prices.

PRACTICE QUESTIONS
1. What *three* types of costs are connected with every business?
2. How is Selling Price defined?
3. Why can larger businesses afford to charge lower prices?
4. List *four* factors that will have an influence on Selling Prices set by business people.
5. You are a chef and owner of a business and the cost of the ingredients of an Irish stew (which is divided into four portions) is as follows:

425 g stewing lamb	@ €2.20 per kg
400 g potatoes	@ 70c per kg
100 g celery	@ 50c per kg
100 g button onions	@ 50c per kg
10 onions	@ 10c each
100 g leeks	@ 55c per kg

(a) Calculate the Total Cost of the ingredients.
(b) Find the Average Cost per portion.
(c) Work out the Selling Price so that the business can achieve a 40% profit on materials.
(d) Calculate the profit (on materials only) of the dish as a whole, in money terms.

Note: Be careful to calculate the cost based on 1,000 g = 1 kg.
    In the case of drink 1,000 ml = 1 litre.

Sample Assignment Briefs

1. You have decided to start your own business. You are required to prepare a cash flow chart for the first six months of trading and a breakeven chart to present to your bank as you require an overdraft facility.

2. Candidates should investigate finance and business controls within an organisation of their choice under the following headings:
   * Brief History, Size, Ownership and Staff Structure.
   * Management Controls which include Planning Controls, Stock Controls, Quality Control, Financial Control, Credit Control.
   * Overall Performance Appraisal.

CHOOSE QUESTION A OR B BUT NOT BOTH

A. Downey and Sons Incorporated produce goods and have recently received worrying cost information.
   One product exists within the range of goods that is making a loss. Financial Cost and Sales information on this product is as follows:

Sales (2,500 units at €120 each)		€300,000
Direct Labour	€200,000	
Direct Materials	€40,000	
Factory Overheads – variable	€10,000	
–fixed	€30,000	€280,000
		€20,000
Selling Expenses – variable	€15,000	
– fixed	€8,000	
Other Fixed Overheads	€6,000	€29,000
Net Loss		€9,000

(i) Make the appropriate pre–calculations to prepare to draw the Breakeven chart.

(ii) Draw the Breakeven chart and include the following details on it:

(a) The Breakeven point.

(b) The 100% Present Capacity position.

(c) The Profit or Loss when 500 units are produced.

(d) The Profit or Loss when 2,000 units are produced.

Comment on your findings.

(iii) What recommendations would you suggest that would improve the Breakeven level and convert the Net Loss to a Net Profit?

B. Based on your knowledge of stock control, analyse the stock control procedures that are operated by a supermarket or superstore in your home locality or wherever is most convenient. (The student should prepare well by summarising the appropriate parts of the text material in Chapter 2.)

3. Freebird Ltd manufactures rail engines and carriages. The business expects cash shortages to occur. The following details apply to the business:

1. Sales are expected to be €2 million in January 2013 and are expected to grow at 3% per month until December 2008. Debtors are allowed one month's credit.

2. The business has €300,000 in the bank in January 2013.

3. The issuing of company shares is expected to raise €600,000 in July.

4. Redundancy payments of €400,000 have to be paid out in May.

5. Purchases are calculated at 20 per cent of sales. The company avails of one month's credit.

6. Wages are calculated at 30 per cent of sales, and paid to employees one month in arrears.

7. Administration costs are expected to amount to €550 per month.

8. The outright purchase of premises is expected in February at a cost of €7.2 million.

9. Government grants of €40,000 will be received every quarter, beginning in March.

10. A tax refund of €3,000 will be received in April.

(a) Prepare a cash flow forecast for Freebird Ltd, for the twelve-month period 1 January to 31 December 2013.

(b) Identify the location of and reasons for any shortfall of cash.

(c) Make appropriate suggestions to management of Freebird Ltd as to how to avoid shortages of cash, based on this twelve-monthly projection.

Sample Questions for Student Research on 'Finance and Business Controls'

1. Can you provide me with a little information about the history, size, ownership and staff structure of the organisation?
2. What types of planning controls are used by the business?
3. Are 'Knowledge Management Systems' used?
4. Is performance appraisal part of the business?
5. What financial controls are used in the business? E.g. breakeven analysis, budgeting, cash flow forecasting, cost analysis (income and expenditure analysis).
6. Are any specific types of computer software used for financial control within the business?
7. What are the main sources of finance in the business? Loans, overdrafts, investor capital, grants, savings? Please specify.
8. How is debt collection managed?
9. How is debt payment managed? Does the business still pay creditors by cheque, or is an online e-payments method used?
10. What terms of trade (credit terms, discounts) are:
    - Offered to debtors.
    - Taken from creditors.
11. How does the business control quality and maintain standards of excellence? E.g. 100 per cent inspection, random sampling, quality circles, observation.
12. Who mainly supplies the business with:
    - Goods?
    - Services?
      (Include office stock)
13. How are stock levels monitored? E.g. EPOS system, stock cards, indexing, MBWA – management by walk around, ordering/reordering.
14. Have understocking or overstocking ever posed a problem for the business? If so, why?

3. Banking, Currencies, Visual Data and Insurance

The Euro and the European Central Bank

There were initially 15 countries in the EU (European Union) but this expanded in more recent years to 27 member states.

MEMBER STATES OF THE EU (YEAR OF ENTRY)

Austria (1995)	Germany (1952)	Netherlands (1952)
Belgium (1952)	Greece (1981)	Poland (2004)
Bulgaria (2007)	Hungary (2004)	Portugal (1986)
Cyprus (2004)	Ireland (1973)	Romania (2007)
Czech Republic (2004)	Italy (1952)	Slovakia (2004)
Denmark (1973)	Latvia (2004)	Slovenia (2004)
Estonia (2004)	Lithuania (2004)	Spain (1986)
Finland (1995)	Luxembourg (1952)	Sweden (1995)
France (1952)	Malta (2004)	United Kingdom (1973)

1 January 2002 marked the launch of euro bank notes and coins. The introduction of the euro as the single currency for around 300 million European citizens was a truly historic event.

The European Central Bank (ECB) has been at the centre of this development. The ECB was first established on 1 June 1998. The German Bundesbank in Frankfurt is the nerve centre of the ECB. It is the governing bank that covers the 12 different countries in the Eurozone (approximately 304 million men, women and children).

The ESCB or European System of Central Banks consists of the ECB and the National Central Banks (NCBs) of each individual member state. Three member states, Denmark, Sweden and the United Kingdom, are part of the ESCB but have opted not to adopt the euro currency.

the euro

On 1 January 2002 the euro banknotes and coins were put into circulation.

...banknotes, coins and more...

the **EURO.**
OUR *money*

The decision-making bodies of the Eurosystem are part of the ECB, namely:

1. The Governing Council – the central decision-making body in charge of monetary policy for the euro area. The Governors of each NCB are members of the Council.
2. The Executive Board.
3. The General Council — for those member states that have not adopted the euro.

The European Union (EU) was originally established as the European Economic Community (EEC) in 1957 by the Treaty of Rome. Transition to European integration began with the Maastricht Treaty in 1992. In 1997, countries wishing to adopt the single European currency had to strive to meet the following economic criteria known as the Maastricht criteria:

- Low inflation.
- Sound public finances.
- Low interest rates.
- Stable exchange rates.
- Political independence of its NCB.

These criteria laid a solid foundation for the new currency and a single monetary policy.

In January 1999, the locking of EMU (European Monetary Union) currencies against the euro marked the official beginning of EMU.

IRREVOCABLY FIXED EXCHANGE RATES

1 euro =	40.3399	Belgian Francs
	1.95583	Deutsche Mark
	340.750	Greek Drachmas
	166.386	Spanish Pesetas
	6.55957	French Francs
	0.787564	Irish Pounds
	1,936.27	Italian Lira
	40.3399	Luxembourg Francs
	2.20371	Dutch Guilders
	13.7603	Austrian Schillings
	200.482	Portuguese Escudos
	5.94573	Finish Markkas

Eleven print works were set up all over the euro area and the first euro coins were produced in August 1999. Approximately 14.5 billion euro bank notes were produced. The Irish mint (Currency Centre) producing euro notes and coins is located in Sandyford, Dublin.

The euro currency was introduced on 1 January 2002. In Ireland both the Irish currency and the euro were legal tender (acceptable in exchange for goods and services) until 9 February 2002. Since then, the euro has replaced the Irish currency.

The Euro and the ECB 2007/2008

As at 1 January 2007 there were 27 member countries of the European Union: Austria, Belgium, Bulgaria, Cyprus, Czech Republic, Denmark, Estonia, Finland, France, Germany, Greece, Hungary, Ireland, Italy, Latvia, Lithuania, Luxembourg, Malta, Netherlands, Poland, Portugal, Romania, Slovakia, Slovenia, Spain, Sweden and the United Kingdom.

The ECB is the central bank for Europe's single currency, the euro. The ECB's main task is to maintain the euro's purchasing power and thus price stability in the euro area.

European Integration

The Euro and Economic and Monetary Union (EMU) 2011

Of the 27 Members States the euro is the single currency shared by (currently) 17 of the European Union's Member States, which together make up the euro area. The introduction of the euro in 1999 was a major step in European integration. Around 330 million EU citizens now use it as their currency.

When the euro was launched on 1 January 1999, it became the new official currency of 11 Member States, replacing in two states the old national currencies, such as the Deutschmark and the French franc. First it was introduced as a virtual currency for cash-less payments and accounting purposes, while the old currencies continued to be used for cash payments and considered as 'sub-units' of the euro. It then appeared in physical form, as banknotes and coins, on 1 January 2002. The euro is not the currency of all EU Member States. Two countries (Denmark and the United Kingdom) agreed an 'opt-out' clause in the Treaty exempting them from participation, while the remainder (many of the newest EU members plus Sweden) do not meet the conditions for adopting the single currency.

The Eurosystem comprises the ECB and the national central banks (NCBs) of those countries which have adopted the euro. The headquarters of the ECB is in Frankfurt, Germany – the financial centre of the European Union.

Refer to **http://ec.europa.eu/economy_finance/euro/index_en.htm.**

The Governing Council

The Governing Council is the main decision-making body of the ECB. It comprises:
- the six members of the Executive Board; and
- the governors of the national central banks (NCBs) from the 13 euro area countries.

Its responsibilities are:
- to adopt the guidelines and take the decisions necessary to ensure the performance of the tasks entrusted to the Eurosystem;
- to formulate monetary policy

for the euro area. This includes decisions relating to monetary objectives, key interest rates, the supply of reserves in the Eurosystem, and the establishment of guidelines for the implementation of those decisions.

The Governing Council usually meets twice a month at the Eurotower in Frankfurt am Main, Germany.

At its first meeting each month, the Governing Council assesses monetary and economic developments and takes its monthly monetary policy decision. At its second meeting, the Council discusses issues mainly related to other tasks and responsibilities of the ECB and the Eurosystem.

The minutes of the meetings are not published, but the monetary policy decision is announced at a press conference held shortly after the first meeting each month. The President, assisted by the Vice-President, chairs the press conference.

Functions of The ECB
(In Co-Operation With The NCBS Jointly Known as
The ESCB – European System of Central Banks)

THE EUROPEAN SYSTEM OF CENTRAL BANKS (ESCB)

The ESCB is made up of the European Central Bank and the national central banks of the Member States. The ESCB's principal aim is to maintain price stability within the EU by way of:

- Defining and implementing the monetary policy of the Union.
- Conducting foreign-exchange operations of the euro vis-à-vis national currencies.
- Holding and managing official foreign-exchange reserves of the Member States.
- Promoting the smooth operation of payment systems.

The ESCB is managed by the decision-making bodies of the ECB. The ECB is therefore responsible for ensuring, through its activities, the missions of the ESCB. The national central banks of the Member States are also an integral part of the ESCB. They act in accordance with the guidelines and instructions issued by the ECB.

The ESCB brings together the ECB and the central banks of all Member States, whether or not they have adopted the euro. The Eurosystem brings together the ECB and the central banks of only those Member States which have adopted the euro. The mission of the Eurosystem is to define and conduct the monetary policy of the euro area.

The instruments used as part of the general ECB functions are:

1. To support and contribute to the general economic policies in the Community with the main objective of price stability.
2. **Open Market Operations in general:** to steer interest rates, manage the liquidity (cash) situation in the market and signal the monetary policy stance within the euro area – the decision on which OMO instrument is to be used lies with the ECB. The executing of the instrument is carried out by individual NCBs. (OMO instruments are listed later.)
3. **Standing Facilities:** The ECB determines the effect of overnight liquidity on market interest rates and signals the general monetary policy stance following these events. The administering of standing facilities are dealt with by NCBs. (Types of standing facilities are listed later.)
4. **Minimum Reserves:** the application of minimum reserves by the ECB is intended to stabilise money market interest rates and to control monetary expansion that can cause inflation.
5. **Counterparties:** a broad range of counterparties participate in the euro system ensuring healthy foreign exchange swaps.
6. **Eligible Assets:** counterparties may borrow from their own NCB by using eligible assets located in another member state as collateral. This eligibility is controlled by the ECB.

EU ministers claim 'progress' on finding a final strategy

Laura Noonan and Sarah Stack
Saturday, October 22 2011

Europe's finance ministers last night claimed to have made 'progress' on a final bid to hammer out a 'comprehensive' solution to the eurozone's debt crisis ahead of a summit of EU leaders tomorrow, but key issues remain. The crisis talks came as the leader of the eurozone's finance ministers group, Jean-Claude Juncker, decried the 'disastrous signals' Europe was sending out by failing to show 'proper functioning leadership'.

The euro's two most powerful countries, France and Germany, remain deeply divided on ways to solve Europe's woes. Their leaders, Nicolas Sarkozy and Angela Merkel, will dine together tonight and attempt to bridge their differences.

Urgency

Yesterday's talks mark the second assembly of Europe's finance ministers in less than a fortnight, a frequency of meetings that underlines the urgency of the crisis despite Europe's many efforts to solve it. Speaking after the meeting ended last night, Finance Minister Michael Noonan said 'progress' had been made on 'all main agenda points' but declined to comment further. It is understood that the meeting adjourned early so decisions could be taken on putting more capital into Europe's banks when ministers from all 27 European countries meet this morning. A grand solution that had been expected tomorrow will now not come until Wednesday at the earliest, after Europe's leaders decided to meet for a second time so they could discuss proposals with their parliaments before taking decisions. The urgency of the situation was highlighted yesterday by a threat from ratings agency Standard & Poor's which warned it would downgrade France and four other countries if Europe slipped back into recession.

'The outside impression is disastrous,' Mr Juncker told reporters as he arrived for yesterday's meetings. 'It does not present an example of superior statesmanship.'

On the way into the meeting, several ministers stressed the need for progress, while IMF chief Christine Lagarde insisted the Europeans would 'find solutions'. Sources last night, however, confirmed that deep divisions remained on one of the central areas of the crisis solution – how to better equip Europe's bailout fund to help struggling countries and reassure markets. The French want the fund, dubbed the European Financial Stability Facility (EFSF), turned into a bank so it can increase its €440bn pile of cash by borrowing more money from the ECB. Yesterday, both German Chancellor Ms Merkel and her finance minister, Wolfgang Schauble, re-iterated their firm opposition to that plan.

'We will stick to the situation as it is in the Treaty that the central bank is not available for state financing,' Mr Schauble told reporters yesterday.

The ECB is itself deeply opposed to lending the money. Other areas to be agreed by Wednesday include how much Europe's banks will have to boost their capital by, as well as the size of the hit investors will have to take on Greek bonds. Meanwhile, the finance ministers confirmed last night that embattled Greece will get the next €8bn instalment of its bailout money.

Source: *Irish Independent*

EU Energy Policy, Climate Change and Global Warming

What is the Kyoto Agreement?

The Kyoto Protocol is an agreement made under the United Nations Framework Convention on Climate Change (UNFCCC) aimed at the 'stabilisation of greenhouse gas concentrations in the atmosphere at a level that would prevent dangerous anthropogenic interference with the climate system'.

Countries that signed up as part of this agreement committed to reduce their emission of carbon dioxide and five other greenhouse gases. This rule now covers over 160 countries globally. As of June 2007, a total of 172 countries and other governmental entities have ratified the agreement. Notable exceptions include the US and Australia. Other countries, like India and China, which have ratified the protocol, are not required to reduce carbon emissions under the present agreement. This treaty expires in 2012, and international talks began in May 2007 on a future treaty to succeed the current one. Countries have to reduce their greenhouse gas emissions or they will be penalised by the UN.

The European Union has agreed policies to tackle climate change that European Commission President Jose Manuel Barroso describes as 'the most ambitious ever made'.

What are the EU's Aims on Climate Change?

Dependence on oil and gas has been a concern. The EU aims to boost wind power and other renewable sources of energy as well as increasing the use of bio-fuels to create a large percentage of the energy used for transportation. The EU wants to get countries to use renewable energy in power generation and heating. EU funding is being made available to countries for research with the aim of bringing down the price of renewable energy and low-carbon technology and finding new ways of increasing energy efficiency. As part of the energy strategy there are plans to encourage the construction of twelve plants that will demonstrate sustainable fossil fuel technologies, such as carbon capture, in action.

Research programmes on nuclear waste management are also a consideration but are controversial. Nuclear power is the cheapest low-carbon source of energy in Europe today. However, there are deep differences between pro- and anti-nuclear member states.

What are the EU's Targets?

The following have all been set as goals to achieve by 2020:

* A 20 per cent reduction in EU greenhouse gas emissions, as compared with 1990 levels, or 30 per cent if other developed nations agree to take similar action.

- An increase in the use of renewable energy, to 20 per cent of all energy consumed. This is a binding target. However, the plan allows flexibility in how each country contributes to the overall EU target.
- A 20 per cent increase in energy efficiency.

Functions and Services of the Central Bank of Ireland

The Central Bank of Ireland was first established in 1943 following the passing of the Central Bank Act 1942. It replaced the Currency Commission, which had functioned as the national currency-issuing authority until then.

In 1999 the bank became part of EMU (European Monetary Union) and together with the other NCBs (National Central Banks) and the ECB (European Central Bank) became part of the Eurosystem (Central Bank Act 1998).

On 1 May 2003 it was renamed and restructured and was then renamed the Central Bank and Financial Services Authority of Ireland (CBFSAI).

Following this, the Central Bank Reform Act 2010, created a new single unitary body, the Central Bank of Ireland, responsible for both central banking and financial regulation. The new structure replaced the previous related entities, the Central Bank and the Financial Services Authority of Ireland (CBFSAI) and the Financial Regulator. The Act commenced on 1 October 2010. View the Central Bank Reform Act 2010 at **www.centralbank.ie.**

The functions of the Central Bank of Ireland currently are to:

1. CONTRIBUTE TO EUROSYSTEM EFFECTIVENESS AND PRICE STABILITY (MONETARY POLICY AND OPERATIONS)

The Central Bank (CB) is responsible for maintaining price stability through monetary policy formulation at ECB level. The CB is also responsible for the effective implementation of monetary policy.

2. CONTRIBUTE TO FINANCIAL STABILITY

The CB has a legal mandate, in both domestic legislation and under the Maastricht Treaty, to contribute to financial stability both in Ireland and across the euro area. A key focus is the resolution of the financial crisis. This includes monitoring overall liquidity for the banking system.

3. ENSURE PROPER AND EFFECTIVE REGULATION OF FINANCIAL INSTITUTIONS AND MARKETS (FINANCIAL REGULATION)

The objective of regulation is to minimise the risk of failure by ensuring compliance with prudential and other requirements. The CB takes a risk-based approach supported by open and challenging dialogue with firms by assertive staff, underpinned by a credible threat of enforcement. The purpose of securities market regulation is to promote an efficient and fair securities market.

Who does the Central Bank Regulate?

The CB regulates:
- Bureaux de change
- Credit institutions
- Credit Unions
- Electronic money institutions
- Funds
- Fund Service Providers
- Insurance/Reinsurance undertakings
- Investment firms
- Moneylenders
- Payment institutions
- Regulated markets
- Retail credit firms/Home reversion firms
- Retail intermediaries
- Approved professional bodies.

All of these financial services providers and funds listed here are required to be either licensed or authorised by the Central Bank of Ireland.

---

4. ENSURE THAT THE BEST INTERESTS OF CONSUMERS OF FINANCIAL SERVICES ARE PROTECTED (CONSUMER PROTECTION)

The objective is to protect customers and investors through conduct of business rules and other measures.

5. PROVIDE INDEPENDENT ECONOMIC ADVICE AND HIGH QUALITY FINANCIAL STATISTICS

The CB contributes to economic development by undertaking economic analysis and research designed to inform economic policy making across a range of areas. A key priority is to provide authoritative economic advice to government by ensuring that such advice is relevant and timely. The provision of high-quality and timely statistical information is essential for this and also to provide a solid basis for decisions.

6. ENSURE EFFICIENT FINANCIAL SERVICES INFRASTRUCTURE TO THE ECONOMY: PAYMENT AND CURRENCY

The CB ensures that payment and securities settlement systems are safe, effective and efficient and that access to such systems is not restricted. The CB plays a strong role in the development of a National Payments Strategy. With regard to currency services, the CB manufactures, issues, stores, processes and authenticates bank notes and coins.

7. MAXIMISE OPERATIONAL EFFICIENCY AND COST EFFECTIVENESS

The CB ensures that the organisation has the capability to deliver the key challenges set out in the Strategic Plan and that the bank's operations are carried out in an effective and efficient manner.

To view the Central Bank of Ireland's Strategic Plan for 2010–2012 refer to:
www.centralbank.ie/about–us/Pages/default.aspx.

Mortgage lending down 53% on last year

Niamh Hennessy   May 2011

Mortgage lending has halved, with an average of just 36 approved per day in the first three months of the year. This compares to 519 approvals a day at the height of the boom in the first quarter of 2006.

Figures from the Irish Banking Federation (IBF) show that in the first quarter of this year 3,259 mortgages were issued, to the total value of €577 million. This is a drop of more than 53% on the same period last year and a fall of 42% on the previous quarter. First-time buyers and mover-purchasers accounted for 77% of the value market, while they made up 67% of the volume. In effect, more than three-quarters of all mortgage credit now issued goes to the home purchasing segments of the market. The average first-time buyer loan was down from €201,516 in the first quarter of last year to €183,543 in the first quarter of 2011. That compares to €212,053 in the first quarter of 2006. The IBF said lenders are reporting 'subdued' underlying demand for new mortgage finance but that

banks are pointing to the need for 'prudent lending', with the focus on the borrower's employment situation and capacity to repay.

IBF chief executive Pat Farrell said: 'The economic situation remains challenging and prudence remains the order of the day. For customers that means manageable borrowing and for financial institutions it means prudent lending.'

Irish Mortgage Corporation director Frank Conway said the figures demonstrate the continued 'wipeout' of the mortgage and property market as consumers remain absent from buying and lenders remain absent from funding.

'This is a meltdown of epic proportions and a trend that is showing little sign of abating,' he said. Mr Conway said Ireland needs banks that can return to funding mortgage requests soon.

'We need our labour market to stabilise before would-be first-time buyers feel confident enough to return to buying,' he said.

Chief executive of the Irish

Brokers Association Ciaran Phelan said that experience among brokers indicated a heightened demand for mortgages in the first quarter of 2011 but a 'dearth of available credit'.

'It's not difficult to see why the property market is struggling with confirmation that the banks are effectively closed to mortgage lending,' he said.

Mr Phelan said the €577m lent represents an almost 95% drop in mortgage advancements compared to the peak in 2006.

'While no one want to go back to those days, this level of available credit will stifle any property or economic stabilisation never mind a recovery,' he said.

Head of residential at Savills Ronan O'Driscoll said the figures show some activity in the housing market. 'Clearly, securing mortgage finance remains a very significant challenge for many people, but those who are buying right now are availing of excellent value in the market,' he said.

Source: www.irishexaminer.com

Central Bank Publishes Revised Consumer Protection Code
19 October 2011

Protections for Consumers Significantly Strengthened

The Central Bank of Ireland today published a revised Consumer Protection Code (2012 Code), which comes into effect from 1 January 2012 for regulated entities including banks, insurance and investment companies and intermediaries. The publication of the revised statutory Code represents the most significant strengthening of protections for consumers of financial institutions since the launch of the initial Code in August 2006.

Bernard Sheridan, Director of Consumer Protection, commented, 'Consumer protection is a key priority for the Central Bank and the publication of the revised Code is the culmination of a significant review and consultation process to strengthen the existing consumer protection framework. A range of significant enhancements have been made to the Code in order to address areas of concern and to ensure that consumers are adequately protected in their dealings with financial entities. These enhancements include additional protections for vulnerable consumers and stricter rules to prevent borrowers in arrears from being harassed.

'The Central Bank is committed to the on-going monitoring of regulated entities' compliance with the Code and we have increased our resources in this area. The Code comes into effect from 1 January 2012 for all regulated entities. However, we recognise that compliance with some of the new and enhanced requirements will require regulated entities to introduce systems and procedural changes and to ensure that all their staff are properly trained to understand and implement the Code. The Central Bank will be cognisant of this for the first six months of our monitoring of compliance with the 2012 Code.'

The revised Code increases the protections for consumers in a number of key areas.

Arrears handling

In the current economic climate, consumers need as much assistance as possible to help them to meet their financial commitments. New rules have been introduced setting out how regulated entities must deal with and treat consumers who are in arrears on a range of loans (including credit cards, personal loans and buy to let mortgages). The 2012 Code introduces protections for these loans similar to those for mortgage arrears which are already covered by the Code of Conduct on Mortgage Arrears.

Contact with consumers

Pressurised selling of financial products to consumers is of particular concern, so unsolicited personal or 'doorstep' visits are now banned.

There are also stricter rules in place to regulate the circumstances in which personal visits can take place.

In addition, in the case of arrears, the 2012 Code limits the number of unsolicited communications with a consumer in arrears to three in each calendar month.

Mis-selling of products

More prescriptive requirements have been introduced in terms of the information that regulated entities must gather under the 'Knowing the Consumer' process, in order to assess whether a product or service is suitable for a particular consumer.

In addition, the 2012 Code sets out that a regulated entity's remuneration arrangements with employees must not impair an employee's assessment of whether a particular product or service is suitable for a consumer and meets their needs and objectives.

The 2012 Code also requires product producers to give detailed information to intermediaries in relation to the investment products they sell on behalf of the product producers. This should aid intermediaries in assessing whether a product is suitable for a consumer.

Vulnerable consumers

Regulated entities must now consider whether there is any evidence of vulnerability on the part of the consumer, for example, a vision or hearing impairment or a lack of knowledge, experience or financial capability, and must provide those identified as vulnerable consumers with the necessary arrangements or assistance to facilitate their dealings with the regulated entity.

Mortgage lending

In order to promote more responsible mortgage lending, the acceptance of self-certified declarations of income by regulated entities has been banned and there are stricter requirements in place for affordability testing.

Transparency

More balanced information must be provided to consumers in advertisements. Where advertisements outline the benefits of a product or service, they must also outline the risks. In addition, key information on products and services must be made prominent in advertisements and must not be obscured.

The 2012 Code also sets out key information that regulated entities must provide to consumers before, during and after the sales process, including information on charges, commission and remuneration arrangements as well as information about the product or service.

Errors and complaints resolution

There are now limited timeframes for regulated entities to resolve errors affecting consumers. Detailed records of complaints from consumers and errors affecting consumers must also be maintained. Regular analysis of errors and complaints is required to ensure that regulated entities identify any potential patterns of consumer detriment.

The publication of the revised Code follows two public consultations in October 2010 and June 2011 seeking views on proposed new and amended Code requirements. Ninety-three submissions were received from interested parties over the course of both consultations and a feedback document has been published with responses to a number of questions and issues raised in the submissions.

Source: 2012 Consumer Protection Code www.centralbank.ie

The Central Bank Monetary Policy Operations

1. OPEN MARKET OPERATIONS

(a) The main Refinancing Operations – concerning refinancing to the financial sector (short-term).

(b) The longer-term Refinancing Operations.

(c) Fine-tuning Operations – this involves managing liquidity in the market and steering interest rates to smooth them following unexpected liquidity changes. Occasionally the ECB will decide whether fine-tuning bilateral operations (two or more countries) are necessary and it will execute the instrument itself.

(d) Structural operations – when the ECB wishes to adjust the structural position of the euro system via the financial sector. The issuance of debt instruments is carried out by the NCBs.

2. STANDING FACILITIES

To provide overnight liquidity to counterparties backed by eligible assets. These can be broken down into:

(a) The marginal lending facility – counterparties can get overnight liquidity from NCBs against eligible assets.

(b) The deposit facility – counterparties can make overnight deposits with the NCBs.

3. MINIMUM RESERVES

NCBs must hold only minimum reserves of cash to avoid too much money being given out – contributing to inflation.

4. ELIGIBLE ASSETS

The types of suitable assets to act as collateral for counterparties loans and the eligibility criteria are established by NCBs, subject to the ECB's approval.

5. BANKER TO GOVERNMENT

Acting as agent for and banker to the government.

6. SUPERVISION OF IRISH FINANCIAL INSTITUTIONS

It is legally responsible for the supervision of most financial institutions in Ireland including banks, building societies and a broad range of non-bank firms, exchanges and collective investment schemes.

7. EURO BANK NOTES AND COINS

Its Currency Centre prints euro bank notes and mints euro coins which are issued into circulation through the banking system. The Central Bank will accept all Irish bank notes and coins for years to come. (*Note*: Other euro area foreign bank notes and coins cannot be accepted and must be exchanged for euros in their own NCB.)

8. BANK REPORTS

The bank reports to the Minister for Finance annually (audited accounts) – its statement on annual accounts is published and is a primary source of financial statistics on the Irish economy. The Governor of the CB appears before the Oireachtas when asked to do so.

9. NET PROFIT

The vast majority of the Central Bank's net profit is paid to the Irish exchequer (Government).

Other responsibilities include:
- Contributing to the maintenance of a stable financial system in Ireland.
- Overseeing the domestic payment and settlement systems.
- Ensuring the provision and integrity of banknotes and coins.
- Managing the investment assets on behalf of the state.
- Acting as agent for and banker to the government.
- Providing advice and guidance on Irish economic policies.
- Serving the public interest – public accountability and external reporting.
- Helping government to draft and redraft legislation at home and EU level.

Functions and Services of Irish Commercial Banks

Government Bailout of Commercial Banks

Commercial banks typically offer a full range of personal and corporate banking services. Irish banks are no exception, with the main two commercial banks being Allied Irish Bank and Bank of Ireland.

In the wake of the global recession and the banking crisis in 2009, Allied Irish Bank (AIB) along with its competitor, Bank of Ireland, accepted a 3.5 billion euro bailout from the government of the Republic of Ireland as a part of the bank recapitalisation scheme. By March 2011 the total sum of the required bailout had risen to 13.3 billion euro. In December 2010, the Irish government took a majority stake in AIB. Following this was effective nationalisation of the bank. The remaining publicly traded shares of AIB are now listed on the Enterprise Securities Market of the Irish Stock Exchange

Typical Functions of Local Commercial Banks

The following are the typical functions of local commercial banks on offer to the public in towns and cities in Ireland:

1. **Selling and management of current accounts:** Personal, student, graduate accounts, international payments, issuing chequebooks and issuing debit cards.
2. **Selling and management of deposit accounts:** Regular, special and fixed-term deposit savings accounts.
3. **Issuing mortgages:** First-time buyer, owner-occupier and buy-to-let mortgages and managing these.
4. **Issuing credit cards**: Also includes managing these.
5. **Issuing loans:** Both business and personal loans, overdrafts, car finance, graduate, student loans, online loans.
6. **Selling insurance:** Home, travel, health, car insurance and life and illness insurance and payment protection.
7. **Selling and management of pensions:** Group, personal, executive, self-employed and retirement pensions (PRSA – personal retirement savings accounts).
8. **Investments.**
9. **Customer bank transfers, cheques and drafts:** Setting up and managing direct debits, standing orders, bank giros, issuing bank drafts and money orders and handling, processing and cashing cheques.
10. **Online banking:** Bill payments (electricity, phone, student fees etc), EFT – electronic funds transfer using SWIFT/IBAN numbers for national and international online money transactions.
11. **Foreign exchange transactions:** Managing these transactions, including changing currencies, issuing and cashing traveller's cheques, euro cheques.

For extra information related to the above topic refer to Chapter 2 'Sources of Finance' and to Chapter 6 'Payments Methods' in this book.

OTHER BANKS IN IRELAND

1. Industrial and Corporate Banks: Bank of Ireland Wholesale Division, HSBC Corporate, Ulster Bank Corporate Division.
2. Merchant Banks: Bank of Ireland Merchant Services – capital markets, AIB Merchant Services (called First Data).

Industrial, corporate and merchant banks provide financial and banking services for the business sector and are regarded as wholesale banks.

How Merchant Banks differ from Commercial Banks

1. They do not deal with the public in general and are therefore wholesale banks.
2. Their services are for investors, large-scale business activities (private sector) and government (public sector).
3. No short-term loans are offered. These banks are only located in prominent city areas – unlike commercial banks they do not have a network of branches.
4. Some of the notable services, other than the regular range of financial and banking services, that are offered to large investors, private sector and public sector customers are:
   (a) The guarantee of the purchase of any issued shares not taken up by shareholders which contributes to the capital of the business – this service is referred to as Underwriting. (The fee is called a Spread.)
   (b) Factoring – the purchasing of debtors to give businesses ready cash for an agreed lower figure than the debtors are worth.
   (c) Leasing – car leases etc.
   (d) They give expert advice and consultation to the private sector, e. g. firms who want to go public, and they liaise with the Stock Exchange on their behalf.
   (e) They take active parts in mergers, take-overs and company rationalisation and liquidation.
   (f) They liaise with government agencies like Forfás, Industrial Development Authority (IDA) and Shannon Development regarding foreign investors.

PRACTICE QUESTIONS
1. When and under what conditions was the euro introduced?
2. How many countries are members of the EU?
3. What is the ECB and what are its functions?
4. Explain the terms:
   (a) ESCB.
   (b) OMO Instrument.
   (c) NCB.
   (d) EMU.
   (e) European integration.
5. What was the Kyoto Agreement?
6. List *three* EU targets aimed at controlling climate change.
7. Explain *five* functions of the Central Bank.
8. List *six* functions of Commercial Banks.
9. Explain *four* ways in which Merchant Banks differ from Commercial Banks.

What was an SSIA?

An SSIA was a Special Savings Incentive Account. This type of account was introduced in 2001 to encourage everyone in the state aged over 18 to start saving. The agreement was that the government would pay out a 25 per cent bonus on the investment if a set amount per month was saved (minimum €12.50, maximum €254 per month). The financial institution would also pay interest to the saver. The scheme was only available to savers from 1 May 2001 to 30 April 2002, allowing people twelve months to open an SSIA account. Savings were to be left in place for five years until their maturity date.

Over one million people had opened SSIAs by the time the scheme closed, many waiting until the last possible day, 30 April 2002. This meant that between 31 May 2006 and 30 April 2007 hundreds of thousands of Irish people experienced a positive and much welcomed maturing of their savings.

What is Funds Administration?

Ireland is now recognised as a centre of excellence in the provision of accounting and administrative services to investment funds. This reputation extends not only to Dublin funds (mainly located in the IFSC, Ireland's International Financial Services Centre) but funds based in other countries including providing administration services for investments to UK, Cayman, Bermuda, the Virgin Islands and the Bahamas.

The Financial Regulatory section of the Central Bank of Ireland is responsible for the regulation of fund administrators and imposes different requirements depending on whether a fund is Irish-incorporated or non-Irish incorporated.

Wealth during the boom in Ireland led to a growing trend of people investing their funds. In response to this, the **hedge funds industry** grew at a fast pace during the Celtic Tiger years when higher returns on investments were almost the norm. These funds were flexible investment funds invested by finance companies (which were called fund administrators) in an effort to enhance returns at lower risk levels. It was the job of the fund administrators to manage these funds.

Financial Mismanagement and Tax Evasion

In recent years there has been a need to create a formal, transparent method of regulating monies in Ireland, probably due to the fallout originating in the misuse of taxpayers' money.

HedgeServ announces 300 new jobs in substantial expansion

Tuesday, 25 October 2011

Minister for Jobs, Enterprise and Innovation, Richard Bruton TD, today welcomed the continued commitment by HedgeServ, a top-ranked global hedge fund administrator, to its Irish operations. The company, located on St Stephen's Green, has increased its workforce by an additional 150 people over the last 12 months, bringing its workforce in Ireland to 230. HedgeServ also announced today that it is on track for continued growth in Ireland with the announcement of an additional 300 jobs into the future.

Welcoming the company's ongoing growth in Ireland, Minister for Jobs, Enterprise and Innovation, Richard Bruton TD said: 'Today's announcement by HedgeServ, a world-leading hedge fund administrator, that it is expanding its operations in Ireland with the creation of 300 new jobs is great news for Ireland and an excellent vote of confidence in our strengths. Jobs are at the very top of this government's agenda, and I am determined to do everything possible to achieve the job creation we so badly need.'

'This means setting highly ambitious targets and undertaking radical change in order to achieve them. It also means targeting sectors where Ireland has advantages, including international financial services. I am determined to build on today's great announcement with a series of radical measures across a range of sectors to get 2 million people back at work in our economy again.'

Jim Kelly, Chairman and Co-Founder of HedgeServ said: 'HedgeServ's growth in Dublin has exceeded all expectations and we are delighted to have been able to hire an additional 150 staff over the last 12 months. Our fast-paced development in Dublin reflects our commitment to answering the global demand for HedgeServ's innovative, high-quality fund administration services. I would like to take this opportunity to thank management and staff at HedgeServ in Dublin for their dedication in making this operation a success.'

Source: Dept. of Jobs, Enterprise and Innovation

The realisation that money had been mismanaged dawned when it was discovered that public money had been used to fund former Taoiseach Charles Haughey's lavish lifestyle. Funds had been invested in an illegal Ansbacher account in the Cayman Islands. These facts emerged in the High Court inspectors' Ansbacher Report, published in 2002.

Other government ministers' financial affairs were also investigated by tribunals of inquiry.

Negotiations with the Revenue Commissioners led to estimates that Haughey may have spent up to £10 million (€12.7 million) during his time in politics (1977 to 1992). Many prominent businessmen were also party to the Ansbacher deposits and other exchanges of monies. Des Traynor, Haughey's accountant, was the mastermind and architect of the elaborate scheme that supported the former Taoiseach's personal finances at the expense of the taxpayer.

Nowadays the Revenue Commissioners and the Financial Regulator both control how monies are managed in the economy.

Taxpayers must file their tax returns on time and pay the monies due. If they do not, they are subject to somewhat draconian sanctions. Non-compliance means that the Revenue charges penalties, and penal interest will be charged on late tax payments. The Revenue Commissioners have also backtracked thirty years and have uncovered monies that were owed on illegal bogus non-residents' accounts and offshore accounts that were held by many taxpayers. This has yielded large tax payments over the last five years or more.

In this climate of zero-tolerance taxpayers are unwilling to take a chance that will cost them money and as a result most people file and pay their taxes on time.

Problems have also been uncovered in banking and financial institutions, including the systematic overcharging of customers. The Financial Regulator (part of the restructured Central Bank of Ireland) now monitors all financial institutions' activities and has the power to prosecute any financial institution on the grounds of mismanagement and illegal financial activities that are against the interests of the consumer. (Refer to Chapter 1, 'The Organisation'.)

The Internet

The Internet was the result of some visionary thinking by people in the early 1960s who saw great potential value in allowing computers to share information on research and development in scientific and military fields. J. C. R. Licklider of Massachusetts Institute of Technology (MIT) first proposed a global network of computers in 1962, and moved over to the Defense Advanced Research Projects Agency (DARPA) in late 1962 to head the work to develop it. Leonard Kleinrock of MIT and later UCLA developed the theory of packet switching, which was to form the basis of Internet connections. Lawrence Roberts of MIT connected a Massachusetts computer with a California computer in 1965 over dial-up telephone lines. This showed that wide area networking was feasible, but also showed that the telephone line's circuit switching was inadequate. Kleinrock's packet switching theory was confirmed. Roberts moved over to DARPA in 1966 and developed his plan for ARPANET. These visionaries – and many more – are the real founders of the Internet.

When Senator Ted Kennedy heard in 1968 that the pioneering Massachusetts company BBN had won the ARPA contract for an 'interface message processor (IMP)', he sent a congratulatory telegram to BBN for their ecumenical spirit in winning the 'interfaith message processor' contract.

The Internet, then known as ARPANET, was brought online in 1969 under a contract let by the renamed Advanced Research Projects Agency (ARPA), which initially connected four major computers at universities in the southwestern US (University of California Los Angeles (UCLA), University of California Santa Barbara (UCSB), Stanford Research Institute and the University of Utah). The contract was carried out by BBN of Cambridge, Massachusetts under Bob Kahn, and went online in December 1969. By June 1970, MIT, Harvard, BBN and Systems Development Corp (SDC) in Santa Monica, California were added to the network and within the next six months Stanford, MIT's Lincoln Labs, Carnegie-Mellon, and Case-Western Reserve University came on board.

Who First Used the Internet?

Charley Kline at UCLA sent the first packets on ARPANET as he tried to connect to Stanford Research Institute on 29 October 1969. The system crashed as he reached the G in LOGIN!

The Internet was designed in part to provide a communications network that would work even if some of the sites were destroyed by nuclear attack. If the most direct route was not available, routers would direct traffic around the network via alternate routes.

The early Internet was used by computer experts, engineers, scientists and librarians. There was nothing friendly about it. There were no home or office personal computers in those days, and anyone who used it, whether a computer professional or an engineer or scientist or librarian, had to learn to use a very complex system.

Did Al Gore Invent the Internet?

According to a CNN transcript of an interview with Wolf Blitzer, American Senator Al Gore said, 'During my service in the United States Congress, I took the initiative in creating the Internet.' Al Gore was not yet in Congress in 1969 when ARPANET started or in 1974 when the term Internet first came into use. Gore was elected to Congress in 1976. In fairness, Bob Kahn and Vint Cerf acknowledge, in a paper entitled 'Al Gore and the Internet', that Gore has probably done more than any other elected official to support the growth and development of the Internet from the 1970s to the present.

Source: www.walthowe.com

What is Broadband?

Broadband is a 'broad bandwidth' connection. It allows a large amount of data to travel through a medium at the same time. Broadband over Power Line (BPL) is a technology that allows Internet data to be transmitted over utility power lines and allows for high-speed Internet access.

What is Mobile Broadband?

Mobile Broadband is a type of wireless internet access that differs from WiFi. Just as the cellular phone revolutionised voice telephony by freeing the user from wires and stationary constraints, mobile broadband is doing the same for high-speed data. Users are no longer confined to desks, no longer inconvenienced with wires, no longer restricted to a stationary environment. Mobile broadband is a step up from local wireless data applications like WiFi, which gets rid of the wire, but not the confinement. Mobile broadband technology provides wide area coverage and works in mobile and fixed environments.

What is Social Networking?

A 'social network site' is a category of websites with profiles, semi–persistent public commentary on the profile, and a traversable publicly articulated social network displayed in relation to the profile.

Source: **www.zephoria.org.**

PROFILE: A profile includes an identifiable handle (either the person's name or details), information about that person (e.g. age, sex, location, interests, etc.). Most profiles also include a photograph and information about last login. Profiles have unique URLs (registered links) that can be visited directly.

TRAVERSABLE, PUBLICLY ARTICULATED SOCIAL NETWORK: Participants have the ability to list other profiles as 'friends' or 'contacts' or some equivalent. This generates a social network graph which may be directed or undirected. This articulated social network is displayed on an individual's profile for all other users to view. Each node contains a link to the profile of the other person so that individuals can move through the network through friends of friends of friends.

Cloud Computing and EU 2020

April 2010

The Role of the Cloud in Delivering EU 2020

Jan Muehlfeit, Chief Executive of Microsoft Europe, delivered a keynote address to IIEA (Institute of International and European Affairs) members on how the EU 2020 strategy for innovation, growth and jobs (the successor to the Lisbon Strategy for Growth and Jobs) can be enhanced and delivered by cloud computing.

According to Minister for Communications, Energy and Natural Resources Eamon Ryan, TD: 'The Irish Government has identified cloud computing as a key driver of our economic renewal. Not only does this emerging technology afford our ICT sector huge opportunities, but it has the potential to transform the way we, in Government and in the wider economy, do business.'

Cloud computing is a new technology where data is outsourced and stored in a secure environment (the cloud) and then provided as a service online, either by subscription or on a pay-on-demand basis to customers.

In his speech, Mr Muehlfeit will deliberate on innovative ways to use the power of technology to help deliver better public services and will address a wide range of important policy issues such as e-health, information privacy and security, and transport.

About the Speaker:

Jan Muehlfeit is the Chairman of Microsoft Europe. Jan Muehlfeit is responsible for Microsoft's engagement with European governments and policy makers. Previously, he was Vice-President for corporate and government strategy, focusing on producing technology solutions for public-sector organisations.

Source: Institute of International and European Affairs

SEMI-PERSISTENT PUBLIC COMMENTS: Participants can leave comments (or testimonials, guestbook messages, etc.) on others' profiles for everyone to see.

Some examples of social network Internet websites are MySpace, Facebook, Friendster, Bebo, YouTube, Cyworld, Mixi, Orkut, Twitter, etc.

High-speed Internet access has allowed for faster image downloads, video downloads and faster message sending and receiving. Some social networking sites are used as a marketing tool.

Websites like www.watchyourspace.ie have been developed by the National Centre for Technology in Education (NCTE) to encourage social networking in an online educational environment. In Ireland the Communications Regulator (Comreg) can fine telecom operators if they are in breach of communications regulations (Communications Regulation Act 2002–2010).

Sony to Bring PlayStation Games to Android

Joe Arico

Sony is looking to expand its gaming services on more portable devices, as the popularity of video games on smartphones continues to grow.

The video game unit at Sony is reportedly in talks to bring the PlayStation Suite, a mobile app for Android tablets and smartphones, to even more devices. PlayStation Suite is currently only available on Sony tablets and one Sony Ericsson smartphone.

Sony's app offers the ability to play original PlayStation titles on today's portable devices. The company stands to benefit from making the games available on several devices because many customers may be playing the games for the first time, while others may be drawn to the titles because they want to revisit old classics.

'This isn't an ecosystem where we want to keep everything within the Sony family,' said Sony executive vice president Kazuo Hirai. 'This is not just for Sony devices.'

Sony has been involved in the portable gaming market for nearly a decade, and recently announced it will launch its system, the PlayStation Vita, in February 2012. However, the Vita will likely cater to hardcore gamers more than the casual fan.

Making older PlayStation titles available across multiple devices sets Sony up with an opportunity to capture casual gamers as well, without spending any additional money making new games to do so.

Smartphone games may not have put an end to the traditional portable gaming market, but they have changed the way companies are going about their business. Even Nintendo, the king of the handheld gaming market, has faced pressure from investors to develop games for the iPhone featuring its trademark characters.

Sony may not be making new games for mobile platforms that are not its own, but if it's successful in licensing older titles for redistribution on Android devices, it may force companies like Nintendo to consider doing the same thing.

Source: www.mobiledia.com/news/113431.html

Apple iPhone 5 rumoured to arrive in 2012; What specs will it have?

Bala Seshan   7 October 2011

In the 'Let's talk iPhone' event, Apple Inc. unveiled the iPhone 4S just to satisfy the feature-hungry fans with basic smartphone specifications. The iPhone 5 remained a mystery after all, but analysts are expecting the Cupertino tech giant to release a 4G LTE iPhone 5 in 2012.

'Apple is saving the iPhone 5 brand for the LTE (Long Term Evolution) version, and the new model won't arrive until the 4G LTE technology is ready to be used in smartphones, which won't be out until next spring,' Will Strauss, president of market research firm Forward Concepts told CNET.

Strauss, who tracks companies such as Qualcomm that deliver the chips for 3G and 4G technology for smartphones, said Apple come out with LTE now. According to him, for Apple's taste, the current implementations of LTE technology in phones like the HTC Thunderbolt are too kludgy, CNET reported.

There are two chip solutions in LTE-capable HTC Thunderbolt, an LTE baseband (modem) chip, and a second one from Qualcomm for 3G voice connections, Strauss said.

Source: *International Business Times* www.ibtimes.com

Tips on Safe Social Networking

Protect your privacy on sites like MySpace, Bebo and Facebook. Social networking is growing in popularity but are you revealing more than you meant to? Social networking should be fun. It allows people to stay in touch online, share fun moments, talk to their beloved and generally exchange personal content online. There are a number of popular social networking websites including Facebook, MySpace and Bebo. They all let you communicate with friends and other online users in one way or another.

Risks

Social networking sites are rapidly becoming a huge target from preying cyber-criminals. They are able to abuse the nature of these sites and gather personal information about its users, information that users themselves are making publicly available. This is known as social engineering. Social engineering is one of the first stages of many cyber-attacks related to identity theft.

These sites are very popular with young people and adults alike. For young people in particular social networking sites can bring together many of the risks associated with being online; online bullying, disclosure of private information, cyber-stalking, access to age-inappropriate content and, at the most extreme, online grooming and child abuse.

For adults there are serious risks too such as loss of privacy and identity theft. Adults too can be victims of cyber-bullying and stalking.

Protect your privacy

You can avoid these risks and enjoy social networking sites by following a few sensible guidelines:

- Don't let peer pressure or what other people are doing on these sites push you into doing something you're not comfortable with. Just because other people post their mobile phone number or birthday, doesn't mean you have to.
- Be wary of publishing any identifying information about yourself. In particular things like: phone numbers, pictures of your home, workplace or school, your address, birthday or full name.
- Pick a user name that doesn't include any personal information. For example, 'joe_glasgow' or 'jane_liverpool' would be bad choices.
- Set up a separate email account that doesn't use your real name and use that to register and receive mail from the site. That way if you want to shut down your connection, you can simply stop using that mail account. This is very simple and quick to do using such providers as Hotmail or Yahoo! Mail. (Other services exist. See the DMOZ directory of free web-based mail services.)
- Use a strong password, using a mixture of letters and numbers.
- Keep your profile closed and only allow your friends to view your profile.
- What goes online, stays online. Don't say anything or publish pictures that might cause you embarrassment later. As a general rule, if you wouldn't say it to your boss or your grandmother, don't say it online.
- Learn how to use the site. Use the privacy features on the site you use to restrict strangers' access to your profile. Be guarded about who you let join your network.
- Be on your guard against phishing scams (suspicious emails looking for personal or banking information to be confirmed). Don't open or answer these. Delete them.

Source: www.getsafeonline.org

What is Second Life?

This is a three-dimensional virtual world on the Internet entirely built and owned by its residents, where citizens can buy property, make friends and trade in their own unique currency (Linden dollars). It was opened to the public in 2003 and now has nearly ten million residents from around the globe. Press conferences and meetings can be held in Second Life – a form of virtual video conferencing. Large multinational companies like Coca-Cola, IBM, Dell, Warner Brothers and Adidas are readily adopting this new virtual world, and all have 'islands' or representations of their offices in Second Life as a representation of their branding – with a view to future business development.

Universities have their own Second Life presence with a virtual library (modelled on the James Joyce Library in University College Dublin). Visitors can use a virtual PC and read e-books, watch Sky News and watch library presentations.

UCD opens Library on Second Life

Marie Boran

University College Dublin (UCD) recently opened the doors of its sixth library, which exists only in Second Life, a popular virtual world on the internet where citizens can buy property, make friends and trade in their own unique currency.

'I attended a conference in Second Life and decided to set up a branch in-world. In between the conference and the opening we also conducted a multi-purpose survey of our real-life clients and found that 30pc would like Second Life-type virtual reference desks. It is early days yet but we get about 40 visits a day,' said Cathal McCauley, project leader for UCD's Second Life Library.

This is one of around 40 libraries that are located on Second Life's Cybrary City Islands, which plays host to the virtual version of existing public and university libraries.

Prominent US universities Berkeley, Stanford and Harvard already have their own Second Life presence.

'We've had instant messaging and blogs for quite some time now so we thought that the virtual world might offer another useful complement to the provision of traditional library services,' said McCauley.

The virtual library is modelled on the James Joyce Library, UCD's main library on the Belfield campus, and was developed with help from the US, UK and Holland.

Although it won't be quite the same as visiting the actual campus library, visitors can use a virtual PC, watch Sky News, read various e-books and watch library presentations.

The aim is to eventually have a staff presence in the virtual library, helping visitors to avail of UCD library services.

Anyone, UCD student or not, can access the library but McCauley told Silicon Republic that depending on services developed in the future, some type of access control may have to be considered.

Irish Independent, July 2007

Can business get a Second Life?

John Kennedy

As a number of sober-suited executives assemble in a plush conference room, they do so safe in the knowledge that no one can eavesdrop on their conversation. This is no ordinary meeting. In reality the executive are sitting at different points around the globe: it is their avatars, internet versions of themselves that are meeting in a virtual world known as Second Life.

This is not a scene from an Arthur C. Clarke novel. This is now. The secure conference room they meet in is provided by a cutting-edge Dublin firm known as V Rising, which in recent months was awarded a grant to conduct a feasibility study into virtual worlds by Enterprise Ireland.

The Second Life phenomenon — a virtual world where people in the form of 'avatars' can go to virtual versions of Dublin, London or Amsterdam and communicate — is beginning to excite the interest of big brand names and entrepreneurs who sense opportunity.

Second Life debuted in 2003 and today boasts over 8.9 million accounts. The virtual world — there are over 30 of them out there — has its own currency known as Linden dollars and has a booming real estate economy. At present a small number of residents earn net incomes from this economy selling anything from apparel to islands and castles.

Big business names like IBM, Dell, Adidas and Warner Brothers have all established 'islands' or representations of their offices in Second Life as an exercise in branding but with an eye on drumming up future business opportunities.

In recent weeks Coca-Cola launched its latest ad campaign with executives attending a red carpet bash in Second Life. When 20th Century Fox unveiled the summer blockbuster *Die Hard 4.0,* it held its press conference in Second Life, actor Bruce Willis's avatar answered journalists' questions; possibly even from the full-time reporter Reuters employs in Second Life.

At the IBM campus in west Dublin where 3,200 people are employed, a team of five at the company's 460-strong IBM.com division works full-time to represent IBM's 'island' on Second Life. Throughout IBM worldwide, more than 3,000 people have Second Life avatars, explained the director of the IBM.com division in Dublin, Hugh O'Byrne.

'You'll find lots of companies up there experimenting,' explains O'Byrne. 'We think it has potential as a way of doing business. We're just experimenting with it ourselves but we see massive potential in the human interaction you can bring. It's a big browsing environment in many ways.'

O'Byrne explains that IBM uses the Second Life environment as a means of providing customer service. 'We have six to 12 people on tap worldwide who will act as concierges 24/7. Their job is to say "hello" to anyone who walks in and guide them through products.'

The IBM office in Second Life also functions as a library as well as an auditorium for seminars, explains David Lallement, of the IBM's Second Life concierge. 'We treat it as a good meeting point but I think the real innovation will come when more people start using voice in Second Life,' he says.

'One customer has asked us to build him a secure meeting room in Second Life and we're going to do it,' adds Greg.
www.independent.ie

ICT and Online Banking

The term 'ICT' means Information and Communication Technologies. In the current information age, advances in world communication have helped to increase globalisation and to make the world a smaller, more accessible place. The main types of ICT that exist today include:

1. The Internet – a worldwide network of computers joined by telecommunication lines.
2. The email facility – both a computer and mobile phone medium allowing us to send and receive electronic information.
3. Video Conferencing – a mode of communication that cuts out the need to travel: a video link allows several people to communicate from different locations, e.g. the 'poshare' video conferencing program.
4. Video Phones – used extensively by journalists to relate news to a newsroom at the touch of a mobile phone button.

What is E-Business?

E-business refers to all business processes that take place across electronic networks. This includes everything from buying and selling goods and services through the World Wide Web to interactive television, to advertising on the net.

Examples are: e-research, e-security, e-property, e-travel and tourism, e-education, e-working (telecommuting – working from home using ICT), e-government, e-health, e-transport and **e-commerce** (an interchange of goods, services or property of any kind through an electronic medium which can be the Internet, or over intranets (websites that can only be accessed within a company or group of companies), using interactive kiosks, using telephones or mobile phones or WAP phones (WAP means Wireless Applications Protocol). The interchange of goods, services or property via WAP phones is known as m-commerce.

B2C Transactions (Business to Consumer)

Online shopping involves the selecting of products from a virtual shopping area and putting them into a virtual shopping basket, paying by credit card and conveniently availing of home delivery of the goods. The provision of new product information to existing and future customers through the electronic medium has indeed revolutionised business to customer transactions.

B2B Transactions (Business to Business)

E-business transactions **between businesses** include the sourcing of new partners and materials helping to open up new markets and provide better customer support.

E-payments and Transfers

WHAT IS ELECTRONIC FUNDS TRANSFER (EFT)?

This refers to the computer-based systems used to perform financial transactions electronically.

The term is used to describe different concepts, including:

* cardholder-initiated transactions, where a cardholder makes use of a payment card
* electronic payments by businesses, including salary payments
* electronic cheque clearing.

EFT takes place when a cardholder uses either a Credit Card or a Debit Card (a regular bank card).

It can take place at an ATM (Automated Teller Machine) or at the point of sale (Electronic Funds Transfer Point of Sale, or EFTPOS).

EFT can also be initiated by the cardholder for mail order, telephone orders or Internet purchases.

The quality standard ISO 8583 often accompanies EFT card-based transactions. The following are the types of transaction that can be carried out by the cardholder:

* Sale – payment for goods or services.
* Refund.
* Withdrawal – from ATM.
* Deposit – lodging money into account via ATM.

- Cashback – with a laser card: pay for goods and get extra cash out of your account at the same time (available from shops and supermarkets).
- Inter-account transfer – transferring money from one account to another account held by the cardholder.
- Payment – transfer of funds to a third party.
- Inquiry – an instant account balance inquiry.
- Administrative – e.g. electronically changing the PIN and other instructions.

The seller can verify the cardholder's signature. The most convenient method of payment, which is commonplace in retail shops, is payment using either a credit card or laser debit card. The cardholder has to punch in a PIN (Personal Identification Number) (chip and pin). Other information on the card is used by the seller via the card issuer, to confirm that the details on the card are valid: for example, the magnetic stripe data, which is not visible to the cardholder, can be checked by the seller.

What is a Debit Card?

A Debit Card is an electronic card issued by a bank that allows bank clients access to their account to withdraw cash or pay for goods and services. It provides an alternative payment method to cash when making purchases. Funds are withdrawn immediately from a cardholder's account.

This removes the need for bank clients to go to the bank to take cash from their account: they can just go to an ATM or pay electronically at merchant locations. This type of card, as a form of payment, also removes the need for cheques, as the debit card immediately transfers money from the client's account to the business account.

They are convenient and secure and easier than writing cheques: you don't need to show ID or pay extra fees. Debit cards are also considered to be a safer form of payment than cheques because a code is required to access the account, whereas cheques can be easily stolen.

Many debit cards are Visa or Mastercard, but there are many other types of debit card, each accepted only within a particular country or region, for example Switch (now Maestro) and Solo in the UK, Carte Bleu in France, Laser in Ireland, EC Electronic Cash (formerly Eurocheque) in Germany, etc.

There are currently two ways in which debit card transactions are processed: Online Debit (also known as PIN Debit) and Offline Debit (also known as Signature Debit).

What is a Credit Card?

A Credit Card is a plastic card, with a magnetic strip, which is issued by a bank or business and which authorises the holder to buy goods or services *on credit*. A high level of interest is charged on these purchases and a statement is issued to the credit card holder every month. The card may be used repeatedly to buy goods and services, subject to a credit limit set by the institution that issued the card to the cardholder. Credit card bills can become very expensive if cardholders do not pay off the amount they owe every month. Interest payments can cause the debt to spiral and become difficult for cardholders to manage.

However, credit cards when used sensibly provide a very convenient way to make purchases and make bookings.

Online bookings of flights, hotel accommodation and car hire is regarded as standard nowadays. A secure PIN can be used at the point of sale terminal to pay for goods and services.

What is 24-hour Banking?

This is the facility available to bank account holders to access their bank account and activate transactions at any time of the day either by phone or online.

Chip and PIN

Chip and PIN is the name given to the initiative based on the EMV standard, which is a group effort between Europay, Mastercard and Visa to establish a compatible standard for secure payments.

In many countries, the use of PIN-validated transactions with EMV smartcard chip readers is being strongly encouraged by the banks as a method of reducing cloned-card fraud, to the extent that cardholder-present transactions will soon not be possible in these countries without knowledge of a PIN, and the POS terminal reading the smart card chip on the card.

What are SSL and S-HTTP?

SSL or Secure Sockets Layer is a cryptographic protocol that helps provide secure communications on the Internet.

It creates a secure connection between a client and a server, over which any amount of data can be sent securely. S-HTTP is designed to transmit individual messages securely. SSL and S-HTTP are therefore complementary rather than competing technologies. Both protocols have been approved by the Internet Engineering Task Force (IETF) as a standard.

What is Western Union?

Western Union is a fast and reliable way to transfer money worldwide in minutes. There are over 280,000 agent locations worldwide in more than 200 countries and territories and people use it to send and receive money.

Complete Online Transaction	Call to Confirm Transaction	Receive Money
Sign in or register. Enter the details of your money transfer. Pay with your Visa or MasterCard credit card.	For your security, operator may need to speak with sender to confirm the transaction.	Receive money at any participating agent location worldwide.

Using Western Union to *send* money from Ireland: for amounts of €1,000 or more, senders must present either one form of primary identification or two forms of non-primary identification, one verifying their name and the other verifying their address. All forms of identification must be current.

Using Western Union to *receive* money from Ireland: persons under 18 years old must have some form of ID (e.g. birth certificate, student ID) and must be accompanied by a guardian who has an acceptable documentary evidence of identity to receive a money transfer payout. The agent will pay on the 'test question' alone for amounts up to €450. The payee must present the correct Money Transfer Control Number (MTCN).

Physical delivery is available by registered mail to street addresses only. If received before 3pm, delivery will be the next day, excluding Saturdays and Sundays.

Receivers must present acceptable documentary evidence of identity.

Primary forms of identification verifying full name include:

1. passport
2. driver's licence
3. national identity card.
4. national age card.

Online Banking/Transactions/Investment

Online banking today allows the customer:

1. To access his or her account, to view balances, to print out online statements – a 24-hour service.
2. To see transaction history.
3. To pay bills.
4. To search for or track a cheque.
5. To top up mobile phones online.
6. To make transfers of money from account to account or out and into an account.
7. To invest in stocks and shares online.
8. To apply for a loan, a mortgage or a credit card online or to get an insurance quote (life policies etc).
9. To avail of foreign exchange facilities online.

AN INTERNET BANKING DEMO

10. To establish an Internet merchant account in order to set up a credit card payment system on a customer's (businesses) web site – transferring credit card details between the bank and customer website and providing a secure certificate to encrypt and protect the credit card details. (The bank and ISP – Internet service provider – will help determine the types of software needed to carry out secure transactions.)

Internet shopping: Eight hours at work on festive shopping

Aoife Dowling   22 September 2011

Workers could spend up to eight hours Christmas shopping online while at work, according to a survey of office workers. Almost 59 per cent of workers have already started their Christmas shopping and could spend the equivalent of a working day shopping online, the Irish Examiner says. The survey carried out by Peninsula Ireland – the employment law consultancy – found that employees may spend close to eight hours between September and 24 December, shopping online during working hours. More than 2,200 calls from line managers were monitored for the study, which found that 64 per cent of employees plan to do Christmas shopping while at work. Managing director of Peninsula Ireland Alan Price said it was totally unacceptable that companies are losing up to a whole working day from online shopping.

'Managers have experienced more and more of their employees spending working time internet shopping. This obviously causes a problem for businesses as their production levels tend to drop in the run up to Christmas.'

Mr Price said the results of the study indicate that employees think it is fine to steal five or ten minutes here and there to do a quick shop on the internet.

Source: www.examiner.ie/business/8-hours-at-work-on-festive-shopping-168337.html

---

PRACTICE QUESTIONS

1. What is an SSIA? List two benefits of SSIAs to the Irish economy.
2. What is Funds Administration?
3. Why have the Revenue Commissioners been described in recent years as 'draconian' in relation to tax evasion?
4. Give a brief history of the Internet.
5. What are Broadband and Mobile Broadband?
6. What is Social Networking?
7. What is Second Life and why is it good for business?
8. What is ICT? Distinguish between e-business and e-commerce.
9. What is EFT? Explain e-payments.

10. Write notes on:
    (i) debit cards
    (ii) credit cards
    (iii) 24-hour banking
    (iv) Chip and PIN
    (v) SSL and S-HTTP
    (vi) Western Union.

Foreign Exchange and Currency Conversion

EMU – European Monetary Union – has meant that Europeans can now travel within the European Community and exchange euros for euros. (Refer to the beginning of this chapter.) Member states that have signed up for EMU and have converted to the euro currency no longer have the inconvenience of watching changing foreign exchange rates in order to figure out different costs of living and value for money in exchange for goods and services. There is now a greater ease of movement of money in EMU countries in particular in relation to travel and among European holiday-makers.

However, the currencies listed in the foreign exchange paper clip are not part of EMU and are denominated against the euro e.g. 1 euro = .9665 dollars and 1 euro = .629 sterling. So for every euro the tourist would only get about 62 British pence.

FOREIGN EXCHANGE RATES

RI Only – (updated: 25/10/2011 09:01:55)

	RATES			
	Notes		Cheques	
Currency	**Sell**	**Buy**	**Sell**	**Buy**
Arab Emirates Dirham	4.9252	5.2559	4.9252	5.2559
Argentinian Peso	5.6501	6.1209	–	–
Australian Dollar	1.2904	1.3696	1.2930	1.3670
Brazilian Real	2.3354	2.5301	–	–
Bulgarian Lev	1.8874	2.0142	–	–
Canadian Dollar	1.3518	1.4348	1.3563	1.4303
Chinese Renminbi	8.4830	9.1899	–	–
Croatia	7.2298	7.7153	–	–
Czech Koruna	23.9957	25.6070	23.9957	25.6070

RATES				
	Notes		Cheques	
Currency	Sell	Buy	Sell	Buy
Danish Krone	7.2238	7.6676	7.2957	7.5957
Egyptian Pound	7.9616	8.6251	-	-
Estonian Kroon	-	-	-	-
Hong Kong Dollar	10.4820	11.1260	10.5740	11.0340
Hungarian Forint	285.2926	304.4501	285.2926	304.4501
Indian Rupee	66.2487	71.7694	66.2487	71.7694
Indonesian Rupiah	11811.8400	12796.1600	-	-
Israeli Shekel	4.9220	5.2255	-	-
Japanese Yen	102.5695	108.8705	103.3200	108.0200
Kenyan Shilling	134.1312	145.3088	-	-
Lithuanian Litas	3.3496	3.5561	-	-
Malaysian Ringgit	4.1913	4.4736	-	-
Mauritius Rupee	38.6126	41.8304	-	-
Mexican Peso	18.0252	19.1365	-	-
Moroccan Dirham	10.8466	11.6896	-	-
New Zealand Dollar	1.6771	1.7801	1.6886	1.7686
Norwegian Krone	7.4642	7.9228	7.5135	7.8735
Omani Riyal	0.5163	0.5509	-	-
Polish Zloty	4.2047	4.4870	4.2265	4.4870
Pound Sterling	0.8461	0.8939	0.8550	0.8850
Romanian Leu	4.1220	4.4888	-	-
Russian Ruble	40.7280	44.1220	-	-
Saudi Arabian Riyal	5.0289	5.3666	-	-
Singapore Dollar	1.7045	1.8093	1.7194	1.7929
South African Rand	10.6490	11.2850	10.7720	11.1620
Swedish Krone	8.8448	9.3882	8.9165	9.3165
Swiss Franc	1.1906	1.2640	1.1974	1.2574
Thai Baht	41.6053	44.1347	41.6268	44.1132
Tunisian Dinar	1.8830	2.0094	-	-
Turkish Lira	2.4358	2.5854	2.4365	2.5847
United States Dollar	1.3481	1.4309	1.3665	1.4135

Ulster Bank Ireland Limited is regulated by the Central Bank of Ireland

Source: www.capitalmarkets.ulsterbank.com

Factors Affecting the Value of a Currency

Many factors have an effect on the value of a country's currency.

1. Economic boom or recession – trade cycle – investors speculate and if there is an upswing in the economic performance of the economy, investors are attracted (together with government grant incentives) to set up and offer jobs. If this trend continues, it signals a rise in the value of the currency.

2. Rising interest rates make it more difficult for people to spend as much because their loans (like mortgages) are higher and they find it difficult to save. This leads to depressed demand for goods and services, closures and unemployment. Investors look unfavourably on this type of economy and the value of the currency falls.

3. Inflation: Sometimes governments find it necessary to devalue a currency when inflation (rising prices) and interest rates are unmanageably high.

Business Information in Graphical Form

Tables

Tabulation is the procedure used to organise raw data (unorganised data usually in note or prose form) into a table. In order to understand the data that is contained in a table, we must differentiate between data and statistics as well as primary and secondary forms of the latter.

(a) Primary Data: is data that has been collected by the investigator personally. He/she knows under what conditions the data was collected and its limitations, e.g. a spending pattern survey carried out by using a questionnaire in a busy street in Dublin.

(b) Secondary Data: is data that already exists and is used by someone else. The conditions under which it was collected or its limitations are not known.

(c) Primary Statistics: are figures that are put into a table and have been collected as part of primary data.

(d) Secondary Statistics: are simply percentages or averages that appear beside the primary statistics in the table – a useful way of analysing primary statistics.

PRACTICE TABULATION QUESTION

Employees in Marshall Company numbered 1,500. The company was organised into three departments, Production, Sales and Administration; 400 people were employed in Production and 630 in Administration. There were 460 young females, 200 young males and 420 senior females employed with the company.

Of those working in the Production Department, 130 were young males, 90 were young females and 100 were senior females. The remaining employees in the department were senior males.

Administration was made up of 220 senior males, 200 senior females and 40 young males, with the remainder young females.

Sales was made up of 120 senior males, 120 senior females and 30 young males, with the remainder young females.

1. Compile a suitable table of information from this raw data detailing:
   (a) Primary statistics – the information above arranged in an organised fashion that is easy to read.
   (b) Secondary statistics to analyse the employment distribution.
2. Comment on your findings.

Steps to tabulate raw data:
1. Decide on the number of rows and columns and whether a total column is needed (not always).
2. The independent variables (males and females categorised) should appear vertically and the dependant variable should appear horizontally (the numbers of employees, categories in Production, in Sales and in Administration, generally are categorised based on being dependant on whether they are male or female).

   Other examples are 'The Profits of Companies' – the companies categorised would be the Independent variables, and profits would be the Dependant variable.

   'Sales over time' – time (in years, months, weeks or days) would be the Independent variable, and sales would change over time (sales = Dependant variable).
3. Clarity and neatness is essential and headings and subheadings should be clearly labelled. A key should be used if wording is too extensive and it overloads and clutters the table.

SOLUTION TO PRACTICE QUESTION

1. Employee Details of Marshall Company

	Production		Sales		Administration		Total	
	No.	%	No.	%	No.	%	No.	%
Sen. F	100	25	120	26	200	32	420	28
Sen. M	80	20	120	26	220	35	420	28
Young M	130	32	30	6	40	6	200	13.3
Young F	90	23	200	42	170	27	460	30.7
	400	100	470	100	630	100	1,500	100

KEY:
Sen.   Senior
M   Males
F   Females

2. Comment

The same number of senior males are employed in the company as females. The largest concentration of senior males appears to be in Administration (35 per cent) with 26 per cent of senior males employed in Sales. The percentage numbers of young males and senior females in Production are 32 per cent and 25 per cent respectively. There is an unusually large number of young females employed in Sales, 42 per cent. The small percentages of young males in Sales and Administration, 6 per cent each, is also noteworthy.

It appears that young females are chosen to promote the business creating a young company image. Possibly the reason for a large number of young males in Production is extra physical strength or other factors such as qualifications. Senior staff are concentrated in all areas, Administration figuring largest in proportion.

More information on company background, products produced or services offered would be necessary to make an accurate comment on the statistics in the table.

Bar Charts

The most common bar charts are:

1. COMPONENT BAR CHARTS

(a) They show the breakdown of the total amount into its component parts.

(b) They show how components of a total change from year to year.

(c) They isolate the component parts of each year's total.

2. PERCENTAGE COMPONENT BAR CHARTS

(a) They are similar to pie charts but are in the shape of a bar.

(b) The parts of the total are shown as a proportionate block of the bar.

(c) The length (magnitude) of the bar is not relevant because each bar is 100 per cent high.

(d) Variations only occur in relative proportional sizes of percentage parts of the bar.

3. MULTIPLE BAR CHARTS

(a) The parts of the component bar are displayed side by side rather than all in the one bar as is the case for a component bar chart.

(b) No Grand Total is shown – all the individual parts would have to be added up.

(c) Comparative heights of each part of the total can be seen at a glance.

Most information can be depicted in one form or another by bar charts.

PRACTICE QUESTION

Given the following information draw:

1. A Component Bar Chart.

2. Three Percentage Component Bar Charts – one for each year.

3. A Multiple Bar Chart.

4. Explore the reasons why one might be more useful than another.

Note: Graph paper should be used to ensure a high level of accuracy.

The breakdown of company X's staff numbers was as follows:

Year 1: Production staff = 180, Sales staff = 75, and Administration staff = 45.
Year 2: Production staff = 200, Sales staff = 80, and Administration staff = 60.
Year 3: Production staff = 150, Sales staff = 60, and Administration staff = 40.

Workings for Percentage Bar Chart, Company X

Year 1 P = 180/300 x 100 = 60%   S = 75/300 x 100 = 25%   A = 45/300 x 100 = 15%
Year 2 P = 200/340 x 100 = 58.8% S = 80/340 x 100 = 23.5%   A = 60/340 x 100 = 17.7%
Year 3 P = 150/250 x 100 = 60%   S = 60/250 x 100 = 24%   A = 40/250 x 100 = 16%

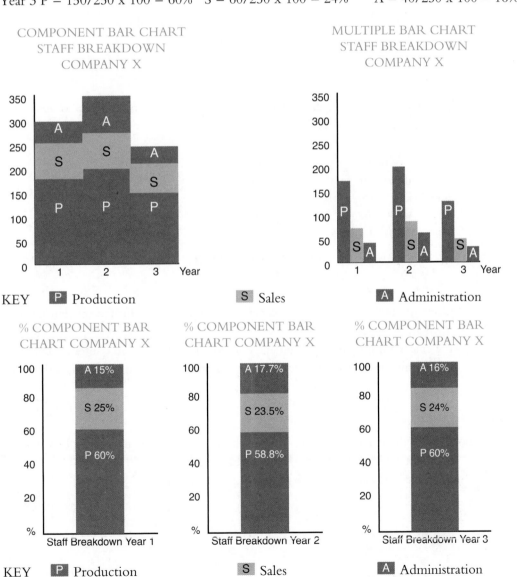

COMPONENT BAR CHART
STAFF BREAKDOWN
COMPANY X

MULTIPLE BAR CHART
STAFF BREAKDOWN
COMPANY X

KEY   P Production   S Sales   A Administration

% COMPONENT BAR
CHART COMPANY X

% COMPONENT BAR
CHART COMPANY X

% COMPONENT BAR
CHART COMPANY X

Staff Breakdown Year 1

Staff Breakdown Year 2

Staff Breakdown Year 3

KEY   P Production   S Sales   A Administration

Pie Charts

Circular diagrams used to show the relative sizes of component elements of a total.
- Use a compass to draw circle.
- Use a protractor to draw the segments of the circle when estimated.

How to calculate measurements to obtain the sizes of the segments of the circle:

(a) If information is given in figures (rather than percentages) use the following formula to obtain the degrees of the circle:

$$\frac{\text{No. of degrees}}{\text{Total Cost or Sales figure}} \qquad \frac{360}{2,000 \text{ (say)}} = .18 \text{ (multiply this by each individual Cost or Sale value to obtain the degrees of the circle)}$$

(b) If information is given in percentages use the following formula to obtain the degrees of the circle:

$$\frac{\text{No. of degrees}}{\text{Total percentage}} \qquad \frac{360}{100\%} = 3.6 \text{ (multiply this by each percentage value to obtain the degrees of the circle)}$$

(c) To get back from degrees of a circle to percentages, divide each degree figure by 3.6.

- Once the pie chart is drawn, percentages are usually indicated in each separate segment of the circle.
- Pie charts are similar to percentage component bar charts in content. However, it is usually easier to see differences in component parts of a pie chart than in a bar chart.

PRACTICE QUESTION

(a) Look at the practice question on bar charts. For part 2 depict the information in the form of three pie charts – one for each year.
(b) Why are these three pie charts not readily comparable?

WORKINGS

To get the degrees of the circle

$$\frac{360°}{300} \quad = \quad 1.2 \quad \text{(multiply this by each part for year 1)}$$

$$1.2 \times 180 \quad = \quad 216°$$

$$1.2 \times 75 \quad = \quad 90°$$

$$1.2 \times 45 \quad = \quad \underline{54°}$$

$$\underline{\underline{360°}}$$

$$\frac{360°}{340} \quad = \quad 1.06 \quad \text{(multiply this by each part for year 2)}$$

$$1.06 \times 200 \quad = \quad 212°$$

$$1.06 \times 80 \quad = \quad 85°$$

$$1.06 \times 60 \quad = \quad \underline{63°}$$

$$\underline{\underline{360°}}$$

$$\frac{360}{250} \quad = \quad 1.44 \quad \text{(multiply this by each part for year 3)}$$

$$1.44 \times 150 \quad = \quad 216°$$

$$1.44 \times 60 \quad = \quad 86°$$

$$1.44 \times 40 \quad = \quad \underline{58°}$$

$$\underline{\underline{360°}}$$

**STAFF BREAKDOWN
COMPANY X Year 1**

**STAFF BREAKDOWN
COMPANY X Year 3**

**STAFF BREAKDOWN
COMPANY X Year 2**

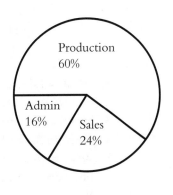

Line Graphs

Many businesses wish to keep track of sales or costs and find the use of a line graph a suitable way of doing this. The following example in Figure 3.1 depicts sales over six months. Line graphs can be linked with Gantt charts (discussed under 'Functions of Management' in Chapter 1). They both depict either sales or cost changes over time. If a target level of sales is anticipated, one can see at a glance whether this level has been reached or not.

Visual display instruments like tables, bar charts, pie charts and line graphs are regularly used by, for example, survey agencies like MRBI or Irish Marketing Surveys to show results of opinion polls or voting trends at election time. Business television programmes and television news use them to show results of information that viewers find easy to interpret at a glance.

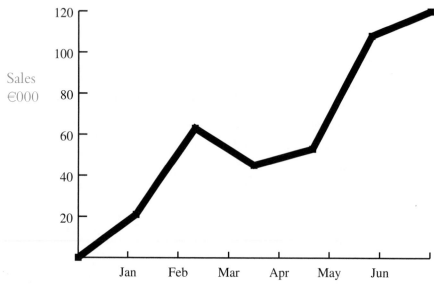

Figure 3.1 Sales Figures over Six Months

Practice Questions

1. What is Tabulation?
2. How is Raw Data defined?
3. How do Primary Data and Primary Statistics differ?
4. How do Secondary Data and Secondary Statistics differ?
5. What steps are involved in drawing a table?
6. How do the *three* types of Bar Charts differ?
7. Which Bar Chart is similar in content (but not in shape) to a Pie Chart?
8. The Breakdown of Company Y's Staff numbers was as follows:

Year	Sales Dept	Production Dept	Administration Dept
Year 1	200	600	150

Year 2	210	500	120
Year 3	205	480	105

You are required to draw:

(a) A Component Bar Chart of the total information.

(b) A Pie Chart for Year 2 only. Show full workings.

(c) A Multiple Bar Chart of the total information.

Business Administration

Portfolio of Coursework (Sample Assignment)

Subjects taken by the students at St Margaret's College are as follows:

Subject	No. of Students 2009
LANGUAGES	
French	850
German	240
Spanish	200
	1,290
INFORMATION TECHNOLOGY	
Comp. Program	300
Computer Applications	250
	550
PROFESSIONAL	
Management	380
Banking	120
Accountancy	190
	690
ACADEMIC	
Leaving Cert	150
Junior Cert	80
Transition Year	31
	261
Total no. students	**2,791**

1. Depict the above data in the following forms:
   (a) A Pie Chart – show full workings.
   (b) A Multiple Bar Chart.
2. Comment on each visual display instrument used to display the data and the trend in the data.

Insurance Against Common Business Risks

The Irish Insurance Federation (IIF) was founded in 1986, and is the representative body for insurance companies in Ireland. The IIF has 62 member companies, which employ over 14,300 people. This includes insurers serving both the domestic market and writing business in overseas markets from a base in Ireland. Collectively, IIF members write over 95 per cent of all life and non-life insurance business in Ireland.

The Irish Insurance Federation is the umbrella organisation for the insurance industry and is used by insurers (insurance companies) to check on the credit rating and solvency of brokers and intermediaries (**www.iif.ie**).

Insurance companies and brokers must register with the Irish Brokers' Association (IBA) (**www.iba.ie**) before they are allowed to operate. Registering with the Irish Insurance Compliance Bureau allows them to be fully bonded and recognised. A brokerage cast outside the IBA fold could not operate unless it was registered with the bureau. Insurance companies are obliged to operate in accordance with the provisions of the Insurance Act 1989 and the regulations that are attached to the Act. Matters relating to non-disclosure of commercial fees and inappropriate business activities can lead to expulsion from the IBA.

An insurer can be an insurance company or a financial institution or a broker that charges a fee called a Premium to insure private individuals and businesses against the risk of accident or theft. Insurers also offer life policies (life assurance) to protect against the risk of serious injury, disability and death.

A Broker is an individual or group of individuals such as the Automobile Association (AA) whose business it is to search around for the best available quote – in this case for motor insurance – and they take a portion of the premium that they quote for themselves (like a middleman).

The Insured, the person or business being insured, can get the value of the lost item back and replace it. A life policy will provide the insurer with peace of mind and will compensate his or her dependants in the case of his or her death. (*Note:* Life policies differ in value.)

An Insurance Policy is the agreement drawn up between the Insurer and the Insured that is presented by the Insurer (e.g. AXA) in the form of a document listing the conditions underpinning the agreement.

Underwriting a Risk is the guarantee given by the insurer to pay compensation to the insured (the extent of compensation is limited by the Principle of Indemnity – discussed later).

Research and Markets: Ireland Insurance Market Intelligence: 2011 Edition

23 February 2011

The insurance industry of Ireland has shown consistent growth of 25.8 per cent over the period of 2002-2007. However from the past two years, Irish insurance industry has registered downfall in its growth rate and the average annual growth rate of the industry has declined to 15.8 per cent for the period of 2002-2009. Changing weather patterns have lead to severe flooding thus affecting the property market adversely. The non-life insurance market sustained an underwriting loss in year 2009 for the first time since 2002, as the insurance industry was hit by both recession and extreme weather events. Positive factors which would support the growth of the industry in the near future are higher demand for automobiles, improving economic growth, demographic advantages, increased awareness towards health measures and an ageing population.

The insurance segment of Ireland is highly concentrated with 98.5 per cent and 92.8 per cent of the market occupied by the top ten life and non-life insurers respectively. The insurance density of Ireland is very high, but has declined in the past two years due to increase in claims. In addition the Irish insurance penetration rate recorded a varying ratio from 2002-2009. The Irish insurance market has a matured set-up; nevertheless, there is evidence of underinsurance and non-insurance in certain segments of the domestic market.

Source: www.businesswire.com

Downgrade forces insurance firms' restrictions

25 October 2011

Three major foreign-owned insurance companies have been restricted from providing cover for state companies.

Three major foreign-owned insurance companies have been restricted from providing cover for Irish state companies as they have been downgraded because Ireland has been demoted by credit rating agencies.

The Irish Insurance Federation has been lobbying Finance Minister Michael Noonan on the issue.

Allianz, Aviva and RSA Insurance represent 40 per cent of the non-life insurance market. Although they are foreign-owned, they have been capitalised in Ireland and have most of their customers here.

As the country has been downgraded, the companies have also been demoted despite meeting the solvency requirements of the Central Bank.

In a letter to the Minister for Finance, seen by RTÉ News, the Irish Insurance Federation says the development has resulted in serious consequences.

One of the effects is that the insurers no longer meet the requirements needed to offer cover

> to Irish state and semi-state companies.
>
> Last week Minister Noonan wrote back to say he was unaware of a specific code of practice or legislation which set minimum criteria. However, it is understood that state bodies do have their own minimum ratings which they set individually.
>
> Source: www.rte.ie/news/2011/1025/insurance-business.html

Common Types of Insurance

The most common insurance policies are:

1. Motor insurance
2. House and contents insurance
3. Business insurance
4. Health insurance
5. Travel insurance
6. Life assurance
7. Other miscellaneous insurances

Motor insurance is compulsory by law (Road Traffic Act 1933) and is broken down into:

(a) Third Party: The insurance company only pays out compensation for the damage to the other vehicle and/or person, but not for damage to your own vehicle.
(b) Third Party, Fire and Theft: Compensation is paid out for third party damage and for burn damage or theft of the vehicle and other appropriate compensation.
(c) Fully Comprehensive: The insurance company will pay compensation for the repair of all vehicles involved in any accident, including your own, as well as personal compensation. If you buy an expensive car, it is likely that parts for it will be expensive and it is best to avail of this type of insurance in this case.

- *Note:* The premiums – payments for motor insurance – will be higher if the driver is younger and regarded as being more risky. Premiums will also be 'loaded' (increased) for larger vehicles and if previous claims have been made.

No Claims Bonus: If a driver continues driving and is lucky enough never to have had an accident, he/she is rewarded with a no claims bonus which rises every subsequent year that the driver has a clear record.

- *Note*: Most insurances have increased substantially due to the high incidence of claims in recent times.

HOUSE AND CONTENTS INSURANCE

Usually when someone decides to buy a house, the house and contents insurance premium is included in the amount repayable to the financial institution with which they take out their mortgage (house loan). People also have the option of insuring their house and contents with separate insurance companies if they prefer. The insurance is usually in case of burglary, fire, etc.

BUSINESS INSURANCE

The most common insurance that businesses in general avail of is Full Public Liability Insurance. This covers them for accidents occurring on or in the vicinity of their premises. Crèches might have high premiums to pay due to the higher risk of children having accidents. Businesses involved in deliveries of any sort, where drivers are frequently parked in busy public areas, are also subject to large premiums.

HEALTH INSURANCE

Three of the main health insurance companies in Ireland include VHI (Voluntary Health Insurance), Quinn Healthcare and Aviva. There are many different types of health cover, such as Plan A, Plan B, Plan C, with variations of these depending of the insurer's choice – the greater the cover, the higher the premium or cost of the health insurance.

Public hospital services themselves are free (doctors and nurses' services). In some cases there are public charges for emergency services and for hospital accommodation, but maternity accommodation in a public ward of a maternity hospital is free.

TRAVEL INSURANCE

Usually tour operators and travel agencies organise baggage and medical insurance for people going abroad on holiday. Banks now provide insurance that covers these types of risk, which cover holiday cancellation, medical and hospital expenses, personal accident, legal expenses, lost baggage, or the cost of getting a person home in case of emergency. Other cover might include winter sports equipment, twenty-four hour emergency medical assistance, missed departure/connection, and loss of passport.

EU IMPLICATIONS FOR TRAVEL INSURANCE – WHAT TO DO IF YOU NEED HELP IN ANOTHER EU COUNTRY

THE EUROPEAN HEALTH INSURANCE CARD

If you are an EU/EEA national and are travelling or staying temporarily in another state of the European Economic Area (EEA) or Switzerland, you are entitled to receive medical care if you become ill or have an accident.

If you are a student or a seconded worker, or if you are entitled to a social security pension in that state, you will be entitled to health care beyond the immediate treatment.

The European Health Insurance Card (EHIC) replaced the E111 form and a number of other 'E' forms including the E128, making it easier for you to get medical care quickly and easily. It is evidence that you are part of a health insurance scheme administered by another state in the EEA/Switzerland. To obtain healthcare with the card, you can go to the nearest public system doctor, public hospital, or other public treatment centre and present your card.

Currently, the European Economic Area (EEA) comprises the 27 member states of the European Union together with Iceland, Norway and Liechtenstein. Your European Health Insurance Card is valid for use throughout any of these countries and in Switzerland.

Refer to **www.citizensinformation.ie.**

Before leaving the country get an EHIC card from your local Social Welfare office, Health Board or doctor.

- **Emergency Care:** In case of emergency only (defined by the doctor) it avoids the need to pay up front. The Social Welfare Department will pay the bill under its own system of payment. This is accepted throughout most of the European Economic Area.
- **Non-emergency Care:** Complications arise for care that is not urgent. The traveller may have to pay for the cost of care abroad but can later claim this money back through the Social Welfare system. Get informed before you go!

LIFE ASSURANCE

This insures a person and his/her family in the event of his/her death or serious injury and it can also provide life savings if the person is willing to pay a higher premium for this provision. A lump sum of money will be paid out to dependants in the event of a person's death.

Many different policies are offered by different insurance companies and brokers and people in general usually avail of the type of policy that suits their own needs.

OTHER MISCELLANEOUS INSURANCES

Most business people who deal in assets will insure their equipment. For example, a hardware equipment hire business would have invested a lot of capital in the assets (equipment) and will insure them because they are the basis of their livelihood, e.g. lawnmowers or diggers for hire etc. Car hire is another business that would probably pay large premiums. Farmers insure their stocks and animals against fire and theft, employers insure their premises against the risk of employee theft or dishonesty (Fidelity Guarantee). Examples would be banks, post offices etc. Marine insurance covers losses which might be suffered while transporting goods by sea.

Insurance Protections and Risk

- Most insurance policies are concerned with the risk of fire, theft, illness or death, and flooding in some cases.
- *Note:* **It is important to enquire into the exact amount of cover that a policy stipulates. In some cases the small print reads 'cover except when loss is due to war or natural disaster' etc.**

- Insurance means that there is a possibility that loss will be incurred and compensation is for the value of that amount only.
- Assurance means a guarantee of a lump sum of money on the death or confirmation of terminal injury of the insured or the maturity of a savings policy after a set number of years.
- Premiums rise as the perceived risks rise. Young people are particularly penalised in the case of motor insurance for drivers under 25 years. Public liability insurance for crèches is high and drivers involved in deliveries also have high insurance premiums to pay.

Principles of Insurance

The Principles of Insurance are concerned with the conditions that create the need to insure, allow for items to be insured and allow for appropriate compensation to be gained, having placed a claim with the insurer.

1. *INSURABLE INTEREST*
You wouldn't insure something unless you had an interest in doing so! The insured must benefit from the existence of what he/she is getting insured and must suffer if it is lost. In short, a value is attached to whatever is being insured. Legal ownership is a prerequisite to this principle.

2. *UTMOST GOOD FAITH*
Trust must exist between the insurer and the insured. If all facts are not disclosed it would lead to a void contract of insurance.

3. *INDEMNITY (SUBROGATION, CONTRIBUTION AND PROXIMATE CLAUSE ARE FOLLOW-ON CONDITIONS TO INDEMNITY).*
Only the loss incurred is compensated – no more. The insured is no better off (no profit gained) than they were prior to the incident that triggered the claim. Life assurance is an exception to this principle.

4. *SUBROGATION*
After the insurance company has paid out the compensation to the insured, the company is entitled to claim against any third party and can take legal action against the person who was responsible (inbuilt in the policy – the insured gives the company permission to do this by signature).

For example: Suppose you're in a car accident and it is clearly not your fault. Your car is wrecked and your neck and back have been injured. Your car insurance policy covers you for both the damage to your car and your personal injuries, so you call your insurance company, file a claim, and they pay all of your expenses relating to the accident. During the course of the claim, your insurance company realises that the other party at fault also has insurance that will cover the damages. Your insurance carrier seeks reimbursement from the other insurance company since the other party it insured was actually at fault for the accident. This process of reimbursing your insurance company for the bills it covered is known as subrogation.

5. CONTRIBUTION

If two different insurance companies are employed, i.e. if the insured is overinsured, the principle of indemnity still applies, and the insured only gets back the loss and no more. A loss is calculated as follows:

Hibernian Insurance and GRE (Guardian Royal Exchange) are both insuring stock in a premises. Hibernian insures €12,000 worth of stock and GRE insures €6,000 worth of stock. €4,000 worth of stock is taken in a burglary.

Hibernian pay out $\dfrac{12,000}{18,000}$ x 4,000 = €2,667

GRE pay out $\dfrac{6,000}{18,000}$ x 4,000 = €1,333

TOTAL €4,000

6. PROXIMATE CAUSE

This refers to the nature of the risk that an item is being insured against. The insurance company always checks the policy to make sure that the risk was insured against before they pay out the compensation.

Proximate cause is a cause which brings about a loss with no other intervening cause breaking the chain of events. For example: A fireman removes undamaged stock from a burning building to avoid it being in the fire. It is stacked in the open yard and subsequently damaged by rain. The question is was the proximate cause of the damage the fire or the rain? The answer is: if the rain damage occurred before the insured had an opportunity to protect it, the proximate cause of the damage would be the fire and fire is covered under a fire policy. However, if the stock was left unprotected for an unreasonably long period, the rain would be a new and independent cause of damage, and damage caused by rain may not be covered under a policy.

Assessing Insurance Requirements in the Current Economic Environment

What is ERM?

Enterprise risk management (ERM) in business is part of strategic planning and includes the methods and processes used by organisations to manage risks and seize opportunities related to the achievement of their objectives. ERM provides a framework for risk management, which typically involves identifying particular events or circumstances relevant to the organisation's objectives (risks and opportunities), assessing them in terms of likelihood and magnitude of impact, determining a response strategy, and monitoring progress.

Risk types include:

- **Hazard risk:** Liability torts, property damage, natural catastrophe.
- **Financial risk:** Pricing risk, Asset risk, currency risk, liquidity risk.
- **Operational risk:** Customer satisfaction, product failure, integrity, reputational risk.
- **Strategic risk:** Competition, social trend, capital availability.

(Refer to Risk Assessment details in Chapter 4 and for Retail Organisations in Chapter 7.)

Insurance needs can be determined when risks have been assessed as part of the organisation's strategic plan. Following the identification of these risks they can then be prioritised in a cost effective manner and appropriate insurance cover can be purchased and put in place in the event of accident or damage to persons or property in the areas identified.

PRACTICE QUESTIONS

1. Write notes on:
   (a) The Irish Insurance Federation.
   (b) The IBA.
   (c) The Irish Compliance Bureau.
2. In accordance with which legal Act are Insurance Companies and Brokers obliged to operate?
3. What is 'Underwriting a Risk'?
4. (a) What is a Premium and what factors will dictate how high or low it is?
   (b) What businesses have to pay higher insurance premiums and why?
5. What are the most common types of insurance policies?
6. With regard to Motor Insurance differentiate between third party, third party fire and theft, and fully comprehensive insurance.
7. What is a No Claims Bonus?
8. What is Public Liability Insurance and who avails of it?
9. Who are the VHI and do they still maintain a monopoly in Ireland?
10. (a) Who provides travel insurance?
    (b) What are the EU implications for Travel Insurance?
11. (a) What is the difference between Insurance and Assurance?
    (b) What is Life Assurance and why is it so important?
12. What is Fidelity Guarantee?
13. List the Principles of Insurance and explain them briefly and clearly.

Insurance Proposal Form

Request a Quote

If you are an existing policyholder click here.

Household quotation details required:

Title | Mr ▼ |

Full Name:

Full Postal Address:

Full Address of property to be insured:

Is this your permanent residence?   Yes ◉   No ○
If no please state details:

Telephone Numbers:

Daytime:

Evening:

Your e-mail address:

Your Date of Birth:

What is your occupation: (including part time occupations)

Please select which type of cover you need: | Buildings Only ▼ |

What is your buildings value?

What is your contents value?

Do you want accidental damage cover?   Yes ○   No ◉

Do you require cover for your personal belongings and valuables outside your home?

Yes ◌ No ◉

If yes please state the sum insured and include details of any individual items worth more than €1,270 (£1,000)

Do you need cover for pedal cycles? *(please tell us how many and the total value)*

Do you have any of the following:

☐ Approved alarm to IŞ 199 standards

☐ Do you have any mortice locks on your outside doors

☐ Do you have smoke detectors fitted?

☐ Are you in a neighbourhood watch area?

Previous claims/losses during the last 5 years:

Date of claim:

Full description of claim/loss:

What is the amount of the payments made to date:

Is the claim settled?　　Yes ◌ No ◉

If there are any other details you feel are relevant, please fill in the following section:

Your home is a Private Residence of standard construction and you have been free of convictions for the last 5 years.

Thank you for taking the time to complete this form, we will reply to you by e-mail with a quotation.

☐ Please tick here if you wish us to post a quotation out to you.

Accident Claim Form

Damage to Both Yours and Another Vehicle

Your Details:

Your Insurance Policy
Number:

Your Name:

E Mail address:

If you are registered for VAT please enter your VAT number here:

Home telephone Number:

Work telephone Number:

Your Vehicle Details:

Registration Number:

Make & Model :
e.g. Ford Escort 1.31

Is the vehicle registered in
your name?

Yes: (•)

No: ( )

Name of any financial institution or hire purchase company with an
interest in the vehicle?

Vehicle Damage...Inspection & Repair Instruction

Please check our approved repairer list before continuing.

Contact name and number to arrange a vehicle inspection:

What is the estimated cost of
repair?

Driver or person last in charge of vehicle

Full name:

Address:

E Mail address:

Date of Birth:

Home telephone Number:

Work telephone Number:

Driving Licence:

Full: ○

Provisional: ◉

Category of Licence:

Did the driver have your permission to drive the vehicle:

Yes: ◉

No: ○

Has the driver ever been convicted of a motoring offence or had any previous accidents?

Yes: ◉

No: ○

Accident details:

In what location did the accident happen:

Please enter the date and time of the accident:

In your view, how did the accident happen:

By how much do you consider yourself to blame?

Select one ▼

Please enter the name/s of any persons (including yourself) who admitted liability verbally or in writing at the scene of the accident:

Name of Garda and station to whom the incident was reported to or investigated by:

Has notice of intention to prosecute been given or summons received?

Yes: ○

No: ◉

If 'yes' give details:

Witness details:

Name:

Address:

Approximate age:

Phone Number:

Witness category: Select one ▼

Details of other vehicles/property involved:

Name of owner:

Name of driver:

Address:

Registration Number of vehicle:

Vehicle Make/Model: e.g. Ford Escort 1.31

Please describe the damage to this vehicle:

Name of other person's Insurance Company:

Other Person's Policy Number:

SUBMIT

Sample Assignment Briefs

QUESTION 1

Choose a Bank or Financial Institution and examine the following aspects of the Institution:

1. The types of loans offered categorised as Short-, Medium-, Long-term.
2. The procedure for getting a loan.
3. The most common services offered and charges incurred relating to personal customers.
4. The most common services offered and charges incurred relating to business customers.

QUESTION 2

Choose an Insurance Company or Broker and do an analysis of the business, examining a range of the following aspects of the organisation:

1. Brief history and organisational structure.
2. The types of insurance policies and cover offered and charges categorised with reference to the section on insurance in this chapter.
3. How the Principles of Insurance tie in with the policies offered.
4. How a claim is handled by the business – process of claim from point of receipt to point of payment.
   - Include in your assignment:
   (a) An Insurance Claim form
   (b) An Insurance Proposal form.

4. Human Resources

Human Resource Management or Personnel Management is concerned with recruiting employees, looking after existing staff needs, dealing with employee grievances and disciplining or dismissing employees if the need arises. This management is also obliged to inform employees of their statutory rights regarding their employment in the organisation and is responsible for drawing up and maintaining documents (attendance records, personnel files and contracts of employment) in the Human Resources Department.

Workforce Planning

This involves forecasting future labour requirements and is based on the estimated 'workforce gap' expected to occur. A workforce gap is the difference between current employee numbers and future requirements. Workforce planning is also referred to as 'Human Resource Planning'. The likely availability of a suitable Labour Supply will dictate whether the workforce gap is bridged.

SHORT-TERM WORKFORCE GAP (UNDER ONE YEAR)

If a female employee has informed her superior that she will be taking maternity leave from a certain date, immediate workforce planning is required. The future temporary worker requirement must be matched by a 'suitable substitute'. This will be based on a suitable future supply of appropriately skilled labour to fill the temporary vacancy. Employee sickness also requires short-term workforce planning. This type of workforce gap can be difficult to bridge because of short notice.

MEDIUM-TERM WORKFORCE GAP (ONE TO FIVE YEARS)

If an employee decides to take a career break (his/her position can be held for a maximum of five years in many state employments), the position must be filled in a temporary capacity. If a company undertakes an assignment or project, it will interview interested and suitably qualified candidates and appoint them for the period of the contract.

LONG-TERM WORKFORCE GAP (OVER FIVE YEARS)

The interviewers would carefully assess any position that would be foreseen as long term. Senior management positions are often (not always) long-term appointments. The suitability of the successful candidate is paramount in the mind of the interviewers. Permanent state jobs tend to fall into this category. Another example would be secondments (explained later in this chapter under the heading 'Internal Sources of Labour').

How to Assess the Workforce Gap

Management normally carries out an 'employee assessment or audit'. This involves analysing the current workforce, taking into account the total number of employees and how they are categorised in terms of their posts of responsibility and their seniority. The diverse skills of each employee should be listed, as well as their qualifications. The future requirements should then be weighed up. Natural wastage (retirement, redundancy and unexpected disability) must be taken into account and the cost of training (if applicable) must be estimated. Some businesses must look carefully at the cost of overtime and the willingness of employees to work overtime. If employee turnover or absenteeism is high, a panel of part-time employees should be available to management to cover requirements.

The Importance of Good Workforce Planning

It is important that managers have the appropriate back-up facilities to cover short-term labour shortfalls. Otherwise the business profile might be damaged and it could affect customer loyalty and/or sales. All workforce planning is difficult and is based on the following factors:

1. Social Factors – people matters – considerations such as whether people's home situations might reduce work effort and contribute to absenteeism.
2. Technological Factors – skills, the need for retraining and the question of whether more labour or less labour is needed based on more modern high-tech equipment being used in the business.
3. Demographic Factors – considerations such as whether an applicant would need to relocate in order to take up the job and the expenses connected with this decision.
4. Political Factors – qualifications and job specification to match with job description as advertised; the recruitment option – open competition and equal opportunity legislation considerations (discussed in the next section).

Fears ease as medical firm creates 79 jobs

Mark Hilliard   Tuesday, 25 October 2011

A town shattered by job concerns received a double boost yesterday as a medical devices firm announced 79 new jobs.

Meanwhile, fears of massive job losses at MBNA in Carrick-on-Shannon are easing, with hopes of a buyer for the Bank of America facility.

Medical devices producer VistaMed revealed plans to invest €7.2m in research and development and in expanding its production capacity, in a move that will almost double its workforce in the Co Leitrim town.

Welcoming the announcement, Jobs, Enterprise and Innovation Minister Richard Bruton described it as a 'significant day for the Irish economy'.

'VistaMed is an Irish company in a regional location taking advantage of Ireland's excellent record in the multinational medical technology sector to drive innovation and employment growth. We need to see more of this,' he said.

Concerns about the future of the Bank of America-owned MBNA in the town have also eased somewhat.

Bank of America announced it was withdrawing from its Irish credit card operation last August, putting 750 jobs under threat.

But it is now understood that a number of companies are interested in purchasing the credit card branch of the bank. An announcement is expected early in the New Year.

Source: *Irish Independent*

Recruitment Options

The methods used to hire labour and to make appointments. Both Internal (recruiting from within the organisation) and External (recruiting from outside the organisation) sources of labour are discussed below.

External Sources of Labour

OPEN COMPETITION

Advertising in newspapers is the most common method used by companies in order to be seen to comply with 'Open Competition' requirements for hiring staff. The advertisement will generally consist of:

1. *THE JOB DESCRIPTION:* This consists of the job title, location, duties attached to the post and any other special features connected with the post.

2. *THE JOB SPECIFICATION:* This refers to the special qualities, qualifications and skills that are sought by the company.

The companies in question will usually refer to their 'policy of equal opportunity' and a closing date for receipt of applications. They will also refer to competitive interviews assessed by interview boards based on appropriate qualifications and applicable work experience. They will state that applications will be treated in strict confidence (complying with the Freedom of Information Act and the Data Protection Act 1988) and in some cases will draw up a set of criteria to shortlist candidates. The statement 'Canvassing will disqualify' may also appear. This type of selection procedure is seen to be fair and non-discriminatory.

STAGES TO BE FOLLOWED IN RECRUITING THROUGH OPEN COMPETITION:

Stage 1: Design of application form for job vacancy.

Stage 2: Evaluation of selection procedure by selection board and management.

Stage 3: Newspaper advertisement.

Stage 4: Application forms are sent to interested parties.

Stage 5: Candidates are shortlisted on the basis of their application, qualifications, suitability and the number of vacancies. References are verified at this stage.

Stage 6: Selected candidates are invited to attend a preliminary interview and/or other qualifying tests (e.g. psychometric tests). The aim is to assess the merits of each candidate. (This does not always apply.)

Stage 7: Subsequent final interviews might be arranged.

Stage 8: Job offers and contracts of employment (which include regulations and conditions of service) are sent to successful candidates. They must sign and return the documents by a set date, if they decide to accept the job offer. The offer is normally subject to the candidate's successful medical examination.

Stage 9: In the case of state jobs the appointments must be sanctioned by the particular government department that the position is connected with.

STAFFING/MANAGEMENT CONSULTANTS

Executive search agencies are often employed by companies to search for and locate suitably qualified candidates for different positions where vacancies arise. It is usually when businesses are head hunting or searching for top-class management candidates that they employ consultants to do the groundwork for them. Head hunting usually involves a business offering the person a more attractive remuneration (wage) than he/she is currently earning. The cost of employing search agencies is usually very high. The recruitment company Marlborough is an example of a company that offers indigenous (within the economy) and multinational clients a range of personnel for their requirements.

EMPLOYMENT AGENCIES

1. Private agencies: are usually relatively expensive to employ but many companies utilise their services.

2. State or semi-state agencies: Foras Áiseanna Saothair (FÁS) is the main government agency providing training and employment services in the country. One of its functions is the provision of a placement service. There is no cost for the service. FÁS grants are often given to businesses if they undertake to recruit FÁS employees for periods of at least thirty-nine weeks.

Internal Sources of Labour

INTERNAL PROMOTIONS

These types of opening are usually advertised on notice boards within the particular establishment where the promotion is due. The criteria to award the promotion are usually based on suitability and merit (the ability and qualifications to do the job), as well as seniority and length of service in the particular area of promotion.

INTERNAL DEMOTIONS

When a person gives up or loses a post of responsibility, the vacancy remaining creates the need for more labour. Usually positions like these are filled from the internal source of labour on the existing staff.

CAREER BREAKS AND SECONDMENTS

When employees take a career break (maximum five years) or if they are granted a secondment away from their usual line of work, this creates temporary vacancies. These vacancies would be, if possible, filled in a temporary capacity by existing part-time staff.

An employee may look for a secondment if they are full-time and permanent employees in state jobs and their aim is to work for another government-run body or for the same government body in a different section. The work must be connected with their main employment and the work experience that is gained from it must be seen to contribute directly to their main employment.

REDEPLOYMENT OR TRANSFERS

- **Redeployment** is the unavoidable transfer of staff to a different location or branch due to closure.
- **Voluntary Transfer** happens when an employee requests a transfer to a different branch.

  The managers in the section that they wish to work in usually request the transfer. Their main employment position is held open (a temporary substitute is recruited) for them while they are on secondment.

Recruiting Options (Informal Methods)

These methods can range from existing staff recommending their friends or relatives as suitable candidates for positions, to sending unrequested CVs, career guidance officer recommendations and media or paper/magazine advertisements to prospective employers.

PRACTICE QUESTIONS

1. Define 'Human Resource Planning'.
2. How does the term 'Human Resource Planning' differ from the term 'Workforce Gap'?
3. Give *one* example each of a short-term, a medium-term, and a long-term Workforce Gap.
4. Define the following terms:
   (a) Employee Audit.
   (b) Natural Wastage.
   (c) Employee Turnover.
5. Why is Workforce Planning so important to managers?
6. How does the term 'External Source of Labour' differ from the term 'Internal Source of Labour'?
7. Make a clear distinction between 'Job Description' and 'Job Specification'. Give *one* example.
8. What do the following terms mean?
   (a) Head Hunting
   (b) Remuneration
   (c) Promotion and Demotion
   (d) Career Break
   (e) Secondment
   (f) Redeployment
   (g) Voluntary Transfer.
9. List the Formal and Informal methods used to recruit staff.

Functions of the Human Resources Department

The term 'Personnel Management' is now generally referred to as Human Resource Management. It can be defined as 'all those who have responsibilities for people matters'. Its purpose is to ensure that the employee has good working conditions. This in the long run helps towards job satisfaction and a pleasant working environment. Human resource management represents the formal recognition of the need for specialist individuals to deal with people management issues.

The Role of the Human Resources Department

The Human Resources Manager or the Personnel Manager's responsibilities include:

1. STAFF WELFARE

The human resource department provides the employee with information on statutory and voluntary employee benefits, and entitlements relating to wages, salaries, hourly and piecework pay rates and temporary/permanent employment.
Statutory benefits: employee benefits underpinned by law. Entitlements and obligatory contributions:

- Maternity leave
- Holidays and holiday pay
- Employment pension schemes
- Sick pay
- Company cars (if applicable).

Voluntary benefits:

- Sports and recreation facilities connected with employment
- Child care facilities
- Health insurance
- Career breaks and secondments
- Option of extra pension subscriptions.

2. STAFF DEVELOPMENT

The 'human factor' determines levels of productivity (efficiency and speed of work). The impact of work conditions on performance has encouraged companies to set up staff seminars and staff development groups made up of a varied staff group to investigate the levels of satisfaction or dissatisfaction with the work environment. This development is an important mechanism that is encouraged by the Human Resource Department in order to keep staff happy. It also gives staff the opportunity to suggest improvements to existing working conditions.

3. STAFF MOTIVATION

Motivation means a stimulus to work hard to achieve objectives and targets.
There are two main types of motivational instruments (reward systems):

- **Extrinsic Motivational Instruments:** These may be monetary rewards such as bonuses or commission, or time off in lieu.
- **Intrinsic Motivational Instruments:** This is explained in Maslow's theory of Hierarchy of Needs.

In 1943 Maslow, a clinical psychologist, analysed human needs in an effort to understand human drives and enthusiasm. His studies became the building blocks of subsequent research on staff motivation, career counselling and the understanding of the human condition. Maslow's Pyramid of Hierarchy of Needs describes how all behaviour is driven by needs. The basic physiological needs are food, shelter and security. Humans must experience security on the lower steps of the ladder to progress to the next step. The need for love, acceptance and recognition is experienced at this stage. The top two steps of the ladder, self-esteem and self-actualisation, are experienced as a result of a positive response, i.e. acceptance, respect, recognition, appreciation and praise.

The understanding of human needs is directly applicable to the analysis of employee behaviour. Appropriate understanding of people and their behaviour within their work environment leads to good worker-manager relations and therefore avoids industrial relations problems, strikes and working to rule (deliberate slow-downs in the workplace).

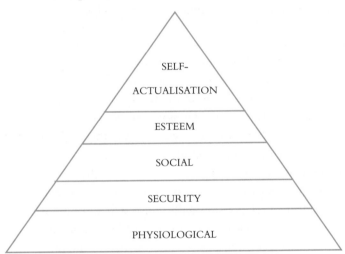

Figure 4.1 Maslow's pyramid of hierarchy of needs

The key terms in describing Maslow's hierarchy with regard to employees might be:

1. Recognition for work done.
2. Appreciation for work done.
3. Respect for employees.
4. Praise.

I have attempted here to interpret each step of the hierarchy in a 'staff needs' context as follows:

1. **Physiological needs:** Maslow's pyramid shows how staff members have material and personal needs.

- Material needs are those physical things like equipment and room space which employees feel they have a right to or ownership of.
- Personal needs, like the manager or superior creating a sense of well-being in the employee – a feeling that needs are being met, their efforts are valued, and that they matter to the organisation.

2. **Security:** When the manager or superior is meeting material and personal needs, it gives the employee a sense of security and well-being.
3. **Social:** This refers to the effective communication flow between the manager and the employee (superior and subordinate).
4. **Esteem:** When employees experience esteem, they realise they are appreciated and respected by their superior, resulting from effective communication flow and praise.
5. **Self-actualisation:** The employee will respond eagerly to positive signs and, in turn, will respond to the manager's or superior's needs. Their self worth will be fully realised, creating greater work effort and stimulating motivation.

Ultimately, the recognition of employees as people, not just as 'work machinery', is the key to good employer-employee relationships.

HERZBERG'S OBSERVATIONS

Frederick Herzberg (1966) observed that:

(a) Highly motivated workers characteristically:
  (i) enjoyed the challenge of the work
  (ii) were involved in the decision-making process
  (iii) gained recognition and were given the opportunity to advance their careers or gain promotion.

(b) Workers with low motivation characteristically:
  (i) were governed by too many rules – oversupervised
  (ii) had a bad relationship with senior staff and superiors
  (iii) were frustrated by workplace attitudes or bullying
  (iv) had a bad relationship with colleagues, leading to low self-esteem
  (v) had a cynical or divisive outlook
  (vi) had poor working conditions.

4. CAREER COUNSELLING

In most organisations induction seminars, in-service courses and training are provided to guide and advise employees how they should approach their jobs. These sessions are organised by the Human Resources Department, which will also readily provide information regarding promotional posts, secondments (already defined) and any other paths that might lead to career advancements if so requested by employees.

Performance Appraisals (feedback on performance) are also offered by the HR department; and training and development may be offered, depending on the needs of the organisation.

5. *Disciplinary procedures and dismissal*

Employees have to adhere to the organisation's rules and regulations regarding behaviour, absenteeism, punctuality etc. If they do not, then the disciplinary procedures laid down will involve:

1. A verbal warning from the employee's immediate superior for an occasional lapse in behaviour or work standards, e.g. being frequently late or swearing at a superior.
2. A formal written warning from the manager following an investigation into the case, if the employee re-offends in the same way, having taken no notice of the verbal warning and where more serious offences have taken place. Usually a copy of this written warning will be sent to the Human Resources Department.
3. A further written warning that dismissal is the next step. This subsequent disciplinary action is based on the unwillingness of the employee to adhere to previous warnings.
4. Management investigating and hearing the employee's case, followed by final warning.
5. Suspension or dismissal.

When employees are hired, they are given a copy of their conditions of employment and this would include a code of conduct which they are expected to follow.

Staff Induction Procedures

Induction is a process by which employees are received and welcomed to the organisation. Induction involves the orientation and training of the employee to allow them to understand and learn about organisational culture. It is a method of formally introducing the employee to their work location and colleagues. A clear understanding of their job, role and responsibilities, and the mission and values of the wider organisation will be provided. The aim is to demonstrate to them how they are interconnected to and interdependent on each other in the organisation. An effective induction process will ensure that the employee is supported in achieving expected performance levels.

It will also ensure that new employees are aware of the importance of team-working and their role within the team and is aimed at ensuring loyalty to the organisation.

Most organisations provide new employees with an employee resource pack. The employee resource pack is designed to assist with the induction process and usually comprises three documents:

- Employee handbook
- Induction guidelines
- Induction checklists.

- To ensure that each employee receives a structured welcome and introduction to their immediate work environment and the wider organisation.
- To outline the organisation's responsibilities and values.
- To assist in the promotion of the culture and philosophy of the organisation.
- To clarify expectations of both employee and employer in relation to codes of conduct, policies and procedures, employee services etc.
- To clarify the employee's role and performance expectations.
- To commence a process of structured feedback on performance.
- To promote an emphasis on customer/client focus.
- To promote an effective work environment.

Different organisations structure their stages of induction according to their needs.

1. **Line or Senior Manager's Introduction:** To make employees feel comfortable (helps them settle in) and supported. Lines of authority are then clearly identifiable to the new employee. The manager outlines and clearly communicates the organisation's policies and procedures.
2. **Department Manager's Introduction:** Employee is introduced to whichever sub-department he/she is assigned to and they are introduced to Department Managers they are to be answerable to. The Department Manager will clarify role expectations and may give information on career advancement or change possibilities like transfers, promotions, secondments.
   Health and safety guidelines are likely to be emphasised as well as the standard codes of conduct and general disciplinary procedures of the organisation.
3. **Workplace Site Induction:** Employees will be taken around the company to familiarise themselves with the layout of a building or a department, with important rooms like staff rooms, toilet facilities etc emphasised.
4. **Scheduled Training and Checklists:** The line manager would keep signed copies of records of training provided during the period of the new employee's probation, often for the duration of one year.
5. **Feedback/Performance Appraisal:** The line manager will monitor, review each new employee's work and act as a mentor to help guide and support them. Reports will be filed on these performance appraisal sessions (one-to-one feedback sessions) to ensure adequate effective and efficient work effort and productivity level is achieved by each new employee.

Risk Assessments and Safe Work Methods

To keep employees, customers, and suppliers safe in any organisation risk assessments should be carried out to determine if any hazards exist and how to deal with these if they are identified. Risk assessments allow organisations to compile their safety statements in line with legislation. Areas of investigation that are common to different occupations include:

- Fire safety
- Manual handling (lifting safely)
- Ergonomics (safe seating positions and equipment usage)
- General hygiene (handwashing)
- Food safety in staff areas
- Staff security
- Protective equipment and clothing.

Most organisations now have first aiders, people trained in the use of defibulators, and fire managers and marshals and develop specific policies and procedures matching each area mentioned. Refer to Chapter 7 for Health and safety initiatives aimed at improving safety in a retail administration environment.

The Health and Safety Authority provides BeSMART, part of the Taking Care of Business initiative developed for small business. This tool is aimed at helping businesses to identify the hazards in the workplace and making the workplace safer.

It is also aimed at helping businesses formulate their own risk assessment and safety statement, in consultation with their employees, as required under health and safety law. Best of all, there is no cost associated with using the tool. Businesses can visit the Health and Safety Authority website and view and listen to a short animated video that gives guidelines regarding how to carry out a risk assessment, using the web-link http://besmart.hsa.ie.

What is Training and Development?

Organisations provide three main types of training:

1. In-service training
2. On-the-job training
3. Off-the-job training.

Usually there are two division dealing with training and development in organisations:
- whole-school requirements, e.g. fire training and first aid
- professional development — upskilling of staff in specific areas of specialisation.

HR managers may decide to do a skills audit to determine the training needs of the staff.

What is Performance Appraisal?

This is when HR managers decide to review the work, skills and qualifications of each staff member one by one by carrying out interviews with them. This is referred to as a Performance Appraisal exercise.

Why Training Courses, Professional Development and Performance Appraisals are Good for Staff Morale and Motivation

- If an employeee upskills, he or she has the potential to diversify his or her work in an organisation to make the work more interesting.
- Employees who improve their skills have a better chance of being in line for promotion.
- Better skills can speed up the work and improve motivation.
- Performance appraisals give feedback to an employee on how efficiently they are working and each session can provide a forum for employees to alert the manager to their needs and wants regarding training and their employment as a whole. This encourages greater self-esteem in the employee.

Staff motivation 'is important for firms'

Tuesday, 4 October 2011

Firms operating across Ireland have been advised of the importance in maintaining motivation levels for staff even when budgets are tight.

Business motivational guru Dave Ulrich told the Irish Times that motivation is tied closely to finding meaning in work, with businesses advised to help employees to see the benefits that their work brings to the organisation and to their clients.

'When employees find meaning from the work that they do, they are more likely to not only be engaged, but feel like they contribute to the company,' Mr Ulrich told the publication.

A professor at the Ross School of Business at the University of Michigan, he made his comments ahead of his speech at the Irish Business and Employer's Confederation (IBEC) HR Leadership Summit 'The Rules of Engagement' that is taking place this week.

Meanwhile, figures from IBEC recently revealed that job creation in Ireland would appear to be on the right track at present, with the fall in employment seen over the last quarter the smallest change since the first three months of 2008.

Source: www.careersportal.ie

PRACTICE QUESTIONS

1. What is the meaning of the term 'Human Resource Management'?
2. Name the functions of the Human Resources Department.
3. What are the differences between Statutory and Voluntary Benefits with regard to Staff Welfare?
4. What is Productivity and why is it so important?
5. What is the meaning of the term 'Motivation'?
6. How are performance appraisal techniques and training and development used to help improve motivation in an organisation?
7. Explain how Maslow's Pyramid of Hierarchy of Needs is applied to staff.

8. What steps are taken by the Human Resources Department regarding the following issues?
   (a) Career Counselling in employment.
   (b) Disciplinary Procedures in employment.
   (c) Training and Development.
   (d) Performance Appraisals.

Purpose of Maintaining Documents in the Human Resources Department

The basic functions of the Human Resources Department that have already been discussed include: the selection, recruitment, training and deployment of suitable types and numbers of employees, as well as staff welfare, staff development, staff motivation, career counselling, staff discipline, staff dismissal and interacting with union representatives to discuss and hopefully solve disputes.

Documents such as employee statistics and personnel files, attendance records (including sick leave taken – both self-certified and medically certified), wage records and job specifications must be kept on record in the Human Resources Department for future reference. Safety and welfare procedures, codes of conduct and disciplinary procedures are also recorded in the department.

1. An employee who leaves the employment will require a job reference and a P45 termination of employment form containing details of pay to take to the next employer.
2. Employee pension rights and payments may need to be reviewed or estimated.
3. Appointment (converting an employee's status from part time to full time) or promotional suitability (an employee's future potential) might need to be reviewed based on qualifications that are kept on record in the department. The manager can assess previous work done by employees and by choosing a suitable candidate can achieve and sustain high job performance to ensure the survival and success of the business (performance appraisal).

   A manager can assess an employee's potential to take on wider responsibilities by referring to their employment records held in the Human Resources Department.
4. An employee's attendance is monitored (with the help of attendance records and time sheets) and the level of absenteeism is noted. It could be a deciding factor with regard to future promotional prospects.

DATE	DAY	TIME	
13/07	Monday	9.00	IN
		13.00	OUT
13/07	Monday	14.00	IN
		17.00	OUT
14/07	Tuesday	–	IN
		–	OUT
14/07	Tuesday	14.00	IN
		17.00	OUT
15/07	Wednesday	9.00	IN
		13.00	OUT
15/07	Wednesday	14.00	IN
		17.00	OUT
15/07	Wednesday	17.45	IN
		19.45	OUT
16/07	Thursday	–	IN
		–	OUT
16/07	Thursday	–	IN
		–	OUT
17/07	Friday	9.00	IN
		13.00	OUT
17/07	Friday	14.00	IN
		17.00	OUT
17/07	Friday	17.30	IN
		21.00	OUT

CLOCK CARD/TIME SHEET

TOTAL BASIC HOURS	BASIC PAY

TOTAL OVERTIME	O/T PAY

TOTAL HOURS	TOTAL GROSS PAY

Innovative computerised IT solutions now exist that allow companies to control labour costs and aim to minimise employee compliance risk and improve workforce productivity.

© CommercialCartoons/www.fotosearch.com

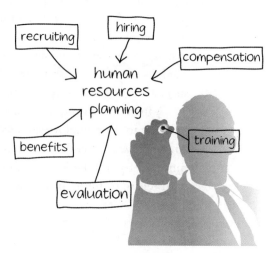

© michaeldb/www.fotosearch.com

Equality and Health and Safety Issues in the Workplace

What is NERA?

The National Employment Rights Authority (NERA) was established under the Social Partnership Agreement 'Towards 2016' to achieve a national culture of employment rights compliance.

NERA provides information to employees and employers through its information unit, monitors employment conditions through its inspection services and can enforce compliance and seek redress.

NERA covers many aspects of employment rights including:

- Wages
- Holidays and Public Holidays
- Working Hours (Organisation of Working Time Act 1997)
- Redundancy
- Dismissal
- Notice.

Refer to **www.employmentrights.ie**.

What is Health, Safety and Welfare in the Workplace?

The Health and Safety Authority (HSA) is a state-sponsored body under the Department of Enterprise, Trade and Employment and has the overall responsibility for the administration and enforcement of health and safety at work in Ireland. It monitors compliance with legislation in the workplace and can take enforcement action, including prosecutions. The health and safety of people at work and of the public affected by work activities is protected by law in the Safety, Health and Welfare at Work Act 2005 (see below).

Employers have an obligation to their employees to ensure a safe work environment with no risks to health. Specific requirements regarding buildings are usually documented in a Safety Statement, which must be made available on request to health and safety inspectors and to employees.

Workplace bullying is also a health and safety issue that can be challenged under the Safety, Health and Welfare at Work Act 2005.

What is the Safety, Health and Welfare at Work Act 2005?

This Act provides for the health and safety of people in the workplace. It is an update on the 1989 Act. It applies to all organisations' employers and employees (including fixed-term and temporary employees) and self-employed people in their workplaces. The Act sets out the rights and obligations of both employers and employees and provides for substantial fines and penalties for breaches of the health and safety legislation.

It contains a list of the following areas for which legal requirements are laid down by the Act:

- Employer's duties.
- Employees' duties.
- Risk assessment and safety statement.
- Protective equipment measures (e.g. for display screen equipment (VDUs)).
- Reporting accidents.
- Health and safety leave (Maternity Protection Act 1994).
- Health and safety and young people.
- Violence in the workplace.
- Bullying (employer and employee code of practice/prevention and resolution of bullying at work).
- Harassment (Employment Equality Acts 1998 and 2004).
- Victimisation.

The Health and Safety Authority (HSA) is responsible for enforcing health and safety at work in Ireland. It provides information to employers, employees and self-employed people on workplace health and safety.

Refer to A Short Guide to The Safety, Health and Welfare at Work Act 2005 at **www.hsa.ie** for further information.

What is Employment Equality?

This is defined as the right, which all workers in the country have, to be treated equally and not to be the subject of employment discrimination.

The Equality Authority is an independent state body in Ireland. It was set up in 1999 to replace the Employment Equality Agency. It provides information to the public on equality legislation and it can, at its discretion, provide legal assistance to people who wish to bring claims to the Equality Tribunal. The Circuit Court deals with claims about gender discrimination.

There are two main pieces of legislation in place in Ireland that set out important rights for citizens and outlaw discrimination when it occurs. They are the Employment Equality Act 1998 (amended 2004) and the Equal Status Act 2000, as amended by the Equality Act 2004. (These Acts are explained below.)

Anyone providing employment opportunities, services or agencies where the public have access must not discriminate on any of nine distinct grounds:

- Gender
- Marital status
- Family status
- Sexual orientation

- Religion
- Age (does not apply to a person under 16)
- Disability
- Race
- Membership of the Traveller community.

Discrimination is described in the Equal Status Act 2000 as the treatment of a person in a less favourable way than another person is, has been or would be treated on any of the above grounds.

Equality Issues/Definitions

What is Positive Action?

Employers have in recent years been encouraged to establish policies and procedures to show that they are taking reasonable steps to demonstrate their commitment to equality and to avoid discrimination in the work environment. Usually these policies and procedures are documented in the form of an equal opportunities policy and grievance procedures (employee complaints procedures) in an employees' handbook, which is usually available from an organisation's human resources department.

Many employers promote 'positive action' by organising anti-racism, anti-harassment and anti-bullying training for staff. The aim is to comply with equality legislation and to avoid discrimination.

For further information refer to **www.eurofound.europa.eu/emire/ireland/positiveaction-ir.**

Definitions of Equality and Ethnicity, Racism and Cultural Diversity

An **ethnic group** is defined by a common identity, kinship, ancestry, culture, history or tradition. The Traveller community is still Ireland's largest ethnic minority, though in recent years immigration has created a multi-ethnic Ireland. Ethnic groups can sometimes be defined on the basis of having a common religion or language, e.g. Protestants and Catholics in Northern Ireland.

- **Ethnicity** describes the membership of a particular racial, national or cultural group and observance of that group's customs, beliefs and language. Ethnic groups can co-exist comfortably with other ethnic groups, e.g. the Chinese community in New York.
- **Racial and religious equality** means promoting equality between different races and people of different religious beliefs, and respecting and understanding cultural diversity, religion and customs.
- **Gender equality** means promoting equality between the sexes.
- **Age equality** means promoting equality for the over-50s.

- **Disability equality** means promoting equality for the disabled.
- **Sexual orientation equality** means promoting equality for non-heterosexual workers (gays, lesbians, bisexuals and transgendered people).
- **Equality regarding marital and family status** means promoting equality for men, women and children in the home.

Workplace Bullying and Sexual Harassment

Sexual harassment is defined as 'unwanted conduct of a sexual nature or other conduct based on sex affecting the dignity of women and men at work'.

Bullying means verbal, physical or psychological aggression engaged in by an employer against employees or by an employee or a group of employees against another employee. It can take the form of intimidation, isolation, victimisation, exclusion, shouting, abusive behaviour, constant criticism or nagging, verbal threats, physical threats, humiliation, excessive controlling behaviour, unreasonable behaviour or task assignment, or posters, banners, emails and emblems that cause offence.

Union Representation in the Workplace

A union is a group of workers who make representations for common work entitlements regarding pay and conditions in the workplace. There are three main types of union:

1. Craft unions – skilled workers, e.g. the Irish Print Union.
2. White collar unions – professional, office and service occupations, e.g. the Teachers' Union of Ireland (TUI).
3. General unions – semi-skilled and unskilled workers, e.g. Services, Industrial, Professional and Technical Union (SIPTU).

The Irish Congress of Trade Unions (ICTU) is the umbrella organisation for most of the bigger unions in Ireland and it represents employees at the social partnership talks. These are talks between government representatives, employer representatives (e.g. IBEC and SFA) and other interested groups, such as the Combat Poverty agency. Pay structures and work conditions are recommended and negotiated and usually a National Wage Agreement (e.g. Partnership 2000) is secured for workers. Public sector workers such as nurses and civil servants are promised incremental pay increases.

Minimum Wage

This is the minimum a worker can legally be paid (usually per hour), in contrast to wages that are determined by the forces of supply and demand in a free market. In most cases, the minimum wage acts as a price floor. Each country sets its own minimum wage laws and regulations, and many countries have no minimum wage. The current minimum wage in Ireland is €8.65 per hour.

New minimum wage rate for Ireland

24 November 2010

Finance minister Brian Lenihan (deceased) confirmed today that Ireland's minimum wage will be reduced to €7.65 per hour.

The €1 an hour reduction from the previous rate of €8.65 was announced today as part of the Government's four-year National Recovery Plan. The change will be effective almost immediately.

The Government said the higher rate of €8.65 was a barrier to job creation, especially for younger, less-skilled workers where unemployment rates were highest.

It was also noted that the €7.65 per hour remains among the highest minimum wage in Europe.

Source: www.businessandleadership.com/economy/item/26885-new-minimum-wage-rate-for

Rates of pay in the Republic of Ireland

PAYMENT OF WAGES

All employees are entitled by law to a payslip. This allows you to check over your total pay before tax and all details of any deductions made from your pay.

RATES OF PAY

- The minimum wage rate for an experienced adult employee is currently €8.65 from 1 July 2011. An experienced adult employee is defined as being over 18 and working for two years or more. The reduced 2011 rate will not apply to current employees; only employees employed after the introduction of the reduced wage.
- The minimum wage, however, doesn't apply to young people under 18 or people in training. If you are **under 18**, the minimum wage is €6.06 per hour.
- From age 18 onwards, you should be paid €6.92 per hour in your first year of employment and €7.79 per hour in your second year of employment.

The National Minimum Wage law does **not** apply to:

- Anyone under 18.
- Anyone employed by a close relative.
- Those serving apprenticeships (training).

WHEN WILL I QUALIFY FOR THE NATIONAL MUNIMUM RATE?

You are automatically entitled to the minimum rate per hour once you have been working for two years at any time over the age of 18.

WHAT CAN BE INCLUDED TO MAKE UP MY PAY?

- Your basic pay.
- Commissions and bonuses which are related to productivity.
- Board and lodgings (if you receive them).

WHAT CAN'T BE INCLUDED?

In restaurant and bar jobs, tips cannot be used by employers to calculate the hourly wage level. Other payments that cannot be included are:

* 'Overtime premium'.
* 'Sunday and public holiday premium'.
* 'Unsociable hours premium'.

Refer to **www.spunout.ie.**

Equal Opportunities in Employment

Employers are legally obliged to adhere to the existing equality legislation when hiring and employing staff, whether they are full-time or part-time. When you are an employee or a prospective candidate your employer **cannot discriminate** against you in any of the following ways:

* **Recruitment procedure**: A discriminatory manner or discriminatory questions during the interview. (You have a right to information through an equality officer if you suspect discrimination has or is taking place.)
* **Access to Employment**: By having different entry requirements for you and for other applicants.
* **Conditions of Employment**: Unequal terms of employment and work conditions, overtime, shift work, transfers or dismissals (except remuneration).
* **Training, Work Experience**: Your employer must provide the same opportunities or facilities for employment counselling and training and work experience as those offered to other employees in similar circumstances.
* **Promotion or Re-grading**: The same access to promotional opportunities must be allowed by your employer as is allowed to similarly qualified or other candidates.

Rights and Responsibilities of Employees and Employers' Obligations and Responsibilities

The main duties of the employee are:

* To be available for work and provide a good service.
* To obey orders from superiors/employers.
* To exercise their work duties with diligence and an acceptable level of efficiency.
* To maintain confidentiality regarding company information.
* To be willing to compensate the employer for any damage caused or wrongful act committed.

The main duties of the employer are:

- To recognise equality issues – equal opportunities related to the workplace, i.e. gender, age, sexual orientation, ethnicity, race, marital status, etc.
- To ensure employees are treated appropriately in the workplace. (Most businesses are covered by full public liability insurance.)
- To adhere to the safety, health and welfare legislation.
- To respect employees' representation by their trade unions.
- To pay employees at an appropriate wage level as agreed by the social partners in national agreements such as Partnership 2000. The social partners include the Government, the Irish Congress of Trade Unions (ICTU), the Irish Business and Employers Confederation (IBEC), the Irish Tourist Industry Confederation (ITIC), the Small Firms Association (SFA), etc.
- To inform workers of their rights regarding their terms of employment by providing employees with a written statement of these terms.
- To provide workers with appropriate minimum notice before the termination of a contract of employment.

The Employer

The following is a checklist of the Irish Employment Acts that apply to the employer:

- Unfair Dismissals Acts 1977-1993
- Payment of Wages Act 1991
- Terms of Employment (Information) Act 1994
- Maternity Protection Act 1995
- Adoptive Leave Act 1995
- Organisation of Working Time Act 1997
- Employment Equality Act 1998.

IRISH EMPLOYMENT ACTS THAT APPLY TO THE EMPLOYER

Equality	Working Hours	Health and Safety
Equality Act 2004 Employment Equality Act 1998 – This Act replaced the Anti Discrimination (Pay) Act 1974 and the Employment Equality Act 1997.	Organisation of Working Time Act 1997.	Safety Health and Welfare at Work Acts 1989 and 2005. General Application Regulations 1993, implementing the EC Framework Directive of 1989.

Maternity Leave	Adoptive Leave	Parental Leave/Force Majeure Leave	Part-Time Employees	Protection of Young Persons
Maternity Protection Act 1994	Adoptive Leave Act 1995	Parental Leave Act 1998	Worker Protection (Regular Part-Time Employees) Act 1991	Protection of Young Persons (Employment) Act 1996

Terms of Employment	Redundancy	Dismissal
Terms of Employment (Information) Act 1994	Redundancy Payments Acts 1967-1991	Unfair Dismissals Acts 1977-1993

Minimum Notice	Disciplinary Procedures	Trade Unions
Minimum Notice and Terms of Employment Acts 1973 & 1991	Labour Relations Commission Code of Practice on Disciplinary Procedures and see LRC website www.lrc.ie	Industrial relations issues are dealt with under the Industrial Relations Acts 1946-1990 and see www.ictu.ie.

What are Employee's Rights?

As an employee, you are entitled to receive certain basic employment rights. Although some industries entitle employees to different rights, the list below is the minimum you should receive.

- **A written statement of terms and conditions of employment:** Whilst the full contract does not have to be in writing, certain terms and conditions of your employment must be stated in writing within two months of starting employment. These would typically include the method of calculating pay and whether or not there is a sick pay scheme in operation. (For fixed-term employees, it would also include in what circumstances your employment will come to an end.)
- **A written statement of pay or 'payslip':** The payslip should set out gross pay and list all the deductions made from it.
- **A minimum wage:** Most experienced adult workers in Ireland are entitled to be paid €8.65 per hour. There are, however, some exceptions to the minimum wage, including those employed by close relatives, people aged under 18 and trainees or apprentices.

There are also certain industries in Ireland where a higher minimum wage applies, including the construction industry.

- **A maximum working week average of 48 hours a week:** The maximum 48-hour week is based on an average calculated over a four-, six-, or twelve-month period, depending on the industry. Your employer must keep a record of how many hours you work.
- **Unpaid breaks during working hours:** You have the right to a 15-minute break if working four and a half hours and a 30-minute break if working six hours.
- **Annual leave from work:** Full-time workers have the right to four working weeks paid annual leave per year. Part-time workers have the right to a proportional amount of annual leave based on the amount of time they work.
- **A minimum amount of notice before dismissal:** You are entitled to a minimum amount of notice if your employment ceases. The minimum amount of notice depends on the length of service.

Source: www.employmentrights.ie.

Note: This information is for information purposes only and is not a legal interpretation.

Employment Law Update (1993–2007)

If you have been out of the workforce in Ireland for some time, you will need to update yourself on changes that have occurred in the field of employment protection. The last decade has seen substantial changes and acquainting yourself with these developments will help you to maximise your rights.

Employment protection developments 1993–2007

The following is a summary of the legislation that has been introduced in this period concerning employment protection:

- *Employment Permits Act 2006.* This Act updates the Employment Permits Act 2003, introducing the Green Card permit and revising the legislation on work permits and spousal permits.
- *Employees (Provision of Information and Consulation) Act 2006.* This legislation sets established minimum requirements for employees' right to information and consultation about the development of their employment's structure and activities. From 4 September 2006 it applies to employers with at least 150 employees, from 23 March 2007 to those with 100 employees and from 23 March 2008 to those with at least 50 employees.

- *Safety, Health and Welfare at Work Act 2005.* This legislation replaced the provisions of the Safety, Health and Welfare Act 1989 when it came into operation on 1 September 2005. It consolidates and updates the existing health and safety law. Changes include the provision for higher fines for breaches of safety legislation.
- *Maternity Protection (Amendment) Act 2004.* This legislation made significant improvements to previous maternity protection legislation including new provisions relating to ante-natal classes, additional maternity leave, breastfeeding, reduction in compulsory period of pre-birth confinement, etc.
- *Equality Act 2004.* This legislation makes significant amendments to the Employment Equality Act 1998 such as providing for extension of the age provisions of that Act to people under the school leaving age (from 16) and those over 65 years. It also amends the Equal Status Act 2000 to extend the definition of sexual harassment and shift the burden of proof from the complainant to the respondent.
- *Protection of Employees on Transfer of Undertakings Regulations 2003.* This legislation applies to any transfer of an undertaking, business or part of a business from one employer to another employer as a result of a legal transfer (including the assignment or forfeiture of a lease) or merger. Employees' rights and entitlements are protected during this transfer.
- *Protection of Employees (Fixed Term Work) Act 2003.* This legislation protects fixed-term employees by ensuring that they cannot be treated less favourably than comparable permanent workers and that employers cannot continually renew fixed term contracts. Under the Act employees can only work on one or more fixed term contracts for a continuous period of four years. After this the employee is considered to have a contract of indefinite duration (e.g. a permanent contract).
- *Organisation of Working Time (Records) (Prescribed Form and Exemptions) Regulations 2001.* The main purpose of this EU Regulation is the requirement by employers to keep a record of the number of hours worked by employees on a daily and weekly basis, to keep records of leave granted to employees in each week as annual leave or as public holidays and details of the payments in respect of this leave. Employers must also keep weekly records of starting and finishing times of employees.
- *Protection of Employees (Part-Time Work) Act 2001* – this replaces the Worker Protection (Regular Part-Time Employees) Act 1991. It provides for the removal of discrimination against part-time workers where such exists. It aims to improve the quality of part-time work, to facilitate the development of part-time work on a voluntary basis and to contribute to the flexible organisation of working time in a manner that takes account of the needs of employers and workers. It guarantees that part-time workers may not be treated less favourably than full-time workers.
- *Carer's Leave Act 2001* – this provides for an entitlement for employees to avail of temporary unpaid carer's leave to enable them to care personally for persons who require full-time care and attention.

- *National Minimum Wage Act 2000* – introduces an enforceable national minimum wage.
- *Employment Equality Act 1998* – prohibits discrimination in a range of employment-related areas. The prohibited grounds of discrimination are gender, marital status, family status, age, race, religious belief, disability, sexual orientation and membership of the Traveller community. The Act also prohibits sexual and other harassment.
- *Parental Leave Act 1998* – provides for a period of unpaid parental leave for parents to care for their children and for a limited right to paid leave in circumstances of serious family illness (force majeure).
- *Organisation of Working Time Act 1997* – regulates a variety of employment conditions including maximum working hours, night work, annual and public holiday leave.
- *Protection of Young Persons (Employment) Act 1996* – replaced previous legislation dating from 1977 and regulates the employment and working conditions of children and young persons.
- *Adoptive Leave Act 1995* – provides for adoptive leave from employment principally by the adoptive mother and for her right to return to work following such leave.
- *Terms of Employment (Information) Act 1994* – updated previous legislation relating to the provision by employers to employees of information on such matters as job description, rate of pay and hours of work.
- *Maternity Protection Act 1994* – replaced previous legislation and covers matters such as maternity leave, the right to return to work after such leave and health/safety during and immediately after the pregnancy.
- *Unfair Dismissals Act 1993* – updates unfair dismissals law and amends previous legislation dating from 1977.

Complaints/Breach of Rights

Employment law in Ireland provides strong protection for employees who feel their rights have been breached. Complaints, disputes and grievances are heard before a Rights Commissioner who will listen to both sides before completing an investigation of the complaint and issuing a recommendation. Recommendations issued by the Rights Commissioner can be binding or non-binding, depending on the type of law under which the case is heard.

Claims under equality legislation are brought to the Equality Tribunal.

Often, disputes between employers and employees can be resolved using mediation. Mediation means that the Labour Relations Commission is contacted and appoints an independent person to meet with both parties and listen to both sides. This free service is available to all employees and employers (except members of the Gardaí, Defence Forces and Prison Services). Meetings are held privately and all discussions are confidential.

How to apply

Requests for mediation services should be made to the Workplace Mediation Service at the Labour Relations Commission.

Complaints, disputes or grievances regarding breaches of employment rights under certain legislation can be heard before a Rights Commissioner. Before you apply to have your complaint heard, you must notify your employer of your intention to contact the Rights Commissioner service. Where legal entitlements are involved, you should try and resolve the matter locally before referring to the Rights Commissioner service.

The application forms must be completed and forwarded to the Labour Relations Commission in advance of a hearing before a Rights Commissioner.

Source: www.citizensinformation.ie

The C and A Machinery

This refers to the processes of Conciliation and Arbitration.

Conciliation is the attempt by a third party to help in the settlement of an industrial dispute by hearing all sides of the dispute and suggesting terms for settlement. The Labour Relations Commission provides a conciliation service.

Arbitration is a way of settling a dispute when both parties to the dispute request a third party to make a decision that they both agree to accept. This would come under the auspices of the Labour Court. Most disputes are settled by conciliation and there is a general unwillingness to refer disputes to arbitration.

The state provides the following specific institutions (all of which have various responsibilities for matters concerning employee relations) that are underpinned by current legislation. Employees can seek help with the appropriate institution to resolve problems that occur in connection with their workplace and/or in connection with alleged discrimination by management against employees in their workplace.

The Labour Relations Commission (LRC)

The purpose of the LRC is 'to promote the development and improvement of Irish industrial relations policies, procedures and practices through the provision of appropriate, timely and effective services to employers, trade unions and employees'. The Labour Relations Commission provides a range of industrial relations advisory and mediation services to meet the needs of employers, employees and their representatives:

The main services are:
- The Conciliation Service
- The Advisory Service Division
- The Rights Commissioner Service
- The Workplace Mediation Service
- Chairing of Joint Industrial Councils (JICs) and Joint Labour Committees (JLCs).

The Minister for Enterprise, Trade and Employment appoints Rights Commissioners on the recommendation of the Labour Relations Commission. They operate as a service of the LRC and are independent in their functions. Rights Commissioners investigate disputes, grievances and claims that individuals or small groups of workers refer under Acts such as the Adoptive Leave Acts 1995 to 2005, Carers Leave Act 2001, Employees (Information and Consultation) Act 2006, Employment Permits Acts 2003 and 2006, Industrial Relations Acts 1969–1990, Industrial Relations (Miscellaneous Provisions) Act 2004, Maternity Protection Acts 1994 and 2004, National Minimum Wage Act 2000, Organisation of Working Time Act 1997, Parental Leave Acts 1998 and 2006, Payment of Wages Act 1991, Protection of Employees (Fixed-Term Work) Act 2003, Protection of Employees (Part-Time Work) Act 2001, Protection of Young Persons (Employment) Act 1996, Safety, Health and Welfare at Work Act 2005, Terms of Employment (Information) Acts 1994 and 2001, Unfair Dismissals Acts 1977 to 2007.

Statutory instruments on a European front include the European Communities (Protection of Employment) Regulations 2000, the European Communities (Protection of Employees on Transfer of Undertakings) Regulations 2003 and the European Communities (European PLC) (Employee Involvement) Regulations 2006.

Advisory services also exist and work with employers, employees and trade unions in non-dispute situations to develop effective industrial relations practices, procedures and structures that best meet their needs. Codes of practice are instruments drafted and put in place by the government to outline recommended practice in certain contexts. While not having the force of law, they can be taken into account in the course of proceedings touching on relevant issues. Section 42 of the Industrial Relations Act 1990 makes provisions for the preparation of draft Codes of Practice by the Labour Relations Commission for submission to the Minister for Enterprise, Trade and Employment.

Refer to www.ibec.ie.

Rights Commissioners Service

The Minister for Enterprise, Trade and Employment appoints Rights Commissioners on the recommendation of the Labour Relations Commission. They operate as a service of the LRC and are independent in their functions. Rights Commissioners investigate disputes, grievances and claims that individuals or small groups of workers refer under legislation with Acts, which include Adoptive Leave Acts 1995 to 2005, Carers Leave Act 2001, Employees (Information & Consultation) Act 2006, Employment Permits Acts 2003 and 2006, Industrial Relations Acts 1969–1990, Industrial Relations (Miscellaneous Provisions) Act 2004, Maternity Protection Acts 1994 and 2004, National Minimum Wage Act 2000, Organisation of Working Time Act 1997, Parental Leave Acts 1998 and 2006, Payment of Wages Act 1991, Protection of Employees (Fixed-Term Work) Act 2003, Protection of Employees (Part-Time Work) Act 2001, Protection of Young Persons (Employment) Act 1996, Safety, Health and Welfare at Work Act 2005, Terms of Employment (Information) Acts 1994 and 2001, and Unfair Dismissals Acts 1977 to 2007. (Refer to www.basis.ie and www.citizensinformation.ie for details on Irish employment acts.)

Statutory instruments on the European front include the European Communities (Protection of Employment) Regulations 2000, the European Communities (Protection of Employees on Transfer of Undertakings) Regulations 2003 and the European Communities (European PLC) (Employee Involvement) Regulations 2006.

Rights Commissioners issue the findings of their investigations in the form of either decisions or non-binding recommendations, depending on the legislation under which a case is referred.

What is the Equality Tribunal?

The Equality Tribunal (also known as the Office of the Director of Equality Investigations) is an impartial body set up by law to decide or mediate complaints under equality legislation. Its functions are quasi-judicial. It hears or mediates claims of unlawful discrimination under the equality legislation. A Tribunal Mediator will facilitate parties to reach a mediated agreement, which is legally binding. Where parties object to mediation, a case will be heard by a Tribunal Equality Officer, who will hear evidence from both parties before issuing a legally binding decision. Where the Tribunal upholds a claim of discrimination, it awards redress and it can direct a person to take a specific action.

What is the Employment Appeals Tribunal?

The Employment Appeals Tribunal is an independent body established to provide a speedy, inexpensive and relatively informal means for adjudicating disputes on employment rights underpinned by various legislation that comes within the Tribunal's scope.

A claim is referred to the Tribunal by way of a completed form containing a statement of the facts and contentions on which the appellant (the person making the claim) intends to rely. There are two types of applications to the Tribunal:

- A direct claim
- An appeal from the Rights Commissioner Service.

Following receipt of a claim, the details are sent to the respondent (the person or company against whom a claim is being made). The respondent is given 14 days to respond to the claim and to complete a notice of appearance. All correspondence to and from both parties is copied to both the appellant and respondent. It is in the appellant's interest to supply as much supporting documentation with his/her claim as possible.

The Tribunal Secretariat sets a date for a hearing and communicates this to both parties. A three-member division of the Tribunal will hear the case. The division will consist of a chairperson, one member representing an employers' group and one member representing the trade union movement.

A party to a claim may appear and be heard in person or may be represented by counsel or a solicitor or by a representative of a trade union or of an employers' organisation, or with the leave of the Tribunal, by any other person.

Following the hearing of the case, the Tribunal will make a determination, which is recorded in a document signed by the chairperson and sealed with the seal of the Tribunal. Written determinations are final and conclusive, subject only to the appropriate avenue of legal appeal to the higher courts

Workplace Mediation Service

Mediation provides an opportunity for those involved to address the issues, explore options and reach a workable outcome through a mutually agreeable course of action. The process is flexible and can be adapted depending on individual situations, but essentially revolves around giving every individual concerned an opportunity to give their side of the story and to work with the other party to find a solution. The process may involve a mix of joint meetings or meetings with the mediator alone. The entire process is focused on every individual involved being comfortable with the process and on the active exploration of potential solutions.

The Labour Court

The Labour Court was established to provide a free, comprehensive service for the resolution of disputes about industrial relations, equality, organisation of working time, national minimum wage, part-time work and fixed-term work matters. In most cases, referral of the case to the Labour Court does not have to be initiated by the parties (i.e. the referral will be made, at the request of the parties, by the Labour Relations Commission).

PRACTICE QUESTIONS

1. Name and briefly explain the main legal Acts that protect employee rights under current legislation.
2. Name the *three* institutional frameworks from which employees can seek help when problems occur in connection with their workplace.
3. What are the functions of the Labour Relations Commission?
4. What are the functions of the Rights Commissioner?
5. How is the right to equality protected under current legislation?
6. What are the functions of the Labour Court?
7. What are the functions of the Employment Appeals Tribunal?

A Brief History of the Trade Union Movement

The concept of trade unionism established itself in the mid-nineteenth century. In Ireland James Larkin founded the ITGWU (Irish Transport and General Workers' Union) in 1909. Employees were poor and dissatisfied with their wages and conditions of employment. Larkin called for a strike in the Dublin Tramways Company in August 1913. Employers locked all ITGWU members out of their places of work. By September 1913, 25,000 people were locked out in Dublin, aptly named the '1913 Lock-out'. This incident marked the beginning of the trade union movement in Ireland.

The Role of a Trade Union in the Workplace at Branch and National Level

A trade union is defined as 'a continuous association of wage earners with the objective of improving or maintaining conditions of employment'. Trade unions fall into three broad groups: employee associations (e.g. SIPTU), employer associations (e.g. IBEC) and trade associations (e.g. the Irish Nurses Organisation, INO).

Employee trade unions are further categorised into three main types in Ireland: Craft unions, General unions, and White Collar unions.

CRAFT UNIONS: are trade unions that protect workers that are in the 'skilled' category. Workers must have a period of apprenticeship appropriate to their work before they will be accepted into the union. Examples of Craft unions are the Electrical Trade Union and the Irish Print Union.

GENERAL UNIONS: are trade unions that cater for semi-skilled and unskilled workers and attract members from different industries. The main general union is the Services, Industrial, Professional and Technical Union (SIPTU), discussed below.

WHITE COLLAR UNIONS: are trade unions catering for professional, office and service occupations. Examples of these unions are the Teachers' Union of Ireland (TUI), Association of Secondary Teachers of Ireland (ASTI), Irish National Teachers' Organisation (INTO) and the National Union of Journalists (NUJ).

The main objectives of trade unions are:

1. To unite employees who have common interests.
2. To secure improvements in members' conditions of employment and rates of pay through negotiation with employers and the government. (Refer to 'Social Partners and Collective Bargaining' discussed below.)
3. To maintain agreed conditions of employment, which include making sure that promises of any pay increases are honoured.
4. To negotiate on behalf of members when disputes arise.
5. To protect their members and strive to ensure security of their jobs.
6. To provide a mechanism allowing members to express any job dissatisfaction and to highlight any developments at local level that might conflict with their job specification and job description (defined earlier).
7. To minimise exploitation of workers.
8. To control activities of members and discipline them if necessary.
9. To provide members with other services like information services regarding pension rights, car insurance schemes and advice regarding any areas of doubt concerning union directives.
10. Training courses for union representatives.

Social Partners and Collective Bargaining

The Social Partners, that is, the unions (on behalf of employees), employers and government representatives collectively discuss and negotiate issues concerning conditions of employment and pay revisions. This is referred to as Collective Bargaining. It replaces individual bargaining, which is generally not very effective and would fail to secure agreement with management on many issues. The conflicts of interest that usually exist between management and workers are best ironed out using the collective bargaining mechanism.

There is no constitutional provision for trade union recognition. This means that employers that are not part of any union themselves are not obliged to recognise employee grievances that are highlighted via the employee trade union.

Why should employers recognise trade unions?

The employee's right to be represented by the union will:

1. Be beneficial for the employee, providing a good degree of security that will lead to better work effort and job satisfaction.
2. Be beneficial for the employee, as it is possible to have proper negotiations over pay and working conditions.
3. Be beneficial for the employer, placing management into a good position to influence union attitudes. There is the possibility for management to create a good atmosphere in the firm by being seen to be fair with regard to decision-making.
4. Be good for the business itself, as a framework exists that can be used to sort out disputes.
5. Minimise the risk of strikes and the occurrences of work-to-rule situations.
6. Be good for all parties, as it imposes certain defined conditions on the conduct of business activities.

Organisations Representing Employees, Employers and the Unemployed

IRISH BUSINESS AND EMPLOYERS' FEDERATION (IBEC)

The Federation of Irish Employers (FIE) and the Confederation of Irish Industry decided to amalgamate in 1993 to form IBEC, the largest employer association in Ireland.

Functions:

1. It represents employers when the Social Partners (unions, employers and government) meet to discuss economic issues and employee/employer disagreements and disputes.
2. IBEC representatives attend important conferences which deal with issues that directly affect employers, and report back to their members who number over 4,000.
3. Economic and Social Policy (involving grant-aid for investment) is a main area of interest and IBEC represents Ireland when representatives take part in meetings of the Union of Industry and Employer Confederations in Europe (UNICE) and at meetings of the European Trade Union Confederation (ETUC) on behalf of its members.
4. It carries out research on behalf of employers.
5. It provides a consultancy service and advises employers on issues like health and safety.
6. It produces publications and provides training for employers.

IRISH SMALL AND MEDIUM ENTERPRISES ASSOCIATION (ISME)

ISME is the main small business lobby group (privately funded) in Ireland that has an input into Social Partner discussions (e.g. National Wage Agreements, Partnership 2000, Towards 2016). It discusses economic issues and other issues that might affect small and medium-sized businesses with the managers of those businesses and with the other Social Partners. It keeps its members up to date with newsletters.

ISME works in close co-operation with the Minister and with 'Enterprise Ireland' the body set up by the Minister, which aims to further promote small and medium-sized indigenous (home) industry.

SMALL FIRMS ASSOCIATION (SFA)

The Small Firms Association represents and provides economic, commercial, employee relations and social affairs advice and assistance to small and medium enterprises (SMEs). There are 7,000 member companies. Information packs on health and safety requirements in the workplace, management training and development, discount schemes, IT management, business and economic trends and employee relations are available to meet the needs of small and medium companies.

Employees are also entitled to be members of an affiliated trade union that represents the employees of that organisation. Employees can make their grievances known through their trade union representatives and can pursue matters until satisfactory resolutions are found.

SERVICES, INDUSTRIAL, PROFESSIONAL AND TECHNICAL UNION (SIPTU)

The beginning of the 1990s saw the birth of a new union, SIPTU, when on 1 January 1990 the amalgamation of the ITGWU and FWUI took place. SIPTU is by far the largest trade union in Ireland. Members of the Irish Transport and General Workers' Union (ITGWU) and the Federated Workers' Union of Ireland (FWUI) were balloted in November 1989 and the amalgamation was the result of the ballot. Other membership groups have been accommodated within the SIPTU structure without difficulty, retaining their distinctive characters, while at the same time benefiting from the additional resources, services and protection that the SIPTU umbrella provides. Groups accommodated in this way were:

- Federation of Rural Workers
- Irish Advertising and Design Associates
- Irish Agricultural Advisory Organisation
- Irish National Painters' and Decorators' Trade Union
- Local Authority Professional Officers
- Medical Laboratory Technologists' Association
- National Association of Transport Employees
- Racing Board Tote Staff Association.

Many other groups of employees are affiliated to and represented by the trade union:

- Association of Artists Ireland
- Association of Irish Composers
- Irish Actors Equity
- Society of Irish Playwrights
- Employees in banking, clerical, administrative, supervisory, sales, hotel/catering and many other occupations.

IRISH NATIONAL ORGANISATION FOR THE UNEMPLOYED (INOU)

This is the lobby group that represents the interests of both the short-term and the long-term unemployed in Ireland. It has significant input into Social Partner discussions and national wage agreements like Partnership 2000. Changing economic circumstances like decisions taken by both the private sector (firms and businesses) and the public sector (government) are the concern of the INOU if they are seen to be a future cause of unemployment. The privatisation of companies (decisions to sell government-owned companies to private firms) can be a major cause of unemployment, as can the proposed withdrawal of foreign companies (e.g. Digital) from the country. In recent years the INOU has had a greater input into decisions that have been made, in particular in relation to Partnership agreements.

Note: Refer to the section on Trade Union Operations at National Level under 'Features of Grievance Procedures' in the next section of this chapter for information on Partnership Agreements.

The Irish Congress of Trade Unions (ICTU)

This is the co-ordinating umbrella body to which many individual trade unions are affiliated. The congress itself is not a trade union, so it has no legal status.

Functions:

1. It provides a framework to co-ordinate the activities of trade unions in Ireland.
2. It consults with government on matters affecting industrial relations – wage agreements etc.
3. It represents collectively the trade union movement with regard to industrial relations, and legislative and administrative matters.
4. At the request of affiliated unions, it may negotiate at national level with employers' organisations on policy and principles relating to pay and conditions of employment.
5. It promotes unity within the trade union movement as a whole.
6. It aims to reconcile views and relationships of unions that have similar classes of workers in their membership.

7. It aims to encourage (in some situations) amalgamation of similar unions to help strengthen their structures.

8. It provides affiliated trade unions with advice and information such as legal advice and educational information and facilities.

Note: Some trade unions are registered with the Registrar of Friendly Societies (now under the control of IFSRA, the Financial Regulator). Some trade unions are registered with both the ICTU and the Registrar.

SAMPLE LIST

Trade Unions affiliated with the ICTU (Source: The Irish Congress of Trade Unions)	Trade Unions Registered with the Registrar of Friendly Societies (Source: The report on the Registry of Friendly Societies, Government Publications Office)
Amalgamated Engineering and Electrical Union Prison Officers' Association Association of Secondary Teachers Ireland (ASTI) Bakery and Food Workers' Amalgamated Union Irish National Teachers' Association (INTO) Mandate (The Union of Retail, Bar & Admin. Workers) Irish Nurses' Organisation National Union of Journalists Teachers' Union of Ireland (TUI) SIPTU National League of the Blind of Ireland	The Association of Electrical Contractors (Ire) Irish Hairdressers' Federation Irish Airline Pilots' Association Irish Bank Officials' Association Irish Postmasters' Union Irish Printing Federation Irish Taxi and Hackney Owners' Association Irish Veterinary Union Licensed Vintners' Association National Bus and Rail Union Retail Jewellers of Ireland

Many more organisations are listed in the source documents mentioned above.

Features of Grievance Procedures

Some trade unions operate at three different levels — workplace level, branch level and national level.

If an employee feels that he/she has been badly treated by colleagues, superiors or 'the system', he/she would:

(a) Bring the grievance to the attention of the workplace union representative/s.

(b) Arrange a meeting with the workplace manager/s.

(c) If a satisfactory resolution is not achieved at this stage the workplace representatives would bring the matter to the attention of the branch union representatives who would request a meeting with the manager/s.

(d) If a satisfactory agreement is not reached at this stage and if a head office governs the workplace, the branch–union representatives would request a meeting with the chief executive or executives based in the head office. (Note: Sometimes this stage structure does not apply depending on the type of organisational structure that exists.)

(e) Having found no resolution the branch representatives would then either:

1. put a strike action motion to the union branch committee that must be voted on; or

2. recommend that the employee refer the matter on to the Labour Relations Commission, which might refer it on to the Labour Court.

Trade Union operations at workplace level

Workplace union representatives are usually called shop stewards. They are elected by fellow staff union members. Their representation involves:

1. Posting union business and information received in the mail on the union bulletin board to keep members informed on current events within the union.

2. Providing staff that wish to join the union with application forms and information regarding subscriptions and collecting subscriptions when applicable. (Many union subs are collected using the DAS method, which means Deduction at Source. The subscriptions are taken directly from their wages, with their approval.)

3. Attending branch meetings approximately once a month and whenever other emergency or special meetings occur. Shop stewards are not paid to attend these meetings on behalf of members.

4. Liaising with union head office.

5. Negotiating with management and representing fellow members when disciplinary and grievance issues arise.

Trade Union operations at branch level

Branch representatives are usually part of the Branch Committee, which includes the Branch Secretary, the Branch Treasurer, and the Equality Officer. These members are elected at the union's AGM (Annual General Meeting). They are made up of employees from different organisations who are employed by the same body located in the same geographical area.

The business of the branch is:

1. To negotiate better terms and conditions for all branch members (all branches). This involves formally meeting with managers of different branches of the organisation to help negotiate fair and better conditions and to help resolve disputes that arise between individual members and management.

2. To manage the internal affairs of the union.

3. To make representations (put forward motions to improve members' pay and conditions) at the Annual Congress held once a year. Delegates who are to attend the Congress are elected at the AGM.

Trade Union operations at national level

Union officers are elected at the Annual Conference. The conference itself is the national forum where motions are put forward, resolutions are passed and union policy is determined. The union's National Executive is the body responsible for ensuring that decisions made at the conference each year are implemented. The people who head the union are full-time employees of the union – called General Officers. They are the President of the union, the Vice-President, the General Secretary, and the Union Treasurer.

THE NATIONAL UNION MEETING

This is a meeting of all the members of the union in the country and is referred to as a Congress or an Annual Conference. A specific number of delegates are put forward and elected from individual branches to attend the Congress and speak on (debate) motions in a public arena before a vote is taken to pass or reject these motions. The motions passed then become resolutions that are later discussed with the other Social Partners, i.e. employer representatives (IBEC, Irish Business and Employers' Confederation), and government representatives. Wage agreements like the Programme for National Recovery 1987, the Programme for Economic and Social Progress (PESP) 1991, and the Programme for Competitiveness and Work (PCW) 1994, were negotiated based on resolutions that were reached at Congress and the Annual Conferences.

Essential Ingredients of a Contract of Employment

A Contract of Employment is an offer in writing of:

(a) Temporary Employment – usually a fixed-term employment contract – usually a maximum commitment of three years or less; or

(b) Permanent Employment.

A temporary contract will contain a statement of the terms and conditions of employment broken down into:

(a) Nature of post of employment – temporary

(b) Duration of employment – annual fixed-term employment (or otherwise)

(c) Duties and extra duties required from time to time

(d)   Working hours

(e)   Salary

(f)   Travel and subsistence allowances (if applicable)

(g)   Holiday entitlements – also referred to as annual leave

(h)   Special leave – e.g. compassionate leave or exceptional circumstances

(i)   Sick leave entitlements

(j)   Notice of termination of employment

(k)   Maternity procedures and entitlements

(l)   Grievance and disciplinary procedures

(m)   Medical examinations (if applicable)

(n)   Declaration and signatures – employee and employer (counter signature)

A Permanent Contract will contain a statement including most of the terms and conditions mentioned above, but will usually also include Probation requirements.

What is the difference between piece-work payment and flat-rate payment?

- Piece-work payment means the employee is paid according to the volume or amount of work he or she completes.
- Flat-rate payment is payment per hour, per day, per week or per month. It is usually a salary-based type of payment.

A Sample Contract of Employment

Dear

We have a temporary vacancy in . . . . and I have pleasure in offering you temporary employment in this post.

A statement of your Terms and Conditions of Employment is enclosed. I should be grateful if you would signify your acceptance of the offer by signing the attached copy of this letter and <u>returning it to</u> . . . .

Your employment is temporary, commencing on Monday 19 June 2XXX and terminating on Friday 28 July 2XXX. The Unfair Dismissals Act 1977–1991 shall not apply to a termination consisting only of the expiry of this term without its being renewed.

Please report for work to . . . . at 9.00 a.m. on . . . . You should bring with you your Income Tax Form P45. As you will see from the attached Terms and Conditions, your salary will be paid monthly, one month in arrears. This payment will be made on the second Friday of each month for any employment with us during the previous month – therefore, you may be with us 6/7 weeks before you receive any payment. If this is likely to cause you any difficulty you should approach your Assistant Manager concerning the arrangement of advance payment of some of your salary.

If you are unable to start on that date, please contact me without delay. If you require further information or clarification on any aspect of this correspondence, please get in touch with myself at ext. . . . .

I would like to take this opportunity to wish you every success and happiness during your period of temporary employment with us.

Yours sincerely,

I accept the temporary position as offered. I acknowledge receipt of a statement of the general terms and conditions of my employment and Staff Rules. I have read these and I accept them as the terms and conditions of my contract of employment with . . . . . . I shall report for duty as requested.

SIGNED: _____   DATE _____

STATEMENT OF TERMS AND CONDITIONS OF EMPLOYMENT – REPUBLIC

1. ## NATURE OF EMPLOYMENT
   You will be employed on a temporary basis.

2. ## SECRECY
   You are required to treat all information gained as a result of your employment with . . . . . as strictly confidential, both during and after your employment with . . . . For this purpose you will be required to sign a Declaration of Secrecy Form.

3. ## WORKING HOURS
   The normal working week is from Monday to Friday inclusive.

   The normal working day may vary, but overtime is calculated on a daily basis in respect of each completed quarter-hour worked in excess of 7.25 hours (exclusive of one hour's lunch-break).

   Your normal starting and finishing times will be advised to you by your Manager/Head of Department.

   Payment for overtime work will be at such rates as are in force from time to time, and is based on completed quarter hours worked in excess of the normal day.

   (Details of eligibility and current overtime rates are available from Managers/Heads of Departments).

4. ## SALARY
   Your salary will be at the rate of . . . . . . per week payable monthly. In addition, overtime is payable at the current agreed rates, at present . . . . . per hour.

5. ## HOLIDAYS
   Provided you have worked at least 120 hours in a calendar month, you will be entitled to holidays at the rate of one and three quarters working days per month worked, this leave to be taken by agreement with your Manager/Head of Department but before six months continuous employment has elapsed.

   If you have worked less than 120 hours in a calendar month you will be entitled to 6 hours paid leave for every 100 hours worked and to proportionately less for periods of less than 100 hours worked provided:

   - you are normally expected to work at least 8 hours per day.
   - you have at least 13 weeks continuous service. These 13 weeks are not included when calculating annual leave entitlements.

   Holiday pay and payment in lieu of accrued holidays on termination of employment will be paid at the rate of . . . . . per day.

   You will be entitled to the same Bank/Public Holidays as permanent Officials, details of which are available from your Manager/Head of Department (if you have worked 120 hours in the 5 weeks preceding the holiday or have 13 weeks continuous employment and are normally expected to work more than 8 hours a week).

6. **<u>BENEFITS NOT APPLYING TO THIS EMPLOYMENT</u>**
You will not have entitlement to benefits applicable to permanent employees,

 e.g. – club subscriptions
     – pension benefits
     – staff loan facilities, etc.

7. **<u>SICK LEAVE</u>**
If you are unable to attend work because of illness, your Manager/Head of Department should be notified as early as possible on the first day.

Where you have cumulative service of one year or more you become entitled to paid certified sick leave up to a maximum of four weeks in any one year. However there will be no pay for absence due to sick leave during the first year of employment. You may be required to see the company doctors or a doctor nominated by the Bank at any stage during your employment. You will be entitled to see any medical report made at the request of the Bank and said report shall not be used by . . . . except for lawful purposes.

8. **<u>NOTICE OF TERMINATION OF EMPLOYMENT</u>**
The Minimum Notice and Terms of Employment Act 1973 will apply to notice of termination by . . . . or by you of your employment. The statutory minimum notice which must be given is one week. . . . . . . reserves the right to give payment in lieu of notice.

9. **<u>MATERNITY</u>**
The Maternity Protection of Employees Act 1981 shall apply to female temporary staff regarding maternity leave and the right to return to work. The requirements in each of sub sections (1) and (2) of Section 22 of the Act are mandatory. (Details available from Personnel Manager.)

10. **<u>GRIEVANCE AND DISCIPLINARY PROCEDURES</u>**
A listing of the principal staff rules is attached. Detailed Grievance and Disciplinary Procedures have been devised to ensure that fair and prompt arrangements exist for dealing with grievance or disciplinary matters. Grievance and Disciplinary Procedures will be provided on request.

11. **<u>ALTERATIONS IN TERMS AND CONDITIONS</u>**
Alterations in your Terms and Conditions of Employment will be advised, normally by general Circular or Memorandum to Branches/Departments, as they occur from time to time.

12. **<u>GENERAL</u>**
It is understood that you will perform, to the best of your ability, all duties assigned to you and will at all times obey all reasonable instructions given to you.

Data Protection Acts 1988 and 2003

The following individuals, firms and other bodies who keep personal information on computer are required to register:

- Public authorities and other public sector bodies
- Financial institutions, insurance companies and individuals or firms whose business consists wholly or mainly in direct marketing or direct mailing, providing credit references or collecting debts
- Any others who keep personal information on computer relating to racial origin, political opinions, religious or other beliefs, sexual life, criminal convictions or health (other than health information on employees kept in the ordinary course of personnel administration and not used or disclosed for any other purpose)
- Those whose business consists wholly or partly in processing personal data on behalf of others.

It is an offence for anyone who is required to register but has not done so to keep personal information on computer.

Note: All those who keep personal information on computer, whether or not they are required to register, must comply with the data protection provisions of the Act from that date.

Application forms for registration, notes on how to register and a Guide to the Act may be obtained from the Office of the Data Protection Commissioner, 74 St Stephen's Green, Dublin 2

The 2003 Act is an act to give effect to directive 95/46 EC of the European Parliament and of the Council of Europe of 24 October 1995 on the protection of individuals. This relates to the processing of personal data and on the free movement of such data, and to amend the Data Protection Act 1988 for that purpose and to provide for related matters.

Refer to: www.irishstatutebook.ie.

Territorial Application of the Data Protection Act

1. If a data controller is **based outside Ireland** and does not use any equipment for data processing (the processing of personal data) in Ireland and does not have any branches or agencies acting on its behalf in Ireland, the data controller is not subject to the Act.
2. If a data controller is **based in Ireland**, then the Act applies.
3. In unclear cases where headquarters are not in Ireland or are in Ireland but carry on all of their activities in other countries, the new European Communities (Data Protection) Regulations, 2001 allows for the replacement of section 23 of the Data Protection Act. In general the regulations apply only to data controllers

established 'in the state' – where equipment is used in Ireland. This does not include Northern Ireland.

4. In general, data controllers in EEA (European Economic Area) countries are subject to data protection laws in the EEA country in which they use equipment to process personal data and in which they are based.

The Services of the Irish Ombudsman

The Ombudsman deals with complaints against government departments, local authorities, the HSE and An Post. The first Ombudsman was appointed in 1984. Ombudsman is a Swedish word meaning 'representative of the people'.

The basis for the services provided by the Ombudsman is the Ombudsman Acts 1980 and 1984/1985. Important features of the Act are as follows:

1. The appointment is made by the President, and the office is held for six years.
2. The Ombudsman can be removed from office by the President due to misbehaviour, incapacity or bankruptcy and must vacate the office on reaching the age of 67 years.
3. The Ombudsman is empowered to make recommendations only – his or her findings are not binding and these recommendations are dealt with in private in the first instance to allow the body concerned to make their own representations.
4. He/she must report on the response of the body complained against and if a response to one of his/her recommendations is not satisfactory he/she may make a special report to the Oireachtas.
5. Excluded from investigation are:
   (a) Cases where the matter is before the courts or where a court decision is being appealed against.
   (b) Cases relating to recruitment or terms and conditions of employment (dealt with by LRC – Labour Relations Commission).
   (c) Cases relating to aliens or naturalisation (emigration).
   (d) Cases relating to prison pardons or sentences or court penalties.
   (e) Cases relating to the administration of prisons.
6. A minister of the government can request that a particular case not be investigated. The Ombudsman must cease his investigation immediately.

The European Ombudsman

The institution of the European Ombudsman was created by the Maastricht Treaty in 1992. The European Parliament elected the first European Ombudsman, Mr Jacob Soderman from Finland, in 1995.

The European Ombudsman investigates and reports on maladministration in the institutions and bodies of the European Community, such as the European Commission, the Council of the European Union and European Parliament based only on complaints made. Only the Court of Justice and the Court of First Instance do not fall within his jurisdiction. Any citizen of the European Union or resident in a member state can lodge a complaint. If an attempt at conciliation fails, the Ombudsman can make recommendations to solve the case. If a problem arises he/she can make a special report to the European Parliament.

Many complaints made to the European Ombudsman concern:

- Administrative delay, lack of transparency or refusal of access to information.
- Work relations between the institutions and their agents, recruitment of staff and the running of competitions.
- Contractual relations between the institutions and private firms, for example in case of abrupt termination of contract.

The European Ombudsman produces an Annual Report to the European Parliament and this is translated into all the official languages of the European Union. He also visits all member states.

PRACTICE QUESTIONS

1. Define the term 'Trade Union'.
2. There are *three* different types of employee unions. What are they?
3. What is the purpose of an employer association?
4. List *five* main objectives of trade unions.
5. Who are the Social Partners and how are they connected with Collective Bargaining?
6. List *three* benefits to employers of recognising trade unions.
7. What is ICTU? List *four* of its functions.
8. Explain the basic differences between the *three* levels at which Trade Unions operate.
9. Write notes on:
   (a) Shop Stewards
   (b) DAS.
10. A Trade Union's Annual Conference displays how it operates formally at National Level. Why is this meeting so important?
11. Give *five* reasons why documents are kept on file in the Human Resources Department.
12. What are the essential ingredients of a Contract of Employment?
13. What is the substance of the Data Protection Act 1998?
14. Write notes on the Ombudsman.

Ombudsman Publishes Case Reports

Date released: 10 January 2008

The Ombudsman, Emily O'Reilly, has today published details on her website of three complaints she has successfully resolved. The Ombudsman periodically publishes case reports on her website in order to further increase public awareness of the wide ranging work of her Office. These case reports will be of interest to public representatives and organisations which provide advice and support to the general public and will encourage them to bring the services of the Office of the Ombudsman to the attention of members of the public who need them.

The three cases now being published relate to the following:

A County Meath pensioner received backdated pension arrears of over €18,000 following a complaint to the Ombudsman. The man complained about the decision of the Department of Social and Family Affairs to award him a reduced pension (75% rate) due to an outstanding unpaid liability for self-employed insurance from 1988 to the date on which he qualified for a State Pension (Contributory). Having examined the Department's file, the Ombudsman did not find a basis to question the Department's decision. However, she noticed from the file that there were gaps in the complainant's social insurance record in the late 1960s. She got additional information from the complainant about his employment record at the time and then asked the Department to investigate whether replacement social insurance contributions were due to him. It turned out that he was due replacement contributions and this resulted in the payment of backdated pension arrears in excess of €18,000 to the man.

A farmer from County Meath will be €60,000 better off as a result of the Ombudsman's intervention in his complaint against the then Department of Agriculture and Food about his application to be accepted as a New Entrant for the Single Farm Payment scheme. In doing so, he asked the Department to exclude the reference years 2000 and 2001 as he would have gained financially if those years were not used for calculating his entitlements.

The Department declined to exclude the reference years in question as it deemed the applicant to be engaged in 'farming activity' during the period but the Ombudsman concluded that the Department had erred in its decision. As a result, the Department agreed to accept him as a New Entrant and excluded the years 2000–2001. The financial difference was very significant. He was granted an annual entitlement of €10,000 for the duration of the scheme (2005–2112). Provided he stays farming, the Ombudsman's intervention will mean a difference of approximately €60,000 to him over the period in question.

A fall of snow was the critical factor in the Ombudsman deciding that a complainant should not have been fined for parking on a yellow box in a car park. The complainant's car was ticketed in a Castlebar Town Council car park. She appealed the decision to the Council but was not successful. The complainant acknowledged that she may not have been parked in a designated parking space but maintained that on the day in question it was snowing and when she arrived at the car park the ground was covered with snow and there was no way of knowing the exact location of the designated parking spaces. Following the Ombudsman's examination of the facts she concluded that a refund should be granted and the Council agreed.

Source: www.ombudsman.gov.ie.

A Sample Student Trade Union Assignment

The Association of Secondary Teachers of Ireland (ASTI)
Compiled by Shane Creedon, Computer Applications and Business student in
Crumlin College 2006–2007

History of Trade Unionism and ASTI

In 1889, the first effort to organise unskilled workers into unions began. Craft unions
had been in place for 150 years before. By 1890, only 7,500 people had been
members of a union. It was slow to grow as owners were opposed to trade unions.
In Ireland, the Irish were concerned with the Land Question, so the rights of
individuals in towns and cities were ignored. People were slow to join, for fear of
being fired. In 1900, the union had more than 60,000 members who were involved
in strikes in Dublin, Cork, Belfast and Wexford.

In the twentieth century, wages were low and there was a lot of unemployment.
People knew that strikes could bring about change. The ITGWU was growing in
size and strikes brought about wage increases. The most notable strike was the 1913
Lock-out.

Trade unions were eventually accepted in the workplace. The membership was
growing, and a number of new, individual unions were being formed in the
workplace in the 1930s. This caused problems both for the workforce and
employers. Different unions wanted to strike for different reasons. There was great
rivalry between unions. A new body of trade unions was set up, the ICTU. This was
because, at a meeting of trade unions in London the ITGWU did not want to
breach Ireland's neutrality. So the ICTU was set up in 1959.

In the 1960s, there was economic growth, and white-collar unions were
beginning to grow. New companies were coming to Ireland and trade unions were
eventually accepted.

In the 1970s, all-out strikes were used to pursue demands. Also, national pay
agreements were introduced. This meant that unions could negotiate with employers.

The ASTI was founded in 1909. It was set up to achieve a system of registration,
an adequate salary scale, reasonable security of tenure and good service pensions. To
have their demands met, they launched a sophisticated lobbying campaign. In 1912,
parliament gave a grant for lay secondary school teachers' salaries of £40,000.
Registration and security provisions were made.

The Molony Committee recommended changes in administration financing.
They wanted wages increased from £180 to £450 per annum. The final offer was
a £40 increase for men and a £30 increase for women. In 1920 the ASTI had their
first strike. In 1923 the first annual delegation took place. In 1924 the Department
of Education was set up, and in 1929 the secondary school superannuation scheme
was set up. The union eventually succeeded in getting a registration of teachers, and
an eight to twelve per cent salary increase. Membership has grown to 14,236 in 1994
and there is now job security for teachers.

ASTI Union Structure

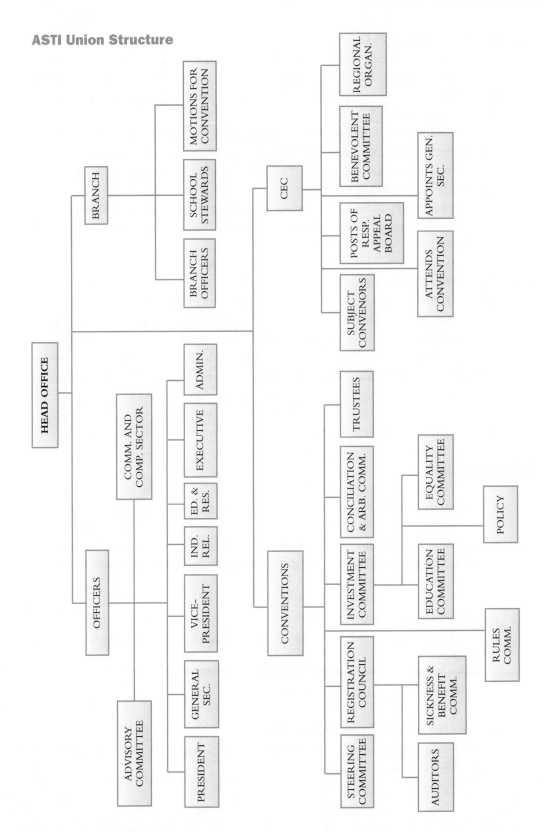

Election Procedures for ASTI

The ASTI is organised in branches of schools in geographical regions. Each school is affiliated to a branch. Members of branches elect a number of their members to the Central Executive Council (CEC). Each branch also elects members as delegates to the Annual Convention.

A standing committee of twenty-three members manages the business of the association. A president is elected at the Annual Convention. The term of office runs from 1 August to 31 July. (He/she is the president-elect for the period running from the Annual Convention to 31 July.)

The Honorary National Organiser and regional organisers are elected by the CEC. A school steward is elected to liaise with the local branch, CEC members and Head Office.

Election of School Stewards

The election of school stewards should take place annually. Each branch arranges that a school steward is elected by the ASTI members of the staff of every school within its area which has more than one teacher who is a member of the association. This election takes place on 1 May of each year. The newly elected school steward, as soon as possible, notifies Head Office using the appropriate form, the Regional Organiser, the Honourable Secretary of his/her branch, and the Hon. secretaries of the branches concerned, of his/her election. The General Secretary informs each school manager of his/her branch, concerning the school steward they elected after 15 May.

Membership of ASTI

There are four classes of membership in the ASTI
- Full membership (for serving lay teachers with the relevant qualifications)
- Associate membership (for lay Higher Diploma or final year college students)
- Emeritus membership (for members who retire on reaching retirement age)
- Honorary life membership (conferred only in recognition of outstanding service to the association).

ELIGIBILITY FOR FULL MEMBERSHIP
- All lay serving assistant teachers who hold qualifications for registration as a secondary teacher
- If they hold a primary university degree
- If they are entitled to become a member.

ELIGIBILITY FOR ASSOCIATE MEMBERSHIP
- H.Dip. in Ed. lay students in their final year or when they have qualified are eligible for associate membership.

ELIGIBILITY FOR EMERITUS MEMBERSHIP

All serving teachers who have retired on reaching the required age, or due to medical grounds, can become an Emeritus member.

APPLICATION FOR MEMBERSHIP

- Fill in the correct application form agreeing to the rules.
- Agree deductions from salary.
- Be proposed and seconded by branch members.
- Pay one-quarter annual subscription for full membership, if not deducted from salary.

INELIGIBLE FOR MEMBERSHIP

- A branch may refuse membership where there is a valid objection by standing committee or CEC.
- Principal teachers with sole power to appoint or dismiss teaching staff are not eligible for membership.
- The decision of the Central Executive Council to accept or reject is final.

Roles and Services of the ASTI

The role of the ASTI is to promote increases in funding for education, and improvements in facilities. It is directly involved in curriculum content and reform. It has direct representation on the National Council for Curriculum and Assessment, Syllabus Committees, the Registration Council, on the Public Services Committee of the ICTU and Posts of Responsibility Appeals Board.

It also represents its members at meetings with the Department of Education, the government and the political parties. Through press releases, conferences and the media, it seeks to improve the teachers' working environment.

At local level, it gives advice on rationalisation, contracts, adequate staffing levels, redeployment and leave entitlements. School stewards, CEC, branch officers and Head Office give advice and information on trade union and professional matters.

ASTI Services

1. It is represented on:
   - School authorities and boards
   - Managerial bodies
   - Government departments
   - Media and general public.
2. It negotiates to:
   - Increase salaries and hourly pay
   - Improve and protect working conditions
   - Secure jobs
   - Develop curriculum

3. It advises on:
   - Career and professional matters
   - Access to information
   - School stewards availability in schools
   - Branch representatives.
4. It gives legal assistance on:
   - Urgent legal counselling
   - Legal expenses.
5. It gives benevolent funds to:
   - Members retiring through illness
   - Dependants of deceased members.
6. It gives sickness benefit:
   - Illness-related expenses
   - Optical and dental benefits
   - Prescribed hearing aid benefits.
7. It gives seminars and training on:
   - Equal opportunities
   - Child abuse
   - Adult education/training
   - Annual Education Conference
   - European Social Fund for schools
   - Training for school stewards and branch officers
   - Health and safety
   - School libraries.
8. It has a contingency fund:
   - For financial benefits for members during disputes.
9. It has a salary protection scheme.
10. It has a car insurance scheme for:
    - Reduced car insurance costs
    - Open to spouses of members.
11. It has publications:
    - *ASTI* monthly journal
    - *Secondary School*, a quarterly educational journal
    - *Nuacht*, current affairs journal
    - *School Year Diary.*
    - Regular publications and leaflets on education matters
12. It has library/information centre for:
    - All members
    - Books and magazines on education
    - Computerised documents
    - Access to educational databases

- Comprehensive media file
- Education and research officer.

13. It has other benefits:
- Rail vouchers
- VHI group scheme
- ASTI credit union.

The ASTI's main aim in 1909 when it started was to:

- Have a registry of teachers
- Adequate salaries
- Employment security
- A good pension scheme.

The ASTI has achieved for secondary school teachers the following:

1. A growth in membership.
2. Salary increases.
3. Job security (protecting employment and redeployment protection for teachers).
4. Pupil:teacher ratio improved.
5. Provisions for disadvantaged students (guidance teachers)
6. Curriculum development (introduction of the Junior and Senior Certificates).
7. Career options (career breaks, job-sharing).

It has done this through successful lobbying, campaigns, public meetings and demonstrations and media publicity to bring about these changes.

Bibliography

ASTI, Members' Handbook.

ASTI, Membership Information.

ICTU, *Understanding Trade Unions: Past & Present*.

Human Resources Worksheet 1

Mini Case Study (Situational Analysis)

Mary Whelan is the young and newly appointed Human Resource Manager at RHS Clothing, a high fashion clothing firm based in Co. Cork. The firm has been expanding over recent years and currently employs a total of 65 staff.

Most of the staff members are semi-skilled machinists and factory floor workers. They make up over three-quarters of the staff. The rest of the staff are office-based, mainly managers and administration staff.

Despite Mary's easy and friendly manner, much suspicion and unease exists among staff regarding piece-work payment and new performance appraisal systems that Mary wants to introduce. Mary believes that these changes will ultimately benefit staff motivation and increase productivity.

Mary aims to create a more employee-centred organisation. Her job will not be easy as a number of what could be viewed as negative features have manifested themselves in the course of time.

* Several layers of supervision have grown.
* A large growth in technical specialists and support staff has occurred.
* A growth in the number of procedures and rules has lead to a good deal of inflexibility.
* A weakening of general decision-making with relatively little input from employees.
* A fall off in the level of innovation.
* Poor communication and duplication of certain activities.

Questions on Case Study

QUESTION 1

a) Give *two* reasons why Mary's plans to introduce piece-work payment has caused suspicion and unease. List *two* benefits of piece-work payment for the employees.

b) What is a performance appraisal system and how are staff members assessed using this system? List *two* ways it could benefit staff.

c) Give *two* other ways in which Mary could motivate her staff.

QUESTION 2

a) Analyse the negative features listed in the case study and give *three* reasons why they may have developed.

b) List *three* ways in which Mary could try to turn the negative features into positive ones.

c) List *two* ways Mary could solve existing communications problems and indicate why you consider them to be good HR practice.

SECOND SECTION

QUESTION 3

a) Distinguish between a short-term, medium-term and long-term workforce gap, giving *one* example of each.

b) List *three* external and *three* internal sources of labour.

c) Explain the main stages to be followed in recruiting through open competition. Refer in your answer to the difference between a job description and a job specification.

QUESTION 4

a) List *two* reasons why staff motivation is key to the successful operation of an organisation.

b) Explain Maslow's theory of hierarchy of needs and list *two* reasons why it is central to HR training and practice. Illustrate your answer appropriately.

c) List *three* types of training used as part of training and development and explain *two* ways in which training can motivate staff.

Human Resources Worksheet 2

Mini Case Study (Situational Analysis)

Free and Easy Holidays Ltd is a travel company located in Galway. The firm has been expanding over recent years and currently employs a total of 65 staff. The last HR manager has recently taken a five-year career break that has caused a workforce gap. The vacancy was filled using the transparent open competition method of recruitment and was filled by a new enthusiastic HR manager, John O'Brien, who wanted to create a better work environment and reduce staff turnover. His plan was first to get to know each member of staff and to introduce new performance appraisal systems. Some negative features had developed in the company in the course of time, before John took over. These included:

- Several layers of supervision had grown.
- Large growth in technical specialists and support staff had occurred.
- Growth in the number of procedures and rules had lead to a deal of inflexibility.
- Weakening of general decision-making with relatively little input from employees
- Fall off in the level of innovation.
- Poor communication and duplication of certain activities.
- John aims to create a more employee-centred organisation but it is true that his job will not be an easy one.

Questions on Case Study

QUESTION 1

a) List the *three* types of workforce gaps that arise in organisations, giving *one* example each. What type of gap has been created due to the departure of this last HR manager? List *three* causes of a high staff turnover.

b) John was recruited and selected by Open Competition? What is it and list the *12 steps* involved in it.

c) What is a performance appraisal system? List *two* ways it could benefit staff and *two* ways it could benefit the organisation.

QUESTION 2

a) Give *one* reason each why the negative features listed in the case study may have developed.

b) Select *three* of the negative features and explain *one* way each in that John can try to turn the negative features into positive ones.

c) Give *two* other ways that John could motivate his staff.

QUESTION 3

HR managers believe that CPD training is essential to maintain a high standard in an organisation in the face of tough competition.

a) List and explain *four* types of training and development available to HR managers.
b) What are the differences between 'creativity' and 'innovation'. List *two* ways that CPD training can positively influence a company in the areas of creativity and innovation. List *two* ways this can help motivate staff.
c) List *three* ways that organisations can use CPD training to help reduce staff turnover?

QUESTION 4

a) List *two* reasons why staff motivation is key to the successful operation of an organisation.
b) Explain Maslow's theory of Hierarchy of Needs and list *two* reasons why is it central to HR training and practice. Illustrate your answer appropriately.
c) Differentiate between Intrinsic Reward Systems and Extrinsic Reward Systems. Give *three* examples each and explain how they can help motivate staff.

Sample Assignment Briefs – Human Resources/Trade Unions

1. Carry out a brief profile of an Irish Trade Union using the following headings as a guide:
   (a) History, size and membership and general purpose of the union.
   (b) Mission Statement.
   (c) Organisational Chart of some aspect of the Trade Union (can be the complete chart, a breakdown of head-office staff or a branch profile or equivalent, e.g. general secretary, vice president of the union, etc.)
   (d) Functions of members mentioned on Organisational Chart(s) explained.
   (e) Union Meetings.
   (f) Grievance Procedures.

2. Analyse the workings of any Human Resources Department using the following headings as a guide:
   (a) History, size and ownership of the business.
   (b) Size and layout of the HR Department (with visuals, staff numbers etc.)
   (c) Organisational Chart of the HR Department and HR staff functions explained.
   (d) Filing methods and general HR Department day-to-day functions/duties.

(e) Recruitment Procedures.

(f) Disciplinary Procedures.

3. The student brief is as follows:

Select and cut out *four* advertisements for various types of jobs from the newspaper.

For each advertisement:

(a) Identify what type of Company or Organisation is advertising.

(b) Identify at what level in the organisation the person will work.

(c) Identify what type of Recruitment Option is being used.

(d) Identify who the applicant will be responsible to and what is the extent of his/her job specification (some imagination and knowledge of the world of work should be evident).

(e) Identify what type of person (qualifications, attributes, skills, experience etc.) is required.

(f) Outline any available information about remuneration with reference to 'flat rate', bonuses, overtime, or other incentives.

Note: The Examiner marking the assignment will take variety of advertisements, clarity of analysis, extent of knowledge, imagination in interpretation and neatness of presentation into consideration.

Sample Questions for Student Research on 'A Trade Union'

1. Could you give me some information on the history of the Trade Union?
2. What is its Mission Statement?
3. Where are the Trade Union offices located, i.e. head office, branches?
4. Is the Trade Union affiliated to the ICTU (Irish Congress of Trade Unions)?
5. How many and what categories of members does the Union have?
6. Could you provide me with an Organisational Chart of the Trade Union? (E.g. President, General Secretary, Assistant General Secretary, etc.)
7. What are their functions?
8. What is the structure in place with regard to union meetings?
9. What grievance procedures can members avail of?

Sample Questions for Student Research on 'The HR Department'

1. When did the business become established? Did it relocate?
2. How many branches/departments are there?

3. What products or services does it offer?
4. What type of ownership is there (e.g. sole trader, partnership, private, public company etc.)?
5. Who owns the business (shareholding)?
6. Could you provide me with an Organisational Chart of staff in the HR Department? If not, can you help me to compile one?
7. Can you explain the basic functions of the staff in the HR Department?
8. What filing systems are used in the HR Department, e.g. alphabetical, numerical, historical, mixture?
9. What are the recruitment procedures of the business, e.g. open competition, agencies used, word of mouth, etc?
10. Could you provide me with a copy of a sample newspaper advert, letters of reply or contracts of employment to include in my project?
11. How do you discipline staff, e.g. reminders (memos), verbal, written warnings, suspensions, dismissals?
12. Do you hold staff development days? If yes, do you think they help to motivate staff and increase work effort?
13. How are the staff motivated – by career advancement/promotions etc?

5. Preparing for Meetings

A meeting is a forum that allows for communication within a group of people.

Role of a Meeting within the Organisation

Meetings are designed to:

1. Allow immediate face-to-face oral exchange, feedback and presentation within a controlled framework, where a chairperson's job is to provide this control and regulation of activities.
2. Help enhance understanding and act as a forum for persuasion.
3. Humanise the context of the organisation's communication channels by opening the parties to personal contact and each other's direct scrutiny and by exposing the characteristics of individual personalities. Open and spontaneous communication is usually encouraged with constructive criticism being paramount to improvements and more satisfactory work arrangements.
4. Spread information quickly and efficiently with full advice on and explanations of business given to participants, to avoid misunderstandings.
5. Create possible decision-making forums usually with detailed discussion before decisions are arrived at, and where previous unfulfilled commitments can be discussed further and sometimes enforced.
6. Iron out difficulties (problem-solving) and promote better 'people relationships' and co-operation.

Different Types of Meeting

Meetings are generally set up by posting a *Notice* informing people where and when the meeting is to be held, together with an *Agenda* briefly detailing what the meeting is about.

1. Informal meetings usually have a chairperson who regulates activities by keeping order and by encouraging contributions to the discussion when necessary. He/she informally guides the discussion along the lines set by the agenda.
2. Formal meetings differ from Informal meetings because as well as the requirements for a Notice to be posted or sent and an Agenda to be drawn up:
   (a) The participants are governed by legal requirements, where they have the right to have an item included on the agenda provided that they give due notice of it to the chairperson.

(b) A sufficient number of participants must be present at the meeting in order to form a *Quorum* (a required number of participants to vote).

(c) The participants usually sign an attendance book to prove that they were present at the meeting.

(d) The participants presiding over the meeting have formal titles like *chairperson* and *secretary*. When these people are not available, 'Acting' participants take their places temporarily.

(e) Formal *Minutes* of the meeting (an accurate summary of proceedings) are taken usually by the secretary.

(f) A formal *Report* of the meeting is usually compiled by the secretary and sent to participants.

(g) The *room layout* of the meeting and the seating arrangements of the participants are sometimes sketched to provide further evidence of attendance and to show that formal procedures were followed.

(The terms written in italics will be discussed later.)

EXAMPLES OF DIFFERENT TYPES OF MEETING

Types of meeting run from the Most Formal to Less Formal to Informal.

The Most Formal meetings are usually Annual General Meetings (AGMs), Annual General Conferences, Board Meetings, Extraordinary General Meetings (EGMs), Department Meetings, Union Meetings, Public Inquiries and Council Meetings.

Less Formal Meetings might be Staff meetings, Club committee meetings, Sub-committee meetings, Task groups and Quality Circle meetings.

Informal meetings might be staff development meetings, authors informally meeting with editors, inter-departmental meetings.

- Formal procedures involve thorough preparation by presiding participants with full written records, official rules of procedure, participant behaviour and rules of law governing the meeting being strictly adhered to.

- Informal arrangements involve informal notes (if any) being taken for reference, with no formal rules for participants and an unstructured procedure being apparent. MBWA, 'Management by walk around', is an informal technique that managers use – they regularly walk around about the workplace and have informal chats with subordinates. It is a deliberate means of stimulating motivation and can help to raise job satisfaction. On the other hand, employees can view it as an intimidating means of motivation.

Note: It is interesting to note that informal meetings can be the key to good organisation because many issues that are discussed informally gain universal agreement before the formal forum is set up. Also input from people who may not wish to voice their opinions or objections in a more public and formal setting can prove to be informative and useful to guide the final decision-making process. It ensures that everyone's needs are considered within the organisation. In short, everyone gets a look in. (Refer to Chapter 1 'The Organisation' where Formal and Informal Organisational Structure is discussed.)

The Functions of Specific Types of Meeting

1. THE AGM

The Annual General Meeting is held once a year by clubs, associations and companies that all shareholders or members are entitled to attend. An invitation is posted or sent to them. The Companies Act requires by law that companies hold an AGM. Officers (i.e. chairperson, vice-chairperson, secretary, treasurer and other typical posts such as publicity officer, equality officer, etc.) are elected or re-elected for the year ahead. Annual reports regarding issues and monies (the financial position of the business including profits/dividends) are dealt with and copies of these are made available to members or participants. Shareholders can question directors openly and satisfy themselves with regard to the current performance of and future plans for the business.

2. AN EGM

An Extraordinary General Meeting is held if a serious turn of events occurs like the possibility of the company going into liquidation. A good example where a meeting like this is required would be if a company merger was envisaged in the near future. This meeting that the board of directors or committee calls notifies all shareholders or members of an EGM to discuss the specific item of business.

3. BOARD MEETINGS

A Board Meeting or Committee Meeting is a meeting of a task force that heads the organisation. The members have delegated authority to make decisions, and can serve as people who can be consulted for the purpose of co-ordinating activities within the organisation. The board members have the authority to carry out the decisions arrived at by them at these meetings. This type of company meeting is underpinned by the Companies Acts 1963–2009.

An MPC is a Monetary Policy Committee meeting that a bank or financial institution might hold to review interest rates and the general financial policy of the institution. It is an example of a type of board meeting.

4. DEPARTMENT MEETINGS

Organisations divide up labour into departments. Usually each department has a 'head of department' and he/she calls internal department meetings that only apply to people directly connected with the department in question. These meetings take place approximately once a month. A review of the past month's activities with regard to that department takes place. Participants make suggestions for change and engage in constructive discussion to allow for improvements within the department. Appropriate statistics and documentation are provided by the head of department to motivate and inform workers present at the meeting.

5. UNION MEETINGS

The different types of Union Representatives are discussed in detail in Chapter 4, 'Human Resources', in the section 'Features of Grievance Procedures'. The corresponding meetings that are presided over by these representatives are:

WORKPLACE UNION MEETINGS

The staff union representative posts a notice and an agenda of the intended meeting on the union notice board. A satisfactory period of notice, usually a week, should be given to staff. Sometimes it is necessary to call an emergency meeting when it is not possible to give this amount of notice to members.

The functions of these meeting are:

1. To keep members informed on current events within the union.
2. To discuss grievances that members wish to raise and to suggest ways that solutions may be found.
3. To decide by majority vote to strike or operate a work to rule in order to gain management's attention, which might result in better pay and conditions of employment.
4. To decide whether disputes at local level should be brought to the attention of the branch representatives.
5. To decide whether disputes might be resolved more quickly by taking the legal route (via the Labour Relations Commission and the Labour Court – discussed in Chapter 4).

BRANCH UNION MEETINGS

The union head office will send individual workplace union representatives notification of branch meetings which take place usually on a monthly basis. Notification is also given of special or emergency meetings from time to time. Usually the branch chairperson, the branch secretary, and from time to time other officers preside over the meeting. All the members of different branches are entitled to attend these meetings and to vote.

The functions of this type of meeting are:

1. To address and discuss grievances resulting in motions being put forward and agreed upon by 'the branch'. These motions must be sanctioned by the Union Executive Body and by the General Officers if they are to be presented as

motions that could be converted into resolutions and become union policy at national level (at the Annual Congress/Conference).

2. To address and discuss problems at local workplace level and decide on options to resolve these disputes to everyone's satisfaction.

3. To discuss issues regarding pay and conditions and discrimination and to put forward motions to deal with local problems in these areas.

4. Each branch holds its individual Annual General Meeting once a year (the functions of an AGM have been discussed previously).

THE NATIONAL UNION MEETING

This is a meeting of all the members of the union in the country and is referred to as a Congress or an Annual Conference. A specific number of delegates are put forward and elected from individual branches to attend the Congress and speak on (debate) motions in a public arena before a vote is taken to pass or reject these motions. The motions that are passed then become resolutions that are later discussed with the other social partners, i.e. employer representatives (IBEC, Irish Business and Employers' Confederation) and government representatives. Wage agreements like the Programme for National Recovery 1987, the Programme for Economic and Social Progress, PESP (1991), the Programme for Competitiveness and Work, PCW (1994), Partnership 2000 and Toward 2016 (2006) were negotiated based on resolutions that were reached at Congress and the Annual Conferences.

6. PUBLIC MEETINGS

Certain European directives and case-law precedents affect the holding and conduct of some meetings. This would apply to public inquires and tribunals, which are types of public meeting. Article 40 of Bunreacht na hÉireann (the Irish Constitution) guarantees the public right to assemble or meet peacefully and without weapons. This right is limited by legislation to protect public order and morality underpinned by the Criminal Justice Public Order Acts of 1994, 2003 and 2006. The law also prevents or controls meetings that are calculated or designed to cause a riot or breach of the peace.

Buying And Living in a Multi-Unit Development Property in Ireland

What are Extraordinary General Meetings (EGMs)?

EGMs are all general meetings of the company other than the AGM.

The Articles will generally outline the process by which an EGM may be held. If the company is a guarantee company not having a share capital, the notice cannot be shorter than 14 days. However, meetings may be convened at shorter notice, only if it so agreed by both the company's auditors and by all the members entitled to attend and vote at the meeting. For example, the articles may state that directors may call an EGM at their own discretion, or that the directors cannot make certain decisions without the approval of members. Under company law there are a number of circumstances where an EGM must be held regardless of what is outlined in the articles of association. In summary, EGMs must be held under the following circumstances:

- Members representing not less than 10 per cent of the voting rights of the company (known as requisitionists) can request that the directors call and hold an EGM by submitting a written request outlining the purpose of the EGM to the company's registered office. The directors are obliged to call an EGM within 21 days of the request and the EGM must be held within two months. If the directors fail to call the EGM, the requisitionists, or any of them representing over half the voting rights of the requisitionists, may convene a meeting which must be held within three months of the date of the original request.
- Where it is not practical to call an EGM or hold it in accordance with the articles of association or the Companies Acts, any member entitled to vote at the meeting may apply to the High Court, and the Court may order that such a meeting be held.
- Where the company's net assets (i.e. total assets less total liabilities) have fallen to 50 per cent or less of its called-up share capital the directors must also convene an EGM.

Source: The National Consumer Agency www.consumerproperty.ie

PRACTICE QUESTIONS

1. (a) Define the meaning of a 'Meeting'.
   (b) List *four* objectives of meetings.
2. What are the main differences between a Formal and an Informal Meeting?
3. Name *five* different types of meetings and explain how they differ.
4. What are the functions of a Workplace Union Meeting?
5. What are the functions of a Branch Union Meeting?
6. What are the functions of a National Union Meeting?
7. What legal Acts underpin public meetings like Tribunals of Inquiry?

Roles, Powers and Duties of Officers at a Meeting

THE CHAIRPERSON

A chairperson regulates activities at a meeting by keeping order and by encouraging contributions to the discussion when necessary. He/she guides the discussion along the lines set by the agenda (in the form of a sequence of business decided in advance). Anything that the chairperson has not been informed about in advance can be referred to under 'Any Other Business' (AOB) if time permits.

In formal meetings, the chairperson has more complex responsibilities and set rules will be applied by him/her.

1. The chairperson will make out a chairperson's agenda that directly corresponds with the main agenda, except personal notes will appear under each item on the main agenda. (A sample is given later.) It provides a personal reference to guide the chairperson when he/she is chairing the meeting. The chairperson's agenda will allow him/her to implement the correct procedure (points of order) that must be observed in convening and constituting the meeting and in the conduct of the debate.

2. In the event of queries or complaints regarding procedure (points of order) the chairperson must give an immediate ruling.

3. He/she must deal firmly and exercise courtesy when participants engage in irrelevancies, long-windedness, interruptions, show a lack of courtesy or use improper language.

4. He/she must regulate proceedings when participants are voting upon issues in order to arrive at a clear-cut decision agreed by a majority.

A well-led meeting can be very productive and effective for the purposes of planning, consultation, problem-solving and decision-making, relaying decisions and instructions, downward and upward briefing (to subordinates and superiors), inter-departmental and cross-departmental liaison.

THE SECRETARY

A secretary would normally:

1. Have 'before-meeting duties' like fixing the date and the time of the meeting and preparing, posting and/or sending out the Notice and the Agenda to interested parties.

2. Be responsible for choosing and preparing the location of the meeting, ensuring appropriate size of venue, good accessibility, appropriate facilities (overhead projectors etc.) and suitable seating arrangements.

3. Have 'during the meeting duties' like making notes and assisting the chairperson regarding clarification of statements made etc.

4. Have 'post-meeting duties' like preparing the Minutes of the meeting based on

the notes taken at the meeting, and might be required to communicate decisions taken based on the discussion at the meeting and/or act on these decisions (this does not always apply).

The functions of the treasurer are:

1. To receive and record subscriptions from members of a club or union and to send the new member a receipt acknowledging receipt of the money.
2. To lodge the money into the appropriate club or union bank account.
3. To pay all club or union bills.
4. To keep the accounts (financial transactions) of the club or union correct and up to date.
5. To prepare a yearly Financial Report for the club or union's AGM and make the report available to members.

Terms Associated with Meetings
(including regulations governing meetings)

1. **CLEAR DAYS:** refers to the time required to convene a meeting, not counting the day the notices are sent out and the day the meeting is held. (An organisation's rules may place a different definition on Clear Days depending on their requirements.)
2. **IN CAMERA:** refers to a meeting that is held in private where the public or the press are not allowed to attend.
3. **A MOTION:** is a proposal put to a meeting. For example, Motion No. 1 might be, 'I propose that Mary Smith be elected as Treasurer of this branch' (usually naming the branch of the organisation). There is usually a 'seconder' to back up the 'proposer'.

     Examples of Motions:
     'propose that the meeting postpone consideration of the subject';
     'propose that the debate be adjourned.'
   Informational proposals can also be cast as motions, e.g. 'I propose to receive the report on the annual accounts given by the treasurer for the year ended . . .'
4. **A PROPOSER:** is a person who puts forward a motion at a meeting.
5. **A SECONDER:** is a person who immediately supports the proposer's motion. A seconder usually signs the minutes of a meeting also.
6. **A RESOLUTION:** If a motion is accepted, but has to be put to superiors or executives, it is referred to as being 'carried'. If, however, it is regarded as a decision, the motion then becomes a 'resolution'.

7. **STANDING ORDERS:** are rules governing the conduct of meetings. A standing order might be invoked to move that a resolution be suspended. (This means that a decision is delayed pending certain conditions.)

8. **AN AMENDMENT:** is a proposal to change the wording of a motion, *before* it is put to a vote.

9. **AN ADDENDUM:** is the change that is made to the wording of a motion *after* a vote has taken place.

10. **SUBSTANTIVE MOTION OR RESOLUTION:** When a motion is changed it becomes a substantive motion that must be voted on again. If carried, it becomes a decision, at which point it is a substantive resolution.

11. **A POINT OF ORDER:** To raise a point of order at a meeting might be to clarify a point that has already been raised or to disagree with it. The point of order should be dealt with immediately by a ruling from the chairperson. Points of Order are designed to ensure:
    (a) that regulations are being observed.
    (b) that the proceedings of the meeting are not later rendered invalid.
    (c) that voting procedures are being adhered to (e.g. making sure that someone who is not entitled to vote does not vote – they are not allowed to manipulate proceedings).

12. **AN 'AD HOC' COMMITTEE:** is one formed for a special purpose.

13. **A QUORUM:** is like a quota – the minimum number of people who must be present at the meeting before the meeting can begin discussions. (Most organisations have rules concerning a quorum for meetings.)

14. **A PROXY:** is a 'stand-in' or the person authorised to act and vote on behalf of a shareholder at an organisation's AGM, with the shareholder's approval. At some company meetings proxies have the right to be present but not to speak.

15. **A SCRUTINEER:** is one who checks the validity of votes on behalf of interested parties, e.g. at elections.

16. **A TELLER:** is a person who counts votes.

17. **A DEBATE:** is a representation of participants' opinions on an item that appears on the Agenda. In a larger forum such as a Conference (Fianna Fáil or Fine Gael Ard Fheis, Teachers' Conferences etc.), motions are debated by different delegates which are then voted on and, if carried, become resolutions. The chairperson is usually the president, vice-president or a prominent leader of the organisation.

18. **THROUGH THE CHAIR:** It is the chairperson's task to guide the meeting through the sequence of short debates. One speaker is allowed to speak at a time. Speakers who wish to interrupt or to argue with others are urged to 'address the chair'. This is a way of controlling interruptions, heckling, and arguments among the participants at the meeting.

19. **AN ADJOURNMENT:** is an interruption in the proceedings of a meeting before they have been completed. It can take the form of an interruption or a postponement to a later date.

(a) If there is a problem regarding the holding of the meeting and the notice to convene has already been issued, the meeting cannot be postponed. The procedure is to hold the meeting, but to propose a motion for an adjournment before any business is done. The secretary may issue an advance notice to members that the adjournment will be proposed, so that they do not waste time coming to the meeting.

(b) If the quorum is a minimum of two people (or higher) and someone leaves, the meeting must be temporarily adjourned because the quorum is lost.

(c) If it is impossible to maintain order, the chairperson will decide to adjourn the meeting.

20. **CASTING VOTE:** When there is an equal number of votes 'for' and 'against', the chairperson has/may have a deciding vote.

21. **ABSTENTION:** The free decision that all members have not to vote either for or against the motion.

22. **'NEM CON':** This is a Latin phrase *nemine contradicente* meaning 'no one voted against the motion' but some members abstained.

23. **UNANIMOUSLY CARRIED:** This means all members voted in favour of the motion.

24. **SINE DIE:** This occurs when a meeting adjourns without fixing a date for the next meeting.

Procedures for Voting at Meetings

Voting is the mechanism used by members of an organisation, club or union to make decisions and to reach agreement regarding motions (proposals) and convey these decisions to members and to the chairperson.

It is often possible to reach agreement without voting at meetings. (Government mostly reach decisions without voting.) At many informal meetings it is not necessary to take a vote. However, when voting is necessary it is important that:

1. The motion (proposal), i.e. the matter for discussion and the point to be decided, be clearly explained and conveyed by the chairperson to the members voting. Voters should know exactly what is being proposed.

2. The regulations governing the meeting are strictly adhered to (discussed previously).

3. Those voting can confirm exactly what was decided.

How is the vote taken?

1. **BY ACQUIESCENCE:** This is the approval of the motion by the members clapping.

2. **BY VOICE (OR ACCLAMATION):** If all those in favour of the motion say 'Aye' and all those against the motion say 'Nay'. The decision has usually been temporarily agreed upon beforehand.

3. ***SHOW OF HANDS:*** The chairperson invites the members to raise a hand, 'All those in favour?' The teller or chairperson counts the votes. Then the chairperson invites 'All those against?' to raise a hand and the chairperson or teller counts these votes. Then the result of the count is declared. This system is based on 'one person, one vote' or if it is allowable a member's proxy will vote on his or her behalf.

4. ***BY PROXY:*** The member nominates a person to vote on his or her behalf (or gives the nominee voting instructions) only if the organisation's rules permit.

5. ***BY POLL:*** After the result of the show of hands, the chairperson must decide whether a poll is required, when members request it. It must either be taken immediately or a date set in the near future. If it is decided to vote by poll, the result of the show of hands must be withdrawn. Individual members then must sign a form (voting paper) indicating their preference 'for or against the motion'. Companies generally vote by poll and in these cases because of shareholdings the system might not necessarily be based on 'one person, one vote'.

6. ***BY BALLOT:*** This is the voting procedure for general and local government elections. Voters tick their preference on a voting paper and place it in a special ballot box. This method of voting is a secret ballot.

7. ***BY DIVISION:*** Members voting walk into different rooms based on 'for' or 'against' preferences and tellers count the numbers and report back to the chairperson. Internal government voting is carried out in this way.

The chairperson declares the result and asks the secretary to include this detail in the minutes of the meeting. The item of business or the debate cannot be reopened for discussion during this meeting. It can, however, be agreed to reschedule it for another time.

Purpose of an Agenda

An Agenda (Latin for 'things to be done') is usually posted or sent out by the secretary, together with the notice, and is a brief description of what the meeting is about. It is usually drawn up in the form of a list of items to be discussed in order of importance.

It informs every participant about:

1. The subject of items to be discussed. Speeches, arguments and questions can be prepared in advance.
2. The order of items to be discussed. This will allow members to attend only when items of interest to them are being discussed.
3. The limited time schedule: the chairperson must make members aware that there is a time limit for debate.

A Sample Combined Notice and Agenda of a Business

The following is the Agenda for the AGM of Maryville Football Club.

Notice of the Annual General Meeting of Maryville Football Club

Notice is hereby given that the sixth Annual General Meeting of Maryville Football Club will be held.

MARYVILLE FOOTBALL CLUB

ANNUAL GENERAL MEETING

Friday 12 November 20XX at 8 p.m.
In Glenstall Hotel, Maryville
AGENDA

1. Apologies for absence.
2. Minutes of the previous AGM.
3. Matters arising from the minutes.
4. Chairperson's Report.
5. Treasurer's Report.
6. Election of Officers.
7. Any Other Business (AOB)
8. Date of next meeting.

Signed:

Frank James
Secretary

MARYVILLE FOOTBALL CLUB

CHAIRPERSON'S AGENDA   NOTES

For the AGM to be held in the Glenstall Hotel
on Friday 12 November 20XX at 8 p.m.

1. *Apologies for absence*
   Mr J. Downey and Ms A. Malone are unable to attend.

2. *Minutes of the previous AGM.*

3. *Matters arising from the minutes*
   Subscriptions: Refer to updated report on estimated
   expected rise in subscriptions and consequent revision
   needed in facilities on the premises.

4. *Chairperson's Report* (attached).

5. *Treasurer's Report* (copy attached).

6. *Election of Officers*
   Proposals for Ms Kathleen Johnson as next year's Secretary
   replacing Mr Harry Black. And Mr Seamus O'Connor
   replacing Regina White as Treasurer.

7. *Any Other Business*
   Item 4: Mr John McCarthy has officially issued his
   resignation as Senior Grounds Supervisor and Mr Frank
   Fahy has been officially appointed to the position.
   Reminder to thank Mr John McCarthy for his years of
   service and to welcome Mr Frank Fahy to the position.
   Item 6: Ms Mary Fox has agreed to organise events and
   presentations at the Club's Annual Dance this year.
   Reminder to thank her.

8. *Date of next meeting*
   Friday 2 February 20XX at Maryville Clubhouse at 8 p.m.
   (subject to agreement).

The Notice sometimes appears in the page preceding the Agenda:

NOTICE

MARYVILLE FOOTBALL CLUB
ANNUAL GENERAL MEETING

Friday 12 November 20XX

At
8 p.m.
in
Glenstall Hotel, Maryville.

Signed:

_____

Frank James
Secretary

Purpose of the Minutes of a Meeting

The minutes of a meeting are a written record of the meeting taken by the secretary (or another nominated person). They are usually taken in the form of shorthand notes and later written up in a formal structure (example given later). The minutes represent a form of reported speech and insignificant outbursts (or personality clashes) are sometimes edited out of the minutes.

The benefits of writing up the minutes of a meeting are:
1. They propose to serve as a complete and concise record of business and as a source of reference regarding details of information, commitments, agreements and disagreements uttered orally by participants.
2. They provide some evidence and back-up and can be referred to regarding conflicts of facts about the meeting, where participants might deliberately forget or distort the account of speeches made at the meeting.

Types of Minutes

1. RESOLUTION MINUTES

Strictly only the decisions that were taken (excluding the debate or objections) will be detailed. These minutes might be used to disguise conflicts of opinion and objections raised. For example 'It was resolved that Maryville Football Club AGM should be held on Friday, 12 November 20XX, at 8 p.m. in Glenstall Hotel, Maryville.'

2. NARRATIVE MINUTES

This is a concise written record of events and debate leading up to the resolutions (decisions) and the resolutions themselves. Participants' speeches, comments, contradictions, agreements and suggestions are noted and participants are held accountable for what they say. The aim is to give a thorough insight into the feelings of participants without unnecessary irrelevant details. For example, 'The Chairperson addressed the meeting and expressed her dissatisfaction that no compromise was reached regarding the formulation of a Company Mission Statement. She referred the meeting to Ms Moloney on this matter. Ms Moloney reported that since the last meeting in April, based on suggestions made to her, she had formulated two sample Mission Statements that she believed would be acceptable to staff. Mr Jones expressed dissatisfaction at not being consulted about the matter. The Chairwoman rejected Mr Jones's complaint out of hand and confirmed that every member of staff had been given detailed information on the requirements. The Chairwoman ordered that a vote be taken on the matter and then requested a show of hands to accept or reject the sample statements. *It was resolved* that sample Mission Statement 2 would serve as the Company Mission Statement for the foreseeable future and would appear in the next company prospectus and future brochures.'

3. ACTION MINUTES

Following decisions (resolutions) taken, the chairperson sometimes has the authority to direct members' actions. This would be in the form of indicating what results are expected following the resolutions and who is responsible for each area. A separate column is often included on the right-hand side of the script to indicate the person who has been appointed to the specific area of authority or who volunteers to perform the duty.

An Example of narrative minutes

MARYVILLE FOOTBALL CLUB

Minutes

These are the minutes of the Maryville Football Club Annual General Meeting held on 12 November 20XX in Glenstall Hotel, Maryville.

Present: All Members accounted for and present.

The meeting commenced at 8 p.m. The Chairperson, Ms Marie O'Donnell, opened the meeting and expressed her satisfaction at the attendance at the meeting. She also spoke of the future envisaged success of the club and future involvements.

1. Apologies for absence.
2. Minutes of the last Annual General Meeting:
   The Secretary Mr Frank James read out the Minutes of the last AGM held on 11 November 1996. The Minutes were then approved and signed by the Chairperson, Ms Marie O'Donnell.
3. Matters arising from the Minutes of last year's AGM:
   The Chairperson referred to the updated report on estimated expected rise in subscriptions and consequent revision needed in facilities on the premises. With reference to the agreed proposal at last year's meetings she referred to the fact that work had already begun on extending the clubhouse and improving the pitch. A new bar and changing area for women would be incorporated in the plans. The cost of the work was detailed and distributed to members and the source of the funding was also detailed in this report.
4. Chairperson's Report:
   A copy of the report was circulated to members and the chairperson referred to the need to review security in the club due to theft of equipment and belongings in the recent past. The Chairperson proposed that 'a special meeting should be held in the club to discuss the matter on 30 November 20XX'. This proposal was seconded by Mr Frank James, Secretary.
5. Treasurer's Report:
   The Treasurer, Ms Regina White, distributed copies of last year's Treasurer's Report and she explained details of outgoing money and incoming money for the last year as well as new subscriptions.
6. Elections of Officers:
   The election of a new Secretary was held as follows:

   Kathleen Johnson was proposed by John Franklin.
   Seconded by Mary Smith.

The election of a new Treasurer was held as follows:

Seamus O'Connor was proposed by Darren Walters.
Seconded by Donnacha O'Neill.

Ms Marie O'Donnell agreed to remain in the position as Chairperson. This was proposed by Frank James and seconded by Seamus O'Connor.

Voting for the elections was by 'a show of hands' and in each case the motions were accepted unanimously.

7. Any Other Business:
    The Chairperson Ms O'Donnell announced the recent resignation of Mr John McCarthy, the senior grounds supervisor. She thanked him for his years of service and she welcomed Mr Frank Fahy to the position. The Chairperson also thanked Ms Mary Fox for agreeing to organise the club's Annual Presentation Night and Dance which is to be held on 7 December 20XX starting at 8 p.m.

8. Date of Next Meeting
    The Chairperson announced that the next regular club meeting would be held on 2 February 20XX at 8 p.m. at the Clubhouse.

Signed: Seconded by
        Marie O'Donnell
        Chairperson
Date: 12 November 20XX

Signed:
        Kathleen Johnson
        Secretary

There was no other business to be discussed and the meeting was brought to a close.

Note: Minutes are sometimes numbered in ascending order (going up) and continue from meeting to meeting. In this example, the last minute is numbered 8, therefore the first minute of the next meeting should be numbered 9.

Purpose of Writing a Report

Reports are generally compiled in response to a request for an investigation of an issue, usually following a meeting. The aim and objectives, as well as findings and recommendations, appear in the report. The aim is referred to as 'the terms of reference'.

A report could be regarded as a fact-finding document, with a lead person or group of experts responsible for compiling it.

DIGIFOTO LTD
Health and Safety Report

Name of Report Writer: Jim White, Health and Safety Officer

Date Report Compiled: 20 June 20XX

Terms of Reference:

To investigate the health and safety risks in the studio area of Digifoto Ltd and the adequacy of its health and safety procedures and to make appropriate recommendations.

Methodology:

- Checklist log kept of a five-week period.
- Manager interviewed.
- Three staff members interviewed.

Findings:

- There is no real health and safety awareness in the organisation. No risk assessment has ever been carried out, and there is no health and safety statement.
- Cables are not stored away – high risk of accident and injury to staff and customers, including floating liquids risk.
- No first aider on site: poorly stocked first aid kit.

Recommendations:

- A risk assessment should be carried out immediately.
- A policy on health and safety and a safety statement should be compiled.
- Liquids should be banned from the studio.
- First aid training should be provided to staff and a dedicated first-aider appointed.
- Fire training should be provided to staff and a fire officer appointed.
- Cables should be tidied carefully out of reach and sight of children where possible.
- General health and safety awareness should be emphasised by managament.

Follow-up meeting to be held on 2 August 20XX.

A Sample Student Summary of Meetings

Compiled by Jean Ryan
Computer Applications and Business student in Crumlin College 2007–2008

Meetings as a Form of Communication

Communication involves the exchange of information between people, and it successfully occurs when the receiver understands what the sender means to convey. In other words, communication is a two-way process which not only requires the message to be received, but also to be understood. Communication is an essential activity for any organisation. The communication process must be both effective and efficient. An effective method, used by organisations to communicate with their employees, is by the means of meetings.

A **meeting** may be defined as the grouping of two or more people to discuss business of common interest. Meetings are a form of oral communication and may be formal or informal. An effective meeting is a highly efficient tool of communication for organisations. It enables organisations to discuss and co-ordinate various activities, give briefs on particular issues, consult with each other, make decisions, solve problems and set future goals and objectives. Formal meetings are conducted under strict guidelines, whereas informal ones are less organised. There are different types of meetings, which may be classified as follows:

1. AGM – Annual General Meeting
2. EGM – Extraordinary General Meeting
3. Board meetings
4. Statutory meetings
5. Executive meetings
6. Consultative meetings
7. (a) Committee meetings
   (b) Sub-committee meetings
8. Review meetings
9. Ad-hoc meetings
10. Inaugural meetings
11. Ordinary meetings
12. Video Conferences

Functions of the Chairperson

- To plan in consultation with the Secretary, the dates and times of the meeting.
- To draw up the Agenda, again in consultation with the Secretary.
- To keep order and prevent disruption.

- To maintain the policies of the organisation.
- When a vote is tied, he/she must use a casting vote.

The Role of the Secretary

- To draw up the Agenda in consultation with the Chairperson.
- To set out the Notice of the Meeting.
- To circulate the Minutes from the previous Meeting (draft minutes).
- To write up the Minutes of a Meeting.
- To plan the next Meeting with the Chairperson.

The Duties of the Treasurer

- To receive yearly subscriptions from members.
- To issue receipts to members.
- To pay the bills on behalf of the organisation.
- To lodge all the organisation's money into bank accounts.
- To keep account books of all transactions made by the organisation.
- To prepare the Financial Report for the AGM.

Notices

NOTICE OF A MEETING

For meetings such as Committee Meetings, General Meetings, or Extraordinary General Meetings, written Notices must be prepared and sent to those entitled to attend. A Notice should contain details of the subject matter, the place, time and date of the meeting.

An Agenda

AN AGENDA OF A MEETING

The secretary, in consultation with the chairperson, is responsible for drawing up the Agenda of a meeting. An agenda is a list of subjects to be covered within the duration of the meeting. A meeting will be far more effective if those attending know in advance what is to be discussed. They will then be able to sort out their ideas, gather data, find out views of colleagues, and come well informed and ready to contribute. It also ensures that every item of importance will be reviewed, and no topic will be overlooked. This is known as meeting preparation, and is of vital importance in order for a meeting to be successful.

The list or programme of items to be discussed at a meeting is generally listed in order of priority, and is usually numbered for easy reference. On the right-hand side of an agenda a space may be included for recording decisions taken on each item of business.

How to Plan for a Meeting

(A simple student account – in the capacity of secretary to the meeting)

1. Before the meeting, I consulted the chairperson about the number of participants expected to attend the proposed meeting in order to choose a suitable room/venue.
2. I decided on the seating arrangement to suit the numbers attending and the general mood of the chairperson (negotiating style) – as this was a type of brainstorming session, where new ideas would be embraced!
   Note: Room layout styles are illustrated in the next section.
3. I made sure that OHP equipment (machine and pens) and Internet/computer facilities would be available to the group as one participant wished to use visual aids (Microsoft Powerpoint).
4. I placed a clip notepad, pen and mineral water at each participant's space.
5. I then checked with the chairperson about the date, time and agenda of the meeting before I posted the notice and agenda in a prominent place, well in advance of the meeting.
6. When everyone was seated and the meeting was about to commence, I put up a poster on the outside of the meeting room door 'Meeting in Progress, Please Do Not Disturb'.

Layout Plan of a Meeting

ROOM LAYOUT

The secretary should always ensure that the meeting room is laid out properly. The chosen meeting room should be laid out in whatever style is appropriate for the size, degree of participation and formality of the meeting.

The way in which the furniture is arranged for meetings can have a big effect on the atmosphere and efficiency. For example, a meeting held round a boardroom table has a completely different atmosphere from one in which participants are free to place their chairs where they wish. The following are eight common arrangements and layouts of the meeting room:

1. Boardroom
2. Round table
3. Negotiating
4. Freestyle
5. Theatre style
6. Schoolroom
7. Horseshoe
8. Herring-bone.

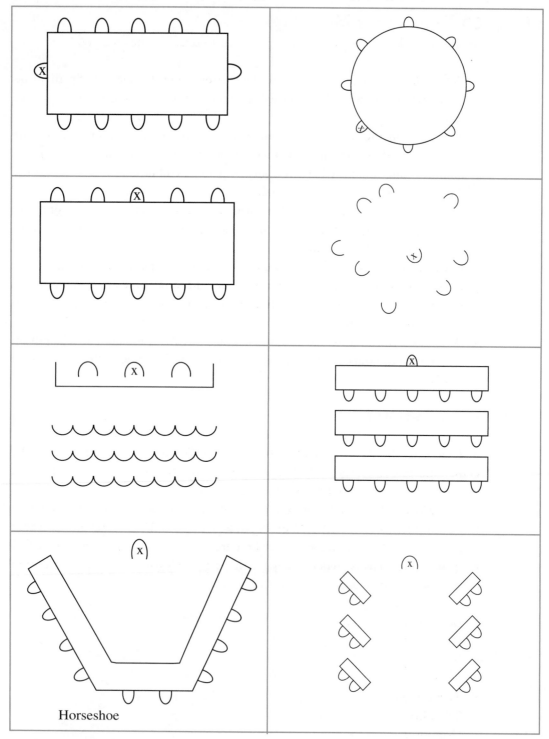

Figure 5.1 Eight arrangements of a meeting (note: X indicates where the Chairperson is seated).

When laying out the plan of the meeting, the following are some of the considerations required to be taken into account beforehand.

(a) The time and place of the meeting should be known well in advance.
(b) Agendas must be circulated well before the date of the meeting.
(c) Minutes must be written up as soon as possible after the meeting.
(d) In relation to the meeting room:
  - Inform reception
  - Put notice on the door notifying that a meeting is in progress
  - Have refreshments available if a long meeting is expected
  - Collect files, reports and attendance sheets
  - Remember spare agendas, paper and shorthand notebook
  - Have graphs and charts (if needed)
  - Redirect incoming calls
  - Locate tape recorder (if required)
  - Check cloakroom facilities available
  - Ensure adequate heating, lighting and ventilation.

In all formal meetings the following seating arrangement is a must. The chairperson must sit in the middle with the secretary sitting on his/her right-hand side, and the treasurer seated on the left.

Minutes of a Meeting

After the closure of a meeting, the secretary has the responsibility of writing up the minutes of the meeting. The minutes of a meeting are a written account of what was discussed and what decisions were taken at a meeting. At a subsequent meeting the minutes should be read, proposed and seconded and then signed by the chairperson when adopted, thus ensuring accuracy. The minutes of a meeting are of extreme importance. If a dispute arises, the court can ask to see the minutes of a meeting. Therefore they must be accurate. With regard to the Companies Act 1963, all companies must keep the minutes of meetings held by directors and shareholders.

Information which should be included in the minutes of a meeting are:

- The type of meeting
- The date, time and place of meeting
- Names in attendance
- Names of absentees
- The approval of previous meeting Minutes, containing signature of chairperson showing/indicating approval
- Summary on matters arising from Minutes

- The resolutions passed or motions rejected
- The adjournment, postponement until a later date, or conclusion of the meeting
- The date of the next meeting (if decided).

Reports

A report is a summary, or an account, of what was investigated, what terms of reference were used and what findings resulted. A report should be laid out and presented clearly to its readers. Reports are needed for many reasons such as:

- Assessment or investigation of a situation
- Recommending a course of action based on findings
- Circulating new information or ideas or work needed to be undertaken
- Keeping others informed of progress on particular projects.

The following are the rules which apply when writing up a report:

Accuracy – the report should be correct and exact.
Brevity – the report should be of a reasonable length.
Clarity – the report should be clear and understandable
Simplicity – the report should be simple, not complicated.

Conclusion

When studying this topic 'Planning Meetings', it became obvious that an effective meeting is an extremely efficient tool in the communication of an organisation. Communication is of vital importance for an organisation in order for it to be successful and gain profits. Meetings inform those within a company of important issues, decisions, problems, goals, objectives and potential new developments. Meetings help to keep those within an organisation up to date with company activities, its financial position and how it compares with competitors.

Meetings – the Top 20

The following are guidelines which directors, chairpersons, managers and supervisors should follow in order to maintain an effective meeting at any hierarchical level.

TOP 10 DOS
Set clear objectives for every meeting.
Circulate agenda and papers in advance.
Complete thorough personal preparation.
Choose a suitable room and lay it out carefully.
Stick firmly to the agenda.
Use visual aids as a help to control discussion.

Time your contributions carefully.

Use the skills and knowledge of all participants.

Use time sensibly throughout.

TOP 10 DON'TS

Don't hold a meeting unless it is really necessary.

Don't invite people who need not attend.

Don't wait for latecomers unless there is a special reason to do so.

Don't let personal feelings affect meeting behaviour.

Don't mix creativity with criticism.

Don't take part in more than one discussion at one time.

Don't force a decision before adequate debate.

Don't argue directly with other participants; debate through the Chair.

Don't, when in the Chair, express your own views unless it is essential to do so.

PRACTICE QUESTIONS

1. Who are the main Officers at a meeting?
2. What are the functions of the Chairperson of a meeting?
3. What is a Chairperson's Agenda? Draft your own example.
4. What are the functions of the Secretary of a meeting?
5. What are the functions of the Treasurer of a meeting?
6. Explain the following terms:
   (a) Motion
   (b) Quorum
   (c) Point of Order
   (d) Through the Chair
   (e) Casting Vote
   (f) Unanimously Carried.
7. What *three* main unwritten rules govern most formal meetings?
8. In what different ways can a vote be taken?
9. What do the following terms mean with regard to meetings?
   (a) Notice
   (b) Agenda
   (c) Minutes.
10. Explain the *three* categories of Minutes of a meeting.
11. What are the reasons for compiling a Report? What headings are normally used?

Sample Assignment Brief – Meetings

1. You are the secretary at a meeting. Explain the plans that you put in place in advance of the meeting. Support your plans with illustrations as appropriate.

2. Having attended the meeting, please submit the following business documents:
   (a) Notice of the meeting.
   (b) Agenda of the meeting.
   (c) Minutes of the meeting (please attach written notes).

Please note – all formal documents should be formally presented, with particular attention paid to layout, spelling and punctuation.

Sample Student Assignment

1. Plans I put in place in advance of the meeting:

- I chose a suitable room that would suit about 15 people.
- I decided on a horseshoe room layout style having consulted with the chairperson.
- I made sure all participants had pen, pencil and paper at their station as well as mineral water.
- I checked with the chairperson regarding equipment that might be needed if any of the participants were giving a presentation (e.g. overhead projector, OHP pens, flipcharts and pens, computer for Powerpoint presentation, TV, video, DVD, CD players). However, none was needed.
- I checked with the chairperson regarding the agenda and the time and length of the proposed meeting and then posted the Notice and Agenda on the main notice board.
- On the day of the meeting, just before it started, I posted a notice on the outside of the meeting room door 'Meeting in Progress, Please Do Not Enter'.

Layout and Seating Plan

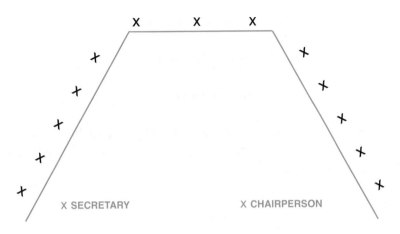

2. a. Notice

NOTICE

A Meeting of the Borris College of Further Education
Fashion Show Committee will take place
on
Thursday 18 October 20XX
at
9.30a.m.
in
Room 1, Top Floor
Borris College

2. b. Agenda

AGENDA

1. Apologies
2. Date, Time, Venue and Refreshments
3. Sponsors, Advertising and Tickets
4. Models and Clothes
5. A.O.B.
6. Date of next meeting

Sign

MEETING IN PROGRESS

PLEASE DO NOT ENTER

2. c. Minutes

Borris College of Further Education

Fashion Show Committee

Minutes of Meeting

These are the minutes of the meeting of the BORCFE Fashion Show Committee that was held on Thursday 18 October 20XX at 9.30a.m. in Room 1, Top Floor, Borris College of Further Education:

PRESENT

Ms Jane Fitzpatrick (Chairperson)
Ms Miriam Ryan (Secretary)
Ms Susan Browne
Ms Fiona White
Mr Joseph Black
Mr Frank Walshe
Ms Joan McCarthy
Ms Vera Lynn
Ms Jacinta Henderson
Ms Gemma McDonnell
Ms Roisin Wren
Mr David George

APOLOGIES

Ms Mary Ryan was unable to attend due to work-related matters.

DATE, TIME, VENUE AND REFRESHMENTS

It was agreed that the show should be staged on 5 December 20XX and that it will commence at 8p.m. with a 7.30p.m. wine and cheese reception. It was also agreed that the interval should happen at 9p.m. for a duration of 15 minutes.

Fiona suggested that the venue should be Jurys Hotel, based on a proposed discount offered by them. She also informed the meeting that she had checked the costs of ramp, host and lighting/music and all amounted to €500.

SPONSORS, ADVERTISING AND TICKETS

It was agreed that the chosen charity would be ISPCC Children's Charity.

Frank agreed to research sponsors by getting a list of existing suppliers to the college.

Susan proposed that an 'event publication' with different sized advertisements might be offered in return for contributions of money, services or goods on the night. Joan said that she would encourage Graphics students to help with the publication. Vera also said she had some desktop publishing skills that might be of use.

Joseph agreed to get the tickets printed for free by a printer he knows.

MODELS AND CLOTHES

It was agreed that there would be six male models and twelve female models, all of whom will be students of the college. Miriam and George agreed jointly to look after the clothes, where some previous student designs could be showcased as well as a good selection of shops. A selection of evening casual, sports and bridal wear could be organised.

Gemma agreed to train the students on Wednesday of each week commencing next week with auditions in the afternoon.

ANY OTHER BUSINESS

Susan agreed to deal with the raffle and to source prizes from different businesses in the city and from staff in the college.

NEXT MEETING

It was agreed that the next meeting will take place on Thursday 25 October at 9.30a.m.

_____

Secretary

_____

Chairperson

_____

Date

6. Processing Business Documents

Definitions and Explanations of Documents and Business Terms including Discounts and VAT

The different types of business organisation discussed in Chapter 1 must all involve themselves in paperwork in order to track transactions. The Documents that are part of everyday business are:

1. LETTERS OF ENQUIRY

The formal procedure for enquiring about a prospective supplier's prices and terms of trade is for the business that is enquiring to write a 'letter of enquiry' stating 'Please send me information on the following good, etc.' This form of enquiry has in recent times been replaced by simply telephoning and the subsequent receipt of a fax including the information asked for.

Email has also replaced the letter of enquiry. It is, however, important to be able to structure any enquiry using the appropriate letter presentation (sample given later).

2. PRICE LISTS AND QUOTATIONS

Customers who do not trade with the business on a regular basis usually ask for a Price List. Regular traders who aim to have future accounts with the business usually request a Quotation.

The Quotation is an important document as it is proof of the prices offered and any trade agreements made between traders that operate on a credit basis (i.e. who do not pay immediately – buyers who have accounts with different suppliers). Accounts are usually set up if the buyer is a regular customer and discounts are built into the transaction.

3. TERMS OF TRADE

These are the trade agreements made between the supplier and the purchaser (seller and buyer) regarding Trade Discounts and Cash/Settlement Discounts, and these are indicated on the Quotation. Sixty days' Credit means that the Supplier allows the buyer approximately two months to pay the Invoice (Bill). Most Suppliers offer 30 days' (or net one month) credit to buyers.

Usually if a bill or invoice is dated 2 June and 60 days' credit is allowed, this means that the buyer does not *strictly* have to pay within 60 days. It does mean, however, that this invoice must be paid by 31 August. The same would apply if the invoice were dated 30 June. A longer payment period is gained if the invoice is dated at the beginning of the month.

The three types of discount that exist are:

(a) Trade Discount: given by suppliers to regular buyers on a long-term basis. This discount is a form of recognition for staying with the same supplier and ensuring them of your continued business. The percentage allowed is often 10%.
(b) Settlement Discount: given only if amounts due are paid within a specific time period (often 14 days); can be between two and five per cent.
(c) Cash Discount (COD): given if the buyer pays cash immediately over the counter (varies depending on the bill).

Most traders 'shop around' and try to get the best quotation possible, keeping an eye of course on quality.

4. PURCHASE ORDER

This is a letter sent from the buyer to the supplier to order a certain amount of goods. The buyer usually keeps one copy to check against the delivery docket and the invoice. Goods are more often ordered directly over the phone and the order is entered into an order book at both the buyer end and the supplier end. This is an important exercise because the volume of transactions in one day makes it impossible to keep a mental track of every order made. This order will subsequently be checked against the delivery docket when the goods arrive. Often Purchase Orders are faxed to the supplier and confirmation of receipt of the fax might be in the form of a return phone call.

5. DELIVERY DOCKETS

These are Dockets that arrive with the goods supplied. When the goods are dispatched (sent out), the warehouse supervisor who releases the goods checks them against the purchase order and retains the top copy of the Delivery Docket. The goods are usually dispatched by road, rail or air transport, and the person delivering the goods asks the person receiving the goods to sign the second copy which duplicates on to a third copy underneath it. The delivery person takes the second copy back to the suppliers' headquarters and this is verification that the goods were delivered. The third copy remains with the goods and the buyer.

6. INVOICES

An Invoice is a bill sent by the supplier to the buyer, charging him/her for the goods that were delivered. A reference Delivery Docket Number and Purchase Order Number (where required) appears on the invoice in order to make it easy to match the documents mentioned.

- Pro-Forma Invoice (PFI): This document looks like an invoice but is only a sample. It gives details of what would appear on a valid invoice to inform the customer, in advance of deciding to purchase, about cost, carriage (transport costs) and VAT charges.
- Cash Invoice: is an invoice given to a buyer if they pay over the counter immediately whether by cash, cheque or credit card.
- Credit Invoice: is an invoice that the supplier sends to the buyer. The buyer is given one, two or three months to pay the bill.

VAT

VAT means value added tax. It appears on invoices. It is an indirect tax levied on goods and services by government. This means it is collected by different parties and paid to the government.

VAT is a regressive tax (it does not take account of the ability to pay). For example, a pensioner and a millionaire might want to buy furniture at a selling price that includes 21 per cent VAT. This 21 per cent will not be reduced for the pensioner.

VAT is charged at different rates for various goods and services:

- **21 per cent:** The standard rate of VAT; all goods and services that do not fall into the reduced-rate categories are charged at this rate. They include alcohol, audio-visual equipment, car parts and accessories, CDs, computers, consultancy services, cosmetics, detergents, diesel, fridges, furniture and furnishings, hardware, jewellery, lawnmowers, machinery, medicines (non-oral), office equipment, pet food, petrol, paper, tobacco, toys, tools, washing machines, bottled water.
- **13.5 per cent**: A reduced rate of VAT for items including fuel (coal, heating oil, gas), electricity, veterinary fees, building and building services, agricultural contracting services, short-term car hire, cleaning and maintenance services.
- **9 per cent:** A new reduced rate of VAT for tourism-related activities including restaurants, hotels, cinemas, hairdressing and newspapers. It applies for the period 1 July 2011 to 31 December 2013.
- **4.8 per cent:** A reduced rate of VAT specifically for agriculture. It applies to livestock (excluding chickens), greyhounds and the hire of horses.
- **0 per cent:** Zero-rated VAT includes all exports, tea, coffee, milk, bread, books, children's clothes and shoes, oral medicine for humans and animals, vegetable seeds and fruit trees, fertilisers, large animal feed, disability aids such as wheelchairs, crutches and hearing aids.

EXEMPT FROM VAT

You do not have to pay any VAT on financial, medical or educational services. You may also not pay VAT for live theatrical and musical performances (except those where food or drink is served during all or part of the performance).

DIFFERENCE BETWEEN EXEMPTION AND ZERO-RATING

If a business person supplies taxable goods or services, including zero-rated ones, they can claim VAT back from the government on their taxable business purchases. However, if someone only supplies exempt goods or services, they cannot reclaim VAT.

Differences between zero-rated VAT and exempt from VAT

Some sellers, such as those who sell goods for charity, are exempt from VAT. They are regarded as non-profit-making organisations and cannot claim VAT back on purchases made. Other sellers, like those selling bread, do not charge VAT because bread is regarded as a necessity. However, because these sellers are officially trading, they are allowed to claim VAT back on their purchases. They are therefore zero-rated suppliers/sellers. Some other zero-rated traders are funeral undertakers and sellers of books and periodicals.

Most goods have VAT levied on them at the point of sale. Goods are usually subject to 21 per cent VAT, and services are usually subject to 13.5 per cent VAT.

Why Cross-check Purchase Orders, Delivery Dockets and Invoices?

Mistakes can sometimes be made, such as:

- The wrong order being delivered (due to a mix-up/mistakes made by the clerk or dispatcher), or
- Too few or too many goods are sent.

If discrepancies are undetected, a business can lose a lot of money, and cost effectiveness is one of the main objectives of successful firms.

- Purchase invoices received are entered into the Purchases Book to keep an account of the volume and type of goods received.
- Sales invoices that are compiled by businesses and sent to their customers are entered into the Sales Book to keep an account of the volume of sales, how many debtors there are, and how much each debtor owes.

What to do when discrepancies are discovered

CREDIT NOTES

A Credit Note is sent by the supplier giving the buyer recognition of credit given for the return of goods due to:

1. The goods being damaged in transit (while being transported), flawed or faulty.
2. An overcharge, when too many goods were delivered and charged for on the invoice. (The delivery does not match the original Purchase Order.)
3. Wrong goods were delivered. (Possibly a mix-up with another customer's order.)

DEBIT NOTES

If a buyer realises that he/she has been undercharged, human nature tells us that the likelihood that the buyer will run to the phone and inform the supplier is fairly slim!

If, however, the supplier detects the mistake, it will be brought to the attention of the buyer and a Debit Note will be sent to the customer to make up the difference, i.e. the undercharge.

A Debit Note is like another invoice that was forgotten about, except for the important difference that it is directly connected with a particular invoice that was sent previously. The reference invoice number will appear on the Debit Note. When the buyer receives the Debit Note, a copy of it can be clipped directly to the corresponding invoice.

STATEMENTS

This is a document that is sent to the buyer to inform him/her about how much is owed to the supplier. It is usually sent out by the supplier every month, listing all the invoices that have been sent out, any Credit Notes and Debit Notes sent out, and any payments made by the buyer.

PRACTICE QUESTIONS

1. What *nine* business documents do businesses send out and receive on a regular basis? Define *each* briefly.
2. Distinguish between a Price List and a Quotation.
3. What are Credit Terms?
4. Name *three* discounts that business people avail of and distinguish clearly between them.
5. What is the difference between a Credit Invoice and a Cash Invoice?
6. Explain in detail what VAT is.
7. What are the differences between 'Zero Rated VAT' and 'Exempt from VAT'?
8. Why is it necessary to match up documents?
9. In each of the following cases, what document is compiled to indicate:
   (a) An undercharge
   (b) A return of goods
   (c) An overcharge
   (d) An omission from an invoice?

SAMPLE QUOTATION

No. 12212

NEERY FIREPLACES LTD
21 REDROSE INDUSTRIAL PARK
KELLS
CO. MEATH

Customer Name: Mr Michael Walsh

Customer Address: Edenfoley Builders Ltd,
                      Athboy,
                      Co. Meath.

Telephone: (042) 431212

Date: 2/5/XX

The following are the terms of agreement that we wish to offer you with the view to doing business with you in the near future.

Terms: 60 Days' Credit
                    Trade Discount 13.5% on all orders
                    Cash/Settlement Discount 5% extra if paid Net one month
                    Carriage paid

- **Prices and the terms of agreement will be reviewed every six months and are subject to change. We ensure that we will give you due notice of any such planned changes.**

We hope that the terms that we are offering you are to your satisfaction and we anticipate trading with you soon.

We will be glad at any time to clarify any queries that you might have regarding our product range.

Yours faithfully

Mary Malone

Mary Malone
Sales Manager

Choosing Suppliers, Pricing and Assessing Quotations

When a person starts in business, he/she may decide to purchase raw materials from suppliers in the local area to minimise transport costs (Carriage).

Carriage Inwards: is a *trading cost* of transportation that suppliers put on bills when they invoice a buyer. The supplier has at this stage already paid the cost.

Carriage Outwards: is an *expense* to a supplier when he/she delivers goods to a buyer and bears the transportation cost.

Quality and Cost Minimisation (keeping costs at a minimum) are both difficult to weigh against each other. It is often said that you pay for what you get. However, it is worthwhile remembering that:

1. If you wish to follow the Economic Route the larger stores are able to sell at cheaper prices (because they buy in bulk and are able to avail of large trade discounts) and a lot of their products are of good quality. This is called an 'Economy of Scale' – one of the benefits of larger-scale operations
2. If you wish to specialise, specialist shops and outlets are relatively more expensive but their turnover is good in their own 'Niche Product Areas'.

It is only with some experience that businesses find suitable suppliers who charge prices that make it cost effective for the business that is buying to trade.

It must be remembered that a Mark-up on cost prices must be estimated and be worthwhile for the business. The cost price must be low enough for the business to sell their products or service successfully at a profit. Breakeven Analysis, discussed in Chapter 2, outlines how a breakeven price can be arrived at.

PRACTICE QUESTIONS
1. What is the difference between Carriage Inwards and Carriage Outwards?
2. Why is it difficult to reach a happy medium between maintaining Quality and keeping Costs down?
3. What is the meaning of the term 'Niche Product Area'?

Example 1: Purchase Order Cash Invoice Exercise and Suggested Solution

Ms Fitzpatrick was redecorating her house and she had previously visited and spoken with a sales consultant in All Weather Paints. She sent a Purchase Order by fax to Jim Smith of All Weather Paints, having written a Letter of Enquiry also addressed to him. Jim faxed the Price List to her and, having delivered the goods, he subsequently sent her the Invoice. Note how the Invoice figures are calculated by reference to the Price List and the Purchase Order.

- When compiling the Invoice it is important to remember that Discount is always subtracted before VAT is added.

LETTER OF ENQUIRY

12 The Lawns
Clonmel
Co. Tipperary
Tel: (0504) 22422
Fax: (0504) 22423

10/7/XX

Mr Jim Smith
All Weather Paints
Weatherfield
Thurles
Co. Tipperary

Dear Jim,

Following our phone conversation, kindly forward to me a current Price List of your products. I hope to purchase some of them in the near future.

Yours truly,

Jane Fitzpatrick

Jane Fitzpatrick

PRICE LIST OF PAINTING AND DECORATING PRODUCTS

ALL WEATHER PAINTS

PRODUCT CODES	DESCRIPTION OF PRODUCTS	VAT	PRICE (in euros)
P(IN) 75	Interior Matt 1 lt	B	7.50
P(IN) 50	Interior Gloss 1 lt	B	9.00
P(IN) 80	Interior Vinyl Silk 1 lt	B	7.50
P(IN) 100	Interior Eggshell (Alkyd) 1 lt	B	11.00
P(IN) 110	Interior Eggshell (Acrylic) 1 lt	B	8.50
P(Ex) 150	Exterior Matt 2.5 lt	B	12.00
P(Ex) 90	Exterior Matt 10 lt	B	37.00
P(Misc) 120	Scrumble Trans Oil Glaze 2.5 lt	B	45.00
Br200	Badger Softener	B	41.00
Br195	Stencil Brush	B	1.50
Br90	Sable Writer	B	7.00
Br12	Paint Brush 1.5 inch pure Bristle	B	6.00
Br14	Paint Brush 2 inch pure Bristle	B	10.00
Br16	Paint Brush 2.5 inch pure Bristle	B	12.00
Br18	Paint Brush 3 inch pure Bristle	B	15.00
Br20	Paint Brush 4 inch pure Bristle	B	25.00
Br22	Paint Brush 6 inch pure Bristle	B	30.00
Sp110	Sea Sponge (Synthetic)	B	7.50
Sp120	Marine Natural Sea Sponge (Lge)	B	40.00
Sp80	Marine Natural Sea Sponge (Sm)	B	30.00
Pap100	Wall Stripper	B	250.00
Pap120	Wallpaper Table	B	15.00
Pap130	Wallpaper Hanging Brush	B	20.00
Pap133	Seam Roller	B	4.50
Sc170	Scaffolding 4ft h x 3.5 ft w	B	72.50
WSp 12	White Spirit (Sm)	B	2.00
WSp 14	White Spirit (Lge)	B	4.75
Ro186	Roller (9 inch)	B	12.50
Ro120	Roller (6 inch)	B	6.50
Ro124	Roller Extension Poll	B	15.00
SERVICE	INTERIOR DESIGNER	A	QUOTE

Large Range of Paints and Wallpaper available

Wallpapers Prices from €10 to €150 per roll

Wallpaper Borders from €10 to €20 per roll

VAT CODES	A = 13.5%		B = 21%

WRITTEN PURCHASE ORDER

12 The Lawns
Clonmel
Co. Tipperary
Tel: (0503) 22422
Fax: (0503) 22423

Date: 15/7/XX

Mr Jim Smith
All Weather Paints
Weatherfield
Thurles
Co. Tipperary

Dear Jim,

Please supply me with the following goods as soon as is convenient.

CODE NUMBER	QUANTITY
P(IN) 80 (Rose Colour)	5 Lt
P(IN) 110 (Rose Colour)	1 Lt
Br195	2
Sp110	1
WSp12	1

Please include on the bill that you are sending to me an amount of €30 plus VAT that I owe your Interior Design Consultant.

When you deliver the goods I will pay cash on delivery. Please phone me in advance to arrange a time of delivery.

Yours truly,

Jane Fitzpatrick

Jane Fitzpatrick

Having received this written purchase order from the cash customer, All Weather Paints allocates an Order Number to it for reference purposes. The Order Number is 4567.

DELIVERY DOCKET

From: All Weather Paints
      Weatherfield
      Thurles
      Co. Tipperary

No: 230
Date: 20/7/XX
Order No: 4567

GOODS:

5 lt Interior Vinyl Silk – Rose Colour	Ref: P(IN) 80
1 lt Interior Eggshell (Acrylic)	Ref: P(IN) 110
2 Stencil Brushes	Ref: Br 195
1 Sea Sponge (Synthetic)	Ref: Sp 110
1 Small Bottle White Spirit	Ref: WSp 12

Received the above goods:

Signed:

Jane Fitzpatrick

CASH SALES INVOICE
ALL WEATHER PAINTS

Weatherfield
Thurles
Co. Tipperary
Telephone: (0504) 21331
Fax: (0504) 21332
VAT No. IE 1234567 D
Purchase Order Number: 4567
Invoice Number: 1101

Ms Jane Fitzpatrick
12 The Lawns
Clonmel
Co. Tipperary

Date: 20/7/XX

Product Code	Q	Description of product	Price p. unit	Vat 13.5%	VAT 21%	Total
P(IN) 80	5 lt	Interior Vinyl Silk-Rose Colour	€7.50 p Lt			€37.50
P(IN) 110	1 lt	Interior Eggshell (Acrylic)	€8.50 p Lt			€8.50
Br 195	2 no.	Stencil Brushes	€1.50 ea.			€3.00
Sp 110	1 no.	Sea Sponge (Synthetic)	€7.50 ea.			€7.50
WSp 12	1 no.	White Spirit (Sm)	€2 ea.			€2.00
SERVICE		Interior Design Service	€30	€30.00		
Totals				€30.00	€58.50	
		Less Cash Discount 5%		€1.50	€2.93	
				€28.50	€55.57	
		Add VAT		€3.85	€11.67	
				€32.35	€67.24	
Total						€99.59
Plus Carriage						€10.00
Total Invoice Price						€109.59

Since Ms Fitzpatrick has agreed to pay cash on receipt of the goods, the Cash Invoice serves as the Delivery Docket and she has been given a 5% Cash Discount because she is paying COD. This type of gesture by a business helps to give the business a competitive edge and entices the customer to return again to purchase goods – maintains consumer loyalty.

Example 2: Credit Invoice Exercise and Suggested Solution

QUESTION

Kelly and Sons Painting and Decorating Subcontractors have been trading regularly with All Weather Paints and can avail of an ongoing 10% Trade Discount which is deducted from every bill irrespective of when it is paid. This agreement was reached when the two parties began trading a long time ago. On 7/8/XX Kelly and Sons placed the following order for goods.

You are required to compile

1. The Purchase Order dated 7/8/XX
2. The Delivery Docket dated 8/8/XX
3. The Credit Invoice dated 10/8/XX

Code No.	Quantity
Br20	5
Sc170	1
P(EX) 150 Magnolia	2 tins
P(IN) 75 White	10 lt
P(IN) 50 White	10 lt
P(IN) 80 White	10 lt

SOLUTION

PURCHASE ORDER

No: 4898

Customer Name: Kelly and Sons Painters & Decorators
Customer Address: Randles Park
Clonmel
Co. Tipperary
Telephone: (0506) 31212

Date: 7/8/XX

TO: Mr Jim Smith
All Weather Paints
Weatherfield
Thurles
Co. Tipperary

Code Ref.	Quantity	Description	VAT Rate (%)	Unit Price
Br 20	5 no.	Paint Brush 4"	B	€25.00 ea.
Sc 170	1 no.	Scaffolding 4'h x 3.5'w	B	€72.50 ea.
P(Ex) 150 Magn	2 tins	Exterior Matt 2.5 lt	B	€12.00 p. lt
P(IN) 75 White	10 lt	Interior Matt 1 lt	B	€7.50 p. lt
P(IN) 50 White	10 lt	Interior Gloss 1 lt	B	€9.00 p. lt
P(IN) 80 White	10 lt	Interior Vinyl Silk 1 lt	B	€7.50 p. lt

Delivery Instructions: Delivery by transit van on 8/8/XX

Signed *Mick Kelly*

Purchasing Officer

DELIVERY DOCKET

From: All Weather Paints
       Weatherfield
       Thurles
       Co. Tipperary

No. 234
Date: 8/8/XX
Order No: 4898

GOODS:

5 no.	Paint Brush 4"	Ref: Br 20
1 no.	Scaffolding 4'h x 3.5'w	Ref: Sc 170
2 lt	Exterior Matt 2.5 lt	Ref: P(Ex) 150 Magn
10 lt	Interior Matt 1 lt	Ref: P(IN) 75 White
10 lt	Interior Gloss 1 lt	Ref: P(IN) 50 White
10 lt	Interior Vinyl Silk 1 lt	Ref: P(IN) 80 White

Received the above goods:

Signed: *Mick Kelly*

CREDIT INVOICE
ALL WEATHER PAINTS

Weatherfield
Thurles
Co. Tipperary

Telephone: (0504) 21331
Fax: (0504) 21332
VAT No. IE 1234567 D
Purchase Order Number: 4898
Invoice Number: 1102

Date 10/8/XX

Kelly and Sons
Painters & Decorators
Randles Park
Clonmel
Co. Tipperary

Product Code	Quantity	Description of Product	Price p. unit	VAT 13.5%	VAT 21%
Br20	5 no.	Paint Brush 4"	€25.00 ea.		€125.00
SC170	1 no.	Scaffolding 4'h x 3.5'w	€72.50 ea.		€72.50
P(Ex) 150 Magnol	2 lt	Exterior Matt 2.5 lt	€12.00 p. lt		€24.00
P(IN) 75 White	10 lt	Interior Matt 1 lt	€7.50 p. lt		€75.00
P(IN) 50 White	10 lt	Interior Gloss 1 lt	€9.00 p. lt		€90.00
P(IN) 80 White	10 lt	Interior Vinyl Silk 1 lt	€7.50 p. lt		€75.00
Total					**€461.50**
		Less Trade Discount 10%			€46.15
					€415.35
		Add VAT			€87.22
Total Invoice Price					**€502.57**

Terms of Trade: Net One Month; Trade Discount 10%, Cash Discount 5%, 14 days 2.5%

Example 3: Routing an Invoice – Student Exercise

This means sourcing an invoice or tracing its origin. It involves compiling the corresponding:
1. Delivery Docket.
2. Purchase Order.
3. Quotation.
4. Letter of Enquiry.

Refer to the appropriate Practice Question at the end of the chapter.

Example 4: Identifying Discrepancies on Orders and Invoices

(includes a Credit Note and Debit Note):

Refer to the All Weather Paints Price List at the beginning of the section:
On 12/8/XX Mary Jones, Limerick Builders Ltd, Main Street, Limerick, telephoned the following order to All Weather Paints:

Quantity	Product Code
10	P(IN) 75 Burnt Sienna
3	Br 195
4	WSp 14

She received the correct goods and checked the Delivery Docket that arrived with the goods to verify this. On 14/8/XX Mary received the Invoice for the goods. However, when she checked the Purchase Order Form she realised that the Invoice stated P(IN) 50 in error. She immediately phoned All Weather Paints and they confirmed the mistake and forwarded the Credit Note to Mary a day later thereby acknowledging the overcharge.

Refer to the All Weather Paints Price List at the beginning of the section:

CREDIT NOTE
ALL WEATHER PAINTS

No: C/N676

Weatherfield
Thurles
Co. Tipperary
Telephone: (0504) 21331
Fax: (0504) 21332
VAT No. IE 1234567 D
Reference Purchase Order Number 2323
Reference Invoice Number 3424

Ms Mary Jones
Limerick Builders Ltd, Main Street, Limerick

Date: 15/8/XX

Date	Details	Price	Total
	Incorrect Product Code P(IN) 50 Burnt Sienna Should be P(IN) 75 Burnt Sienna Subsequent Overcharge	10 x €2.50	€25.00
	Add VAT @ 21%		5.25
	TOTAL CREDIT GIVEN		€30.25

Important Note:

As already mentioned, Credit Notes are also sent by suppliers when a buyer returns damaged goods or goods which were not ordered.

Example 5: Debit Note – Question and Solution

Refer to the All Weather Paints Price List at the beginning of the section:

On 20/8/XX Mary Jones, Limerick Builders Ltd, Main Street, Limerick, telephoned the following order to All Weather Paints:

Quantity	Product Code
14	P(EX) 90 Magnolia
1	P(EX) 150 Magnolia

She received the goods the day after she phoned and she checked the Delivery Docket to verify that she had received all the goods she had ordered. She received the Invoice for the goods the next day and realised that Product Code P(EX) 150 had not been charged for. She received a phone call from Jim Smith, All Weather Paints, that day to inform her of the error. He said that he would send on a Debit Note to rectify the undercharge, and this arrived two days later.

DEBIT NOTE

ALL WEATHER PAINTS **No: D/N389**

Weatherfield
Thurles
Co. Tipperary

Telephone:(0504) 21331
Fax: (0504) 21332
VAT No. IE 1234567 D
Reference Purchase Order Number 2848
Reference Invoice Number 3797

Date: 24/8/XX

Ms Mary Jones
Limerick Builders Ltd
Main Street
Limerick

Date	Details	Price	Total
	Item omitted from Invoice No. 3797		
	P(EX) 150 – undercharge	1 x €12.00	€12.00
	Add VAT @ 21%		€2.52
	TOTAL		€14.52

Important Notes:

Once an Invoice is sent out it cannot be changed. This is why Credit Notes and Debit Notes play such an important part in the correction of errors when traders are engaged in transactions.

• In the last two examples, Trade Discount was not allowed to Limerick Builders.

Payment Methods

Money is legal tender, that is, a means of payment that must be accepted by law in return for payment of a debt. The most common payment methods to date are payments by:

1. CHEQUE (CHEQUE CARD VALIDATION)

A Cheque Card is given to all creditworthy current account holders. It is nearly always requested by the shop or outlet to verify the authenticity of the cheque – to ensure that the cheque will not 'bounce' (not enough money in the account to meet it). If there is a shortfall in the account the bank will allow the account to go into debt (the red) because they trust the customer to restore the balance in the account to a credit balance (money in the account) as soon as possible. So if you have a cheque card to accompany cheques, any embarrassment will be avoided.

2. CREDIT CARD

Payment using a credit card is immediately validated by computer (e.g. in super-markets) or with card number via phone or Internet.

Credit cards are generally given to creditworthy customers. The bank or financial institution sets a Credit Limit and it allows the customer to use the money reserve whenever he or she needs to do so. However, a set minimum amount of the debt must be cleared when the Statement of Account arrives at the end of the month. Otherwise large amounts of interest will accrue on the debt.

When a credit card is used to deposit and withdraw funds the chip and PIN facility is very convenient for the customer. Nowadays most shops and business outlets have machines allowing a customer to pay for goods or services by inserting their credit card into the desktop card machine and keying in their PIN number. This increases the negative balance on the credit card – in other words the customer's debt – but it is a very convenient payment method.

3. CHARGE CARDS

Charge cards are issued by businesses to their regular customers, allowing them a money reserve that is based on the same principle as credit cards. The difference is that the customer is confined to shopping in that store or business when availing of the money reserve. The shop issues the customer with a bill and a minimum amount of the debt must be paid off at the end of the month to avoid large interest charges.

Credit and Charge Cards are very useful if the bills received are managed tightly. They give the customer a sense of security always knowing that money is available if needed (positive cash flow). On the other hand, they can work out to be a debt-generating habit, that is, prone to getting out of control.

4. CASH AVAILABILITY FROM BANKS OR FINANCIAL INSTITUTIONS (PLASTIC CARDS/ATM)

Some people refer to the ATMs (Automatic Teller Machines) jokingly as 'The Hole in the Wall' or 'The Drink Link'. Most are open twenty-four hours a day. This method of using the Plastic Card, keying in a PIN Number (Personal Identification Number) and withdrawing money is, nowadays, the most convenient and common method of withdrawing cash. Cash can also be lodged in this way by using a Lodgment Envelope. During office hours, cash can also be withdrawn using a Withdrawal Docket in the bank or financial institution.

5. INTERNET/24-HOUR BANKING, CODE CARDS, ATM/LASER CARDS/DEBIT CARDS AND CASHBACK

This type of payment method is common nowadays when transacting in business. ATM cardholders can register for 24-hour banking and using a registration number and secret PIN number can access their accounts either online or on the phone instead of having to visit the bank or financial institution.

Options that are available include funds transfer (EFT, discussed in Chapter 3) from one account to another and bill payments. The cardholder has to key in his or her secret PIN number and for security reasons to verify numbers that either appear on a code card or that are part of the PIN number.

The extra facilities available with an ATM card makes it simple and convenient to pay bills and transfer funds using only the computer keyboard or the phone.

There is now a Laser facility on ATM cards that allows cardholders to pay bills in shops, for example the shopping bill at the checkout. Instead of having to go to the ATM machine the customer can simply pay with their ATM debit card (Laser card) and can opt to get cash back with their change. This money is taken straight out of the cardholder's bank account at the checkout. Customers can also pay using Online Debit (also known as PIN Debit) or Offline Debit (also known as Signature Debit)

Businesses are increasingly using these methods to pay their creditors and other overheads like phone and electricity bills.

6. BANK GIRO/CREDIT TRANSFER

The method used to pay a person to whom you owe money (creditor) by bank transaction (filling in a bank giro form) allowing for the transfer of money direct into the creditor's account. It avoids having to wait for a cheque and the inconvenience of having to get to a bank to lodge it.

7. BANK DRAFT/MONEY ORDER

If you do not have a cheque book, buying a bank draft in the bank will allow you to send money safely by post. The person or firm named on the draft will be paid by lodging it to their own bank account.

8. POSTAL ORDER

Postal Orders can be purchased from Post Offices if you do not have a cheque book and you need to pay a smaller sum of money to a creditor. They are a similar type of payment method to bank drafts. The banks, however, handle small as well as larger sums of money.

9. DIRECT DEBIT MANDATE

The Direct Debit Mandate is under the control of the financial institution that sets it up for the customer. It cannot be cancelled without the agreement of the financial institution. Most mortgages (house loans – long-term loans) are paid off by direct debit. The money is taken out of the bank account that the customer nominates. If the customer defaults on payment, there is a risk that, for example, their house might be repossessed by the bank or financial institution the mortgage is taken out with.

10. STANDING ORDER

A Standing Order is under the control of the customer. The customer can cancel the Standing Order at any time. Short-term and medium-term loans are usually paid off by the customer setting up a Standing Order allowing the institution (for example, the credit union) to take the money that is owed to it out of the customer's bank account.

11. INTERNATIONAL BANK TRANSFER

Depositing and withdrawing funds by International Bank Transfer is a more expensive way of transferring funds to foreign bank accounts than by using the online transfer method (with a debit card/code card).

IBAN is the identification number of the bank account that is used for foreign money transactions.

12. WHAT IS WESTERN UNION?

It is an alternative method of sending a money transfer online, making it possible to send money abroad from Ireland or receive money from Ireland in another country (see Chapter 3).

13. WHAT IS PAYPAL?

Paypal is how individuals and businesses send and receive money online – it is a fast, easy and secure way of making online payments.

- **For buyers**: customers can choose to pay with their credit card, debit card or bank account. They can make secure purchases without revealing their credit card number or financial information.
- **For sellers**: sellers accept credit cards, debit cards, and bank account payments for low transaction fees. It is possible to add Paypal to a customer's website in minutes, no downtime required.

Millions of active online shoppers use this payment method. It is also possible to shop using Paypal on eBay (a type of online auction room) and this makes it possible to trade with thousands of merchants worldwide.

14. NETELLER

This is a money transfer system that allows transfer between merchants and individuals. It is an online payment service used in particular for gambling transactions. This system of payment is commonly used in the gambling industry in North America, e.g. for poker accounts and accessing and using winnings acquired from gambling in casinos, etc.

15. TRAVELLER'S CHEQUES

When people travel abroad they usually bring enough money with them but do not carry it in cash. Instead, they change it into Traveller's Cheques and keep receipts of them in a different location in case they are lost or stolen. They are only accepted by banks for cash. In the foreign country the bank will convert the cheques at the current exchange rate into the foreign country's currency. The adoption of the euro currency in many countries has lessened the need to carry Travellers' Cheques because cash can be withdrawn using Bank Cards at ATM machines in these countries. Bank charges for these services can, however, be expensive and there is also a risk of travellers losing Bank Cards.

16. EUROCHEQUES (EUROCHEQUE CARD VALIDATION)

The difference between Traveller's Cheques and Eurocheques is that Eurocheques are like regular cheques where the Eurocheque Book holder can write cheques in foreign currency and the amount when reconverted into euros will be taken out of the Eurocheque holder's bank account.

It means that the person writing these cheques has to be absolutely sure of the exchange rate and sure that there are enough funds in his/her account to meet the amounts written on the cheques. The accompanying validation card is always requested by those accepting the cheques as a guarantee that the bank regards the customer as creditworthy and reliable in this regard.

Example 6: Statements of Account and Cheques – Questions and Solutions

A Statement of Account is a document that is sent out by the supplier to inform the debtor (person that owes money) how much money he/she owes or if anything is owed at all. If too much is paid, it will indicate this too. Most businesses send out monthly statements to their debtors.

In the case of Bank Statements, the customer can request weekly Statements of Account and in this case the balance on the account will be shown as well as other bank charges, withdrawals and lodgments.

Statement of Account Example – Question and Solution

PRACTICE QUESTION

Kelly and Sons traded with All Weather Paints in the month of July and received the following documents and made the following payments during the month:

Documents Received:

4/7/XX Invoice Number 1181	€250.20
18/7/XX Invoice Number 1311	€100.80
6/7/XX Credit Note Number 1767	€28
20/7/XX Credit Note Number 1858	€18.50
29/7 XX Invoice Number 1102	€476.68
31/7/XX Debit Note D/N 865	€26.14

Payments made:

2/7 XX Kelly wrote a cheque for €100

• Kelly and Sons had a carry forward balance of €200 from June.

You are required to:

(a) Show the Cheque that was sent by Kelly and Sons on 2/7/XX.

(b) Compile the Statement of Account for the month of July.

SOLUTION

(a) Cheque

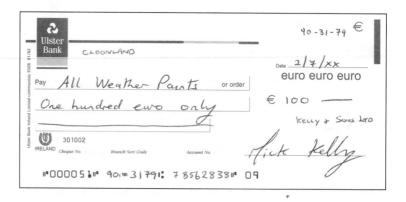

• Cheque Guarantee Card will usually be requested to back up the cheque and to verify the signature.

(b) Statement of Account

All Weather Paints
Weatherfield
Thurles
Co. Tipperary

Statement

To: Kelly and Sons   **Date:** 2 August 20XX
     Painter and Decorator   **No.** 89
     Randles Park
     Clonmel
     Co. Tipperary

Date	Ref No	Details	Debit €	Credit €	Balance €
1/7/XX	–	C/f	–	–	200.00
2/7/XX	121214356	Cheque	–	100.00	100.00
4/7/XX	1181	Invoice	250.20	–	350.20
6/7/XX	1767	Credit Note	–	28.00	322.20
18/7/XX	1311	Invoice	100.80	–	423.00
20/7/XX	1858	Credit Note	–	18.50	404.50
29/7/XX	1102	Invoice	476.68	–	881.18
31/7/XX	865	Debit Note	26.14	–	907.32

Cheque, Bank Giro Form and Petty Cash Voucher

Cheque

Bank Giro Form

DATE_____   LODGMENT/BANK GIRO CREDIT TRANSFER

AIB Bank
Teller's Brand
and initials

ACCOUNT:

Ref:

Paid in by:

€ Notes

Coins
1 & 2 €

Other
Coins

Total Cash

Cheques
etc.
As per
Back

SORTING CODE NUMBER   ACCOUNT NUMBER   TRANS/CODE

93-51-31   89   €

Please do not write or mark below this line or fold this voucher   euro euro euro

⑊500050⑊ 93⑊5131⑊   ⑊ 89

**Petty Cash
Voucher**

PETTY CASH VOUCHER

Date:————————   No:————————

Purchase(s) :   **AMOUNT**

	£	P
TOTAL OF PURCHASES :		

Signed:_____

Authorised by:_____

Sample Assignment Brief – Business Documents

Suggested Outline for Assignment

Basic layout of pages:

1. Title page.
2. Introduction.
3. Aims, Objectives and Methodology.
4. History, Size, Ownership, Products or Services of Organisation (Branches/ National/International)
5. Sketch or Photo of Organisation and/or Logo.
6. Accounts Department: number of staff, how many males and females, and basic functions.

7. Day-to-day routine regarding handling of Business Documents in the Organisation.
8. List of Documents. Include a *List of Actual Documents* included in the project (collected by the learner from a business) with the *definition of each and an analysis of the transactions on each of the documents presented*. (Suggestion: present the documents or photocopies of them back-to-back in poly pockets or a plastic folder.)

These are the documents that should be included in the project:
a. Price List
b. Quotation
c. Purchase Order Form
d. Delivery Docket
e. Invoice – Sales or Purchases (identify whether they are Sales Invoices or Purchase Invoices – ask who is selling to whom or who is buying from whom).
f. Credit Notes – Sales or Purchase Credit Notes (ask: who is sending back damaged goods or was there an overcharge?)
g. Debit Notes (ask: was there an undercharge? Who undercharged whom?)
h. Statement of Account – a list of transactions during (usually) a month
i. Payment Methods – cheque payments or receipts (try to get an example of a cheque or other payment methods used to pay creditors or received from debtors, e.g. online transfer of funds/Internet banking?).

Suggestion: Try to link the order, delivery and invoice with the statement of account where possible.
Note: These headings should be converted into a questionnaire when a learner is compiling primary data, i.e. trying to collect the information and the documents.
The project can also be supported using suitable up-to-date secondary data from sources like the Internet, business leaflets, journals or books and periodicals with particular reference to business documents and transacting in business.

1. Conclusion
2. Bibliography
3. Appendix – include the Questionnaire that was used.

PRACTICE QUESTION 1

Yvonne's Boutique, Harold's Cross Road, Dublin 6 (VAT Number 943126) purchased the following items from Fashion House, Dame Street, Dublin 2 (VAT Number 23165).

10 Handbags @ €25 each
30 Leather Belts @ €15 each (Ref: 62)
28 Hair Clips @ €5 each (Packet number: 101)

Draw up the following documents based on this information:

(a) Purchase Order, no. 231, date 26/4/XX
(b) Delivery Docket, no. 561, date 28/4/XX
(c) Invoice, no. 326, date 28/4/XX

VAT = 21%

(d) Yvonne found that 15 leather belts were scratched and so she returned all 15 of them. You are required to make the appropriate adjustment by compiling the Credit Note no. 846, date 4/5/XX that was sent out.
(e) Draft the Statement Number 922, dated 7/5/XX that Fashion House sent to Yvonne's Boutique.
(f) Draft the Bank of Ireland Cheque dated 10/5/XX that Yvonne's Boutique sends to Fashion House to clear the balance on the account.

Note: In the office the exercise would be to locate and match up the documents.

(b) Write your own account of what you think the Supplier's Office Procedures would have entailed from the moment the Letter of Enquiry was sent. Explore and expand on the ways the Order could have first been received, the Delivery Instructions up to and including when the Invoice was sent out and received by the buyer.

PRACTICE QUESTION 2

(a) Route the following Invoice:

INVOICE

ALL WEATHER PAINTS
Weatherfield
Thurles
Co. Tipperary

Telephone: (0504) 21331
Fax: (0504) 21332
VAT No. IE 1234567 D
Purchase Order Number: 4568
Invoice Number: 1102

Date 10/8/XX

Kelly and Sons
Painters & Decorators
Randles Park
Clonmel
Co. Tipperary

Product Code	Quantity	Description of Product	Price p. unit	VAT 13.5%	VAT 21%
P(IN) 80	5 lt	Interior Vinyl Silk – Rose Colour	€7.50 p. lt		€37.50
P(IN) 110	1 lt	Interior Eggshell (Acrylic)	€8.50 p. lt		€8.50
WSp 12	1 no.	White Spirit (Sm)	€2.00 ea.		€2.00
Br22	5 no.	Paint Brush 6"	€30.00 ea.		€150.00
P(IN) 75 White	10 lt	Interior Matt 1 lt	€7.50 p. lt		€75.00
P(IN) 50 White	10 lt	Interior Gloss 1 lt	€9.00 p. lt		€90.00
P(IN) 80 White	10 lt	Interior Vinyl Silk 1 lt	€7.50 p. lt		€75.00
Total					€438.00
		Less Trade Discount 10%			€43.80
					€394.20
		Add VAT			€82.78
Total Invoice Price					€476.98

PRACTICE QUESTION 3

Jim's Drapery, Mary Street, Cork (VAT Number 43434342 K) purchased the following from Fashion House, Dame Street, Dublin 2 (VAT Number 23165).

35 Handbags @ €25 each
45 Leather belts @ €15 each (ref: 62)
10 Hand and face towel sets @ €25 each set
20 Sun caps at €5.50 each
* Trade discount allowed is 15%
* VAT is charged at 21%

You are required to:

(a) Draft the Invoice that Fashion House sent out to Jim's Drapery – Invoice No. 2343, date 23/7/XX.

(b) Fashion House realised on the day after they sent the Invoice that the Purchasing Manager in Jim's Drapery had phoned Fashion House, after the above order was taken, to order an extra 10 sun caps. This extra order had not been included in the Invoice.

Based on this information you are required to complete the Debit Note No. 2425 and date it appropriately to rectify the omission.

(c) Given that the following additional documents were sent by Fashion House to Jim's Drapery and the following payments were made by Jim's Drapery in July, compile the July Statement of Account and show the correct balance that is owing.

Documents Received

Date	Document	Amount
1/7/XX	Invoice No. 2020	€300.00
2/7/XX	Invoice No. 2031	€400.50
18/7/XX	Invoice No. 2158	€80.50
20/7/XX	Credit Note C/N1255	€30.50

Payments made

Date	Document	Amount
3/7/XX	Cheque No. 10005	€400.00
20/7/XX	Cheque No. 10010	€100.00

The Carry Forward Balance from the previous month was €233.55.

Purchases Book, Sales Book and VAT Returns

Purchase Invoices, Sales Invoices, Credit Notes and Debit Notes are the documents used to compile VAT (Value Added Tax) Returns every two months.

Purchases are divided into:

1. Non-resale items – items that are purchased but not sold back to the public, like office furniture or mobile phones, used as part of the daily business routine. Goods that are hired, insurance bills and accountants' invoices are also non-resale items.

2. Resale items – items that are purchased and resold back to the public, such as builder's blocks, because they are going to be used to build a house that will be sold to the public later.

• Make sure to categorise purchases correctly in this way.

Sometimes small businesses enter their Purchases Returns (Credit Notes) into their Purchases Book together with Purchases, but *write them in red* to denote that they must be subtracted from Purchases. The same applies to VAT on Purchases and Purchases Returns (Credit Notes).

A self-employed sales distributor made the following purchases in March and April 20XX. His VAT registration number is IE 5678785 T.

10/3/XX	Purchased €40 worth of diesel from Grange Service Station (VAT included @ 21%).
15/3/XX	Purchased a mobile phone from NCA Mobile Phone Shop which cost €39.00 inclusive of VAT @ 21%.
24/4/XX	Purchased a computer from Filine Technology costing €899.00 inclusive of VAT @ 21%.
25/4/XX	Truck cleaned – a full valet provided by Valetet cost €55.00 inclusive of VAT @ 13.5%. 13.5% VAT is charged because it is a purchase of a service as opposed to a purchase of goods.
20/3/XX	Returned the mobile phone because it was faulty and received a full refund and a Credit Note.
15/4/XX	Purchased bread and confectionery wholesale from Betterbuy Bake to resell to his own customers. The bill was €2,277 inclusive of VAT. There is no VAT on bread. However, there is 21% VAT on confectionery. €130 of the €2,277 was confectionery.

Sometimes only the selling price is quoted on the invoice so it is important to be able to convert back to the figure before VAT and to find the VAT itself. The *quick* way to do this is:

Take €40 divided by 121% = €33.06

(the figure before VAT) also known as the net figure.

Take €33.06 multiplied by 21% = €6.94

(the VAT itself).

Take the entry required for 15/4/XX – the following is the breakdown.

€2,277 *minus* €130 = €2,147.

- So €2,147 is the cost of the bread (no VAT)
- €130 divided by 121% = €107.44 (the figure before VAT) and €107.44 multiplied by 21% = €22.56 (the VAT itself)
- Check:

	Bread	**Confectionery**
	€2,147	€107.44
VAT	0	€ 22.56
Total		€2,277

Note that this entry is recorded under 'Resale' in the next section.

- *Note:* You enter the invoices into your own books by allocating your own Invoice Reference Number to them in the order that you locate them. Only Invoices, Credit Notes and Debit Notes that are dated in March or April can be included in the March/April VAT Returns.
- (Purchase Invoices received as well as Returns, i.e. Credit Notes received, are entered here in this case. This is not always feasible because the larger the business, the greater the need to have individual Purchases Returns and Sales Returns Books.)

Sample extract from a Sales Distributor's Book (Jim Jones)

- The self-employed sales distributor made sales in March and April 20XX and the transactions are shown in the Sales Book as follows:

Jim Jones
PURCHASES BOOK

March/April 20XX

Date	Details	Inv/Cn No.	0%	Non-Resale 21%	13.5%	0%	Resale 21%	13.5%	VAT
10/3/XX	Purch Grange Service St	201		33.06					6.94
15/3/XX	Purch NCA Mobile Ph Shop	202		32.23					6.77
24/4/XX	Purch Filine Tech & Computers	203		742.98					156.03
25/4/XX	Purch Valetet	204			48.88				6.11
20/3/XX	*Return NCA Mobile Ph Shop*	*205*		*32.23*					6.77
15/4/XX	Purch Betterbuy Bake	206					2147.00	107.44	22.56
Mar/Apr Totals				**776.04**	**48.88**		**2147.00**	**107.44**	**191.64**

Purchases VAT = €191.65

- Check:

	Net	(Selling Prices) VAT	Gross
Non Resale (21%)	776.04	162.97	939.01
Non Resale (13.5%)	48.88	7.00	55.88
Resale (21%)	107.44	22.56	130.00
Resale (13.5%)	0	0	
Total VAT on purchases		192.53	

Sample extract from a Self-employed Sales Distributor's Sales Book

Sales Book: Jim Jones
March/April 20XX

Date	Details Inv/Dn No.		0%	Net 21%	13.5%	VAT	€(Gross) Selling Prices
2/3/XX	Franco's	121	32.00	12.00		2.52	46.52
14/3/XX	Betterbuy A/c	122	1172.00		40.42	5.46	1217.47
14/3/XX	Commission	122		182.43		38.31	220.74
20/4/XX	Patricia's Deli	123	30.00	15.00		3.15	48.15
15/3/XX	*Betterby A/c Debit Note*	*124*	*15.00*			*0.00*	*15.00*
	Mar/Apr Totals		**1249.00**	**249.85**		**49.44**	

Summary of March/April VAT Return 20XX – Purchases and Sales

Purchases VAT Figure	€192.53	(Rounded to €192)
Sales VAT Figure	49.44	(Rounded to €49)
VAT Reclaimable (Repayable)	143.09	(Rounded to €143)

- Since the VAT on purchases is higher than the VAT on sales, the sales distributor can claim back the difference – €143.09. (Rounded to €143)
- If the VAT on purchases had been lower than the VAT on sales, the sales distributor would have had to pay the difference to the Revenue section of government.

A Sample Euro VAT Form

In all correspondence please quote:

Registration No: IE

Notice No: 02782366-16579P

Period:

Office of the Revenue Commissioners
Collector-Generals Division
Sarsfield House
Francis Street
Limerick

17808 181010 17520 180878 030802VAT3EE

Enquiries: 1890 203070

Payment due by:

VAT 3 RETURN

Please print one figure only in each space using a black or blue ball-point pen.

1. VAT

€ : ENTER WHOLE EUROS ONLY

VAT on sales* T1   4 9 •00

VAT on purchases* T2   1 9 3 •00
*See notes part 1 overleaf

OFFICE USE ONLY	
AMD A1 ☐	GCD: 014
O/S A2 ☐	UNIT: 101
DRS	CSZ: I

Net Repayable   OR   Net Payable

T4   1 4 3 •00   T3   —————— •00
(Excess of T2 over T1)   (Excess of T1 over T2)

2. TRADING WITH OTHER EU COUNTRIES

Total goods to other EU countries   Total goods from other EU countries

E1   ——————— •00   E2   ——————— •00

3. BANK DETAILS FOR REPAYMENTS/REFUNDS

SORT CODE B1 ☐ ☐ ☐   ACCOUNT NUMBER B2 ☐

Only complete if you have not previously advised us of account details or you wish to amend previously submitted details.
Any repayment of VAT will be repaid to the bank or building society account as notified.

I declare that this is a correct return of Value Added Tax for the period specified:–

Signed:– *Jim Jones*   Status:– *Director*   Date:– *19th May xxxx*

PRACTICE QUESTIONS

1. What books are required to be written up in order to do a VAT return?
2. A self-employed bread sales agent, John Ryan, has the following Purchases and Sales for May–June 20XX, VAT Number 48567591K

Purchases (Purchases Invoices and Credit notes)	**Sales** (Sales Invoices)
5/5/XX €40 Trailer Service Station (VAT 21%)	2/5/XX Mary's Deli €500 (VAT 21%)
6/5/XX €980 Computer Literate (VAT 21%)	8/6/XX Superbuy €1,000
	(VAT €800 @ 13.5% €200 @ 0%)
15/6/XX €20 Trailer Service Station (VAT 21%)	10/6/XX Monalisa €550 (VAT 21%)
16/6/XX €1,000 Betterbuys – Bread for resale (VAT 0%)	20/6/XX Monalisa €550 (VAT 21%)
17/6/XX €29 Return of Bread to Betterbuy (Credit Note) (VAT 0%)	26/6/XX Superbuy €950 (VAT 0%)

All figures above are *inclusive* of the VAT stated

You are required to:

(a) Enter each transaction into the appropriate books and make appropriate pre-calculations.

(b) Complete the VAT return for John Ryan for the period May–June 20XX.

Note: Be careful to categorise purchases in resale/non-resale form and do a summary of the return before you enter anything in the VAT return form itself.

Sample Assignment

PART 1 (Kelly & Sons Ltd Question): .

PRICE LIST OF PAINTING AND DECORATING PRODUCTS

ALL WEATHER PAINTS

PRODUCT CODES	DESCRIPTION OF PRODUCTS	VAT	UNIT PRICE *per tin, per bottle, each etc.*
P(IN) 75	Interior Matt 1 lt tin	B	€7.50
P(IN) 50	Interior Gloss 1 lt tin	B	€9.00
P(IN) 80	Interior Vinyl Silk 1 lt tin	B	€7.50
P(IN) 100	Interior Eggshell (Alkyd) 1 lt tin	B	€11.00
P(IN) 110	Interior Eggshell (Acrylic) 1 lt tin	B	€8.50
P(Ex) 150	Exterior Matt 2.5 lt tin	B	€12.00
P(Ex) 90	Exterior Matt 10 lt tin	B	€37.00
P(Misc) 120	Scrumble Trans Oil Glaze 2.5 lt tin	B	€45.00
Br200	Badger Softener	B	€41.00
Br195	Stencil Brush	B	€1.50
Br90	Sable Writer	B	€7.00
Br12	Paint Brush 1.5" pure bristle	B	€6.00
Br14	Paint brush 2" pure bristle	B	€10.00
Br16	Paint brush 2.5" pure bristle	B	€12.00
Br18	Paint brush 3" pure bristle	B	€15.00
Br20	Paint brush 4" pure bristle	B	€25.00
Br22	Paint brush 6" pure bristle	B	€30.00
Sp110	Sea Sponge (Synthetic)	B	€7.50
Sp120	Marine Natural Sea Sponge (Lge)	B	€40.00
Sp80	Marine Natural Sea Sponge (Sm)	B	€30.00
Pap100	Wall Stripper	B	€250.00
Pap120	Wallpaper Table	B	€15.00
Pap130	Wallpaper Hanging Brush	B	€20.00
Pap133	Seam Roller	B	€4.50
Sc170	Scaffolding 4' h x 3.5' w	B	€70.00
WSp12	White Spirit (Sm)	B	€2.00
WSp14	White Spirit (Lge)	B	€4.75
Ro186	Roller (9")	B	€12.50
Ro120	Roller (6")	B	€6.50
Ro124	Roller Extension Pole	B	€15.00
SERVICE	INTERIOR DESIGNER	A	QUOTE

Large range of paints and wallpaper available   VAT   A = 13.5%

CODES B = 21%

Wallpaper prices from €10 to €150 per roll

Wallpaper borders from €10 to €20 per roll

You are employed as a sales clerk in the offices of All Weather Paints, Weatherfield, Thurles, Co. Tipperary.

On 29 July 20XX you receive an order from Kelly and Sons, Painters & Decorators, Randles Park, Clonmel, Co. Tipperary, for the following:

Code No.	Quantity
P(Ex) 150 Magnolia	12 tins
P(IN) 75 White	10 tins
Br12	8
Br14	8
Br20	4
P(Misc) 120	2

QUESTIONS

1. Enter this information on a Purchase Order Form and for use in your firm.
2. Prepare an Invoice to send to Kelly and Sons, dated 30 July 20XX, Invoice Number 1343 and assume it is posted that day. Apply a 10% Trade Discount and VAT at 21%.
3. On 2 August 20XX Kelly and Sons receive the goods. Draft the Delivery Docket.
4. They discovered that 2 of the items, Code Number Br20, are damaged, as well as finding that 2 tins of the items Code Number P(Ex) 150 Magnolia are Gloss Code P(IN) 50. The damaged items were returned and the other items were simply exchanged. Kelly himself is unhappy with the service on this occasion.
   (i) Draft the letter of complaint that he sends to you in All Weather Paints
   (ii) Prepare the document you would send him to rectify the mistake dated 5 August 20XX, Document Number 2454.
5. Prepare the Statement of Account at the end of the month.
6. Prepare the cheque which Kelly and Sons send to pay for the goods on 10 September 20XX.

PART 2 (FRANK'S NEWSAGENT'S QUESTION):

Read the following Purchase Order and also study the corresponding Invoice that follows it.

ORDER FORM

FRANK'S NEWSAGENT'S
Main Street, Monaghan.

Order no: 3335/20

BOOKSTORE SUPPLIES
Main Street, Ennis.

Date: 10 July 20XX

QUANTITY	DESCRIPTION	PRICE €
20	Financial Extracts, Pelican, Byrne and Smyth ISBN 2322	15.50
10	DIY Domestic, Pelican, Lee and Lee ISBN 1451	9.50
5	Painting and Decorating, Folens, Rodgers and O'Rourke ISBN 2828	12.20
12	Feathered Friends, O'Brien Publishers, O'Neill and O'Neill ISBN 2222	6.50

INVOICE

BOOKSTORE SUPPLIES
Main Street, Ennis.
Tel: (0503) 23244
Fax: (0503) 23245
VAT No: 1212435F

Invoice No: 1010
Order No: 3335/20

FRANK'S NEWSAGENT'S
Main Street, Monaghan.

Date: 15 July 20XX

QUANTITY	DESCRIPTION	UNIT COST €	TOTAL €
19	Financial Extracts, Pelican, Byrne and Smyth ISBN 2322	15.00	285.00
10	DIY Domestic, Pelican, Lee and Lee ISBN 1451	9.50	95.00
5	Painting and Decorating, Folens, Rodgers and O'Rourke ISBN 2828	12.20	70.00
12	Feathered Friends, O'Brien Publishers, O'Neill and O'Neill ISBN 2222	6.50	78.00

With reference to Order Number 3335/20 and Invoice Number 1010:

(a) Assume that the prices on the Order form are correct. Note the discrepancies and work out the correct total. Exclude VAT and Discount.

(b) State whether an overcharge or undercharge occurred and name the appropriate document to correct the mistake.

(c) Finish off the incorrect Invoice Number 1010, above, and leave it in its uncorrected form by sub-totalling it, deducting 12% Trade Discount and adding VAT at 21%.

(d) Compile the document that will rectify the mistakes occurring in part (b), above, and deduct 12% Trade Discount and add 21% VAT. (Document Number 1586 dated 17 July 20XX.)

(e) If on 1/7/XX a balance of €212.40 exists on Frank's Newsagent's account and if a further two Invoices and one Credit Note were sent to Frank's Newsagent's as follows:

22 July 20XX	Invoice Number 1888	€345.50
23 July 20XX	Invoice Number 2898	€100.20
25 July 20XX	Credit Note Number 1090	€20.20

and if €400 was paid by cheque on 30 July 20XX (cheque number 10058) by Frank's Newsagent's to Bookstore Supplies. Compile the Frank's Newsagent's Statement of Account dated 31 July 20XX. Use the blank documents that can be duplicated on the following pages.

Blank Documents that can be Duplicated

SAMPLE QUOTATION

No:

Supplier Name:

Customer Name:

Customer Address:

Telephone:

Date:

The following are the items of agreement that we wish to offer you with the view to doing business with you in the near future.

Terms:

- **Prices and the terms of agreement will be reviewed every 6 months and are subject to change. We ensure that we will give you due notice of any such planned changes.**

We hope that the terms that we are offering you are to your satisfaction and we anticipate trading with you soon.

We will be glad at any time to clarify any queries that you might have regarding our product range.

Yours faithfully

_____

Sales Manager

LETTER OF ENQUIRY

Customer Address:

Date:

Supplier Name and Address:

Dear

Following our phone conversation, kindly forward to me a current Price List of your products. I hope to purchase some of them in the near future.

Yours truly

PURCHASE ORDER

No:

Customer Name:
Customer Address:

Telephone: **Date:**
To:

Code Ref	Quantity	Description	Vat Rate (%)	Unit Price

Delivery Instructions: Delivery by   on

Signed: _____
        Purchasing Officer

DELIVERY DOCKET

From:

No:
Date:
Order No:

Goods:	**Quantity**	**Description**	**Code No.**

Received the above goods:

Signed: _____

INVOICE

Supplier name and address:

Telephone:
Fax:
VAT No:
Purchase Order No:
Invoice No:
Date:

Customer Name and Address:

Product Code	Q	Description of product	Price p. unit	VAT 13.5%	VAT 21%	Total

Total

Less Trade Discount
Add VAT

Total Invoice Price

Terms of Trade:

CREDIT NOTE   **Credit Note No:**

Supplier Name and Address:

Telephone:
Fax:
VAT No:
Reference Purchase Order Number:
Reference Invoice Number:

Date:

Customer Name and Address:

DATE	Q	DETAILS	PRICE	TOTAL

Add VAT @ 21%

Total Credit given

DEBIT NOTE   **Debit Note No:**

Supplier Name and Address

Telephone:
Fax:
VAT No:
Reference Purchase Order Number
Reference Invoice Number

Date:

Customer Name and Address:

DATE	Q	DETAILS	PRICE	TOTAL

Add VAT @ 21%

TOTAL

STATEMENT OF ACCOUNT

Supplier Name and Address

Statement

To:

Date:
No:

Date	Ref No.	Details	Debit €	Credit €	Balance €

7. Retail Administration

The Retail Sector

As we know the retail sector is in the tertiary sector, and includes many service-type organisations within the sector. There are over 20,000 food and non-food retail enterprises in Ireland, with 240,000 employees. The enterprises consist of Irish and international companies but are mostly SMEs (small and medium-sized enterprises). They have all invested heavily in their businesses in the last decade. Since 2007 due to the recession, the retail market has shrunk by over one fifth in value terms. Retailers have cut prices, but their costs have not fallen due to inflexible rents, property service charges, local authority charges and hourly pay rates. Retailing provides a range of specialised careers such as merchandising, supply-chain management, finance, IT and purchasing. Retailing is highly competitive as anyone can open a shop in Ireland. If retailers can source suppliers and materials locally, they will prioritise this and are interested in serving the customer.

Refer to **www.retailireland.ie.**

Forfás Report on the Structure of Irish Retailing

OVERVIEW OF THE RETAIL SECTOR

Retailing is defined as the means by which goods and services are provided to consumers in exchange for payment. Retailing thus excludes wholesaling and business-to-business selling. Retailing can be segmented into three distinct categories:

- Predominantly Food Stores
- Predominantly Non-Food Stores
- Non-Store Retailing.

The following is a description of the elements of these categories as used in the report.

PREDOMINANTLY FOOD STORES

Hypermarkets

Hypermarkets are very large retail outlets, which are defined by the OECD as over 2,500 sq. metres, but which are typically much bigger. For example, the average size of new hypermarkets in Europe is typically 7,500 sq. metres. Hypermarkets carry a wide range of food and non-food items. Hypermarkets are sometimes referred to as Superstores, though Superstores focus primarily on food. They are normally sited on the periphery of towns and cities.

Supermarkets

In the main, supermarkets are 1,500 to 2,500 sq metres and are on the edge of towns or town centre locations. Supermarkets contain much of the product ranges and customer services of hypermarkets.

Symbol Groups

Symbol groups are a group of outlets, that are generally independently owned, operating under a symbol name and co-operating to gain purchase cost savings and, in some instances, develop own-label products. Symbol groups are essentially managed or grouped around a wholesaler.

Convenience Stores

Convenience stores are small stores, such as forecourt shops and small supermarkets, with a wide food and non-food product range. They are often part of a Symbol Group and sometimes offer a range of own-brand products. These stores are characterised by convenient town, city or suburban locations, generally have extended opening hours and are used mainly for 'top-up' shopping.

Category Management

The practice of category management is increasingly used by large-scale retailers and involves developing a category or range of processes including product development, consumer marketing, promotions to maximise the yield from that category.

Category Killers

Category killers exist where large retail outlets offer a specialised product range in substantial depth but not in breadth.

Independent Stores

These include specialists such as greengrocers, bakers, fish shops, delicatessens as well as large general grocery stores such as family-owned Spar, Mace, Supervalu or Londis stores, and are typically owner-managed.

Discounters

These are retail outlets that offer a range of goods while focusing on offering substantial discounts over other retailers. Discounters are referred to as 'hard' or 'soft' depending on the levels of discounts provided. Own-label products and dry goods often feature significantly in these outlets.

PREDOMINANTLY NON-FOOD STORES

Department Stores

Department stores are typically large city centre shops, generally multi-storey, offering a range of clothing, footwear, personal care and household products. Areas within department stores may be franchised to specialist operators and leading brands.

Boutiques

Boutiques are typically small, single outlets specialising in one manufacturer's products, or a specialist range of clothing and other merchandise.

Multiples

Non-food multiples are supermarket size outlets selling mainly clothing and footwear, but occasionally other items, e.g. sports goods. These shops tend to be at the lower end of the clothing market in price terms, whereas department stores are in the middle to upper price ranges.

Factory Outlets

These are outlets selling the products of a factory, typically branded goods such as clothing.

NON-STORE RETAILING

This sector traditionally includes mail order, door-to-door, vending machines and repairs to products. However, the boundary between this sector and store retailing is becoming blurred as store retailers develop into non-store selling via the Internet, telephone selling and TV shopping.

Supply Chain

The supply chain is the sequence of companies or individuals involved in the process by which raw materials are transformed into products and delivered to the retail outlets for consumer markets. Historically, manufacturers delivered their products to individual stores using their own transport, distribution agents or wholesalers, or some combination of these. This results in numerous deliveries to shops by many suppliers which is seen as ineffective and inefficient.

In other countries, where appropriate to market conditions, RDCs (Regional Distribution Centres) and Consolidation Centres have evolved to simplify the distribution system and rationalise deliveries to stores. This aim is to maximise the use of full loads, and optimise the efficiency of the distribution system.

The function of the RDC is to consolidate the products of various suppliers into deliveries for individual stores and thereby minimise the deliveries to individual stores. To improve the efficiencies of RDCs, consolidation centres are used to receive part loads from suppliers and to consolidate supplies into full loads for delivery to RDCs.

A key feature of the food retail sector in Ireland is the current emergence of a centralised distribution structure amongst major retailers.

The OECD define supermarkets as stores ranging in size from 400 sq. metres to 2,499 sq. metres.

Source: *www.forfas.com*

Weak start to 2011 for retailing – Retail Ireland

Monday, 28 February 2011

Retail Ireland, the IBEC group that represents the retail sector, today said that new CSO retail sales figures for January show a weak start for retailing in 2011. The group said the political parties that form the new government must follow through on election commitments to support the retail sector, reduce business costs and get people back to work.

Retail Ireland director Torlach Denihan said: 'The value of core retail sales (excluding cars and bars) fell year-on-year by 1.5 per cent in January. The Budget hit pay packets in January and this had a major negative impact on spending towards the end of the month especially.

'Last year was the third year in a row in which the value of core retail sales fell and the cumulative decline is now over 20 per cent. The sector needs urgent action from the incoming government. While prices have been cut to the bone, the cost of running a shop has not fallen.

'The key challenge facing the incoming government is to restore consumer confidence and boost spending in the economy. To safeguard jobs in the retail sector urgent reform is needed to reduce key business costs, such as rent, labour costs and commercial rates, and improve access to credit.

'Legislation to address unsustainable commercial rents is needed urgently. The next Attorney General should immediately review the issue of upward only rent review clauses, with a view to clearing the way for new legislation to abolish them.

'The rules for setting wages in the retail grocery sector are destroying jobs and are unnecessary because of the national minimum wage. The ongoing review of these rules must lead to a major overhaul in the system.'

Source: www.ibec.ie

Future skills requirements of the wholesale and retail sector

10 May 2010

The Forfás report entitled 'Future Skills Needs of the Wholesale and Retail Sector' assessed the skills requirements of the wholesale and retail sector in Ireland over the period to 2016, and identified actions required to meet these skills needs.

Attracting and developing talent in the wholesale and retail sector will enhance productivity and drive competitiveness. Minister for Lifelong Learning Seán Haughey TD, launched the above Expert Group report on skills needs for the wholesale retail sector.

While employment growth is not forecast to return to the wholesale and retail sector in the short term, the sector continues to provide significant employment accounting for over 14 per cent of jobs in the country, according to a new report published today by the Expert Group on Future Skills Needs. 'Future Skills Needs of the Wholesale and Retail Sector' finds that the industry will continue to be a relatively high turnover sector in comparison to the rest of the economy, and will provide important opportunities for people that have lost their jobs to re-engage with the labour market. It is also a vital sector for entrepreneurship and small Irish businesses offering a broad spectrum of career paths to people at all skill levels.

Launching the report, the Minister for Lifelong Learning, Seán Haughey TD, highlighted the importance of the sector to the Irish economy, commenting, 'Wholesale and retail is one of the most vital sectors to any economy. Most people interact with it on a daily basis. It accounts for 11 per cent of value-added in the economy, directly employs 272,000 people and is highly connected with other sectors such as transport, storage, business services, ICT and agriculture. Developing the skills base of the workforce can drive innovation and enhance productivity in the sector, benefit the wider economy, provide a multitude of career paths for people with relatively low levels of qualifications and make a significant contribution towards the upskilling targets of the National Skills Strategy.'

Source: www.forfas.ie/publication/search.jsp?ft=/publications/2010/Title,6228,en.php
or
www.skillsireland.ie/publication/egfsnSearch.jsp?ft=/publications/2010/title,6230,en.php

What are the Retail Planning Guidelines?

The RPGs are guidelines provided by the Government to guide:
1. Local authorities when they are preparing development plans and assessing applications for planning permission
2. Retailers and developers in formulating their development proposals.

These guidelines were revised in 2005 and now contain new policies regarding large retail warehouses (underpinned by Section 28 of the Planning and Development Act 2000).

In 2005 the government agreed to change the planning laws, clearing the way for furniture stores like the Swedish giant Ikea to open in Ireland. The 6,000 square metre cap (limit) on shop size was removed. This applies only in Dublin and the eight gateway towns that were identified as designated for urban regeneration or redevelopment. This change will not affect grocery shops and only affects those selling durable goods.

Most Ikea stores around Europe are four times bigger than the maximum size previously allowed in Ireland (64,000 square metres). Environment Minister Dick Roche was criticised by many and accused of setting policy to suit one company.

ADVANTAGES OF THE CHANGE TO THE RPGS:
1. More consumer choice
2. Greater retail price competition
3. Urban regeneration
4. Greater direct employment and spin-off services.

DISADVANTAGES:

1. Increased risk of traffic congestion
2. Danger that smaller retailers may go out of business
3. Smaller suppliers may go out of business.

IKEA opened a new store in Belfast in November 2007 and (as part of government urban regeneration policy) will open another in Ballymun, Dublin in 2008.

Critics include ISME (the Irish Small and Medium Enterprises Association) and RGDATA (the organisation representing retail grocers). They said that government policy set a bad precedent for many Irish businesses that invest in urban regeneration.

The Competition Authority believed that the decision was a positive one for Irish consumers' choices and price competition.

More information is available at **www.irishspatialstrategy.ie** and at **www.environ.ie**.

What was the Groceries Order (Restrictive Practices) 1987?

This was an order that banned the selling of goods at below their invoice price (i.e. it banned below-cost selling). It was introduced in 1987 to prevent small shops being driven out of business by large supermarket chains.

The ban was lifted in 2005 when the then Minister for Enterprise announced the end to the Groceries Order (Restrictive Practices). At the same time the minister promised to strengthen the Competition Act to stop unfair price discrimination and to ban 'hello money'.

ADVANTAGES OF LIFTING THE BAN:

1. The National Consumer Agency believed that less well off households who spend more on groceries stood to benefit most.
2. Lower prices for consumers.
3. The market is now more in line with the natural laws of competition/demand and supply.

DISADVANTAGES OF LIFTING THE BAN:

1. The risk of dominance by a small number of large retailers.
2. RGDATA believed that large multiples would engage in pricing gimmicks and practices reintroducing the idea of loss leaders into Irish retailing.
3. FDII (Food and Drink Industry Ireland) were concerned about fair trade and that the Irish food industry and retailers may operate in a regime with dominance in the marketplace and predatory pricing.

4. The ICMSA (the Irish Creamery Milk Suppliers Association) were concerned that aggressive discounting by retailers could be detrimental to farmers and producers.

5. While that order existed it helped shopping competition to thrive and facilitated real competition in the grocery retail sector. Now there is the risk that multiple retailers will use below-cost selling to further increase their profitability and put smaller competitors out of business.

Different Types of Retail Outlet in Ireland

1. A franchise – the purchase of the right to run a business, usually using a group symbol or name and its shop layout and trading method/characteristics. The business support network is available to the franchise to allow for maximum efficiency and porfitability. Example: Garvey's SuperValu, Limerick.

2. Irish multi-generation family concerns – Arnotts, Clearys, Dunnes Stores, Heatons.

3. Multi-national giants (European retail groups) – BHS, Marks & Spencers, Boots, Dixons, Currys.

4. Multiples – the Musgrave Group (started life in 1876 as a family owned shop in Cork run by two Co. Leitrim brothers – it is still a family run concern). Musgrave rapidly expanded its Centra and Supervalu operations in the 1990s, thereby quadrupling its business. Other symbol groups include Londis and Spar. These shops are franchised out by Musgrave and owned by independent operators. Ninety per cent of the stock, however, is sourced from Musgrave.

5. Other Multiples are Tesco and Dunnes Stores.

6. Other Food Retailers/grocery sector – SuperQuinn.

Multiples

These are large business operations. Some oversee the operations of multiple shops that are franchised out by it, e.g. the Musgrave Group. Multiple shops are shops that have branches throughout a region or a country e.g. Supervalu, Londis, Centra.

The characteristics of multiples are:

1. Similar range of products and prices available in each branch.
2. Similar branch layout and appearance.
3. Central control of purchasing in Head Office.
4. Independent manager and sometimes owner (in the case of franchises) per branch hired by head office.
5. No credit offered to the public.

ADVANTAGES

1. No bad debts because no credit purchases by public.
2. Bulk buying means trade discounts can be gained and competitive selling prices offered to public.
3. Slow selling products can be transferred to other policy branches where demand is greater.

DISADVANTAGES

1. No credit given to customers.
2. Less personal consumer attention.
3. Local managers have less input into decision-making at head office.

Department stores, hypermarkets and superstores

A department store consists of a number of shops, each called a department, housed under the one roof. It is a spacious building with specialised shops/departments dealing in hardware, cosmetics, clothing, furniture, toys etc. The department store also offers other services to the consumer such as restaurant facilities, coffee shops, post-office and banking services. Examples are Arnotts, Clearys, Roches Stores.

Hypermarkets are large stores with a large area of square footage, which usually have only one floor and deal in groceries, cosmetics and a large selection of household goods depending on the time of the year. Examples are Dunnes Stores, Cornelscourt, Dublin and Lidl (German).

Superstores are large stores that deal in a very large variety of housewares, clothes, food and in recent times different departments on different floor levels. Many Dunnes Stores outlets would fall into this category.

ADVANTAGES

1. Parking and improved infrastructure, giving the public ease of access and convenience.
2. Bulk buying means that companies get trade discounts. This results in lower and more competitive selling prices which are attractive to the public.
3. A wide range of goods and services are at hand under the one roof, making it easy for the customer.
4. Open display leads to impulse buying, and this is good for sales.

DISADVANTAGES

1. Lack of personal service to public.
2. Large population and catchment area needed for centre to be a success.
3. Goods may become damaged more quickly, due to open display.
4. Goods are generally mass produced and little attention is given to detail. Home-produced goods are less common.

Acquisition shopping as it should be

Paul O'Kane

The Background

Brothers Thomas and Stuart Musgrave opened their first shop in Cork in 1876. They set up their business as a partnership in 1887, trading as Musgrave Brothers. Seven years later it became a limited company.

The Church of Ireland brothers had an abhorrence of alcohol. Articles of association prevented the company from buying, selling or manufacturing alcoholic liquor. This was why the Musgrave-owned Metropole Hotel in Cork didn't obtain a bar licence until 1956.

By 1899 the company had a turnover of over £67,000 – almost €8.5m in today's terms. By the mid-1920s Musgrave was almost exclusively a wholesale business and by the 1930s it was selling to retailers all over Munster.

In the early 1950s Jack Musgrave took over the reins. Musgrave obtained the VG franchise for Ireland from the Netherlands in 1958 for a nominal £1. By the 1970s Musgrave narrowed its focus, eliminating sweet manufacturing in 1977 and its tea business in 1972. It began opening massive cash and carries in the 1970s and by 1977 turnover was almost £30m.

In 1979 Musgrave began to change its VG stores into the new 'voluntary multiples' it had developed, SuperValu and Centra. By 1990 Musgrave had turnover of £380m and pre-tax profit of £9.9m. The group grew rapidly in the '90s, moving into Northern Ireland and into Spain in 1994. In 2000 it paid almost stg£90m to German food distributor REWE for an effective 43% holding in Budgens.

Despite being a €3.5bn operation Musgrave remains a family company: Thomas and Stuart's descendants still own 76% of the firm.

It's a long way from tea blending, boiled sweets and small shopkeepers.

The acquisition of the British retailer Budgens will transform the Musgrave group. Adding Budgens to Musgrave will grow the company's annual sales from €2.3bn to €3.5bn at a stroke and the move also sets the pattern for future growth at the company, according to Musgrave group managing director Seamus Scally. Although Musgrave also has a business in Spain, Britain will now be the focus for expansion.

Musgrave has owned a stake in Budgens since August 2000 when it acquired a 28% shareholding in the business and convertible loan stock which gave a total effective holding of 43% for €138m. Ten days ago it agreed to buy the remainder of the business for €275m in a deal that values Budgens at €492m. During Musgrave's two years as a minority shareholder with board representation, Scally

said the Irish company 'saw nothing that discouraged us from taking the remaining stock'.

Musgrave which started life 126 years ago as a family-owned shop in Cork run by two Co. Leitrim brothers, has finally arrived in the British market. In a way the company's huge success in Ireland in recent years has forced it to look east. During the 1990s Musgrave quadrupled its business by rapidly expanding both its Centra and SuperValu operations. These fascias replaced the VG stores that had been operated by Musgrave and its partners.

'We have 22–23% of the retail market in the Republic so the opportunity for significant growth here is fairly limited,' according to Scally. 'We're building a successful business in the North and felt that the British market most suited us.' Last year the company made pre-tax profits of €47m on sales of €2.27bn.

SuperValu and Centra have made Musgrave a 'virtual multiple', as although the group doesn't physically own any shops in Ireland it has a presence throughout the country. The company has used this system to its advantage when dealing with media, government and regulators. Its executives will argue that small shopkeepers who are part of Centra or SuperValu struggle daily against big bad multiples such as Tesco and Dunnes. But in fact Musgrave is a large multiple, albeit one that uses a franchise-like model. The shops are owned by independent operators but typically more than 90% of stock is sourced from Musgrave. It also advises on site selection, store layout, staffing and training.

The so-called independent grocery sector, which includes symbol groups such as Centra, SuperValu, Londis and Spar, now has 45–50% of the Irish market, according to Scally. While the sector has been aided by the expansion of almost all symbol operators, Musgrave has been responsible for most of the growth. During the 1990s, at a time when Musgrave and its 'small grocers' were threatened by a powerful new arrival in the shape of Tesco, the Cork-based group quadrupled its turnover.

Despite talk of the threat from the multiples, SuperValu and Centra have blossomed, due in part to the public's willingness to pay over the odds for convenience. The group hopes to continue its success by building a new type of convenience operation in Britain. 'The convenience sector was not particularly well done in the UK. It's a stg£100bn market but the independent sector has less than 20%.'

Scally said shortly after Musgrave began to research the British market they came across Budgens and were impressed by the quality of

its stores and its track record. 'They [Budgens] are very close to the business and they see opportunities and gaps created by the multiples when they move to large centres.'

Budgens has 245 outlets in the south of England, mostly convenience stores. It has been adding 15 to 20 shops a year and Musgrave hopes to continue the expansion. Unlike its Irish parent, Budgens actually owns most of its stores, although it also has a small franchise operation. Scally said Musgrave had no plans to sell any Budgens stores to franchisees as 'the [Budgens] model was working very well' but added that building the franchise operation would be 'speeded up'.

The acquisition will leave Musgrave with debts of €450m–€500m. Scally said the acquisition would result in a debt to EBITDA ratio of 3.5. 'That could be considered on the high side but in 2000 the ratio was 2.9 and by 2001 it had been reduced to 2.3. There's a very strong cash flow in this business.'

Scally admits that given the debt incurred as a result of the Budgens deal, Musgrave will probably not be in a position to make another large acquisition in the short term. 'All going well, after about five years we would take a big bite again.'

Budgens is a publicly quoted operation but Musgrave, which is committed to remaining private, intends to cancel the listing. There will be some savings from delisting but the deal offers few synergies as Musgrave has no existing British business and Budgens will be run as a separate entity. Scally said there may be benefits in terms of buying as the group would now have sales of €3.5bn in Britain and Ireland.

While the real expansion focus has shifted to Britain, Scally believes there is still room for organic growth in the Republic.

'We're adding Centra stores at the rate of 20 a year and we see that happening for the next five years at least, while SuperValu is growing by about five to six stores a year and that will also continue. That expansion should get us another 1–2% market share.'

But having invested so much in the deal, the real growth story over the next five years has to be Budgens. 'It's growing at 5% on a like for like basis, which is an attractive proposition. But Budgens has only stg£500m of sales in a £100bn market, that's only about half a per cent of the market. It's much easier to grow that in percentage terms than it is when you have 15–20% of the market.'

If Musgrave's future is to stay bright, that future has to be British.

Courtesy of the *Sunday Tribune*

Retail Co-Operatives

Some Co-operatives, such as Thurles Co-operative Creamery Limited, have had a retail outlet attached to the Co-op. In this they sell fresh produce as well as a range of household items to the public. Retail Co-operatives like this are listed in the 'Registrar of Friendly Societies' under the section 'Industrial and Provident Societies – Dairy Section'. Other Co-operatives, such as Knitwear Co-ops, can also have shops attached to them. They are listed under the Other Productive Societies section of the same publication.

The Impact of the Size and Type of a Retail Organisation

1. OWNERSHIP

The larger retail organisation usually has an ownership structure consisting of shareholders, are private or public limited companies or, in recent times, are multi-national companies, e.g. Tesco, Boots, Currys, Dixons. Multiples, department stores, hypermarkets and superstores also generally have this type of ownership structure.

The smaller shop/newsagent can be a sole trader or a partnership. Specialised shops are smaller and are usually units in shopping centres, with independent ownership per unit. Franchises benefit from the symbol group name and support network. Consumer confidence helps the business run efficiently.

The larger retail organisations are highly competitive, and have been mostly responsible for putting the smaller corner store, drapery etc. out of business. However, they have provided a larger variety of choice for the consumer, employment for people and modern facilities for greater convenience.

2. PROFIT SHARING

The small retail outlet, shop, newsagent, either claims all profit for himself/herself, if they are a sole trader, or if it is a partnership, profits will be divided in agreed ratios, according to the Deed of Partnership. (Refer to the section on partnerships in Chapter 1.) There is a greater possibility of owners/shareholders making greater profits in larger retail outlets, because investment capabilities are much greater with more investors as well as bulk buying abilities and the ability to avail of large trade discounts. This means that costs per unit sold are minimised and sales are maximised. They also have the added advantages of reputation. Moreover, advertising in the large outlet is cheaper per unit sold. These benefits due to larger size are called Economies of Scale and are the reasons why larger retail outlets can generate greater profits, despite these profits having to be divided out between the shareholders, usually in line with their profit-sharing ratios.

The large retail outlets that are owned by multi-nationals repatriate profits (bring back profits to their own countries) and this is not good for the economy of the country in which the stores are located. There is also the danger that businesses like the British multi-nationals will in time move back to their home country, causing a large loss of jobs in the country in which they have temporarily located. This is why establishing home-based Irish retail businesses, that start off small and have the possibility of becoming larger with time and track-record, is very much encouraged. This will lead to home-based profits and Irish jobs will then be guaranteed.

3. MANAGEMENT

In general, the larger retail outlet has a head office with Chief Executives and Assistant Executives who monitor the activities of the different branches. Area managers are usually allocated certain branches in a part of the country and each branch has a Manager, Assistant Manager and Supervisors in different departmental areas.

The bigger the retail organisation, the more complex the management structure will be (see Figure 7.1). The smaller retail outlet will probably have one manager who is the owner and possibly an Assistant Supervisor who will monitor activities in the shop/ newsagent/corner shop when the owner is not present. (See tall and flat organisational charts in Chapter 1.)

4. ADMINISTRATION

The larger retail outlet will find it cost-effective to employ more modern technology to complete jobs more quickly and efficiently. Most administrative activities are likely to be computerised. There will generally be specialised areas that deal with administration, for example personnel department, sales and marketing department, buying and stores, financial and accounting, etc. (Refer to the functions of management in Chapter 1.)

The smaller retail outlet will not be subdivided into departments and therefore the administration of the business will be probably confined to one office with one secretary or clerk in charge of all paperwork. There will be fewer employees and wages and bookkeeping might be done manually rather than by computer.

5. STAFFING

The staff structure of the larger retail outlet will be more complex than the small outlet. The larger outlet is likely to have a taller organisational structure, which means that a greater number of lines of authority exist and there is a greater variety of subordinates. Employees are usually directly answerable to one superior, who may be a supervisor or sub-manager. The large departmental structure leads to many heads of department. The smaller retail outlet has a smaller organisational staff structure, where staff are usually within close spatial proximity, and owner, supervisor, and usually a small number of other employees with one secretary/clerk make up the total staff. (Refer to Chapter 1.)

Factors that Affect the Location of a Retail Outlet

Retail outlets usually take the following factors into account when they decide to locate:

1. *POPULATION AND MARKET SIZE* – The larger the population in the catchment area, the greater the demand for goods.
2. *INFRASTRUCTURE* – The road network and accessibility to transport – rail, bus – will make it convenient for shoppers and will stimulate demand.
3. *PROXIMITY TO BACK-UP SERVICES AND SUPPLIERS* – Reordering, repairs and maintenance services as well as suppliers should be located nearby, otherwise time and transport costs will pose a problem.
4. *PROXIMITY TO SKILLED LABOUR SUPPLY* – Local skilled labour is an advantage, as travelling expenses will not have to be paid to them and punctuality will be ensured in most cases.
5. *EXCESS LAND AREA/SPACE SURROUNDING OUTLET* – This applies more to the larger retail outlet, with the aim of providing car park space for customers, which is a major advantage with regard to convenience for the customer.
6. *PLANNING LAWS* – Planning permission and by-law considerations have to be taken into account when a retailer is considering setting up his/her business.
7. *CONSIDERING THE LOCATION OF THE NEAREST COMPETITOR* – The business should weigh up whether the competitor will have a significantly adverse effect on sales, or whether the business is diverse enough and popular enough to maintain consumer loyalty and not be affected by the competitor's location.
8. *GOVERNMENT LEGISLATION* – Tax incentives, if available, will encourage a business to locate in a particular area.

The Impact of Location on a Retail Outlet

When a retail outlet successfully locates, having taken into account the factors above, they set out with the aim of maximising sales and demand and minimising costs, thereby maximising profits. Successful location can lead to:

1. Higher profits, and plans to expand.
2. Higher demand for labour – employment.
3. Higher wages for employees and greater purchasing power as a result, as well as job satisfaction.

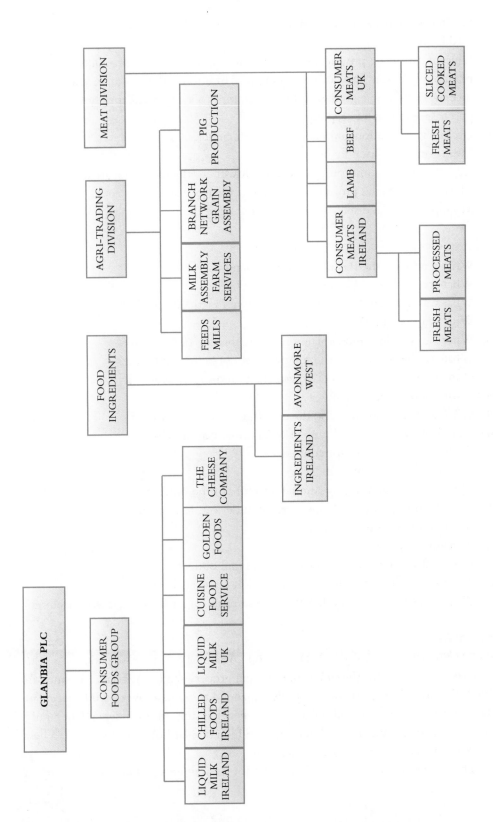

Figure 7.1 An Organisational Chart of a Large Retail Organisation

4. Greater usage of technology and computers – modern laser cash registers, credit card facilities.

5. Diversification of products – modification and improved products including branding goods, as well as new techniques to interest the customer and provide incentives to buy, e.g. discount cards, stamps to avail of cheaper holidays or to purchase goods at a cheaper price.

6. Greater specialisation and management efficiencies.

7. More consumer-friendly policy.

8. Advertising per unit output will be lower as the business grows so more advertising and sales promotion methods might be used.

9. More professional display of goods encouraging impulse buying.

PRACTICE QUESTIONS

1. Write a note on the Retail Sector in Ireland.
2. What are the Retail Planning Guidelines?
3. What was the Groceries Order (Restrictive Practices) 1987?
4. What is a Franchise?
5. What is a Multiple and explain briefly the history of Musgraves.
6. What are the advantages and disadvantages of being a multiple?
7. How do department stores, hypermarkets and superstores differ?
8. What is a retail co-operative?
9. What are the advantages and disadvantages attached to them?
10. Explain how the size and type of retail outlet can influence:
    (a) the type of ownership required.
    (b) how profits are divided.
    (c) the management organisational structure of the outlet.
11. Explain how the size and type of retail outlet can influence:
    (a) administration procedures.
    (b) staffing levels.
12. What factors influence the location of a retail outlet?
13. What are the implications of good location on a retail outlet?
14. What is EPOS and how do EPOS Systems impact on retailers? (Refer to Chapter 2.)

What is RGDATA?

RGDATA (Retail, Grocery, Dairy and Allied Traders Association) is the representative body for the independent retail grocery sector in Ireland. Formed in 1942, the organisation has since rapidly expanded to include over 4,000 grocers in the Ireland. Its main aim and objective is to provide support for independent family grocers, while encouraging and developing a high standard of retailing, equal to best European practice and competitor standards.

The activities undertaken by RGDATA for its members include:

- The monitoring of new or impending legislation which effects the grocery trade
- Lobbying the government when necessary
- Providing support to members
- Offering ongoing advice and publications to members
- Countering adverse media content with a more balanced view
- Offering planning support, contesting the scale and location of shopping centres and multiple branches.

To ensure that the organisation is informed of the latest retail developments in Ireland and mainland Europe, RGDATA is a member of:

- The International Federation of Grocers' Associations (IFGA).
- The Irish Business and Employers' Confederation (IBEC).
- The Irish Council of the European Movement (ICEM).
- Joint Labour Committee.
- Senate Electoral Panel.
- European Federation of Independent Retailers (UGAL).

RGDATA operates from its headquarters in Blackrock, Co Dublin. Composed of a board of directors representing all grocery interests in the retail trade, it always has an in-depth grocery market outlook and considerable experience to draw on.
Refer to **www.rgdata.ie.**

What is Retail Ireland?

Retail Ireland is the national representative body for the entire retail sector. It is a branch of IBEC (Irish Business Employers Confederation). It represents Irish and international department stores, DIY, electrical retailers, fashion and footwear retailers, major supermarket groups, symbol groups and a range of specialist retailers.

Mace is a convenience store symbol group operated in the UK and Ireland. The stores are independently owned and join the group, paying a fee for marketing and branding support and purchasing their stock from the brand owner.

The following were detailed proposals made to the Government by Retail Ireland in support of the retail sector:

- **Consumer spending:** To help the customer side of retail by implementing policies recommended by IBEC in its document 'Delivering the Jobs Agenda' – aimed at boosting employment and so increase consumer spending.
- **Rents:** To introduce legislation to address high rents.
- **Wages**: To abolish the JLC – Joint Labour Committee system of regulated wage agreements and maintain the national minimum wage at €7.65.
- **Bank Credit:** To get credit flowing to businesses by introducing a loan guarantee scheme for SMEs.

- **Rates**: Introduce a property tax to fund local authority services allowing a 25 per cent reduction in commercial rates.

Legal Aspects of Retailing

What Makes a Contract Valid?

A contract is an agreement enforceable by law that retailers, wholesalers, customers and anyone in business must concern themselves with. The following features must exist if a contract is deemed to be valid:

1. *OFFER AND ACCEPTANCE*

In order to ascertain whether an agreement exists, the offer must be clear, complete and unconditional. The agreement must match the offer exactly and must be communicated to the person who is offered it within a specific time limit in order for it to be legally effective. The offer and acceptance are valid if they are made by word, in writing or by conduct.

- **By Word:** In the retail trade, it is very rare that agreements are made orally. An example would be giving goods to a customer who says they will return in an hour's time to pay for them. A better example is the oral agreement that a tenant makes agreeing to pay the required rent to a landlord or landlady.
- **By Conduct:** In the retail trade, a customer in a supermarket or shop who fills their shopping basket with goods is by his or her actions offering to buy the goods. When the checkout assistant accepts the money for the goods, he or she is accepting the offer by actions or conduct.
- **In Writing:** When a retailer signs a 'terms of trade' agreement, agreeing to pay the sales agent at the end of every month or when they sign a lease agreement when leasing the business vehicle, the retailer has made payment agreements, the terms of which are outlined in writing.

2. *CONSIDERATION*

This is the **price** agreed by the parties to the contract. It is the medium of payment whether in the form of goods (barter) or money, a loss or responsibility that is given by one party and subsequently taken by the other party in return for goods or services rendered.

For example Mary offers to purchase Jim's house for €100,000. The €100,000 is the consideration. Even if the house is worth more it is the agreed price that is the consideration. In the retail sector, when the customer indicated his or her intention and offer to purchase by actions and by handing the checkout assistant €100, this is the consideration for the contract. When the checkout assistant takes the money this is the acceptance involved in the contract.

3. CONTRACTUAL CAPACITY

The parties engaging in the agreement must have the capacity to make the contract. The age of majority is 21 years. Anyone entering into a contract with a party below this age is not legally bound to fulfil a contract when it concerns the repayment of money, unless special conditions are attached to it. The contract would be regarded as null and void.

For example in a supermarket, a checkout assistant accepting €5 from a two-year-old child for sweets would not render the transaction valid because of the child's age.

4. INTENTION TO CREATE LEGAL RELATIONS

The intention of the parties concerned that a legal contract exists must be clear. If you agree to visit a person's house at a particular time on a particular date, this is not a legal contract. 'Intention' alone does not constitute a contract, however.

For example if I go into a supermarket or shop with the intention of buying items and I return home having bought nothing, I am not legally bound to fulfil any contract because the other features of Contract Law have not been adhered to in this case.

5. LEGALITY OF OBJECT

Some contracts must be in a specific form in writing before they are accepted as being valid. Direct debit mandates and standing orders (discussed in Chapter 2) must be signed before they are accepted. Hire purchase agreements and leases must also be structured in a particular form and signed by the customer of the person entering into the contract.

For example if a retailer wishes to insure his premises against fire and theft he/she must sign a specifically worded insurance form that is issued to him/her by the insurance company with details of what the insurance does and does not cover.

The Implied Conditions that Underlie a Contract for a Sale of Goods under the Sale of Goods and Supply of Services Act 1980

The following conditions are implied in all sale agreements, unless specifically stated:

1. MERCHANTABLE QUALITY

It is presumed that all goods for sale are of merchantable quality. This means that if any serious fault exists in the goods, the buyer can take action against the seller for a breach of the implied condition of sale. (Exceptions: a motor vehicle dealer where both parties agree that the vehicle requires repair before use.)

2. SALE BY SAMPLE

If, for example, a retailer gives a potential customer a sample of the goods on sale, it is reasonable to presume that the goods that will be received by the buyer will correspond (as far as is practicably possible) with the sample. This could be applied to the sale of paint – with colour cards being the sample – or curtains – where sample materials would be provided by the shop assistant.

3. SALE BY DESCRIPTION

For example, if a firm that fits windows and doors has a brochure with photos and descriptions of the different types of designs available. The buyer receives a door or window that does not fit the original description of the item that he/she agreed to buy. Then the buyer can take action against the seller for breach of the implied condition of sale.

4. FIT FOR PURPOSE

Often when customers are buying, they are relying on the knowledge, expertise and advice of the seller. When a customer informs a seller of the reasons why the goods are required, the implication exists that the seller is verifying that the goods or services are fit for the purpose for which they are going to be used. The buyer can take action against the seller for breach of the implied condition of sale.

5. IMPLIED WARRANTY

When an advertisement for goods or a service appears, and extra conditions are guaranteed with the purchase, such as after sales service, the buyer can take action if these conditions are not honoured.

Another example of a warranty is a guarantee that goods or services will be delivered or provided at the agreed date and time. When a situation occurs where goods are delivered late, the buyer cannot refuse to take them, but he can sue the seller for a decrease in sales and a loss of earnings as a result of the late delivery.

Other Consumer Considerations Relating to the Sale of Goods:

RECOGNITION OF CONSUMER RIGHTS AND REDRESS FOR THE CONSUMER: Statements like 'no liability accepted for faulty goods' CANNOT be publicly displayed and lead to prosecution. Recognition of consumer rights must take precedence.

If the consumer has a reason for complaint he/she must act promptly. Otherwise delays in examining the goods would weaken the case and imply that the fault was caused after the goods were purchased or the service was given.

What is the National Consumer Agency?

The National Consumer Agency (formerly the Office of the Director of Consumer Affairs) is an independent office established by law in Ireland to protect the rights of consumers. The National Consumer Agency (NCA) was set up on an interim basis in May 2005 and established on a statutory basis in May 2007 (underpinned by Consumer Protection Act 2007). It has a general function of promoting consumer welfare and is responsible for investigating, enforcing and encouraging compliance with consumer law. The NCA took over the functions and powers of the Office of the Director of Consumer Affairs and has even more extensive functions and powers.

FUNCTIONS OF THE NATIONAL CONSUMER AGENCY

The main functions of the NCA are to:

- Promote and protect the interests and welfare of consumers.
- Enforce the relevant consumer law.
- Encourage compliance with the relevant law.
- Investigate suspected offences under any of the relevant laws.
- Refer cases to the Director of Public Prosecutions where appropriate.

In carrying out its functions, the NCA can advise and make recommendations on any legislation or policy which concerns or is likely to impact on consumer protection and welfare. The NCA also has the power to make proposals for new legislation. The NCA must be consulted about decisions that affect consumers.

The Minister for Jobs, Enterprise and Innovation sets out which bodies the NCA must co-operate with, such as:

- The Commission for Energy Regulation (which makes decisions about electricity and gas prices)
- Comreg (which regulates the telecommunications and postal industry).

The NCA has the power to enforce consumer legislation, to pursue their investigations and to apply to the courts for search warrants. The NCA may exchange relevant information with the Competition Authority, the Gardaí, the Director of Corporate Enforcement, the Revenue Commissioners, the Central Bank of Ireland or other people the Minister specifies.

SPECIFIC FUNCTIONS OF THE NATIONAL CONSUMER AGENCY

The NCA is also obliged to:

- Work with and consult consumer groups and representatives and co-operate with other authorities who are concerned with consumer protection.
- Promote the development of alternative dispute resolution (ADR) procedures as a means of resolving consumer disputes.
- Conduct or commission research (or support voluntary bodies to do this).
- Promote public awareness and conduct public information campaigns for the

purpose of educating and advising consumers in relation to consumer protection and welfare (or support voluntary bodies to do this).

- Promote educational initiatives and activities relating to consumer information and awareness and advice, when requested by any Minister or public body or education or training institution (or support voluntary bodies to do this).
- Review and approve relevant codes of practice.
- Prepare and publish guidelines to traders.
- Promote and encourage the establishment of quality assurance schemes by traders.
- Perform the functions previously carried out by the Director of Consumer Affairs.

Refer to **www.djei.ie** and **www.consumerconnect.ie.**

What is The Consumer Protection Act 2007?

The Consumer Protection Act 2007 came into effect in Ireland on 1 May 2007.

1. ESTABLISHMENT OF THE NATIONAL CONSUMER AGENCY

The Act provided for the establishment of the National Consumer Agency. It put the EU Directive on unfair commercial practices into national law and it made various changes to our consumer laws. It also repealed certain older consumer laws, some of which dated from the 19th century.

2. UNFAIR COMMERCIAL PRACTICES

The Consumer Protection Act 2007 provides for its implementation of the EU Unfair Commercial Practices Directive (Directive 2005/28/EC of 11 May 2005) in Ireland deals with unfair business–to–consumer commercial practices, (it does not apply to dealings between businesses). Refer to **www.isitfair.eu.**

3. UNFAIR, MISLEADING AND AGRESSIVE TRADING PRACTICES SOMETIMES BANNED

The Act provides that a range of unfair, misleading and aggressive trading practices are banned if they would be likely to cause appreciable impairment of the average consumer's ability to make an informed choice in relation to the product concerned and would cause the average consumer to make a decision about a transaction that they would not otherwise make. Practices are banned, therefore, if they meet two conditions: if they are unfair, misleading or aggressive and if they are likely to distort the consumer's choice.

4. PRICE DISPLAY REGULATIONS

The Consumer Protection Act 2007 gives the Minister the power to make regulations requiring that the prices of certain products be displayed in a specific manner. For example, they could provide that prices of certain products must be displayed inclusive of charges, fees and taxes.

5. PRICE CONTROLS

The Prices Acts 1958-1972 gave the Minister for Jobs, Enterprise and Innovation a range of powers to set maximum prices. The Act *repeals all of these powers* except the power to control prices in emergency situations. It provides that the power to control prices in emergency situations must be exercised by the government and not the Minister.

6. PYRAMID SELLING

The Pyramid Selling Act 1980 was repealed by the Consumer Protection Act 2007 and replaced by new provisions. These provisions ban participation in pyramid schemes and inducing others to participate. They also ban the establishment, operation or promotion of these schemes and increase the penalties for breaking the law. The new penalties for offences relating to pyramid schemes involve a fine of up to €150,000 and a prison term of up to five years.

7. CODES OF PRACTICE

The Consumer Protection Act 2007 provides for the recognition of codes of practice drawn up by traders or groups of traders and for the NCA to approve such codes. It also provides that the NCA may issue guidelines to traders about consumer protection and welfare, commercial practices, quality assurance schemes and codes of practice.

8. CASUAL TRADING LICENCES

The Act gives power to the Minister to introduce statutory guidelines for local authorities in regard to the issuing of casual trading licences. Non-statutory guidelines were issued to local authorities in July 2005 and again in July 2006, with a view to their being implemented on a voluntary basis.

9. ENFORCEMENT

Previously, the Office of the Director of Consumer Affairs could either try to get voluntary compliance with consumer legislation or take legal action. In the case of misleading practices, the Director could apply to the High Court for an injunction. The Consumer Protection Act 2007 provides for a range of other enforcement mechanisms to be available to the NCA.

10. ROLE OF THE CENTRAL BANK

The Central Bank of Ireland has a role in enforcing the provisions of the Consumer Protection Act 2007 in the financial services area. The NCA and the Central Bank are required to have a co-operation agreement setting out their respective roles.

11. WHISTLEBLOWERS PROTECTION

The Act provides protection for people who report breaches of the legislation to the NCA.

12. REDRESS FOR INDIVIDUAL CONSUMERS

Anyone, including the NCA, may apply to the Circuit Court or the High Court for an order prohibiting any practice (with some small exceptions) which is unlawful under the Consumer Protection Act 2007. If an individual takes such an action, notice must be given to the trader and to the NCA. It is not necessary to show loss or damage as a result of the trader's actions.

If a trader is convicted of an offence under the Act, consumers may sue the trader for damages. It is open to the court to require the trader to pay damages to a consumer who has suffered loss as a result of the trader's actions. Such a compensation order may be instead of, or in addition to, any fine or penalty the court imposes on the trader.

13. PENALTIES

The Act provides for a range of penalties for the various offences. The maximum fine for a first offence is €3,000 and €60,000 for proven convictions on indictment. There are higher fines for repeat offenders.

Refer to **www.djei.ie** and **www.consumerconnect.ie.**

The Consumers' Association of Ireland (CAI)

The Consumers' Association of Ireland is a voluntary body which aims to inform, represent and protect Irish consumers. The Consumers' Association is Ireland's independent, self-funded and non-profit organisation, founded in 1966 and registered with charity status. It provides an advice and information service for consumers. The Consumers' Association also campaigns for improved consumer legislation.

It produces *Consumer Choice* magazine and members can subscribe to it and keep themselves aware of consumer issues and changes in legislation regarding consumer rights. Refer to **www.consumerconnect.ie.**

The Advertising Standards Authority for Ireland (ASAI)

The Advertising Standards Authority is a voluntary self-regulatory body of advertising practitioners, which deals with complaints about standards of advertising. There are voluntary codes of standards and you may complain about breaches of those standards. These codes are on Advertising Standards and on Sales Promotion Practice. Refer to **www.asai.ie.**

European Consumer Organisation

EUROPEAN CONSUMER CENTRE (ECC)

The European Consumer Centre provides a free information and advice service on consumer rights in the EU. It is part of an EU-wide network of consumer centres and it can help you to solve consumer disputes arising in other Member States of the EU. It does this by trying to solve the dispute directly and, if this fails, by referring your case to an Alternative Dispute Resolution organisation in the other Member State. The Office of the Director of Consumer Affairs and the European Commission jointly finance the Centre. Refer to **www.eccireland.ie.**

Health and Safety in Retailing

HACCP

Training must be provided to ensure food safety in retail outlets. Since 1998 it has been a legal requirement for all food businesses to have a food-safety management system based on the principle of HACCP. Under current legislation, a 'food business' is defined as '…any undertaking, whether for profit or not and whether public or private, carrying out any or all of the following: preparation, processing, manufacturing, packaging, storing, transportation, distribution, handling or offering for sale or supply of foodstuffs'. For comprehensive information on HACCP and food safety refer to Chapter 1.

Health And Safety Initiatives Aimed at Improving Safety in a Retail Administration Environment

1. FIRE SAFETY

Retailers should ensure that fire-safety regulations are adhered to and fire-safety drills are carried out on a regular basis. All staff including Fire Managers and Fire Marshalls should be trained and identified to all staff with fire safety reports given to staff on regular occasions. Fire exits should be clearly marked with easy access to extinguishers in line with the organisation's policies and procedures.

To maintain excellent fire safety in the retail outlet, organisations must meet the requirements of The Safety Health and Welfare at Work Act 2005 and the Fire Services Act 1981 (2003). Legislation places responsibility upon the 'person having control of premises to guard against the outbreak of fire and to ensure the safety of persons on the premises in the event of an outbreak of fire, insofar as is reasonably practicable whether such an outbreak has occurred or not. Knowledge of legislation and record-keeping would be essential. A Fire Safety Register should be set up and maintained also.

A typical list of initiatives might include training in:

- Evacuation procedures.
- How to react in an emergency situation.
- Equipment: Detection and alarm systems, fire-fighting equipment.
- Emergency lighting.
- Assisting the Fire Brigade.
- Management responsibilities and staff fire-safety training.
- Role of Fire Marshals.
- Fire-chemistry classes.

2. FOOD SAFETY

Retailers should ensure adequate staff training on food hygiene, including hand washing, separating raw food from cooked food to prevent diseases, such as E. coli and salmonella.

3. PROTECTIVE EQUIPMENT AND CLOTHING

Retailers should ensure that eye protection and safety clothing is worn by staff when necessary, in line with the business's policies and procedures.

4. FIRST AID/DEFIBULATOR TRAINING

This includes locating of first aid equipment, identifying the staff specifically trained to use it and the procedure to evacuate.

5. STAFF SECURITY

In case of robbery, staff should be trained appropriately to follow appropriate procedures if there is an attack or assault and to be aware of where panic alarm buttons are located.

6. GENERAL HYGIENE

Retailers should ensure that staff are aware of and practise good personal hygiene including regular hand-washing techniques.

7. MANUAL HANDLING

Staff in retailing should be trained appropriately how to safely lift equipment, if necessary, using safety techniques for manual handling, to ensure their personal physical safety.

8. ERGONOMICS

Retailers should provide appropriate office seating, computer visors etc for those working on computers or who are in seated positions for long periods of time. Regular breaks should be arranged in line with the retail organisation's staff and safety policies.

RISK ASSESSMENT TO ASSESS SAFE WORK METHODS IN RETAILING

Businesses can visit the Health and Safety Authority website and view a video that gives guidelines on how to carry out a risk assessment using the following web-link **http://besmart.hsa.ie.**

Refer to risk assessments and safe work methods in Chapter 4.

Retail

Traditionally, retail is not viewed as a high-risk sector and it is not targeted specifically in any Health and Safety Authority compliance-inspection programmes.

The retail sector comes under NACE category G (the retail sales statistical index), Wholesale/Retail trade; repair of vehicles, personal and household goods. This sector recorded three fatalities in 2006, making it the fifth-largest sector for fatalities that year.

Two of these accidents particularly related to construction activities. The accident triggers were a) fall from a height, b) loss of control of a machine, and c) other. One accident involved a member of the public, and one worker fatality was to a non-Irish national (other EU).

There were four fatalities in 2003, four in 2004, and eight in 2005.

Causes of accidents

The proportion of accidents due to manual handling is particularly high in the wholesale and retail trade (47 per cent). Injury arising from 'manual handling' includes 'lifting and carrying', 'pushing and pulling' and 'twisting and turning of the body' is much more significant in this sector.

Wholesale and retail also suffers a high proportion of incidents associated with 'mobile handling devices' such as barrows and pallet trucks (9 per cent) and 'objects and packaging in storage areas' (9 per cent).

The second most frequently reported accident trigger is 'slips, trips, falls'. This trigger accounts for over 17 per cent of all accidents reported from this sector. Together, 'manual handling' and 'slips, trips, falls' triggered over 60 per cent of all the reported accidents in 2006. Also the proportion of sprain and strain injuries is over 40 per cent in the wholesale and retail trade.

Understanding a complex sector

When considering the retail sector, one must remember that there are many sub-categories of retail where particular risks may be quite different, e.g. the risks will vary substantially between a pharmacy and an off-licence, between a newsagents and an electrical shop.
In some cases it may prove necessary to produce very specific sectoral guidance.

Market research

In December 2005 the HSA commissioned a national survey of micro businesses (with under ten employees) in the retail sector. This information may be of assistance in formulating strategies to effect improved safety and health across the entire retail sector.

Source: **www.hsa.ie/eng/Your_Industry/Retail**

Processing Customer Complaints in Retailing

Quality and first-rate customer service should be high on every retailer's agenda. When retailers who care for their brand pay attention to complaints and look for feedback to identify the root causes of issues and concerns, they then retain customer loyalty and secure repeat business.

Document Control Strategy to Process Customer Complaints, Queries and Product Returns

1. MANUAL METHODS

Information on Customer complaints and customer concerns can be captured as follows:

- By documenting verbal customer complaints at (Customer Service desks).
- By encouraging customers to voluntarily fill in Customer Feedback Survey forms available in-store and online.
- To document general complaints in-store or on a forecourt of a service station for example.

This will allow for trend reports to be produced by the retailer. These reports can be used by the retailer to:

- Improve the problem resolution process.
- Identify opportunities for improvement in the retail outlet and eradicate the causes of customer dissatisfaction.
- Assure the consistent delivery of exceptional service and give the retailer the ability to identify opportunities to further improve the overall customer experience.

2. COMPUTERISED METHODS

Computerised complaints management systems (CMS) exist and these IT companies offer systems to enable the retailer to capture complaints, compliments and general queries across all areas of the business. These CMS systems are user-friendly, often website-based, and allow for:

- Customers to quickly and simply report issues via the company's website.
- Social media interaction: e.g. information sent via Facebook etc.
- Staff in the retail outlet to rapidly track and enter complaints information ensuring that regulatory and commercial timescales are adhered to.
- Prompt handling and resolution of complaints.

- Prompt answering of queries.
- Translation of different languages.

The same systems can be used to handle queries and to generate information on product returns also. The IT company would provide IT support, but the retailer would be responsible for the management of the system's information.

PRACTICE QUESTIONS

1. What is RGDATA?
2. Write a note on Retail Ireland.
3. What constitutes a valid contract?
4. What is the Sale of Goods and Supply of Services Act 1980 and what conditions of sale are implied by this Act?
5. Write a note on the National Consumer Agency.
6. List *eight* provisions of the Consumer Protection Act 2007.
7. Write a note on the Consumers' Association of Ireland (CAI).
8. Write a note on the Advertising Standards Authority for Ireland (ASAI).
9. Write a note on the European Consumer Centre (ECC).
10. List and explain *eight* Health and Safety initiatives aimed at improving safety in a retail administration environment.
11. Explain the document control strategies (manual and computerised) that could be used to process customer complaints, queries and product returns.

Retail Administration

Portfolio of Coursework – Sample Assignment

A CASE STUDY OF AN ORGANISATION

Note: Students should refer to Chapter 1, in particular how students can research organisations, SWOT and PEST analyses before attempting this assignment.

Choose an organisation with which you are familiar or one that will be easy to approach for information and examine a range of the following aspects of the organisation:

- Location
- Structure (organisational chart)
- Ownership
- Environmental factors (PEST plus Competition – refer to Chapter 1)
- Staffing

- Administration
- Stock control
- Pricing strategy

Note: Any other details given are extra and will earn marks for initiative and originality.

- Work placements can be chosen for analysis.

A Retail Case Study – A School Bookshop

Introduction

This case study aims to explore how a retail outlet, in this case a bookshop/school book supplier, started business and progressed to its current state. Areas of analysis will include the history of the business, its start-up characteristics, advertising, pricing, costs, factors affecting location, safety, health and hygiene procedures and the life cycle of the business. An analysis of its strengths and weaknesses will be carried out. Future opportunities or plans will be enquired into and threats to the business will be pin-pointed. Finally, an analysis of political, economic, social and technological factors that affect the business, or have affected it in the past, will be carried out.

History of the Business

The business was originally established in June 1988. It was located in a first-floor rented unit over a bank in the main street of a small town in Ireland. The owners then decided to relocate at street level in another rented unit on the main street.

The son of the previous owners now owns the shop and has been trading as a sole trader since May 1995. The shop unit in which the business is now located, which was previously a drapery/wool shop, has a larger floor area – 45 square metres approximately.

Set-Up Procedure and Qualifications or Work Experience Necessary to be Successful

Before occupying the unit, it was necessary to invest €15,000 to refurbish it completely. Included in this cost figure was the cost of improvements including ceiling, carpets, walls and lights. The layout of the unit had to be changed completely to make it suitable for a bookshop.

The owner concluded that previous experience of the school retail trade is not absolutely essential for success in retailing. However, some knowledge of the retail trade with regard to books together with appropriate work experience with educational printers, publishers or suppliers like Folens would be an advantage.

Experience in receiving orders (types of orders) and previous knowledge of teachers' margins (how many books they might order and under what criteria they order), and publishers' margins would give the entrepreneur wishing to specialise in school supplies (as opposed to more general books) the edge.

Market Research

The daughter of the former owners also takes an active part in the business and undertook the market research. She investigated other bookshops and realised while carrying out this fieldwork that this town was the only town in the region that didn't have a school supplier.

Insurance/Health and Safety Considerations

The business is covered by full Public Liability insurance.

Advertising Before and After Opening

It was estimated that €300 approximately was spent on printing flyers while renovations were being carried out on the unit. These were distributed around the locality. Shortly after opening, an intensive marketing strategy was undertaken by the owners in schools. They provided in-school demonstrations of products, backed up by a catalogue and back-to-school prices quoted for teachers. Most of the arrangements for meeting teachers were made through the principals in the schools and teachers were often invited back to the shop to view the products if time did not allow for it during the day. Long hours after normal trading hours were spent working in order to gain the existing market share.

Expert personal selling techniques and follow-up phone calls, as well as call-in procedures used in order to secure sales, were regarded as key methods of gaining business.

Change in Work Philosophy, Advertising and Target Market

The owners decided to adopt a different work ethos that incorporated a change of emphasis on product range and mix. There was to be more direct selling to schools. The visiting of schools was a major generator of business. Twenty to twenty-five schools are now ordering and buying from the shop whereas two years ago this was not the case.

In more recent times, as well as keeping up the momentum with regard to personal selling, the business has also purchased advertisements in local publications and sports clubs, and has sponsored jerseys for local soccer clubs. The shop holds a January and May Sale, and the January Sale appears to be the most effective.

ORGANISATIONAL CHART

Functions of Staff

1. MANAGING DIRECTOR

The managing director controls the financial affairs of the business as he is a qualified accountant. He is responsible for the monthly management of accounts. Once a year he submits his tax and VAT returns to be signed off by a firm of accountants. He also takes an active part in the running of the shop and the marketing of products.

2. SALES AND MARKETING MANAGER

The function of the Sales and Marketing Manager is to take charge of the overall marketing of products. She is directly involved in selling to schools, wholesale ordering, dealing with customers, agreeing the end-of-day till balance with opening cash and sales for the day and many other day-to-day routine business dealings.

Ordering is done during the day and in the evening. The efficient suppliers' fax lines are open in the evening and at night after business hours. This facilitates the ordering procedure, particularly at peak trading times of the year.

3. FULL-TIME AND PART-TIME SALES ASSISTANTS

Both of those employees are employed in the peak summertime period only. They are responsible for looking after customer needs, handling cash and other means of payment as well as keeping an account of order requirements. They are also responsible for keeping the shop tidy and in good order.

Business Hours, Type of Stock for Sale, Suppliers and Trading Cycle

Regular business hours are from 9.30am to 6pm Monday to Saturday.

The product and service range consists of:

1. School books (new and second-hand), school stationery and school supplies (arts and crafts).
2. Office and general stationery.
3. Novels and other books (adult, children's, educational materials for younger age groups).
4. Services such as photocopying, faxing and laminating.

The stationery suppliers are Musgraves, Easons, Deales and Morton. The school book and other book suppliers and publishers are: Modern Languages (who have a shop and act as wholesalers), Fallons, Folens, Gill & Macmillan, Educational Company, Celtic Press, AIS, Veritas, Mentor Press, Exemplar Press and Topics Publications.

A large proportion of the annual turnover is generated in the period from 1 June to 30 September. This is mainly due to the demand for school supplies during this time. It is during this time that the demand for the two extra employees occurs every year.

With regard to the life cycle of the business, from 1995 to 1998 has been a 'Growth' stage and the business has not reached its peak as yet – that is, the 'Mature' stage of the life cycle.

October, November and December see a peak in demand for novels in the run-up to Christmas. The Christmas peak generally runs into January when a sale of goods is displayed in the shop front. January is also busy because of the Honours to Pass or vice versa changes in schools and the demand for revision titles and exam papers.

February to May is the off-peak period and this time is used to plan for the forthcoming peak period. If any alterations need to be made to the way the business runs or to its premises, this is the time to make them.

Factors affecting Location

THE REASONS FOR THE CHOICE OF LOCATION

1. The town was the only town in the region that did not have a school supplier.
2. The young population meant that a sustained demand for schoolbooks existed in the region.
3. Previous experience in an upstairs location proved that street level was a priority for a retail outlet specialising in schoolbooks and supplies.

THE PROBLEMS WITH THE LOCATION

1. It is not close enough to suppliers. (Many suppliers won't deliver due to distance from Dublin.) Costs in terms of time and money are incurred because of delivery problems.
2. There is a shortage of adequate parking along the main street. This is one of the explanations for the stunted growth in retailing along the main street.
3. The lack of passing trade might also be caused by the commercial underdevelopment of the main street.
4. There are threats of future competition because of the relative closeness of the town to busy shopping areas.

Daily and End-of-Day Routine Regarding Cash and Stock Control, as well as General Yearly Stock Control

Every day, the delivery dockets are checked against deliveries and then later checked against order forms and invoices received from the suppliers. When ordering is completed every evening, it is necessary to count the cash. The procedure referred to as 'Agreeing the Till' is undertaken. The control of cash is a priority in a retail outlet.

There are three stock-takes each year, one on 31 May, the second at the end of September/beginning of October, and the third in February/March. Everything in the shop is counted. Then the school order forms are counted and checked against stock.

A minimum stock holding is best in the area of school books because syllabi change yearly and surplus stock would be be impossible to sell into the school year and make a loss.

Pricing Policy

1. The retail outlet has no control over the prices of school books, other general books or novels. The publishers and suppliers have complete control over this. Retail shops, however, get 35 per cent commission on novels and 20 per cent commission on the sale of school books.

2. As regards stationery, the shop can price up from cost higher than the margin set by the suppliers. In this case a 40–45 per cent mark-up is worthwhile.

Quality and Quality Control

Customers demand that when buying a new book it must look untouched. As near to this as possible applies to second-hand books. School books have to be current and on the book list and in reasonably good condition.

Regarding 'returns' there is often the pretence that the book was bought in the retail outlet whereas in fact a price sticker indicates to the contrary. This is referred to as 'Swop Pretence'.

The customer will dictate the standards regarding quality, and will not buy the book or supply unless it conforms to a certain level of quality.

European Regulations

Novels published in the UK will be priced in both sterling and euro on the price form. Currently there is no VAT on books, however this could change depending on European regulations.

A SWOT Analysis of the Business

STRENGTHS

* Location at street level on a main street.
* Family-run business, therefore security and customer loyalty through family links.

- Only school supplier in the town.
- School loyalty – unwritten guarantee of business.
- Good relationship with banks.

Weaknesses

- Shop layout and size.
- Parking problems.
- Passing trade problem due to underdevelopment of the main street.
- Schoolbook returns are approximately 5 per cent.
- Delivery problems on supplier side, and time and cost of delivering to schools.
- Stock out too often – need to review stocking procedure.

Opportunities

- Expansion will depend on future competition in and near the area.
- Possible further diversification of product and service range.

Threats

- Other similar shops in nearby towns, as well as existing and planned shopping complexes where people can shop for everything including school books.
- The decision to make outlets on the main street residential rather than commercial premises. Passing trade would be virtually non-existent if this happened and would adversely affect the business.

A PEST Analysis of the Business

Political Factors

Family links and good relationships with banks, Chamber of Commerce, clubs that the business sponsored, publishers and authors are factors that positively influence the business.

Economic Factors

- The 'boom' in the economy has meant more houses being built in the area and therefore a larger school-going population which translates into a higher demand for school books and supplies and other book store products and services.
- More finance is readily available from banks and financial institutions and interest rates are relatively low, so the cost of borrowing for renovations is low.
- More money has allowed the business to expand its range of products and services and to diversify.

Social Factors

- The change in the style of selling was part of a new work ethos fuelled by 'the competitive urge'. The success of the marketing strategy that has been employed since 1995 has brought in more customers. Personal selling has achieved the objective of gaining customer confidence as well as convincing them to sample the diverse product and service range that is readily available either in the shop, or which can be ordered in.

TECHNOLOGICAL FACTORS

* The business has made use of a new computerised ordering system called 'EROS' which is operated via Eason's Bookshop's modem. The procedure involves ordering through a bar code or by typing the title or author. The message is sent through via phone link, and provides an efficient and prompt service.

Conclusion

This sample retail case study of a bookshop has highlighted the importance of interpersonal skills and personality in the path to securing future business. Personal selling together with the knowledge that a sustainable market share exists and the youthful ambition to succeed describes adequately the work that was undertaken by the owners. The doubling of turnover since 1995 is evidence of the success of the venture. The diversification of products and services together with the structural improvements that were made to the unit equally contributed to the business's success to date. Finally, despite the weaknesses that were listed, it is encouraging to see how a zestful, refreshing and ambitious marketing strategy can be successful.

PRACTICE QUESTIONS

1. What are the Retail Planning Guidelines?
2. What was the Groceries Order (Restrictive Practices) 1987?
3. What is a Symbol Group?
4. What is a Franchise?
5. Define 'Multiples' with reference to retail outlets and explain their characteristics.
6. What are the advantages and disadvantages of being a Multiple?
7. How do Department Stores, Hypermarkets and Superstores differ?
8. What is a Retail Co-operative? What are the advantages and disadvantages of retail co-operatives?
9. Explain how the size and type of retail outlet can influence:
   a) the type of ownership required
   b) how profits are divided
   c) the management organisational structure of the outlet.
10. Explain how the size and type of retail outlet can influence:
    a) administration procedures
    b) staffing levels.
11. What factors influence the location of a retail outlet?
12. What are the implications of good location for a retail outlet?

13. What is EPOS and how do EPOS systems impact on retailers? (Refer to Chapter 2.)

14. What is RGDATA?

15. List and explain the conditions that must exist for a contract to be valid.

16. What is the Sale of Goods and Supply of Services Act 1980 and what conditions of sale are implied by this Act?

17. What is consumer redress? List three organisations or institutions that consumers can turn to in order to gain redress.

18. Write a note on the Consumer Association of Ireland (CAI).

19. What are the main conditions that underpin the Consumer Information Act 1978?

20. Write a note on the Small Claims Court.

21. What are the main functions of the Director of Consumer Affairs?

8. Sample Exam Papers

Business Administration

Time Allowed: 2 hours

- Answer 10 out of 12 questions in Section A.
- Answer two out of three questions in Section B.

Section A

- Answer 10 out of 12 questions in this section.

1. List *four* environmental features that affect an organisation.

2. What are Quality Circles?

3. How does the Formal Organisation differ from the Informal Organisation?

4. List *three* functions of the Human Resources Department in an organisation.

5. With regard to meetings, what is a motion?

6. Explain the term EPOS.

7. Illustrate, by sketching, the differences between a Component Bar Chart and a Multiple Bar Chart.

8. What is Factoring?

9. In each of the following cases, what document is compiled in order to indicate:
   (a) An undercharge
   (b) A return of goods
   (c) An overcharge
   (d) An omission from an invoice?

10. With regard to Communication, what is the difference between 'Effectiveness' and 'Efficiency'?

11. Who are the Social Partners and what is Collective Bargaining?

12. What is the purpose of a Cash Flow Chart?

Section B

- Answer two out of three questions from this section.

1. (a) Draw the Control Network Diagram and the Gantt Chart.
   (b) Explain how quality control in business is maintained by linking the two illustrations mentioned in (a) to the four most widely used quality control measures.
   (c) Write a note on three quality marks that you are familiar with.

2. (a) Explain the procedures to convert from an Unlimited Partnership to a Private Limited Company.
   (b) What is the purpose of the Deed of Partnership and how is it connected with 'The Partnership Act 1890'?
   (c) What is the difference between the 'Certificate of Incorporation' and the 'Trading Certificate'?

3. (a) Explain the Principles of Insurance.
   (b) Write a note on each of the following:
     i. IBA.
     ii. Premium.
     iii. Comprehensive Insurance.
     iv. Fidelity Guarantee.
     v. Life Assurance.

Business Administration

Time Allowed: 2 Hours

- Answer 10 out of 12 questions in Section A.
- Answer two out of three questions in Section B.

Section A

- Answer 10 out of 12 questions in this section. (Two marks each)

1. List *two* purposes of the ICTU.

2. List *two* reasons for differences between a tall and a flat organisational pyramid. Illustrate.

3. List *three* benefits of a tight credit control policy.

4. With regard to insurance what is the meaning of Indemnity?

5. What is the 'Deed of Partnership?

6. List *three* Quality Awards.

7. What does a Gantt Chart measure?

8. What is a Certificate of Incorporation?

9. What is the meaning of 'Credit Terms'?

10. Name *three* common room layout arrangements made before a meeting.

11. What type of organisation is a Credit Union?

12. Give *one* Irish example each of the following:
    * A non-trading state body.
    * A trading semi-state body.

Section B

* Answer two questions from this section. (10 marks each)

1. (a) How do price lists differ from quotations?
   (b) Write a note on each of the following:
       i. Terms of trade.
       ii. Discounts given in business.
   (c) Examine the price list given (attached). The following was the order faxed to All Weather Paints from McCarthy & Sons Ltd., Cruises Street, Limerick on 21/1/XX.

       2 PIN 75 purple
       4 PIN 80 white
       6 PIN 110 yellow
       5 Sp 110
       Interior Design Service (from a previous job, to be included in next invoice) €35 net figure. (VAT rates are indicated on the price list.)

   Based on the information given:
   i. Compile the Invoice number 2200 sent to McCarthy & Sons Ltd., on 21/1/XX.

ii. Compile the business document sent to McCarthy & Sons Ltd., document number 511, on 22/1/XX when McCarthy returned five damaged tins of the six paint tins code PIN 110.

iii. Draft the January Statement of Account dated 31/1/XX, if McCarthy's balance owed to All Weather Paints for January 20XX was €200 and the following additional transactions had taken place in January:

- 4/1/XX Invoice number 2008 – €150 (Received by McCarthy).
- 14/1/XX Cheque Payment number 1000013 made to All Weather paints – €50.
- 18/1/XX Invoice number 2100 – €160.

2. (a) Give *one* example each of a short-term, medium-term and long-term workforce (workforce) gap.
   (b) Distinguish between the terms 'Job Description' and 'Job Specification'.
   (c) Explain and illustrate Maslow's pyramid of Hierarchy of Needs.

3. (a) List and briefly explain the *six* main functions of management.
   (b) Explain the differences between *three* different types of minutes that are taken at meetings.
   (c) Write a note on the following terms used at meetings:
      i. An Addendum
      ii. A Resolution
      iii. Standing Order
      iv. A Quorum.

PRICE LIST OF PAINT PRODUCTS
ALL WEATHER PAINTS

WEATHERFIELD, THURLES, CO. TIPPERARY
VAT NO. 2345678D   **ALL PRICES QUOTED ARE IN EURO**

PRODUCT CODES	DESCRIPTION OF PRODUCTS	VAT	PRICE
P(IN) 75	Interior Matt 1lt	B	7.50
P(IN) 50	Interior Gloss 1lt	B	9.00
P(IN) 80	Interior Vinyl Silk 1lt	B	7.50
P(IN) 100	Interior Eggshell (Alkyd) 1 lt	B	11.00
P(IN) 110	Interior Eggshell (Acrylic) 1 lt	B	8.50
P(Ex)150	Exterior Matt 2.5 lt	B	12.00
P(Ex)90	Exterior Matt 10lt	B	37.00
P(Misc)120	Scrumble Trans Oil Glaze 2.5 lt	B	45.00
Br200	Badger Softener	B	41.00
Br195	Stencil Brush	B	1.50
Br90	Sable Writer	B	7.00
Br12	Paint Brush 1.5 inch, pure bristle	B	6.00
Br14	Paint Brush 2 inch, pure bristle	B	10.00
Br16	Paint Brush 2.5 inch, pure bristle	B	12.00
Br18	Paint Brush 3 inch, pure bristle	B	15.00
Br20	Paint Brush 4 inch, pure bristle	B	25.00
Br22	Paint Brush 6 inch, pure bristle	B	30.00
Sp 110	Sea Sponge (Synthetic)	B	7.50
Sp 120	Marine Natural Sea Sponge (Lge)	B	40.00
Sp80	Marine Natural Sea Sponge (Sml)	B	30.00
Pap100	Wall Stripper	B	250.00
Pap120	Wallpaper Table	B	15.00
Pap130	Wallpaper Hanging Brush	B	20.00
Pap133	Seam Roller	B	4.50
Sc170	Scaffolding 4ft h x 3.5 ft w	B	70.00
WSp 12	White Spirit (Sm)	B	2.00
WSp 14	White Spirit (Lge)	B	4.75
Ro186	Roller (9 Inch)	B	12.50
Ro120	Roller (6 Inch)	B	6.50
Ro124	Roller Extention Poll	B	15.00
SERVICE	INTERIOR DESIGNER	A	QUOTE

Large Range of Paints and Wallpaper available

VAT CODES   A = 13.5%   B = 21%

Retail Administration, Summer 2011

Please answer four out of five of the following questions.
All structured questions are awarded 15 marks each.

1. (a) Why is the Command Function of Management so important in
        business. (5 marks)
    (b) List and explain the remaining *five* Functions of Management (10 marks)

2. Write short notes on the following:
    (a) The Sale of Goods & Supply of Services Act 1980.
    (b) The meanings of the terms:
        Franchise.
        Symbol Groups.
    (c) ICTU and IBEC.
    (d) The National Consumer Agency.
    (e) *Four* types of Stock Control. (3 marks each)

3. (a) Explain with *one* example each what is a PEST plus C Analysis
        of a Retail Outlet. (9 marks)
    (b) List and explain *three* benefits of a well located retail outlet. (6 marks)

4. (a) What are the Retail Planning Guidelines? (5 marks)
    (b) List *three* arguments for and *three* arguments against the changes
        that took place in the RPG's some years ago (refer to the set
        up of IKEA in Ireland). (10 marks)

3. Cash Flow Chart Question
    The following are the expected inflows and outflows of money from 1 Jan
    2012 to June 30 2012 for Michael Browne Ltd. The expected cash balance at
    1 Jan was €1000.

    1. Expected Sales

Month	Cash €	Credit €
January	2300	1000
February	2000	1500
March	3000	1800
April	2800	1400
May	3300	1500
June	3500	1900

2.   Expected Expenses

	Jan	Feb	Mar	Apr	May	Jun
Purchases (credit)	700	1500	1300	1000	1000	1000
Cash purchases	300	2000	800	1000	1100	1400
Wages	1000	1000	1000	1000	1500	1500
Purchase of Office Equipment		7000				
Rent and Rates	300	300	350	350	350	350
Administration	70	60	60	60	60	65

3.   Purchases are on credit, where one month's credit is taken from suppliers.
4.   Debtors are allowed two month's credit.
5.   Commission is 2% of total sales and is paid to employees one month in arrears.
6.   A yearly light and heat bill of €2000 is payable quarterly in arrears, with the first payment starting in February.
7.   The lag in the payment of wages is one month.
8.   Administration expenses are payable a month in arrears.
9.   Any other expenses are paid out in the month incurred.

Based on the information given, you are required to:
(a) Compile a Cash Flow Forecast for Michael Browne Ltd for the period from 1 Jan 2012 to June 30 2012.   (9 marks)
(b) Identify *two* sources of the expected shortfall of cash.   (3 marks)
(c) Recommend any *two* provisions that should be put in place to avoid any shortfalls of cash.   (3 marks)

Retail Administration, Summer 2006

Answer four out of the following five structured questions.

1. (a) List *six* Functions of Management.
    (b) Explain *four* of these functions and how they might relate to a Retail Organisation.
    (c) List *two* factors that a retailer would take into account when deciding on where to locate.

2. (a) What is a Quality Circle?
   (b) List and explain *four* ways that retailers use to control quality in an effort to maintain quality standards.
   (c) List *three* standard quality marks and in each case indicate who certifies them.

3. (a) What was the Grocery Orders Act?
   (b) Why was it featured in the media in recent times?
   (c) How will the changes regarding the Act affect:
       1. Retailers
       2. Consumers?

4. Write a short note on *each* of the following:
   (a) The Sale of Goods and Supply of Services Act.
   (b) The Consumer Association of Ireland.
   (c) The Director of Consumer Affairs.
   (d) EPOS.
   (e) Cash flow forecasts.

5. John Rene Men's Fashion Ltd. delivered the following goods to Top Hat Men's Shop Ltd on 5/5/06. (The following figures are selling prices inclusive of VAT @ 21%.)
   15 pairs of Clark's Men's Shoes €428
   5 Louis Copeland Men's Suits €1500
   5 boxes of Men's Assorted Accessories (sunglasses, ties, etc.) €600

   (a) Work back to the figures before VAT was added, i.e the net figures.
   (b) Construct the Invoice (Number 20567) incorporating a 10% trade discount and then add the VAT.
   (c) Distinguish between the use of a Credit Note and a Debit Note.
   (d) John Rene Men's Fashion Ltd undercharged Top Hat Men's Shop Ltd by €30 (inclusive of VAT). Draft the appropriate document number 296A, sent on 6/5/06.
   (e) On 10/5/06 Top Hat Men's Shop Ltd paid €1000 to John Rene Men's Fashion Ltd and paid off another €400 on 20/5/06. Draft the Statement of Account dated 31/5/06 that John Rene Men's Fashion Ltd sent to Top Hat Men's Shop Ltd, taking into account that the opening balance of €200 existed on 1/5/06.

Retail Administration, Summer 2007

This exam paper contains five structured questions.
Candidates must attempt to answer four out of five questions.

1. (a) What are the RPGs?   (5 marks)
    (b) Why have they featured in the media?   (5 marks)
    (c) What are the arguments for and against changing the RPGs?   (5 marks)

2. (a) What is the role of the Ombudsman?   (5 marks)
    (b) Explain *two* main functions of the Director of Consumer Affairs. (4 marks)
    (c) Briefly list and explain the main *three* functions of Management. (6 marks)

3. (a) Write notes on the following:
    *   The Sale of Goods Act 1980
    *   The effect of Contract Law on the Retailer
    *   EPOS systems
    *   The difference between a Multiple and a Symbol Group
    *   The meaning of a Franchise.   (15 marks)

4. (a) Carry out a PEST plus C analysis of a Retail Outlet of your choice.

                                                                                                         (8 marks)

    (b) What is a SWOT analysis and why would a manager consider it important to
         carry one out often in a Retail Outlet?   (7 marks)

Brian O' Driscoll, Thomond Park, Limerick purchased the following items from
Limerick Sports Store, Mulgrave Street, Limerick:

Code	Quantity	Description	Price per unit	VAT
GS	10	Gum Shields	€15	21%
MJ	20	Munster Jerseys	€50	21%
KHS	20	Knee High Socks	€8	21%

Brian avails of a 10% trade discount.
Brian's telephone number is 061 959595, if there are any queries with his order.
Draw up the following documents based on this information:
(a) Purchase Order, number 666, date 10/10/2007   (3 marks)
(b) Delivery Docket, number 789, date 12/10/2007   (3 marks)

(c) Invoice, number 484, date 12/10/2007   (5 marks)
VAT is charged @ 21%.

(d) Brian found that 12 jerseys were ripped so he returned all 12 of them. You are required to make the appropriate adjustment by compiling the Credit Note number 137, date 28/10/2007 that was sent out.   (4 marks)

Retail Administration

Time allowed: 2 hours.

Please answer four out of the following five questions.

1. Read the following extract and answer the questions that follow it.

Michael Jordan is Managing director of Leoware Ltd., a large multiple which incorporates multiple shops. A department store and hypermarket are located near one of the Limerick multiple shops. This did not seem to affect business, however. Michael believed that a mixture of consumer loyalty and a good marketing strategy were the reasons why the market share had not been affected. The future plan was to diversify and to do so Michael planned to look for either medium-term or long-term sources of finance. Michael planned to make other improvements in the business such as tightening up the credit control policy in the business. This should help profitability and cash flow.

(a) How do multiples, department stores and hypermarkets differ? Give a clear explanation.
(b) In the context of retailing what is the meaning of 'to diversify'?
(c) Distinguish between medium-term and long-term sources of finance. Give *two* examples of each.
(d) Outline the impact of a business' credit control policy on the profitability of a retail outlet.

2. (a) Define the meaning of 'Trade Union'.
   (b) Distinguish between the role of a Trade Union at:
      i. Workplace level.
      ii. Branch level.
      iii. National level.

3. (a) With reference to stock control, what factors will affect a business that wishes to maintain an optimum level of stock? Explain these implications in your own words.

(b) Differentiate between minimum stock and maximum stock and the problems with both.

4. Beauty Depot Supplies Ltd. delivered the following goods to Mary French & Company Ltd., Beauty Salon on 8/8/XX. (The following figures are selling prices inclusive of VAT.)

   10 Boxes Maljay Moisturiser €500
   15 Boxes Disposable Electrolysis Equipment €200
   1 Box Sunbed Bulbs €120

(a) Work back to the figures before VAT was added, i.e. the net figures.

(b) Construct the invoice (number 18564) incorporating a 10% trade discount and then add the VAT at 21%.

(c) Distinguish between the use of a credit note and a debit note.

(d) Beauty Depot Supplies Ltd., undercharged Mary French & Co. by €20 (figure inclusive of VAT at 21%). Draft the appropriate document that was sent to Mary French & Co. to correct the mistake – document number 35878, sent on 9/8/XX.

(e) On 10/8/XX Mary French & Co. paid €100 to Beauty Depot and paid off another €100 on 20/8/XX. Draft the Statement of Account dated 31/8/XX that Beauty Depot sent to Mary French & Co. taking into account that the opening balance of €50 existed on 1/8/XX.

5. Write notes on the following:

(a) Sale of Goods Act 1980.

(b) Roles of the Irish Ombudsman.

(c) Roles of the Director of Consumer Affairs.

(d) Indemnity (in the context of Insurance).

(e) Control – one of the functions of management.